David Hume

The History of England Vol. I VIII

From the Invasion of Julius Caesar to the Revolution in 1688

David Hume

The History of England Vol. I VIII
From the Invasion of Julius Caesar to the Revolution in 1688

ISBN/EAN: 9783741169045

Manufactured in Europe, USA, Canada, Australia, Japa

Cover: Foto ©ninafisch / pixelio.de

Manufactured and distributed by brebook publishing software (www.brebook.com)

David Hume

The History of England Vol. I VIII

THE

HISTORY

OF

ENGLAND.

VOL. II.

THE
HISTORY
OF
ENGLAND,

FROM THE

INVASION OF JULIUS CÆSAR

TO

The REVOLUTION in 1688.

In EIGHT VOLUMES.

By DAVID HUME, Esq;

VOL. II.

A NEW EDITION, with the AUTHOR's last
CORRECTIONS and IMPROVEMENTS.

To which is prefixed,
A short ACCOUNT of his LIFE, written by himself.

LONDON:
Printed for T. CADELL, in the Strand.
MDCCLXXXVI.

CONTENTS
OF THE
SECOND VOLUME.

CHAP. X.
RICHARD I.

The king's preparations for the crusade—— Sets out on the crusade—— Transactions in Sicily—— King's arrival in Palestine—— State of Palestine—— Disorders in England—— The king's heroic actions in Palestine———His return to Palestine——— Captivity in Germany——War with France—— The king's delivery——Return to England—— War with France---Death——and character of the king——Miscellaneous transactions of this reign. Page 1

CHAP. XI.
JOHN.

Accession of the king - His marriage——War with France——Murder of Arthur, duke of Britanny ——The king expelled from all the French provinces——The king's quarrel with the court of Rome——Cardinal Langton appointed archbishop

of

CONTENTS.

of Canterbury — Interdict of the kingdom — Excommunication of the king — The king's submission to the pope — Discontents of the barons — Insurrection of the barons — Magna Charta — Renewal of the civil wars — Prince Lewis called over — Death — and character of the king. Page 39

APPENDIX II.

The FEUDAL and ANGLO-NORMAN GOVERNMENT and MANNERS.

Origin of the feudal law — Its progress — Feudal government of England — The feudal parliament — The commons — Judicial power — Revenue of the crown — Commerce — The church — Civil Laws — Manners. 101

CHAP. XII.

HENRY III.

Settlement of the government — General pacification — Death of the protector — Some commotions — Hubert de Burgh displaced — The bishop of Winchester minister — King's partiality to foreigners — Grievances — Ecclesiastical grievances — Earl of Cornwall elected king of the Romans — Discontent of the barons — Simon de Mountfort earl of Leicester — Provisions of Oxford — Usurpation of the barons — Prince Edward

CONTENTS.

ward——*Civil wars of the barons*——*Reference to the king of France*——*Renewal of the civil wars*——*Battle of Lewes*——*House of commons*——*Battle of Evesham, and death of Leicester*——*Settlement of the government*——*Death*——*and character of the king*——*Miscellaneous transactions of this reign.* Page 143

CHAP. XIII.
EDWARD I.

Civil administration of the king——*Conquest of Wales*——*Affairs of Scotland*——*Competitors for the crown of Scotland*——*Reference to Edward*——*Homage of Scotland*——*Award of Edward in favour of Baliol*——*War with France*——*Digression concerning the constitution of parliament*——*War with Scotland*——*Scotland subdued*——*War with France*——*Dissentions with the clergy*——*Arbitrary measures*——*Peace with France*——*Revolt of Scotland*——*That kingdom again subdued*——*again revolts*——*is again subdued*——*Robert Bruce*——*Third revolt of Scotland*——*Death*——*and character of the king*——*Miscellaneous transactions of this reign.* 232

CHAP. XIV.
EDWARD II.

Weakness of the king——*His passion for favourites*——*Piers Gavaston*——*Discontent of the barons*——*Murder of Gavaston*——*War with Scotland*——*Battle*

CONTENTS.

——*Battle of Bannockburn*——*Hugh le Despenser*——*Civil commotions*——*Execution of the earl of Lancaster*——*Conspiracy against the king*——*Insurrection*——*The king dethroned*——*Murdered*——*His character*——*Miscellaneous transactions in this reign.* Page 327

CHAP. XV.

EDWARD III.

War with Scotland——*Execution of the earl of Kent*——*Execution of Mortimer, earl of March*——*State of Scotland*——*War with that kingdom*——*King's claim to the crown of France*——*Preparations for war with France*——*War*——*Naval victory*——*Domestic disturbances*——*Affairs of Britanny*——*Renewal of the war with France*——*Invasion of France*——*Battle of Crecy*——*War with Scotland*——*Captivity of the king of Scots*——*Calais taken.* 371

CHAP. XVI.

Institution of the garter——*State of France*——*Battle of Poictiers*——*Captivity of the king of France*——*State of that kingdom*——*Invasion of France*——*Peace of Bretigni*——*State of France*——*Expedition into Castile*——*Rupture with France*——*Ill success of the English*——*Death of the prince of Wales Death*——*and character of the king*——*Miscellaneous transactions in this reign.* 447

THE

THE HISTORY OF ENGLAND.

CHAP. X.

RICHARD I.

The king's preparations for the crusade—Sets out on the crusade—Transactions in Sicily—King's arrival in Palestine—State of Palestine—Disorders in England—The king's heroic actions in Palestine—His return from Palestine—Captivity in Germany—War with France—The king's delivery—Return to England—War with France—Death—and character of the king—Miscellaneous transactions of this reign.

THE compunction of Richard for his undutiful behaviour towards his father was durable, and influenced him in the choice of his ministers and servants after his accession. Those who had seconded and favoured his rebellion, instead of meeting with that trust and honour which they expected, were surprised

CHAP.
X.

1189.

to find that they lay under difgrace with the new king, and were on all occafions hated and defpifed by him. The faithful minifters of Henry, who had vigoroufly oppofed all the enterprizes of his fons, were received with open arms, and were continued in thofe offices which they had honourably difcharged to their former mafter [a]. This prudent conduct might be the refult of reflection; but in a prince, like Richard, fo much guided by paffion, and fo little by policy, it was commonly afcribed to a principle ftill more virtuous and more honourable.

RICHARD, that he might make atonement to one parent for his breach of duty to the other, immediately fent orders for releafing the queen-dowager from the confinement in which fhe had long been detained; and he entrufted her with the government of England till his arrival in that kingdom. His bounty to his brother John was rather profufe and imprudent. Befides beftowing on him the county of Mortaigne in Normandy, granting him a penfion of four thoufand marks a year, and marrying him to Avifa, the daughter of the earl of Glocefter, by whom he inherited all the poffeffions of that opulent family; he increafed this appanage, which the late king had deftined him, by other extenfive grants and conceffions. He conferred on him the whole eftate of William Peverell, which had efcheated to the crown: He put him in poffeffion of eight caftles, with all the forefts and honours annexed to them: He delivered over to him no lefs than fix earldoms, Cornwal, Devon, Somerfet, Nottingham, Dorfet, Lancafter, and Derby: And endeavouring, by favours, to fix that vicious prince in his duty, he put it too much in his power, whenever he pleafed, to depart from it.

The king's preparation for the crufade.

THE king, impelled more by the love of military glory than by fuperftition, acted, from the beginning of his

[a] Hoveden, p. 655. Bened. Abb. p. 517. M. Paris, p. 107.

reign,

RICHARD I.

reign, as if the sole purpose of his government had been the relief of the Holy Land, and the recovery of Jerusalem from the Saracens. This zeal against infidels being communicated to his subjects, broke out in London on the day of his coronation, and made them find a crusade less dangerous, and attended with more immediate profit. The prejudices of the age had made the lending of money on interest pass by the invidious name of usury: Yet the necessity of the practice had still continued it, and the greater part of that kind of dealing fell every where into the hands of the Jews; who, being already infamous on account of their religion, had no honour to lose, and were apt to exercise a profession, odious in itself, by every kind of rigour, and even sometimes by rapine and extortion. The industry and frugality of this people had put them in possession of all the ready money, which the idleness and profusion, common to the English with other European nations, enabled them to lend at exorbitant and unequal interest. The monkish writers represent it as a great stain on the wise and equitable government of Henry, that he had carefully protected this infidel race from all injuries and insults; but the zeal of Richard afforded the populace a pretence for venting their animosity against them. The king had issued an edict, prohibiting their appearance at his coronation; but some of them bringing him large presents from their nation, presumed, in confidence of that merit, to approach the hall in which he dined: Being discovered, they were exposed to the insults of the bystanders; they took to flight; the people pursued them; the rumour was spread, that the king had issued orders to massacre all the Jews; a command so agreeable was executed in an instant on such as fell into the hands of the populace; those who had kept at home were exposed to equal danger; the people, moved by rapacity and zeal, broke into their houses,

CHAP. houses, which they plundered, after having murdered the
X. owners; where the Jews barricadoed their doors, and
1189. defended themselves with vigour, the rabble set fire to the
houses, and made way through the flames to exercise their
pillage and violence; the usual licentiousness of London,
which the sovereign power with difficulty restrained, broke
out with fury, and continued these outrages; the houses
of the rich citizens, though Christians, were next attacked and plundered; and weariness and satiety at last put
an end to the disorder: Yet, when the king impowered
Glanville, the justiciary, to enquire into the authors of
these crimes, the guilt was found to involve so many of
the most considerable citizens, that it was deemed more
prudent to drop the prosecution; and very few suffered
the punishment due to this enormity. But the disorder
stopped not at London. The inhabitants of the other
cities of England, hearing of this slaughter of the Jews,
imitated the example: In York, five hundred of that nation, who had retired into the castle for safety, and found
themselves unable to defend the place, murdered their
own wives and children, threw the dead bodies over the
walls upon the populace, and then setting fire to the
houses, perished in the flames. The gentry of the neighbourhood, who were all indebted to the Jews, ran to the
cathedral, where their bonds were kept, and made a
solemn bonfire of the papers before the altar. The compiler of the Annals of Waverley, in relating these events,
blesses the Almighty for thus delivering over this impious
race to destruction [b].

THE ancient situation of England, when the people
possessed little riches and the public no credit, made it impossible for sovereigns to bear the expence of a steady or
durable war, even on their frontiers; much less could
they find regular means for the support of distant expedi-

[b] Gale's Collect. vol. iii. p. 165.

tions

RICHARD I.

tions like those into Palestine, which were more the result of popular frenzy than of sober reason or deliberate policy. Richard, therefore, knew that he must carry with him all the treasure necessary for his enterprize, and that both the remoteness of his own country and its poverty made it unable to furnish him with those continued supplies which the exigencies of so perilous a war must necessarily require. His father had left him a treasure of above a hundred thousand marks; and the king, negligent of every consideration but his present object, endeavoured to augment this sum by all expedients, how pernicious soever to the public, or dangerous to royal authority. He put to sale the revenues and manors of the crown; the offices of greatest trust and power, even those of forester and sheriff, which anciently were so important[c], became venal; the dignity of chief justiciary, in whose hands was lodged the whole execution of the laws, was sold to Hugh de Puzas, bishop of Durham, for a thousand marks; the same prelate bought the earldom of Northumberland for life[d]; many of the champions of the cross, who had repented of their vow, purchased the liberty of violating it; and Richard, who stood less in need of men than of money, dispensed, on these conditions, with their attendance. Elated with the hopes of fame, which in that age attended no wars but those against the infidels, he was blind to every other consideration; and when some of his wiser ministers objected to this dissipation of the revenue and power of the crown, he replied, that he would sell London itself, could he find a purchaser[e]. Nothing indeed could be a stronger proof how negligent he was of all future interests in comparison of the crusade, than his selling, for so small a sum as 10,000 marks, the vassalage of

---

[c] The sheriff had anciently both the administration of justice and the management of the king's revenue committed to him in the county. See Hale of Sheriff's Accounts.
[d] M. Paris, p. 109.   [e] W. Heming. p. 519. Knyghton, p. 2401.

CHAP. X.

1189.

Scotland, together with the fortresses of Roxborough and Berwic, the greatest acquisition that had been made by his father during the course of his victorious reign; and his accepting the homage of William in the usual terms, merely for the territories which that prince held in England[f]. The English, of all ranks and stations, were oppressed by numerous exactions: Menaces were employed, both against the innocent and the guilty, in order to extort money from them: And where a pretence was wanting against the rich, the king obliged them, by the fear of his displeasure, to lend him sums which, he knew, it would never be in his power to repay.

BUT Richard, though he sacrificed every interest and consideration to the success of this pious enterprize, carried so little the appearance of sanctity in his conduct, that Fulk, curate of Neuilly, a zealous preacher of the crusade, who from that merit had acquired the privilege of speaking the boldest truths, advised him to rid himself of his notorious vices, particularly his pride, avarice, and voluptuousness, which he called the king's three favourite daughters. *You counsel well,* replied Richard; *and I hereby dispose of the first to the Templars, of the second to the Benedictines, and of the third to my prelates.*

RICHARD, jealous of attempts which might be made on England during his absence, laid prince John, as well as his natural brother Geoffrey, archbishop of York, under engagements, confirmed by their oaths, that neither of them should enter the kingdom till his return; though he thought proper, before his departure, to withdraw this prohibition. The administration was left in the hands of Hugh, bishop of Durham, and of Longchamp, bishop of Ely, whom he appointed justiciaries and guardians of the realm. The latter was a Frenchman of mean birth, and of a violent character; who by art and address

[f] Hoveden, p. 662. Rymer, vol. I. p. 64. M. West. p. 257.

had

had infinuated himfelf into favour, whom Richard had
created chancellor, and whom he had engaged the pope
alfo to inveft with the legantine authority, that, by
centering every kind of power in his perfon, he might
the better enfure the public tranquillity. All the military and turbulent fpirits flocked about the perfon of
the king, and were impatient to diftinguifh themfelves
againft the infidels in Afia; whither his inclinations, his
engagements, led him, and whither he was impelled by
meffages from the king of France, ready to embark in
this enterprize.

CHAP. X.

1189.

THE emperor Frederic, a prince of great fpirit and
conduct, had already taken the road to Paleftine at the
head of 150,000 men, collected from Germany and all
the northern ftates. Having furmounted every obftacle
thrown in his way by the artifices of the Greeks and the
power of the infidels, he had penetrated to the borders of
Syria; when, bathing in the cold river Cydnus during
the greateft heat of the fummer-feafon, he was feized with
a mortal diftemper, which put an end to his life and his
rafh enterprize[a]. His army, under the command of his
fon Conrade, reached Paleftine; but was fo diminifhed
by fatigue, famine, maladies, and the fword, that it
fcarcely amounted to eight thoufand men; and was unable to make any progrefs againft the great power, valour, and conduct of Saladin. Thefe reiterated calamities attending the crufades had taught the kings of
France and England the neceffity of trying another road
to the Holy Land; and they determined to conduct their
armies thither by fea, to carry provifions along with them,
and, by means of their naval power, to maintain an open
communication with their own ftates, and with the weftern
parts of Europe. The place of rendezvous was appointed
in the plains of Vezelay, on the borders of Burgundy[b];

1190. 24th June.

[a] Bened. Abb. p. 558.   [b] Hoveden, p. 660.

Philip

CHAP. X.

1190.

Philip and Richard, on their arrival there, found their combined army amount to 100,000 men[1]; a mighty force, animated with glory and religion, conducted by two warlike monarchs, provided with every thing which their several dominions could supply, and not to be overcome but by their own misconduct, or by the unsurmountable obstacles of nature.

King sets out on the crusade.

THE French prince and the English here reiterated their promises of cordial friendship, pledged their faith not to invade each other's dominions during the crusade, mutually exchanged the oaths of all their barons and prelates to the same effect, and subjected themselves to the penalty of interdicts and excommunications, if they should ever violate this public and solemn engagement. They then separated; Philip took the road to Genoa, Richard that to Marseilles, with a view of meeting their fleets, which were severally appointed to rendezvous in these harbours. They put to sea; and, nearly about the same time, were obliged, by stress of weather, to take shelter in Messina, where they were detained during the whole winter. This incident laid the foundation of animosities which proved fatal to their enterprize.

14th Sept.

RICHARD and Philip were, by the situation and extent of their dominions, rivals in power; by their age and inclinations, competitors for glory; and these causes of emulation, which, had the princes been employed in the field against the common enemy, might have stimulated them to martial enterprizes, soon excited, during the present leisure and repose, quarrels between monarchs of such a fiery character. Equally haughty, ambitious, intrepid, and inflexible, they were irritated with the least appearance of injury, and were incapable, by mutual condescensions, to efface those causes of complaint which unavoidably arose between them. Richard, candid, sin-

[1] Vinisauf, p. 305.

cere,

were, undesigning, impolitic, violent, laid himself open, on every occasion, to the designs of his antagonist; who, provident, interested, intriguing, failed not to take all advantages against him: And thus, both the circumstances of their disposition in which they were similar, and those in which they differed, rendered it impossible for them to persevere in that harmony, which was so necessary to the success of their undertaking.

THE last king of Sicily and Naples was William II. who had married Joan, sister to Richard, and who, dying without issue, had bequeathed his dominions to his paternal aunt, Constantia, the only legitimate descendant surviving of Roger, the first sovereign of those states who had been honoured with the royal title. This princess had, in expectation of that rich inheritance, been married to Henry VI. the reigning emperor[k]; but Tancred, her natural brother, had fixed such an interest among the barons, that, taking advantage of Henry's absence, he had acquired possession of the throne, and maintained his claim, by force of arms, against all the efforts of the Germans[l]. The approach of the crusaders naturally gave him apprehensions for his unstable government; and he was uncertain, whether he had most reason to dread the presence of the French or of the English monarch. Philip was engaged in a strict alliance with the emperor his competitor: Richard was disgusted by his rigors towards the queen-dowager, whom the Sicilian prince had confined in Palermo; because she had opposed with all her interest his succession to the crown. Tancred, therefore, sensible of the present necessity, resolved to pay court to both these formidable princes; and he was not unsuccessful in his endeavours. He persuaded Philip that it was highly improper for him to interrupt his enterprize against the infidels, by any attempt against a Christian state: He

CHAP. X.

1190.

Transactions to Sicily.

[k] Bened. Abb. p. 580.   [l] Hoveden, p. 663.

restored

CHAP. X.

1191.

3d October.

restored queen Joan to her liberty; and even found means to make an alliance with Richard, who stipulated by treaty to marry his nephew, Arthur, the young duke of Britanny, to one of the daughters of Tancred [a]. But before these terms of friendship were settled, Richard, jealous both of Tancred and of the inhabitants of Messina, had taken up his quarters in the suburbs, and had possessed himself of a small fort, which commanded the harbour; and he kept himself extremely on his guard against their enterprizes. The citizens took umbrage. Mutual insults and attacks passed between them and the English: Philip, who had quartered his troops in the town, endeavoured to accommodate the quarrel, and held a conference with Richard for that purpose. While the two kings, meeting in the open fields, were engaged in discourse on this subject, a body of those Sicilians seemed to be drawing towards them; and Richard pushed forwards, in order to enquire into the reason of this extraordinary movement [b]. The English, insolent from their power, and inflamed with former animosities, wanted but a pretence for attacking the Messinese: They soon chased them off the field, drove them into the town, and entered with them at the gates. The king employed his authority to restrain them from pillaging and massacring the defenceless inhabitants; but he gave orders, in token of his victory, that the standard of England should be erected on the walls. Philip, who considered that place as his quarters, exclaimed against the insult, and ordered some of his troops to pull down the standard: But Richard informed him by a messenger, that, though he himself would willingly remove that ground of offence, he would not permit it to be done by others; and if the French king attempted such an insult upon him, he should not succeed but by the utmost

[a] Hoveden, p. 676, 677. Bened. Abb. p. 615.   [b] Bened. Abb. p. 608.

effusion

effusion of blood. Philip, content with this species of haughty submission, recalled his orders [a]: The difference was seemingly accommodated; but still left the remains of rancour and jealousy in the breasts of the two monarchs.

TANCRED, who, for his own security, desired to inflame their mutual hatred, employed an artifice, which might have been attended with consequences still more fatal. He showed Richard a letter, signed by the French king, and delivered to him, as he pretended, by the duke of Burgundy; in which that monarch desired Tancred to fall upon the quarters of the English, and promised to assist him in putting them to the sword, as common enemies. The unwary Richard gave credit to the information; but was too candid not to betray his discontent to Philip, who absolutely denied the letter, and charged the Sicilian prince with forgery and falsehood. Richard either was, or pretended to be, entirely satisfied [b].

LEST these jealousies and complaints should multiply between them, it was proposed, that they should, by a solemn treaty, obviate all future differences, and adjust every point that could possibly hereafter become a controversy between them. But this expedient started a new dispute, which might have proved more dangerous than any of the foregoing, and which deeply concerned the honour of Philip's family. When Richard, in every treaty with the late king, insisted so strenuously on being allowed to marry Alice of France, he had only sought a pretence for quarrelling; and never meant to take to his bed a princess suspected of a criminal amour with his own father. After he became master, he no longer spake of that alliance: He even took measures for espousing Berengaria, daughter of Sanchez, king of Navarre, with whom he had become enamoured during his abode in

[a] Hoveden, p. 674. Brompton, p. 1195. [b] Ibid. p. 688. Bened. Abb. p. 642, 643.

Guienne:

CHAP. X.

1191.

Guienne: Queen Eleanor was daily expected with that princess at Messina: And when Philip renewed to him his applications for espousing his sister Alice, Richard was obliged to give him an absolute refusal. It is pretended by Hoveden, and other historians, that he was able to produce such convincing proofs of Alice's infidelity, and even of her having born a child to Henry, that her brother desisted from his applications, and chose to wrap up the dishonour of his family in silence and oblivion. It is certain, from the treaty itself, which remains, that, whatever were his motives, he permitted Richard to give his hand to Berengaria; and having settled all other controversies with that prince, he immediately set sail for the Holy Land. Richard awaited some time the arrival of his mother and bride; and when they joined him, he separated his fleet into two squadrons, and set forward on his enterprize. Queen Eleanor returned to England; but Berengaria, and the queen-dowager of Sicily, his sister, attended him on the expedition.

10th April.

THE English fleet, on leaving the port of Messina, met with a furious tempest; and the squadron, on which the two princesses were embarked, was driven on the coast of Cyprus, and some of the vessels were wrecked near Limisso in that island. Isaac, prince of Cyprus, who assumed the magnificent title of Emperor, pillaged the ships that were stranded, threw the seamen and passengers into prison, and even refused to the princesses liberty, in their dangerous situation, of entering the harbour of Limisso. But Richard, who arrived soon after, took ample vengeance on him for the injury. He disembarked his troops; defeated the tyrant, who opposed his landing; entered Limisso by storm; gained next day a second victory; obliged Isaac to surrender at discretion;

and

and established governors over the island. The Greek prince, being thrown into prison and loaded with irons, complained of the little regard with which he was treated: Upon which, Richard ordered silver fetters to be made for him; and this emperor, pleased with the distinction, expressed a sense of the generosity of his conqueror [v]. The king here espoused Berengaria, who, immediately embarking, carried along with her to Palestine the daughter of the Cypriot prince; a dangerous rival, who was believed to have seduced the affections of her husband. Such were the libertine character and conduct of the heroes engaged in this pious enterprize!

THE English army arrived in time to partake in the glory of the siege of Acre or Ptolemais, which had been attacked for above two years by the united force of all the Christians in Palestine, and had been defended by the utmost efforts of Saladin and the Saracens. The remains of the German army, conducted by the emperor Frederic, and the separate bodies of adventurers who continually poured in from the West, had enabled the king of Jerusalem to form this important enterprize [x]: But Saladin, having thrown a strong garrison into the place under the command of Caracos, his own master in the art of war, and molesting the besiegers with continual attacks and sallies, had protracted the success of the enterprize, and wasted the force of his enemies. The arrival of Philip and Richard inspired new life into the Christians; and these princes, acting by concert, and sharing the honour and danger of every action, gave hopes of a final victory over the infidels. They agreed on this plan of operations: When the French monarch attacked the town, the English guarded the trenches: Next day, when the English prince conducted the assault, the French

[v] Bened. Ab. p. 650. Ann. Waverl. p. 164. W. Heming. p. 523. Vinisauf, p. 318.
[x] Vinisauf, p. 269. 271. 279.

succeeded

CHAP. X.

1191.

succeeded him in providing for the safety of the assailants. The emulation between those rival kings and rival nations produced extraordinary acts of valour: Richard in particular, animated with a more precipitate courage than Philip, and more agreeable to the romantic spirit of that age, drew to himself the general attention, and acquired a great and splendid reputation. But this harmony was of short duration; and occasions of discord soon arose between these jealous and haughty princes.

State of Paleſtine.

THE family of Boüillon, which had firſt been placed on the throne of Jeruſalem, ending in a female, Fulk, count of Anjou, grandfather to Henry II. of England, married the heireſs of that kingdom, and tranſmitted his title to the younger branches of his family. The Anjevin race ending alſo in a female, Guy de Luſignan, by eſpouſing Sibylla, the heireſs, had ſucceeded to the title; and though he loſt his kingdom by the invaſion of Saladin, he was ſtill acknowledged by all the Chriſtians for king of Jeruſalem[y]. But as Sibylla died without iſſue, during the ſiege of Acre, Iſabella, her younger ſiſter, put in her claim to that titular kingdom, and required Luſignan to reſign his pretenſions to her huſband, Conrade, marquis of Monferrat. Luſignan, maintaining that the royal title was unalienable and indefeazable, had recourſe to the protection of Richard, attended on him before he left Cyprus, and engaged him to embrace his cauſe[z]. There needed no other reaſon for throwing Philip into the party of Conrade; and the oppoſite views of theſe great monarchs brought faction and diſſention into the Chriſtian army, and retarded all its operations. The Templars, the Genoeſe, and the Germans, declared for Philip and Conrade; the Flemings, the Piſans, the knights of the hoſpital of St. John, adhered to Richard

[y] Vinſauf, p. 131. [z] Trivet, p. 114. Vinſauf, p. 342. W. Hemming. p. 524.

and

and Lusignan. But notwithstanding these disputes, as the length of the siege had reduced the Saracen garrison to the last extremity, they surrendered themselves prisoners; stipulated, in return for their lives, other advantages to the Christians, such as the restoring of the Christian prisoners, and the delivery of the wood of the true cross [a]; and this great enterprize, which had long engaged the attention of all Europe and Asia, was at last, after the loss of 300,000 men, brought to a happy period.

BUT Philip, instead of pursuing the hopes of farther conquest, and of redeeming the holy city from slavery, being disgusted with the ascendant assumed and acquired by Richard, and having views of many advantages, which he might reap by his presence in Europe, declared his resolution of returning to France; and he pleaded his bad state of health as an excuse for his desertion of the common cause. He left, however, to Richard ten thousand of his troops, under the command of the duke of Burgundy; and he renewed his oath never to commence hostilities against that prince's dominions during his absence. But he had no sooner reached Italy than he applied, it is pretended, to pope Celestine III. for a dispensation from this vow; and when denied that request, he still proceeded, though after a covert manner, in a project, which the present situation of England rendered inviting, and which gratified, in an eminent degree, both his resentment and his ambition.

IMMEDIATELY after Richard had left England, and begun his march to the holy land, the two prelates, whom he had appointed guardians of the realm, broke out into animosities against each other, and threw the king-

CHAP. X.

1191.
11th July.

Disorders in England.

[a] This true cross was lost in the battle of Tiberiade, to which it had been carried by the crusaders for their protection. Rigord, an author of that age, says, that after this dismal event, all the children who were born throughout all Christendom, had only twenty or twenty-two teeth, instead of thirty or thirty-two, which was their former complement, p. 14.

CHAP. X.
1191.

dom into combustion. Longchamp, presumptuous in his nature, elated by the favour which he enjoyed with his master, and armed with the legantine commission, could not submit to an equality with the bishop of Durham: He even went so far as to arrest his colleague, and to extort from him a resignation of the earldom of Northumberland, and of his other dignities, as the price of his liberty [b]. The king, informed of these dissentions, ordered, by letters from Marseilles, that the bishop should be reinstated in his offices; but Longchamp had still the boldness to refuse compliance, on pretence that he himself was better acquainted with the king's secret intentions [c]. He proceeded to govern the kingdom by his sole authority; to treat all the nobility with arrogance; and to display his power and riches with an invidious ostentation. He never travelled without a strong guard of fifteen hundred foreign soldiers, collected from that licentious tribe, with which the age was generally infested: Nobles and knights were proud of being admitted into his train: His retinue wore the aspect of royal magnificence: And when, in his progress through the kingdom, he lodged in any monastery, his attendants, it is said, were sufficient to devour, in one night, the revenue of several years [d]. The king, who was detained in Europe longer than the haughty prelate expected, hearing of this ostentation, which exceeded even what the habits of that age indulged in ecclesiastics; being also informed of the insolent, tyrannical conduct of his minister; thought proper to restrain his power: He sent new orders, appointing Walter archbishop of Rouen, William Mareshal earl of Strigul, Geoffrey Fitz-Peter, William Briewere, and Hugh Bardolf, counsellors to Longchamp,

[b] Hoveden, p. 665. Knyghton, p. 2403. [c] W. Heming. p. 518. [d] Hoveden, p. 680. Bened. Abb. p. 616. 700. Brompton, p. 1193.

and commanding him to take no measure of importance without their concurrence and approbation. But such general terror had this man impressed by his violent conduct, that even the archbishop of Roüen and the earl of Strigul durst not produce this mandate of the king's; and Longchamp still maintained an uncontrouled authority over the nation. But when he proceeded so far as to throw into prison Geoffrey, archbishop of York, who had opposed his measures, this breach of ecclesiastical privileges excited such an universal ferment, that prince John, disgusted with the small share he possessed in the government, and personally disobliged by Longchamp, ventured to summon, at Reading, a general council of the nobility and prelates, and cite him to appear before them. Longchamp thought it dangerous to entrust his person in their hands, and he shut himself up in the Tower of London; but being soon obliged to surrender that fortress, he fled beyond sea, concealed under a female habit, and was deprived of his offices of chancellor and chief justiciary; the last of which was conferred on the archbishop of Roüen, a prelate of prudence and moderation. The commission of legate, however, which had been renewed to Longchamp by pope Celestine, still gave him, notwithstanding his absence, great authority in the kingdom, enabled him to disturb the government, and forwarded the views of Philip, who watched every opportunity of annoying Richard's dominions. That monarch first attempted to carry open war into Normandy; but as the French nobility refused to follow him in an invasion of a state which they had sworn to protect, and as the pope, who was the general guardian of all princes that had taken the cross, threatened him with ecclesiastical censures, he desisted from his enterprize, and employed against England the expedient of secret policy and intrigue. He debauched prince John from his allegiance; promised him his sister Alice in marriage; offered to give him

CHAP. X.

1192.

possession of all Richard's transmarine dominions; and had not the authority of queen Eleanor, and the menaces of the English council, prevailed over the inclinations of that turbulent prince, he was ready to have crossed the seas, and to have put in execution his criminal enterprizes.

The king's heroic actions in Palestine.

THE jealousy of Philip was every moment excited by the glory which the great actions of Richard were gaining him in the east, and which, being compared to his own desertion of that popular cause, threw a double lustre on his rival. His envy, therefore, prompted him to obscure that fame which he had not equalled; and he embraced every pretence of throwing the most violent and most improbable calumnies on the king of England. There was a petty prince in Asia, commonly called *The old man of the mountain*, who had acquired such an ascendant over his fanatical subjects, that they paid the most implicit deference to his commands; esteemed assassination meritorious, when sanctified by his mandate; courted danger, and even certain death, in the execution of his orders; and fancied, that when they sacrificed their lives for his sake, the highest joys of paradise were the infallible reward of their devoted obedience [*]. It was the custom of this prince, when he imagined himself injured, to dispatch secretly some of his subjects against the aggressor, to charge them with the execution of his revenge, to instruct them in every art of disguising their purpose; and no precaution was sufficient to guard any man, however powerful, against the attempts of those subtle and determined ruffians. The greatest monarchs stood in awe of this prince of the assassins (for that was the name of his people; whence the word has passed into most European languages), and it was the highest indiscretion in Conrade, marquis of Montserrat, to offend and

[*] W. Hemlng. p. 532. Brompton, p. 1243.

affront

RICHARD I.

affront him. The inhabitants of Tyre, who were governed by that nobleman, had put to death some of this dangerous people: The prince demanded satisfaction; for, as he piqued himself on never beginning any offence [f], he had his regular and established formalities in requiring atonement: Conrade treated his messengers with disdain: The prince issued the fatal orders: Two of his subjects, who had insinuated themselves in disguise among Conrade's guards, openly, in the streets of Sidon, wounded him mortally; and when they were seized and put to the most cruel tortures, they triumphed amidst their agonies, and rejoiced that they had been destined by heaven to suffer in so just and meritorious a cause.

Every one in Palestine knew from what hand the blow came. Richard was entirely free from suspicion. Though that monarch had formerly maintained the cause of Lusignan against Conrade, he had become sensible of the bad effects attending those dissentions, and had voluntarily conferred on the former the kingdom of Cyprus, on condition that he should resign to his rival all pretensions to the crown of Jerusalem [g]. Conrade himself, with his dying breath, had recommended his widow to the protection of Richard [h]; the prince of the assassins avowed the action in a formal narrative which he sent to Europe [i]; yet on this foundation, the king of France thought fit to build the most egregious calumnies, and to impute to Richard the murder of the marquis of Montferrat, whose elevation he had once openly opposed. He filled all Europe with exclamations against the crime; appointed a guard for his own person, in order to defend himself against a like attempt [k]; and endeavoured, by these shallow artifices, to cover the infamy of attack-

[f] Rymer, vol. I. p. 71. [g] Vinisauf, p. 391. [h] Brompton, 1243. [i] Rymer, vol. i. p. 71. Tilver, p. 124. W. Heming. p. 544. Diceto, p. 660. [k] W. Heming. p. 538. Brompton, p. 1245.

CHAP.
X.

1192.

ing the dominions of a prince, whom he himself had deserted, and who was engaged with so much glory in a war, universally acknowledged to be the common cause of Christendom.

But Richard's heroic actions in Palestine were the best apology for his conduct. The Christian adventurers under his command determined, on opening the campaign, to attempt the siege of Ascalon, in order to prepare the way for that of Jerusalem; and they marched along the sea-coast with that intention. Saladin purposed to intercept their passage; and he placed himself on the road with an army, amounting to 300,000 combatants. On this occasion was fought one of the greatest battles of that age; and the most celebrated, for the military genius of the commanders, for the number and valour of the troops, and for the great variety of events which attended it. Both the right wing of the Christians, commanded by d'Avesnes, and the left, conducted by the duke of Burgundy, were, in the beginning of the day, broken and defeated; when Richard, who led on the main body, restored the battle; attacked the enemy with intrepidity and presence of mind; performed the part both of a consummate general and gallant soldier; and not only gave his two wings leisure to recover from their confusion, but obtained a complete victory over the Saracens, of whom forty thousand are said to have perished in the field[1]. Ascalon soon after fell into the hands of the Christians: Other sieges were carried on with equal success: Richard was even able to advance within sight of Jerusalem, the object of his enterprize; when he had the mortification to find, that he must abandon all hopes of immediate success, and must put a stop to his career of victory. The crusaders, animated with an en-

[1] Hoveden, p. 698. Bened. Abb. p. 677. Diceto, p. 662. Brompton, p. 1114.

thusiastic

thusiastic ardor for the holy wars, broke at first through all regards to safety or interest in the profecution of their purpofe; and trusting to the immediate assistance of heaven, set nothing before their eyes but fame and victory in this world, and a crown of glory in the next. But long abfence from home, fatigue, difeafe, want, and the variety of incidents which naturally attend war, had gradually abated that fury, which nothing was able directly to withstand; and every one, except the king of England, expressed a defire of fpeedily returning into Europe. The Germans and the Italians declared their refolution of defifting from the enterprize: The French were still more obstinate in this purpofe: The duke of Burgundy, in order to pay court to Philip, took all opportunities of mortifying and oppofing Richard [m]: And there appeared an abfolute neceffity of abandoning for the prefent all hopes of farther conqueft, and of fecuring the acquifitions of the Chriftians by an accommodation with Saladin. Richard, therefore, concluded a truce with that monarch, and ftipulated, that Acre, Joppa, and other feaport towns of Paleftine, fhould remain in the hands of the Chriftians, and that every one of that religion fhould have liberty to perform his pilgrimage to Jerufalem unmolefted. This truce was concluded for three years, three months, three weeks, three days, and three hours; a magical number, which had probably been devifed by the Europeans, and which was fuggefted by a fuperftition well fuited to the object of the war.

THE liberty, in which Saladin indulged the Chriftians, to perform their pilgrimages to Jerufalem, was an eafy facrifice on his part; and the furious wars which he waged in defence of the barren territory of Judea, were not with him, as with the European adventurers, the refult of fuperftition, but of policy. The advantage indeed of

[m] Vinifauf. p. 380.

fcience,

CHAP. X.
1192.

science, moderation, humanity, was at that time entirely on the side of the Saracens; and this gallant emperor, in particular, displayed, during the course of the war, a spirit and generosity, which even his bigotted enemies were obliged to acknowledge and admire. Richard, equally martial and brave, carried with him more of the barbarian character; and was guilty of acts of ferocity, which threw a stain on his celebrated victories. When Saladin refused to ratify the capitulation of Acre, the king of England ordered all his prisoners, to the number of five thousand, to be butchered; and the Saracens found themselves obliged to retaliate upon the Christians by a like cruelty [a]. Saladin died at Damascus soon after concluding this truce with the princes of the crusade: It is memorable, that, before he expired, he ordered his winding-sheet to be carried as a standard through every street of the city; while a crier went before, and proclaimed with a loud voice, *This is all that remains to the mighty Saladin, the conqueror of the East.* By his last will he ordered charities to be distributed to the poor, without distinction of Jew, Christian, or Mahometan.

The king's return from Palestine.

THERE remained, after the truce, no business of importance to detain Richard in Palestine; and the intelligence which he received, concerning the intrigues of his brother John, and those of the king of France, made him sensible, that his presence was necessary in Europe. As he dared not to pass through France, he sailed to the Adriatic; and being shipwrecked near Aquileia, he put on the disguise of a pilgrim, with a purpose of taking his journey secretly through Germany. Pursued by the governor of Istria, he was forced out of the direct road to England, and was obliged to pass by Vienna; where his expences and liberalities betrayed the monarch in the

[a] Heveden, p. 697. Bened. Abb. p. 673. M. Paris, p. 115. Vinisauf. p. 346. W. Heming. p. 531.

habit

RICHARD I. 23

habit of the pilgrim; and he was arrested by orders of Leopold, duke of Austria. This prince had served under Richard at the siege of Acre; but being disgusted by some insult of that haughty monarch, he was so ungenerous as to seize the present opportunity of gratifying at once his avarice and revenge; and he threw the king into prison. The emperor Henry VI. who also considered Richard as an enemy, on account of the alliance contracted by him with Tancred, king of Sicily, dispatched messengers to the duke of Austria, required the royal captive to be delivered to him; and stipulated a large sum of money as a reward for this service. Thus the king of England, who had filled the whole world with his renown, found himself, during the most critical state of his affairs, confined in a dungeon, and loaded with irons, in the heart of Germany [a], and entirely at the mercy of his enemies, the basest and most sordid of mankind.

THE English council was astonished on receiving this fatal intelligence; and foresaw all the dangerous consequences which might naturally arise from that event. The queen-dowager wrote reiterated letters to pope Celestine, exclaiming against the injury which her son had sustained; representing the impiety of detaining in prison the most illustrious prince that had yet carried the banners of Christ into the Holy Land; claiming the protection of the apostolic see, which was due even to the meanest of those adventurers; and upbraiding the pope, that, in a cause where justice, religion, and the dignity of the church, were so much concerned, a cause which it might well befit his holiness himself to support by taking in person a journey to Germany, the spiritual thunders should so long be suspended over those sacrilegious offenders [b]. The zeal of Celestine corresponded not to the

CHAP. X.

1192.
  about December.

1193.

Captivity in Germany.

[a] Chron. T. Wykes, p. 35. 75, 76, &c.
[b] Rymer, vol. i. p. 71, 73, 74,

impatience

CHAP. X.

1193.

War with France.

impatience of the queen-mother; and the regency of England were, for a long time, left to struggle alone with all their domestic and foreign enemies.

The king of France, quickly informed of Richard's confinement by a message from the emperor [q], prepared himself to take advantage of the incident; and he employed every means of force and intrigue, of war and negotiation, against the dominions and the person of his unfortunate rival. He revived the calumny of Richard's assassinating the marquis of Montferrat; and by that absurd pretence, he induced his barons to violate their oaths, by which they had engaged, that, during the crusade, they never would, on any account, attack the dominions of the king of England. He made the emperor the largest offers, if he would deliver into his hands the royal prisoner, or at least detain him in perpetual captivity: He even formed an alliance by marriage with the king of Denmark, desired that the ancient Danish claim to the crown of England should be transferred to him, and solicited a supply of shipping to maintain it. But the most successful of Philip's negotiations was with prince John, who, forgetting every tye to his brother, his sovereign and his benefactor, thought of nothing but how to make his own advantage of the public calamities. That traitor, on the first invitation from the court of France, suddenly went abroad, had a conference with Philip, and made a treaty, of which the object was the perpetual ruin of his unhappy brother. He stipulated to deliver into Philip's hands a great part of Normandy [r]; he received, in return, the investiture of all Richard's transmarine dominions; and it is reported by several historians, that he even did homage to the French king for the crown of England.

In consequence of this treaty, Philip invaded Normandy; and by the treachery of John's emissaries, made

[q] Rymer, vol. I. p. 70.   [r] Ibid. p. 85.

himself

himself master, without opposition, of many fortresses, Neuf-chatel, Neaufle, Gisors, Pacey, Ivreé: He subdued the counties of Eu and Aumale; and advancing to form the siege of Roüen, he threatened to put all the inhabitants to the sword, if they dared to make resistance. Happily, Robert earl of Leicester appeared in that critical moment; a gallant nobleman, who had acquired great honour during the crusade, and who, being more fortunate than his master in finding his passage homewards, took on him the command in Roüen, and exerted himself, by his exhortations and example, to infuse courage into the dismayed Normans. Philip was repulsed in every attack; the time of service from his vassals expired; and he consented to a truce with the English regency, received in return the promise of 20,000 marks, and had four castles put into his hands, as security for the payment[s].

PRINCE John, who, with a view of encreasing the general confusion, went over to England, was still less successful in his enterprizes. He was only able to make himself master of the castles of Windsor and Wallingford; but when he arrived in London, and claimed the kingdom as heir to his brother, of whose death he pretended to have received certain intelligence, he was rejected by all the barons, and measures were taken to oppose and subdue him[t]. The justiciaries, supported by the general affection of the people, provided so well for the defence of the kingdom, that John was obliged, after some fruitless efforts, to conclude a truce with them; and before its expiration, he thought it prudent to return into France, where he openly avowed his alliance with Philip[u].

MEAN while, the high spirit of Richard suffered in Germany every kind of insult and indignity. The French ambassadors,

[s] Hoveden, p. 730, 731. Rymer, vol. I. p. 82.
p. 724.   [t] W. Heming. p. 556.
[u] Hoveden,

CHAP. X.

1193.

CHAP. ambassadors, in their master's name, renounced him as a
X. vassal to the crown of France, and declared all his fiefs
1193. to be forfeited to his liege-lord. The emperor, that he
might render him more impatient for the recovery of his
liberty, and make him submit to the payment of a larger
ransom, treated him with the greatest severity, and reduced him to a condition worse than that of the meanest
malefactor. He was even produced before the diet of the
empire at Worms, and accused by Henry of many crimes
and misdemeanors; of making an alliance with Tancred,
the usurper of Sicily; of turning the arms of the Crusade
against a Christian prince, and subduing Cyprus; of
affronting the duke of Austria before Acre; of obstructing
the progress of the Christian arms by his quarrels with the
king of France; of assassinating Conrade, marquis of
Montferrat; and of concluding a truce with Saladin, and
leaving Jerusalem in the hands of the Saracen emperor *.
Richard, whose spirit was not broken by his misfortunes,
and whose genius was rather rouzed by these frivolous or
scandalous imputations; after premising, that his dignity
exempted him from answering before any jurisdiction,
except that of heaven; yet condescended, for the sake of
his reputation, to justify his conduct before that great
assembly. He observed, that he had no hand in Tancred's elevation, and only concluded a treaty with a
prince, whom he found in possession of the throne: That
the king, or rather tyrant of Cyprus, had provoked his
indignation by the most ungenerous and unjust proceedings; and though he chastised this aggressor, he had not
retarded a moment the progress of his chief enterprize:
That if he had at any time been wanting in civility to the
duke of Austria, he had already been sufficiently punished
for that sally of passion; and it better became men, embarked together in so holy a cause, to forgive each other's

* M. Paris, p. 161. W. Hemingf. p. 556.

infirmities,

infirmities, than to purſue a ſlight offence with ſuch unrelenting vengeance: That it had ſufficiently appeared by the event, whether the king of France or he were moſt zealous for the conqueſt of the Holy Land, and were moſt likely to ſacrifice private paſſions and animoſities to that great object: That if the whole tenor of his life had not ſhown him incapable of a baſe aſſaſſination, and juſtified him from that imputation in the eyes of his very enemies, it was in vain for him, at preſent, to make his apology, or plead the many irrefragable arguments which he could produce in his own favour: And that, however he might regret the neceſſity, he was ſo far from being aſhamed of his truce with Saladin, that he rather gloried in that event; and thought it extremely honourable, that, though abandoned by all the world, ſupported only by his own courage and by the ſmall remains of his national troops, he could yet obtain ſuch conditions from the moſt powerful and moſt warlike emperor that the Eaſt had ever yet produced. Richard, after thus deigning to apologize for his conduct, burſt out into indignation at the cruel treatment which he had met with; that he, the champion of the croſs, ſtill wearing that honourable badge, ſhould, after expending the blood and treaſure of his ſubjects in the common cauſe of Chriſtendom, be intercepted by Chriſtian princes in his return to his own country, be thrown into a dungeon, be loaded with irons, be obliged to plead his cauſe, as if he were a ſubject and a malefactor; and, what he ſtill more regretted, be thereby prevented from making preparations for a new cruſade, which he had projected, after the expiration of the truce, and from redeeming the ſepulchre of Chriſt, which had ſo long been profaned by the dominion of infidels. The ſpirit and eloquence of Richard made ſuch impreſſion on the German princes, that they exclaimed loudly againſt the conduct of the emperor; the pope threatened him with excommunication; and Henry, who had hearkened to the propoſals

CHAP.
X.
1193.
The king's delivery.

posals of the king of France and prince John, found that it would be impracticable for him to execute his and their base purposes, or to detain the king of England any longer in captivity. He therefore concluded with him a treaty for his ransom, and agreed to restore him to his freedom for the sum of 150,000 marks, about 300,000 pounds of our present money; of which 100,000 marks were to be paid before he received his liberty, and sixty-seven hostages delivered for the remainder [r]. The emperor, as if to gloss over the infamy of this transaction, made at the same time a present to Richard of the kingdom of Arles, comprehending Provence, Dauphiny, Narbonne, and other states, over which the empire had some antiquated claims; a present which the king very wisely neglected.

1194.
4th Feb.

THE captivity of the superior lord was one of the cases provided for by the feudal tenures; and all the vassals were in that event obliged to give an aid for his ransom. Twenty shillings were therefore levied on each knight's fee in England; but as this money came in slowly, and was not sufficient for the intended purpose, the voluntary zeal of the people readily supplied the deficiency. The churches and monasteries melted down their plate, to the amount of 30,000 marks; the bishops, abbots, and nobles, paid a fourth of their yearly rent; the parochial clergy contributed a tenth of their tythes: And the requisite sum being thus collected, queen Eleanor, and Walter archbishop of Roüen, set out with it for Germany; paid the money to the emperor and the duke of Austria at Mentz; delivered them hostages for the remainder; and freed Richard from captivity. His escape was very critical. Henry had been detected in the assassination of the bishop of Liege, and in an attempt of a like nature on the duke of Louvaine; and finding himself extremely obnoxious to the German princes on account

[r] Rymer, vol. i. p. 84.

of these odious practices, he had determined to seek support from an alliance with the king of France; to detain Richard, the enemy of that prince, in perpetual captivity; to keep in his hands the money which he had already received for his ransom; and to extort fresh sums from Philip and prince John, who were very liberal in their offers to him. He therefore gave orders that Richard should be pursued and arrested; but the king, making all imaginable haste, had already embarked at the mouth of the Schelde, and was out of sight of land, when the messengers of the emperor reached Antwerp.

CHAP. X.

1194.

The joy of the English was extreme on the appearance of their monarch, who had suffered so many calamities, who had acquired so much glory, and who had spread the reputation of their name into the farthest East, whither their fame had never before been able to extend. He gave them, soon after his arrival, an opportunity of publicly displaying their exultation, by ordering himself to be crowned anew at Winchester; as if he intended, by that ceremony, to reinstate himself in his throne, and to wipe off the ignominy of his captivity. Their satisfaction was not damped, even when he declared his purpose of resuming all those exorbitant grants, which he had been necessitated to make before his departure for the Holy Land. The barons also, in a great council, confiscated, on account of his treason, all prince John's possessions in England; and they assisted the king in reducing the fortresses which still remained in the hands of his brother's adherents [r]. Richard, having settled every thing in England, passed over with an army into Normandy; being impatient to make war on Philip, and to revenge himself for the many injuries which he had received from that monarch [s]. As soon as Philip heard of the king's deli-

King's return to England. 20th March.

[r] Hoveden, p. 737. Ann. Waverl. p. 165. W. Heming. p. 540.
[s] Hoveden, p. 740.

verance

CHAP. X.
1194.
War with France.

verance from captivity, he wrote to his confederate, John, in these terms: *Take care of yourself: The devil is broken loose*[a].

WHEN we consider such powerful and martial monarchs, inflamed with personal animosity against each other, enraged by mutual injuries, excited by rivalship, impelled by opposite interests, and instigated by the pride and violence of their own temper; our curiosity is naturally raised, and we expect an obstinate and furious war, distinguished by the greatest events, and concluded by some remarkable catastrophe. Yet are the incidents, which attended those hostilities, so frivolous, that scarce any historian can entertain such a passion for military descriptions as to venture on a detail of them: A certain proof of the extreme weakness of princes in those ages, and of the little authority they possessed over their refractory vassals! The whole amount of the exploits on both sides is, the taking of a castle, the surprise of a straggling party, a rencounter of horse, which resembles more a rout than a battle. Richard obliged Philip to raise the siege of Verneüil; he took Loches, a small town in Anjou; he made himself master of Beaumont, and some other places of little consequence; and after these trivial exploits, the two kings began already to hold conferences for an accommodation. Philip insisted, that, if a general peace were concluded, the barons on each side should, for the future, be prohibited from carrying on private wars against each other: But Richard replied, that this was a right claimed by his vassals, and he could not debar them from it. After this fruitless negotiation, there ensued an action between the French and English cavalry at Fretteval, in which the former were routed, and the king of France's cartulary and records, which commonly at that time attended his person, were taken. But this victory

[a] Hoveden, p. 739.

leading

leading to no important advantages, a truce for a year was at last, from mutual weakness, concluded between the two monarchs.

During this war, prince John deserted from Philip, threw himself at his brother's feet, craved pardon for his offences, and by the intercession of queen Eleanor, was received into favour. *I forgive him,* said the king, *and hope I shall as easily forget his injuries, as he will my pardon.* John was incapable even of returning to his duty, without committing a baseness. Before he left Philip's party, he invited to dinner all the officers of the garrison, which that prince had placed in the citadel of Evreux; he massacred them during the entertainment; fell, with the assistance of the townsmen, on the garrison, whom he put to the sword; and then delivered up the place to his brother.

The king of France was the great object of Richard's resentment and animosity: The conduct of John, as well as that of the emperor and duke of Austria, had been so base, and was exposed to such general odium and reproach, that the king deemed himself sufficiently revenged for their injuries; and he seems never to have entertained any project of vengeance against any of them. The duke of Austria, about this time, having crushed his leg by the fall of his horse at a tournament, was thrown into a fever; and being struck, on the approaches of death, with remorse for his injustice to Richard, he ordered, by will, all the English hostages in his hands to be set at liberty, and the remainder of the debt due to him to be remitted: His son, who seemed inclined to disobey these orders, was constrained by his ecclesiastics to execute them [b]. The emperor also made advances for Richard's friendship, and offered to give him a discharge of all the debt, not yet paid to him, provided he

[b] Rymer, vol. I. p. 81. 102.

would

CHAP. X.

1195.

would enter into an offensive alliance against the king of France; a proposal which was very acceptable to Richard; and was greedily embraced by him. The treaty with the emperor took no effect; but it served to rekindle the war between France and England before the expiration of the truce. This war was not distinguished by any more remarkable incidents than the foregoing. After mutually ravaging the open country, and taking a few insignificant castles, the two kings concluded a peace at Louviers, and made an exchange of some territories with each other[c].

1196. Their inability to wage war occasioned the peace: Their mutual antipathy engaged them again in war before two months expired. Richard imagined, that he had now found an opportunity of gaining great advantages over his rival, by forming an alliance with the counts of Flanders, Toulouse, Boulogne, Champagne, and other considerable vassals of the crown of France[d]. But he soon experienced the insincerity of those princes; and was not able to make any impression on that kingdom, while governed by a monarch of so much vigour and activity as Philip. The most remarkable incident of this war was the taking prisoner in battle the bishop of Beauvais, a martial prelate, who was of the family of Dreux, and a near relation of the French king's. Richard, who hated that bishop, threw him into prison, and loaded him with irons; and when the pope demanded his liberty, and claimed him as his son, the king sent to his holiness the coat of mail which the prelate had worn in battle, and which was all besmeared with blood: And he replied to him, in the terms employed by Jacob's sons to that patriarch, *This have we found: Know now whether it be thy son's coat or no*[e]. This new war between England and France,

[c] Rymer, vol. I. p. 91. [d] W. Heming. p. 549. Brompton, p. 1273. Rymer, vol. I. p. 94. [e] Genesis, chap. xxxvii. ver. 32. M. Paris, p. 118. Brompton, p. 1273.

though

RICHARD I.

though carried on with such animosity, that both kings frequently put out the eyes of their prisoners, was soon finished by a truce of five years; and immediately after signing this treaty, the kings were ready, on some new offence, to break out again into hostilities; when the mediation of the cardinal of St. Mary, the pope's legate accommodated the difference [f]. This prelate even engaged the princes to commence a treaty for a more durable peace; but the death of Richard put an end to the negotiation.

VIDOMAR, viscount of Limoges, a vassal of the king's, had found a treasure, of which he sent part to that prince as a present. Richard, as superior lord, claimed the whole; and, at the head of some Brabançons, besieged the viscount in the castle of Chalus, near Limoges, in order to make him comply with his demand [g]. The garrison offered to surrender; but the king replied, that, since he had taken the pains to come thither and besiege the place in person, he would take it by force, and would hang every one of them. The same day, Richard, accompanied by Marcadée, leader of his Brabançons, approached the castle in order to survey it; when one Bertrand de Gourdon, an archer, took aim at him, and pierced his shoulder with an arrow. The king, however, gave orders for the assault, took the place, and hanged all the garrison, except Gourdon, who had wounded him, and whom he reserved for a more deliberate and more cruel execution [h].

THE wound was not in itself dangerous; but the unskilfulness of the surgeon made it mortal: He so rankled Richard's shoulder in pulling out the arrow, that a gangrene ensued; and that prince was now sensible that his life was drawing towards a period. He sent for Gour-

[f] Rymer, vol. I. p. 109, 110. p. 113. [h] Ibid. [g] Hoveden, p. 791. Knyghton, don,

CHAP. X.

1199.

don, and asked him, *Wretch, what have I ever done to you, to oblige you to seek my life?*—*What have you done to me?* replied coolly the prisoner: *You killed with your own hands my father and my two brothers; and you intended to have hanged myself: I am now in your power, and you may take revenge, by inflicting on me the most severe torments: But I shall endure them all with pleasure, provided I can think that I have been so happy as to rid the world of such a nuisance*[1]. Richard, struck with the reasonableness of this reply, and humbled by the near approach of death, ordered Gourdon to be set at liberty, and a sum of money to be given him; but Marcadée, unknown to him, seized the unhappy man, flayed him alive, and then hanged him.

6th April, Death.

Richard died in the tenth year of his reign, and the forty-second of his age; and he left no issue behind him.

and character of this king.

THE most shining part of this prince's character are his military talents. No man, even in that romantic age, carried personal courage and intrepidity to a greater height; and this quality gained him the appellation of the lion-hearted, *cœur de lion*. He passionately loved glory, chiefly military glory; and as his conduct in the field was not inferior to his valour, he seems to have possessed every talent necessary for acquiring it. His resentments also were high; his pride unconquerable; and his subjects, as well as his neighbours, had therefore reason to apprehend, from the continuance of his reign, a perpetual scene of blood and violence. Of an impetuous and vehement spirit, he was distinguished by all the good, as well as the bad qualities, incident to that character: He was open, frank, generous, sincere, and brave; he was revengeful, domineering, ambitious, haughty, and cruel; and was thus better calculated to dazzle men by the splendour of his enterprizes, than either to promote

[1] Hoveden, p. 791. Brompton, p. 1277. Knyghton, p. 2413.

RICHARD I.

their happiness or his own grandeur, by a sound and well regulated policy. As military talents make great impression on the people, he seems to have been much beloved by his English subjects; and he is remarked to have been the first prince of the Norman line that bore any sincere regard to them. He passed however only four months of his reign in that kingdom: The crusade employed him near three years; he was detained about fourteen months in captivity; the rest of his reign was spent either in war, or preparations for war, against France; and he was so pleased with the fame which he had acquired in the East, that he determined, notwithstanding his past misfortunes, to have farther exhausted his kingdom, and to have exposed himself to new hazards, by conducting another expedition against the infidels.

CHAP. X.

1199.

THOUGH the English pleased themselves with the glory which the king's martial genius procured them, his reign was very oppressive, and somewhat arbitrary, by the high taxes which he levied on them, and often without consent of the states or great council. In the ninth year of his reign, he levied five shillings on each hyde of land; and because the clergy refused to contribute their share, he put them out of the protection of law, and ordered the civil courts to give them no sentence for any debts which they might claim [h]. Twice in his reign he ordered all his charters to be sealed anew, and the parties to pay fees for the renewal [i]. It is said that Hubert, his Justiciary, sent him over to France, in the space of two years, no less a sum than 1,100,000 marks, besides bearing all the charges of the government in England. But this account is quite incredible, unless we suppose that Richard made a thorough dilapidation of the demesnes of the crown, which it is not likely he could do with any advantage after his

Miscellaneous transactions of this reign.

[h] Hoveden, p. 743. Tyrrel, vol. II. p. 563. [i] Prynne's Chronol. Vindic. tom. i. p. 1173.

CHAP. X.

1199.

former refumption of all grants. A king, who poffeffed fuch a revenue, could never have endured fourteen
months captivity, for not paying 150,000 marks to the
emperor, and be obliged at laft to leave hoftages for a
third of the fum. The prices of commodities in this
reign are alfo a certain proof, that no fuch enormous fum
could be levied on the people. A hyde of land, or
about a hundred and twenty acres, was commonly let at
twenty fhillings a year, money of that time. As there
were 243,600 hydes in England, it is eafy to compute
the amount of all the landed rents of the kingdom. The
general and ftated price of an ox was four fhillings; of
a labouring horfe the fame; of a fow, one fhilling; of
a fheep with fine wool, ten-pence; with coarfe wool,
fix-pence [m]. Thefe commodities feem not to have advanced in their prices fince the conqueft [o], and to have
ftill been ten times cheaper than at prefent.

RICHARD renewed the fevere laws againft tranfgreffors
in his forefts, whom he punifhed by caftration and putting out their eyes, as in the reign of his great-grand-
father. He eftablifhed by law one weight and meafure
throughout his kingdom [*]: A ufeful inftitution, which
the mercenary difpofition and neceffities of his fucceffor
engaged him to difpenfe with for money.

THE diforders in London, derived from its bad police,
had rifen to a great height during this reign; and in the
year 1196, there feemed to be formed fo regular a confpi-
racy among the numerous malefactors, as threatened the
city with deftruction. There was one William Fitz-
Ofbert, commonly called *Longbeard*, a lawyer, who had
rendered himfelf extremely popular among the lower rank
of citizens; and, by defending them on all occafions, had

[m] Hoveden, p. 745. [o] See note [A] at the end of the volume.
[n] M. Paris, p. 109, 134. Trivet, p. 127. Ann. Waverl. p. 165.
Hoveden, p. 774.

acquired

RICHARD I.

acquired the appellation of the advocate or saviour of the poor. He exerted his authority, by injuring and insulting the more substantial citizens, with whom he lived in a state of hostility, and who were every moment exposed to the most outrageous violences from him and his licentious emissaries. Murders were daily committed in the streets; houses were broken open and pillaged in day-light; and it is pretended, that no less than fifty-two thousand persons had entered into an association, by which they bound themselves to obey all the orders of this dangerous ruffian. Archbishop Hubert, who was then chief justiciary, summoned him before the council to answer for his conduct; but he came so well attended, that no one durst accuse him, or give evidence against him; and the primate, finding the impotence of law, contented himself with exacting from the citizens hostages for their good behaviour. He kept, however, a watchful eye on Fitz-Osbert; and seizing a favourable opportunity, attempted to commit him to custody; but the criminal, murdering one of the public officers, escaped with his concubine to the church of St. Mary le Bow, where he defended himself by force of arms. He was at last forced from his retreat, condemned, and executed, amidst the regrets of the populace, who were so devoted to his memory, that they stole his gibbet, paid the same veneration to it as to the cross, and were equally zealous in propagating and attesting reports of the miracles wrought by it[e]. But though the sectaries of this superstition were punished by the justiciary[f], it received so little encouragement from the established clergy, whose property was endangered by such seditious practices, that it suddenly sunk and vanished.

[e] Hoveden, p. 765. Diceto, p. 691. Neubrig. p. 492, 493.
[f] Gervase, p. 1551.

CHAP.
X.

1199.

It was during the crusades, that the custom of using coats of arms was first introduced into Europe. The knights, cased up in armour, had no way to make themselves be known, and distinguished in battle, but by the devices on their shields; and these were gradually adopted by their posterity and families, who were proud of the pious and military enterprizes of their ancestors.

King Richard was a passionate lover of poetry: There even remain some poetical works of his composition: And he bears a rank among the Provençal poets or *Trobadores*, who were the first of the modern Europeans that distinguished themselves by attempts of that nature.

CHAP. XI.

JOHN.

Accession of the king —— His marriage —— War with France —— Murder of Arthur duke of Britanny —— The king expelled the French provinces —— The king's quarrel with the court of Rome —— Cardinal Langton appointed archbishop of Canterbury —— Interdict of the kingdom —— Excommunication of the king —— The king's submission to the pope —— Discontents of the barons —— Insurrection of the barons —— Magna Charta —— Renewal of the civil wars —— Prince Lewis called over —— Death —— and character of the king.

THE noble and free genius of the ancients, which made the government of a single person be always regarded as a species of tyranny and usurpation, and kept them from forming any conception of a legal and regular monarchy, had rendered them entirely ignorant both of the rights of *primogeniture* and a *representation* in succession; inventions so necessary for preserving order in the lines of princes, for obviating the evils of civil discord and of usurpation, and for begetting moderation in that species of government, by giving security to the ruling sovereign. These innovations arose from the feudal law; which, first introducing the right of primogeniture, made such a distinction between the families of the elder and younger brothers, that the son

CHAP. XI.
1190.

of the former was thought entitled to succeed to his grandfather, preferably to his uncles, though nearer allied to the deceased monarch. But though this progress of ideas was natural, it was gradual. In the age of which we treat, the practice of representation was indeed introduced, but not thoroughly established; and the minds of men fluctuated between opposite principles. Richard, when he entered on the holy war, declared his nephew, Arthur duke of Britanny, his successor; and by a formal deed, he set aside, in his favour, the title of his brother John, who was younger than Geoffrey, the father of that prince [a]. But John so little acquiesced in that destination, that, when he gained the ascendant in the English ministry, by expelling Longchamp, the chancellor and great justiciary, he engaged all the English barons to swear, that they would maintain his right of succession; and Richard, on his return, took no steps towards restoring or securing the order which he had at first established. He was even careful, by his last will, to declare his brother John heir to all his dominions [b]; whether, that he now thought Arthur, who was only twelve years of age, incapable of asserting his claim against John's faction, or was influenced by Eleanor, the queen-mother, who hated Constantia, mother of the young duke, and who dreaded the credit which that princess would naturally acquire if her son should mount the throne. The authority of a testament was great in that age, even where the succession of a kingdom was concerned; and John had reason to hope that this title, joined to his plausible right in other respects, would ensure him the succession. But the idea of representation seems to have made, at this time, greater progress in France than in England: The barons of the transmarine provinces,

[a] Hoveden, p. 677. M. Paris, p. 112. Chron. de Dunst. p. 43. Rymer, vol. I. p. 66. 68. Benedict. Abb. p. 619. [b] Hoveden, p. 791. Trivet, p. 138.

Anjou,

Anjou, Maine, and Touraine, immediately declared in favour of Arthur's title, and applied for affiſtance to the French monarch as their ſuperior lord. Philip, who deſired only an occaſion to embarraſs John, and diſmember his dominions, embraced the cauſe of the young duke of Britanny, took him under his protection, and ſent him to Paris to be educated, along with his own ſon Lewis [c]. In this emergence, John haſtened to eſtabliſh his authority in the chief members of the monarchy; and after ſending Eleanor into Poictou and Guienne, where her right was inconteſtible, and was readily acknowledged, he hurried to Roüen, and having ſecured the dutchy of Normandy, he paſſed over, without loſs of time, to England. Hubert, archbiſhop of Canterbury, William Mareſchal, earl of Strigul, who alſo paſſes by the name of earl of Pembroke, and Geoffrey Fitz-Peter, the juſticiary, the three moſt favoured miniſters of the late king, were already engaged on his ſide [d]; and the ſubmiſſion or acquieſcence of all the other barons put him, without oppoſition, in poſſeſſion of the throne.

THE king ſoon returned to France, in order to conduct the war againſt Philip, and to recover the revolted provinces from his nephew, Arthur. The alliances which Richard had formed with the earl of Flanders [e], and other potent French princes, though they had not been very effectual, ſtill ſubſiſted, and enabled John to defend himſelf againſt all the efforts of his enemy. In an action between the French and Flemings, the elect biſhop of Cambray was taken priſoner by the former; and when the cardinal of Capua claimed his liberty, Philip, inſtead of complying, reproached him with the weak efforts which he had employed in favour of the biſhop of Beau-

[c] Hoveden, p. 792. M. Paris, p. 137. M. Weſt. p. 263. Knyghton, p. 2414. [d] Hoveden, p. 793. M. Paris, p. 137. [e] Rymer, vol. I. p. 114. Hoveden, p. 794. M. Paris, p. 138.

yais, who was in a like condition. The legate, to show his impartiality, laid at the same time the kingdom of France and the dutchy of Normandy under an interdict; and the two kings found themselves obliged to make an exchange of these military prelates.

NOTHING enabled the king to bring this war to a happy issue so much as the selfish, intriguing character of Philip, who acted in the provinces that had declared for Arthur, without any regard to the interests of that prince. Constantia, seized with a violent jealousy that he intended to usurp the entire dominion of them[f], found means to carry off her son secretly from Paris: She put him into the hands of his uncle; restored the provinces which had adhered to the young prince; and made him do homage for the dutchy of Britanny, which was regarded as a rere-fief of Normandy. From this incident, Philip saw that he could not hope to make any progress against John; and being threatened with an interdict on account of his irregular divorce from Ingelburga, the Danish princess, whom he had espoused, he became desirous of concluding a peace with England. After some fruitless conferences, the terms were at last adjusted; and the two monarchs seemed in this treaty to have an intention, besides ending the present quarrel, of preventing all future causes of discord, and of obviating every controversy which could hereafter arise between them. They adjusted the limits of all their territories; mutually secured the interests of their vassals; and, to render the union more durable, John gave his niece, Blanche of Castile, in marriage to prince Lewis, Philip's eldest son, and with her the baronies of Issoudun and Graçai, and other fiefs in Berri. Nine barons of the king of England, and as many of the king of France,

[f] Hoveden, p. 795.

were

were guarantees of this treaty; and all of them swore, that, if their sovereign violated any article of it, they would declare themselves against him, and embrace the cause of the injured monarch [t].

JOHN, now secure, as he imagined, on the side of France, indulged his passion for Isabella, the daughter and heir of Aymar Tailleffer, count of Angouleme, a lady with whom he had become much enamoured. His queen, the heiress of the family of Glocester, was still alive: Isabella was married to the count de la Marche, and was already consigned to the care of that nobleman; though, by reason of her tender years, the marriage had not been consummated. The passion of John made him overlook all these obstacles: He persuaded the count of Angouleme to carry off his daughter from her husband; and having, on some pretence or other, procured a divorce from his own wife, he espoused Isabella; regardless both of the menaces of the pope, who exclaimed against these irregular proceedings, and of the resentment of the injured count, who soon found means of punishing his powerful and insolent rival.

JOHN had not the art of attaching his barons either by affection or by fear. The count de la Marche, and his brother the count d'Eu, taking advantage of the general discontent against him, excited commotions in Poictou and Normandy; and obliged the king to have recourse to arms, in order to suppress the insurrection of his vassals. He summoned together the barons of England, and required them to pass the sea under his standard, and to quell the rebels: He found that he possessed as little authority in that kingdom as in his transmarine provinces. The English barons unanimously replied, that they would not attend him on this expedition, unless he would pro-

CHAP. XI.

1200.

The king's marriage.

1201.

[t] Norman. Duchessall, p. 1055. Rymer, tom. I. p. 117, 118, 119. Hoveden, p. 814. Chron. Dunst. vol. i. p. 47.

mise,

mise to restore and preserve their privileges[h]: The first symptom of a regular association and plan of liberty among those noblemen! But affairs were not yet fully ripe for the revolution projected. John, by menacing the barons, broke the concert; and both engaged many of them to follow him into Normandy, and obliged the rest, who staid behind, to pay him a scutage of two marks on each knight's fee, as the price of their exemption from the service.

The force which John carried abroad with him, and that which joined him in Normandy, rendered him much superior to his malcontent barons; and so much the more, as Philip did not publickly give them any countenance, and seemed as yet determined to persevere steadily in the alliance, which he had contracted with England. But the king, elated with his superiority, advanced claims, which gave an universal alarm to his vassals, and diffused still wider the general discontent. As the jurisprudence of those times required, that the causes in the lord's court should chiefly be decided by duel, he carried along with him certain bravos, whom he retained as champions, and whom he destined to fight with his barons, in order to determine any controversy which he might raise against them [i]. The count de la Marche, and other noblemen, regarded this proceeding as an affront, as well as an injury; and declared, that they would never draw their sword against men of such inferior quality. The king menaced them with vengeance; but he had not vigour to employ against them the force in his hands, or to prosecute the injustice, by crushing entirely the nobles who opposed it.

This government, equally feeble and violent, gave the injured barons courage as well as inclination to carry farther their opposition: They appealed to the king of France;

[h] Annal. Burton. p. 262. [i] Ibid.

France; complained of the denial of justice in John's court; demanded redress from him as their superior lord; and entreated him to employ his authority, and prevent their final ruin and oppression. Philip perceived his advantage, opened his mind to great projects, interposed in behalf of the French barons, and began to talk in a high and menacing style to the king of England. John, who could not disavow Philip's authority, replied, that it belonged to himself first to grant them a trial by their peers in his own court; it was not till he failed in this duty, that he was answerable to his peers in the supreme court of the French king[b]; and he promised, by a fair and equitable judicature, to give satisfaction to his barons. When the nobles, in consequence of this engagement, demanded a safe-conduct, that they might attend his court, he at first refused it: upon the renewal of Philip's menaces, he promised to grant their demand; he violated this promise; fresh menaces extorted from him a promise to surrender to Philip the fortresses of Tillieres and Boutavant, as a security for performance; he again violated this engagement; his enemies, sensible both of his weakness and want of faith, combined still closer in the resolution of pushing him to extremities; and a new and powerful ally soon appeared to encourage them in their invasion of this odious and despicable government.

THE young duke of Britanny, who was now rising to man's estate, sensible of the dangerous character of his uncle, determined to seek both his security and elevation by an union with Philip and the malcontent barons. He joined the French army, which had begun hostilities against the king of England: He was received with great marks of distinction by Philip; was knighted by him; espoused his daughter Mary; and was invested not only

[b] Philipp. lib. vi.

CHAP. XI.

1203.

in the dutchy of Britanny, but in the counties of Anjou and Maine, which he had formerly refigned to his uncle [l]. Every attempt fucceeded with the allies. Tillieres and Boutavant were taken by Philip, after making a feeble defence: Mortimar and Lyons fell into his hands almoft without refiftance. That prince next invefted Gournai; and opening the fluices of a lake, which lay in the neighbourhood, poured fuch a torrent of water into the place, that the garrifon deferted it, and the French monarch, without ftriking a blow, made himfelf mafter of that important fortrefs. The progrefs of the French arms was rapid, and promifed more confiderable fuccefs than ufually in that age attended military enterprizes. In anfwer to every advance which the king made towards peace, Philip ftill infifted, that he fhould refign all his tranfmarine dominions to his nephew, and reft contented with the kingdom of England; when an event happened, which feemed to turn the fcales in favour of John, and to give him a decifive fuperiority over his enemies.

YOUNG Arthur, fond of military renown, had broken into Poictou at the head of a fmall army; and paffing near Mirebeau, he heard, that his grandmother, Queen Eleanor, who had always oppofed his interefts, was lodged in that place, and was protected by a weak garrifon, and ruinous fortifications [m]. He immediately determined to lay fiege to the fortrefs, and make himfelf mafter of her perfon: But John, rouzed from his indolence by fo preffing an occafion, collected an army of Englifh and Brabançons, and advanced from Normandy with hafty marches to the relief of the queen-mother. He fell on Arthur's camp before that prince was aware of the danger; difperfed his army; took him prifoner, together with the count de la Marche, Geoffrey de Lufignan, and the moft confiderable of the revolted barons; and returned in

[l] Trivet, p. 142. [m] Ann. Waverl. p. 167. M. Weft. p. 264.

triumph

triumph to Normandy. Philip, who was lying before Arques in that dutchy, raised the siege and retired, upon his approach. The greater part of the prisoners were sent over to England; but Arthur was shut up in the castle of Falaise.

THE king had here a conference with his nephew; represented to him the folly of his pretensions; and required him to renounce the French alliance, which had encouraged him to live in a state of enmity with all his family: But the brave, though imprudent, youth, rendered more haughty from misfortunes, maintained the justice of his cause; asserted his claim, not only to the French provinces, but to the crown of England; and, in his turn, required the king to restore the son of his elder brother to the possession of his inheritance. John, sensible, from these symptoms of spirit, that the young prince, though now a prisoner, might hereafter prove a dangerous enemy, determined to prevent all future peril by dispatching his nephew; and Arthur was never more heard of. The circumstances which attended this deed of darkness were, no doubt, carefully concealed by the actors, and are variously related by historians: But the most probable account is as follows: The king, it is said, first proposed to William de la Bray, one of his servants, to dispatch Arthur; but William replied, that he was a gentleman, not a hangman; and he positively refused compliance. Another instrument of murder was found, and was dispatched with proper orders to Falaise; but Hubert de Bourg, chamberlain to the king, and constable of the castle, feigning that he himself would execute the king's mandate, sent back the assassin, spread the report that the young prince was dead, and publickly performed all the ceremonies of his interment: But finding, that the

CHAP. XI.

1203.
18 August.

Murder of Arthur duke of Brittany.

Bretons

CHAP. XI.
1203.

Bretons vowed revenge for the murder, and that all the revolted barons persevered more obstinately in their rebellion, he thought it prudent to reveal the secret, and to inform the world that the duke of Britanny was still alive, and in his custody. This discovery proved fatal to the young prince: John first removed him to the castle of Roüen; and coming in a boat, during the night-time, to that place, commanded Arthur to be brought forth to him. The young prince, aware of his danger, and now more subdued by the continuance of his misfortunes, and by the approach of death, threw himself on his knees before his uncle, and begged for mercy: But the barbarous tyrant, making no reply, stabbed him with his own hands; and fastening a stone to the dead body, threw it into the Seine.

ALL men were struck with horror at this inhuman deed; and from that moment the king, detested by his subjects, retained a very precarious authority over both the people and the barons in his dominions. The Bretons, enraged at this disappointment in their fond hopes, waged implacable war against him; and fixing the succession of their government, put themselves in a posture to revenge the murder of their sovereign. John had got into his power his niece, Eleanor, sister to Arthur, commonly called *the Damsel of Britanny*; and carrying her over to England, detained her ever after in captivity [t]: But the Bretons, in despair of recovering this princess, chose Alice for their sovereign; a younger daughter of Constantia, by her second marriage with Guy de Thouars; and they entrusted the government of the dutchy to that nobleman. The states of Britanny, meanwhile, carried their complaints before Philip as their liege lord, and demanded justice for the violence commit-

[t] Trivet, p. 145. T. Wykes, p. 36. Ypod. Neust. p. 459.

JOHN.

led by John on the person of Arthur, so near a relation, who, notwithstanding the homage which he did to Normandy, was always regarded as one of the chief vassals of the crown. Philip received their application with pleasure; summoned John to stand a trial before him; and on his non-appearance passed sentence, with the concurrence of the peers, upon that prince; declared him guilty of felony and parricide; and adjudged him to forfeit to his superior lord all his seignories and fiefs in France [r].

CHAP. XI.
1203.

THE king of France, whose ambitious and active spirit had been hitherto confined, either by the sound policy of Henry, or the martial genius of Richard, seeing now the opportunity favourable against this base and odious prince, embraced the project of expelling the English, or rather the English king, from France, and of annexing to the crown so many considerable fiefs, which, during several ages, had been dismembered from it. Many of the other great vassals, whose jealousy might have interposed, and have obstructed the execution of this project, were not at present in a situation to oppose it; and the rest either looked on with indifference, or gave their assistance to this dangerous aggrandizement of their superior lord. The earls of Flanders and Blois were engaged in the holy war: The count of Champagne was an infant, and under the guardianship of Philip: The dutchy of Britanny, enraged at the murder of their prince, vigorously promoted all his measures: And the general defection of John's vassals made every enterprize easy and successful against him. Philip, after taking several castles and fortresses beyond the Loire, which he either garrisoned or dismantled, received the submissions of the count of Alençon, who deserted John, and delivered up all the places under his command to the French: Upon which Philip

The king expelled from the French provinces.

[r] W. Heming. p. 435. M. West. p. 264. Knyghton, p. 2410.

VOL. II.   E   broke

CHAP. XI.

1203.

broke up his camp, in order to give the troops some repose after the fatigues of the campaign. John, suddenly collecting some forces, laid siege to Alençon; and Philip, whose dispersed army could not be brought together in time to succour it, saw himself exposed to the disgrace of suffering the oppression of his friend and confederate. But his active and fertile genius found an expedient against this evil. There was held at that very time a tournament at Moret in the Gatinois; whither all the chief nobility of France and the neighbouring countries had resorted, in order to signalize their prowess and address. Philip presented himself before them; craved their assistance in his distress; and pointed out the plains of Alençon, as the most honourable field in which they could display their generosity and martial spirit. Those valorous knights vowed, that they would take vengeance on the base parricide, the stain of arms and of chivalry; and putting themselves, with all their retinue, under the command of Philip, instantly marched to raise the siege of Alençon. John, hearing of their approach, fled from before the place; and in the hurry abandoned all his tents, machines, and baggage, to the enemy.

THIS feeble effort was the last exploit of that slothful and cowardly prince for the defence of his dominions. He thenceforth remained in total inactivity at Rouen; passing all his time, with his young wife, in pastimes and amusements, as if his state had been in the most profound tranquillity, or his affairs in the most prosperous condition. If he ever mentioned war, it was only to give himself vaunting airs, which, in the eyes of all men, rendered him still more despicable and ridiculous. *Let the French go on*, said he, *I will retake in a day what it has cost them years to acquire*[a]. His stupidity and indolence appeared so extraordinary, that the people endeavoured to

[a] M. Paris, p. 146. M. West. p. 266.

account for the infatuation by forcery, and believed, that he was thrown into this lethargy by fome magic or witchcraft. The Englifh barons, finding that their time was wafted to no purpofe, and that they muft fuffer the difgrace of feeing, without refiftance, the progrefs of the French arms, withdrew from their colours, and fecretly returned to their own country[f]. No one thought of defending a man, who feemed to have deferted himfelf; and his fubjects regarded his fate with the fame indifference, to which, in this preffing exigency, they faw him totally abandoned.

JOHN, while he neglected all domeftic refources, had the meannefs to betake himfelf to a foreign power, whofe protection he claimed: He applied to the pope, Innocent III. and entreated him to interpofe his authority between him and the French monarch. Innocent, pleafed with any occafion of exerting his fuperiority, fent Philip orders to ftop the progrefs of his arms, and to make peace with the king of England. But the French barons received the meffage with indignation; difclaimed the temporal authority affumed by the pontiff; and vowed, that they would, to the uttermoft, affift their prince againft all his enemies: Philip, feconding their ardour, proceeded, inftead of obeying the pope's envoys, to lay fiege to Chateau Gaillard, the moft confiderable fortrefs which remained to guard the frontiers of Normandy.

CHATEAU GAILLARD was fituated partly on an ifland in the river Seine, partly on a rock oppofite to it; and was fecured by every advantage, which either art or nature could beftow upon it. The late king, having caft his eye on this favourable fituation, had fpared no labour or expence in fortifying it; and it was defended by Roger de Laci, conftable of Chefter, a determined officer,

[f] M. Paris, p. 146. M. Weft. p. 264.

CHAP. XI.

1204.

at the head of a numerous garrison. Philip, who despaired of taking the place by force, purposed to reduce it by famine; and that he might cut off its communication with the neighbouring country, he threw a bridge across the Seine, while he himself with his army blockaded it by land. The earl of Pembroke, the man of greatest vigour and capacity in the English court, formed a plan for breaking through the French entrenchments, and throwing relief into the place. He carried with him an army of 4000 infantry and 3000 cavalry, and suddenly attacked, with great success, Philip's camp in the night-time; having left orders, that a fleet of seventy flat-bottomed vessels should sail up the Seine, and fall at the same instant on the bridge. But the wind and the current of the river, by retarding the vessels, disconcerted this plan of operations; and it was morning before the fleet appeared; when Pembroke, though successful in the beginning of the action, was already repulsed with considerable loss, and the king of France had leisure to defend himself against these new assailants, who also met with a repulse. After this misfortune, John made no farther efforts for the relief of Chateau Gaillard; and Philip had all the leisure requisite for conducting and finishing the siege. Roger de Laci defended himself for a twelvemonth with great obstinacy; and having bravely repelled every attack, and patiently borne all the hardships of famine, he was at last overpowered by a sudden assault in the night-time, and made prisoner of war, with his garrison [t]. Philip, who knew how to respect valour even in an enemy, treated him with civility, and gave him the whole city of Paris for the place of his confinement.

WHEN this bulwark of Normandy was once subdued, all the province lay open to the inroads of Philip; and the king of England despaired of being any longer able to

[t] Triveт, p. 144. Gul. Brito, lib. 7. Ann. Waverl. p. 168.

defend

defend it. He secretly prepared vessels for a scandalous flight; and that the Normans might no longer doubt of his resolution to abandon them, he ordered the fortifications of Pont de l'Arche, Moulineaux, and Montfort l'Amauri to be demolished. Not daring to repose confidence in any of his barons, whom he believed to be universally engaged in a conspiracy against him, he entrusted the government of the province to Archas Martin and Lupicaire, two mercenary Brabançons, whom he had retained in his service. Philip, now secure of his prey, pushed his conquests with vigour and success against the dismayed Normans. Falaise was first besieged; and Lupicaire, who commanded in this impregnable fortress, after surrendering the place, inlisted himself with his troops in the service of Philip, and carried on hostilities against his ancient master. Caen, Coutance, Seez, Evreux, Baïeux soon fell into the hands of the French monarch, and all the lower Normandy was reduced under his dominion. To forward his enterprizes on the other division of the province, Gui de Thouars, at the head of the Bretons, broke into the territory, and took Mount St. Michael, Avranches, and all the other fortresses in that neighbourhood. The Normans, who abhorred the French yoke, and who would have defended themsevles to the last extremity, if their prince had appeared to conduct them, found no resource but in submission; and every city opened its gates, as soon as Philip appeared before it. Roüen alone, Arques, and Verneüil determined to maintain their liberties; and formed a confederacy for mutual defence. Philip began with the siege of Roüen: The inhabitants were so inflamed with hatred to France, that, on the appearance of his army, they fell on all the natives of that country, whom they found within their walls, and put them to death. But after the French king had begun his operations with success, and had taken some of their

CHAP.
XI.

1205.
18 June.

their outworks, the citizens, seeing no resource, offered to capitulate, and demanded only thirty days to advertise their prince of their danger, and to require succours against the enemy. Upon the expiration of the term, as no supply had arrived, they opened their gates to Philip [w]; and the whole province soon after imitated the example, and submitted to the victor. Thus was this important territory re-united to the crown of France, about three centuries after the cession of it by Charles the Simple to Rollo, the first duke: And the Normans, sensible that this conquest was probably final, demanded the privilege of being governed by French laws; which Philip, making a few alterations on the ancient Norman customs, readily granted them. But the French monarch had too much ambition and genius to stop in his present career of success. He carried his victorious army into the western provinces; soon reduced Anjou, Maine, Touraine, and part of Poictou [x]; and in this manner, the French crown, during the reign of one able and active prince, received such an accession of power and grandeur, as, in the ordinary course of things, it would have required several ages to attain.

JOHN, on his arrival in England, that he might cover the disgrace of his own conduct, exclaimed loudly against his barons, who, he pretended, had deserted his standard in Normandy; and he arbitrarily extorted from them a seventh of all their moveables, as a punishment for the offence [y]. Soon after he forced them to grant him a scutage of two marks and a half on each knight's fee for an expedition into Normandy; but he did not attempt to execute the service for which he pretended to exact it. Next year, he summoned all the barons of his realm to attend him on this foreign expedition, and collected ships

[w] Trivet, p. 147. Ypod. Neust. p. 459.   [x] Trivet, p. 149.
[y] M. Paris, p. 146. M. West p. 265.

from

JOHN.

from all the sea-ports; but meeting with opposition from some of his ministers, and abandoning his design, he dismissed both fleet and army, and then renewed his exclamations against the barons for deserting him. He next put to sea with a small army, and his subjects believed, that he was resolved to expose himself to the utmost hazard for the defence and recovery of his dominions: But they were surprized, after a few days, to see him return again into harbour, without attempting any thing. In the subsequent season, he had the courage to carry his hostile measures a step farther. Gui de Thouars, who governed Britanny, jealous of the rapid progress made by his ally, the French king, promised to join the king of England with all his forces; and John ventured abroad with a considerable army, and landed at Rochelle. He marched to Angers; which he took and reduced to ashes. But the approach of Philip with an army threw him into a panic; and he immediately made proposals for peace, and fixed a place of interview with his enemy: But instead of keeping this engagement, he stole off with his army, embarked at Rochelle, and returned, loaded with new shame and disgrace, into England. The mediation of the pope procured him at last a truce for two years with the French monarch [a]; almost all the transmarine provinces were ravished from him; and his English barons, though harassed with arbitrary taxes and fruitless expeditions, saw themselves and their country baffled and affronted in every enterprize.

In an age, when personal valour was regarded as the chief accomplishment, such conduct as that of John, always disgraceful, must be exposed to peculiar contempt; and he must thenceforth have expected to rule his turbulent vassals with a very doubtful authority. But the government, exercised by the Norman princes, had wound

[a] Rymer, vol. I. p. 141.

CHAP.
XI.
1206.

up the royal power to so high a pitch, and so much beyond the usual tenor of the feudal constitutions, that it still behoved him to be debased by new affronts and disgraces, ere his barons could entertain the view of conspiring against him, in order to retrench his prerogatives. The church, which, at that time, declined not a contest with the most powerful and most vigorous monarchs, took first advantage of John's imbecility; and, with the most aggravating circumstances of insolence and scorn, fixed her yoke upon him.

1207.

The king's quarrel with the court of France.

THE papal chair was then filled by Innocent III. who, having attained that dignity at the age of thirty-seven years, and being endowed with a lofty and enterprizing genius, gave full scope to his ambition, and attempted, perhaps more openly than any of his predecessors, to convert that superiority, which was yielded him by all the European princes, into a real dominion over them. The hierarchy, protected by the Roman pontiff, had already carried to an enormous height its usurpations upon the civil power; but in order to extend them farther, and render them useful to the court of Rome, it was necessary to reduce the ecclesiastics themselves under an absolute monarchy, and to make them entirely dependant on their spiritual leader. For this purpose, Innocent first attempted to impose taxes at pleasure upon the clergy; and in the first year of this century, taking advantage of the popular frenzy for crusades, he sent collectors over all Europe, who levied, by his authority, the fortieth of all ecclesiastical revenues for the relief of the Holy Land, and received the voluntary contributions of the laity to a like amount[a]. The same year Hubert, archbishop of Canterbury, attempted another innovation, favourable to ecclesiastical and papal power: In the king's absence, he

[a] Rymer, vol. I. p. 119.

summoned,

JOHN. 57

summoned, by his legantine authority, a synod of all the English clergy, contrary to the inhibition of Geoffrey Fitz-Peter, the chief justiciary; and no proper censure was ever passed on this encroachment, the first of the kind, upon the royal power. But a favourable incident soon after happened, which enabled so aspiring a pontiff as Innocent, to extend still farther his usurpations on so contemptible a prince as John.

CHAP. XI.
1207.

HUBERT, the primate, died in 1205; and as the monks or canons of Christ-church, Canterbury, possessed a right of voting in the election of their archbishop, some of the juniors of the order, who lay in wait for that event, met clandestinely the very night of Hubert's death, and, without any congé d'elire from the king, chose Reginald, their sub-prior, for the successor; installed him in the archi-episcopal throne before midnight; and having enjoined him the strictest secrecy, sent him immediately to Rome, in order to solicit the confirmation of his election[b]. The vanity of Reginald prevailed over his prudence; and he no sooner arrived in Flanders, than he revealed to every one the purpose of his journey, which was immediately known in England[c]. The king was enraged at the novelty and temerity of the attempt, in filling so important an office without his knowledge or consent: The suffragan bishops of Canterbury, who were accustomed to concur in the choice of their primate, were no less displeased at the exclusion given them in this election: The senior monks of Christ-church were injured by the irregular proceedings of their juniors: The juniors themselves, ashamed of their conduct, and disgusted with the levity of Reginald, who had broken his engagements with them, were willing to set aside his election[d]: And all men concurred in the design of remedying the false

[b] M. Paris, p. 148. M. West. p. 166. [c] Ibid.
[d] M. West. p. 166.

measures

CHAP. XI.
1207.

measures which had been taken. But as John knew that this affair would be canvassed before a superior tribunal, where the interposition of royal authority in bestowing ecclesiastical benefices was very invidious; where even the cause of suffragan bishops was not so favourable as that of monks; he determined to make the new election entirely unexceptionable: He submitted the affair wholly to the canons of Christ-church; and departing from the right claimed by his predecessors, ventured no farther than to inform them privately, that they would do him an acceptable service if they chose John de Gray, bishop of Norwich, for their primate[e]. The election of that prelate was accordingly made without a contradictory vote; and the king, to obviate all contests, endeavoured to persuade the suffragan bishops not to insist on their claim of concurring in the election: But those prelates, persevering in their pretensions, sent an agent to maintain their cause before Innocent; while the king, and the convent of Christ-church, dispatched twelve monks of that order to support, before the same tribunal, the election of the bishop of Norwich.

Thus there lay three different claims before the pope, whom all parties allowed to be the supreme arbiter in the contest. The claim of the suffragans, being so opposite to the usual maxims of the papal court, was soon set aside: The election of Reginald was so obviously fraudulent and irregular, that there was no possibility of defending it: But Innocent maintained, that though this election was null and invalid, it ought previously to have been declared such by the sovereign pontiff, before the monks could proceed to a new election; and that the choice of the bishop of Norwich was of course as uncanonical as that of his competitor[f]. Advantage was therefore taken of

[e] M. Paris, p. 149. M. West. p. 266. Chron. de Mailr. p. 182.
[f] M. Paris, p. 155.

this subtlety for introducing a precedent, by which the fee of Canterbury, the most important dignity in the church after the papal throne, should ever after be at the disposal of the court of Rome.

While the pope maintained so many fierce contests, in order to wrest from princes the right of granting investitures, and to exclude laymen from all authority in conferring ecclesiastical benefices, he was supported by the united influence of the clergy, who, aspiring to independence, fought, with all the ardour of ambition, and all the zeal of superstition, under his sacred banners. But no sooner was this point, after a great effusion of blood, and the convulsions of many states, established in some tolerable degree, than the victorious leader, as is usual, turned his arms against his own community, and aspired to centre all power in his person. By the invention of reserves, provisions, commendams, and other devices, the pope gradually assumed the right of filling vacant benefices; and the plenitude of his apostolic power, which was not subject to any limitations, supplied all defects of title in the person on whom he bestowed preferment. The canons which regulated elections were purposely rendered intricate and involved: Frequent disputes arose among candidates: Appeals were every day carried to Rome: The apostolic see, besides reaping pecuniary advantages from these contests, often exercised the power of setting aside both the litigants, and, on pretence of appeasing faction, nominated a third person, who might be more acceptable to the contending parties.

This present controversy about the election to the see of Canterbury afforded Innocent an opportunity of claiming this right; and he failed not to perceive and avail himself of the advantage. He sent for the twelve monks deputed by the convent to maintain the cause of the bishop of Norwich; and commanded them, under the penalty

of

CHAP. XL.

1207.
Cardinal Langton appointed archbishop of Canterbury.

of excommunication, to chuse for their primate cardinal Langton, an Englishman by birth, but educated in France, and connected, by his interest and attachments, with the see of Rome [e]. In vain did the monks represent, that they had received from their convent no authority for this purpose; that an election, without a previous writ from the king, would be deemed highly irregular; and that they were merely agents for another person, whose right they had no power or pretence to abandon. None of them had the courage to persevere in this opposition, except one, Elias de Brantefield: All the rest, overcome by the menaces and authority of the pope, complied with his orders, and made the election required of them.

INNOCENT, sensible that this flagrant usurpation would be highly resented by the court of England, wrote John a mollifying letter; sent him four golden rings set with precious stones; and endeavoured to enhance the value of the present, by informing him of the many mysteries implied in it. He begged him to consider seriously the *form* of the rings, their *number*, their *matter*, and their *colour*. Their form, he said, being round, shadowed out Eternity, which had neither beginning nor end; and he ought thence to learn his duty of aspiring from earthly objects to heavenly, from things temporal to things eternal. The number four, being a square, denoted steadiness of mind, not to be subverted either by adversity or prosperity, fixed for ever on the firm basis of the four cardinal virtues. Gold, which is the matter, being the most precious of metals, signified Wisdom, which is the most valuable of all accomplishments, and justly preferred by Solomon to riches, power, and all exterior attainments. The blue colour of the saphire represented Faith; the

[e] M. Paris, p. 156. Ann. Waverl. p. 169. W. Heming. p. 553. Knyghton, p. 1415.

verdure

verdure of the emerald, Hope; the redness of the ruby, Charity; and the splendour of the topaz, Good Works[h]. By these conceits, Innocent endeavoured to repay John for one of the most important prerogatives of his crown, which he had ravished from him; conceits probably admired by Innocent himself: For it is easily possible for a man, especially in a barbarous age, to unite strong talents for business with an absurd taste for literature and the arts.

JOHN was inflamed with the utmost rage when he heard of this attempt of the court of Rome[i]; and he immediately vented his passion on the monks of Christchurch, whom he found inclined to support the election made by their fellows at Rome. He sent Fulk de Cantelupe, and Henry de Cornhulle, two knights of his retinue, men of violent tempers and rude manners, to expel them the convent, and take possession of their revenues. These knights entered the monastery with drawn swords, commanded the prior and the monks to depart the kingdom, and menaced them, that, in case of disobedience, they would instantly burn them with the convent[k]. Innocent prognosticating, from the violence and imprudence of these measures, that John would finally sink in the contest, persevered the more vigorously in his pretensions, and exhorted the king not to oppose God and the church any longer, nor to prosecute that cause for which the holy martyr St. Thomas had sacrificed his life, and which had exalted him equal to the highest saints in heaven[l]: A clear hint to John to profit by the example of his father, and to remember the prejudices and established principles of his subjects, who bore a profound veneration to that martyr, and regarded his merits as the subject of their chief glory and exultation.

[h] Rymer, vol. i. p. 139. M. Paris, p. 155. [i] Rymer, vol. i. p. 143. [k] M. Paris, p. 156. Trivet, p. 151. Ann. Waverl. p. 169. [l] M. Paris, p. 157.

INNOCENT,

INNOCENT, finding that John was not sufficiently tamed to submission, sent three prelates, the bishops of London, Ely, and Worcester, to intimate, that if he persevered in his disobedience, the sovereign pontiff would be obliged to lay the kingdom under an interdict[m]. All the other prelates threw themselves on their knees before him, and entreated him, with tears in their eyes, to prevent the scandal of this sentence, by making a speedy submission to his spiritual father, by receiving from his hands the new-elected primate, and by restoring the monks of Christ-church to all their rights and possessions. He burst out into the most indecent invectives against the prelates; swore by God's teeth, his usual oath, that if the pope presumed to lay his kingdom under an interdict, he would send to him all the bishops and clergy in England, and would confiscate all their estates; and threatened, that if thenceforth he caught any Romans in his dominions, he would put out their eyes, and cut off their noses, in order to set a mark upon them which might distinguish them from all other nations[n]. Amidst all this idle violence, John stood on such bad terms with his nobility, that he never dared to assemble the states of the kingdom, who, in so just a cause, would probably have adhered to any other monarch, and have defended with vigour the liberties of the nation against these palpable usurpations of the court of Rome. Innocent, therefore, perceiving the king's weakness, fulminated at last the sentence of interdict, which he had for some time held suspended over him[o].

Interdict of the kingdom.

THE sentence of interdict was at that time the great instrument of vengeance and policy employed by the court of Rome; was denounced against sovereigns for the lightest offences; and made the guilt of one person involve the

[m] M. Paris, p. 157. [n] Ibid. [o] Ibid. Trivet, p. 152.
Ann. Waverl. p. 170. M. West. p. 268.

ruin

ruin of millions, even in their spiritual and eternal welfare. The execution of it was calculated to strike the senses in the highest degree, and to operate with irresistible force on the superstitious minds of the people. The nation was of a sudden deprived of all exterior exercise of its religion: The altars were despoiled of their ornaments: The crosses, the reliques, the images, the statues of the saints, were laid on the ground; and, as if the air itself were profaned, and might pollute them by its contact, the priests carefully covered them up, even from their own approach and veneration. The use of bells entirely ceased in all the churches: The bells themselves were removed from the steeples, and laid on the ground with the other sacred utensils. Mass was celebrated with shut doors, and none but the priests were admitted to that holy institution. The laity partook of no religious rite, except baptism to new-born infants, and the communion to the dying: The dead were not interred in consecrated ground: They were thrown into ditches, or buried in common fields; and their obsequies were not attended with prayers, or any hallowed ceremony. Marriage was celebrated in the church-yards [p]; and that every action in life might bear the marks of this dreadful situation, the people were prohibited the use of meat, as in Lent, or times of the highest penance; were debarred from all pleasures and entertainments; and were forbidden even to salute each other, or so much as to shave their beards, and give any decent attention to their person and apparel. Every circumstance carried symptoms of the deepest distress, and of the most immediate apprehension of divine vengeance and indignation.

THE king, that he might oppose *his* temporal to *their* spiritual terrors, immediately, from his own authority, confiscated the estates of all the clergy who obeyed the

[p] Chron. Dunst. vol. i. p. 51.

interdict;

CHAP.
XI.
1207.

interdict[q]; banished the prelates, confined the monks in their convent, and gave them only such a small allowance from their own estates as would suffice to provide them with food and raiment. He treated with the utmost rigour all Langton's adherents, and every one that showed any disposition to obey the commands of Rome: And in order to distress the clergy in the tenderest point, and at the same time expose them to reproach and ridicule, he threw into prison all their concubines, and required high fines as the price of their liberty[r].

AFTER the canons which established the celibacy of the clergy were, by the zealous endeavours of archbishop Anselm, more rigorously executed in England, the ecclesiastics gave, almost universally and avowedly, into the use of concubinage; and the court of Rome, which had no interest in prohibiting this practice, made very slight opposition to it. The custom was become so prevalent, that, in some cantons of Switzerland, before the reformation, the laws not only permitted, but, to avoid scandal, enjoined the use of concubines to the younger clergy[s]; and it was usual every where for priests to apply to the ordinary, and obtain from him a formal liberty for this indulgence. The bishop commonly took care to prevent the practice from degenerating into licentiousness: He confined the priest to the use of one woman, required him to be constant to her bed, obliged him to provide for her subsistence and that of her children; and though the offspring was, in the eye of the law, deemed illegitimate, this commerce was really a kind of inferior marriage, such as is still practised in Germany among the nobles; and may be regarded by the candid as an appeal from the tyranny of civil and ecclesiastical institutions, to the more virtuous and more unerring laws of nature.

[q] Ann. Waverl. p. 170.   [r] M. Paris, p. 158. Ann. Waverl. p. 170.   [s] Padre Paolo, Hist. Conc. Trid. lib. 1.

THE

JOHN

THE quarrel between the king and the see of Rome continued for some years; and though many of the clergy, from the fear of punishment, obeyed the orders of John, and celebrated divine service, they complied with the utmost reluctance, and were regarded, both by themselves and the people, as men who betrayed their principles, and sacrificed their conscience to temporal regards and interests. During this violent situation, the king, in order to give a lustre to his government, attempted military expeditions against Scotland, against Ireland, against the Welsh[1]; and he commonly prevailed, more from the weakness of his enemies, than from his own vigour or abilities. Meanwhile, the danger to which his government stood continually exposed from the discontents of the ecclesiastics, encreased his natural propension to tyranny; and he seems to have even wantonly disgusted all orders of men, especially his nobles, from whom alone he could reasonably expect support and assistance. He dishonoured their families by his licentious amours; he published edicts, prohibiting them from hunting feathered game, and thereby restrained them from their favourite occupation and amusement[a]; he ordered all the hedges and fences near his forests to be levelled, that his deer might have more ready access into the fields for pasture; and he continually loaded the nation with arbitrary impositions. Conscious of the general hatred which he had incurred, he required his nobility to give him hostages for security of their allegiance; and they were obliged to put into his hands their sons, nephews, or near relations. When his messengers came with like orders to the castle of William de Braouse, a baron of great note, the lady of that nobleman replied, That she would never entrust her son into the hands of one

CHAP. XI.

1207.

1208.

[1] W. Heming. p. 556. Ypod. Neust. p. 460. Knyghton, p. 2420.
[a] M. West. p. 268.

VOL. II.   F   who

who had murdered his own nephew, while in his custody. Her husband reproved her for the severity of this speech; but, sensible of his danger, he immediately fled with his wife and son into Ireland, where he endeavoured to conceal himself. The king discovered the unhappy family in their retreat; seized the wife and son, whom he starved to death in prison; and the baron himself narrowly escaped, by flying into France.

1209.

The court of Rome had artfully contrived a gradation of sentences; by which she kept offenders in awe; still afforded them an opportunity of preventing the next anathema by submission; and, in case of their obstinacy, was able to refresh the horror of the people against them, by new denunciations of the wrath and vengeance of heaven. As the sentence of interdict had not produced the desired effect on John, and as his people, though extremely discontented, had hitherto been restrained from rising in open rebellion against him, he was soon to look for the sentence of excommunication: And he had reason to apprehend, that, notwithstanding all his precautions, the most dangerous consequences might ensue from it. He was witness of the other scenes, which, at that very time, were acting in Europe, and which displayed the unbounded and uncontrouled power of the papacy. Innocent, far from being dismayed at his contests with the king of England, had excommunicated the emperor Otho, John's nephew *; and soon brought that powerful and haughty prince to submit to his authority. He published a crusade against the Albigenses, a species of enthusiasts in the south of France, whom he denominated heretics; because, like other enthusiasts, they neglected the rites of the church, and opposed the power

* M. Paris, p. 160. Triv, 154. M. West. p. 269.

and

and influence of the clergy: The people from all parts of
Europe, moved by their superstition and their passion for
wars and adventures, flocked to his standard: Simon de
Montfort, the general of the crusade, acquired to himself a sovereignty in these provinces: The count of
Toulouse, who protected, or perhaps only tolerated, the
Albigenses, was stripped of his dominions: And these sectaries themselves, though the most innocent and inoffensive of mankind, were exterminated with all the circumstances of extreme violence and barbarity. Here were
therefore both an army and a general, dangerous from
their zeal and valour, who might be directed to act
against John; and Innocent, after keeping the thunder
long suspended, gave at last authority to the bishops of
London, Ely, and Worcester, to fulminate the sentence
of excommunication against him [s]. These prelates obeyed; though their brethren were deterred from publishing,
as the pope required of them, the sentence in the several
churches of their dioceses.

No sooner was the excommunication known, than the
effects of it appeared. Geoffrey, archdeacon of Norwich, who was entrusted with a considerable office in the
court of exchequer, being informed of it while sitting on
the bench, observed to his colleagues the danger of serving
under an excommunicated king; and he immediately left
his chair, and departed the court. John gave orders to
seize him, to throw him into prison, to cover his head
with a great leaden cope; and by this and other severe
usage, he soon put an end to his life [t]: Nor was there
any thing wanting to Geoffrey, except the dignity and
rank of Becket, to exalt him to an equal station in
heaven with that great and celebrated martyr. Hugh de
Wells, the chancellor, being elected, by the king's appointment, bishop of Lincoln, upon a vacancy in that

CHAP.
XI.

1209.

Excommuni-
cation of
the king.

[s] M. Paris, p. 159. M. West. p. 270.   [t] M. Paris, p. 159.

CHAP. XI.
1207.

see, defired leave to go abroad, in order to receive confecration from the archbifhop of Roüen; but he no fooner reached France, than he haftened to Pontigny, where Langton then refided, and paid fubmiffions to him as his primate. The bifhops, finding themfelves expofed either to the jealoufy of the king, or hatred of the people, gradually ftole out of the kingdom; and at laft there remained only three prelates to perform the functions of the epifcopal office [a]. Many of the nobility, terrified by John's tyranny, and obnoxious to him on different accounts, imitated the example of the bifhops; and moft of the others who remained were, with reafon, fufpected of having fecretly entered into a confederacy againft him [b]. John was alarmed at his dangerous fituation; a fituation which prudence, vigour, and popularity might formerly have prevented, but which no virtues or abilities were now fufficient to retrieve. He defired a conference with Langton at Dover; offered to acknowledge him as primate, to fubmit to the pope, to reftore the exiled clergy, even to pay them a limited fum as a compenfation for the rents of their confifcated eftates. But Langton, perceiving his advantage, was not fatisfied with thefe conceffions: He demanded that full reftitution and reparation fhould be made to all the clergy; a condition fo exorbitant, that the king, who probably had not the power of fulfilling it, and who forefaw that this eftimation of damages might amount to an immenfe fum, finally broke off the conference [b].

1212.

THE next gradation of papal fentences was to abfolve John's fubjects from their oaths of fidelity and allegiance, and to declare every one excommunicated who had any commerce with him, in public or in private; at his

[a] Ann. Waverl. p. 170. Ann. Marg. p. 14. [a] M. Paris, p. 162. M. Weft. p. 270, 271. [b] Ann. Waverl. p. 171.

table,

table, in his council, or even in private conversation^c: And this sentence was accordingly, with all imaginable solemnity, pronounced against him. But as John still persevered in his contumacy, there remained nothing but the sentence of deposition; which, though intimately connected with the former, had been distinguished from it by the artifice of the court of Rome; and Innocent determined to dart this last thunderbolt against the refractory monarch. But as a sentence of this kind required an armed force to execute it, the pontiff, casting his eyes around, fixed at last on Philip, king of France, as the person into whose powerful hand he could most properly entrust that weapon, the ultimate resource of his ghostly authority. And he offered the monarch, besides the remission of all his sins and endless spiritual benefits, the property and possession of the kingdom of England, as the reward of his labour ^d.

It was the common concern of all princes to oppose these exorbitant pretensions of the Roman pontiff, by which they themselves were rendered vassals, and vassals totally dependant, of the papal crown: Yet even Philip, the most able monarch of the age, was seduced, by present interest, and by the prospect of so tempting a prize, to accept this liberal offer of the pontiff, and thereby to ratify that authority, which, if he ever opposed its boundless usurpations, might, next day, tumble him from the throne. He levied a great army; summoned all the vassals of the crown to attend him at Roüen; collected a fleet of 1700 vessels, great and small, in the sea-ports of Normandy and Picardy; and partly from the zealous spirit of the age, partly from the personal regard universally paid him, prepared a force, which seemed equal to the greatness of his enterprize. The king, on the other

^c M. Paris, p. 161. M. West, p. 270.   ^d M. Paris, p. 162.
M. West. p. 272.

CHAP. XL.
1213.

hand, issued out writs, requiring the attendance of all his military tenants at Dover, and even of all able-bodied men, to defend the kingdom in this dangerous extremity. A great number appeared; and he selected an army of 60,000 men; a power invincible, had they been united in affection to their prince, and animated with a becoming zeal for the defence of their native country [e]. But the people were swayed by superstition, and regarded their king with horror, as anathematized by papal censures: The barons, besides lying under the same prejudices, were all disgusted by his tyranny, and were, many of them, suspected of holding a secret correspondence with the enemy: And the incapacity and cowardice of the king himself, ill-fitted to contend with those mighty difficulties, made men prognosticate the most fatal effects from the French invasion.

PANDOLF, whom the pope had chosen for his legate, and appointed to head this important expedition, had, before he left Rome, applied for a secret conference with his master, and had asked him, whether, if the king of England, in this desperate situation, were willing to submit to the apostolic see, the church should, without the consent of Philip, grant him any terms of accommodation [f]? Innocent, expecting from his agreement with a prince so abject both in character and fortune, more advantages than from his alliance with a great and victorious monarch, who, after such mighty acquisitions, might become too haughty to be bound by spiritual chains, explained to Pandolf the conditions on which he was willing to be reconciled to the king of England. The legate, therefore, as soon as he arrived in the north of France, sent over two knights templars to desire an interview with John at Dover, which was readily granted: He there represented to him, in such strong, and probably

[e] M. Paris, p. 163. M. West. p. 171. [f] M. Paris, p. 161.

JOHN.

in such true colours, his lost condition, the disaffection of his subjects, the secret combination of his vassals against him, the mighty armament of France, that John yielded at discretion [e], and subscribed to all the conditions which Pandolf was pleased to impose upon him. He promised, among other articles, that he would submit himself entirely to the judgment of the pope; that he would acknowledge Langton for primate; that he would restore all the exiled clergy and laity, who had been banished on account of the contest; that he would make them full restitution of their goods, and compensation for all damages, and instantly consign eight thousand pounds, in part of payment; and that every one outlawed or imprisoned for his adherence to the pope, should immediately be received into grace and favour [h]. Four barons swore, along with the king, to the observance of this ignominious treaty [i].

BUT the ignominy of the king was not yet carried to its full height. Pandolf required him, as the first trial of obedience, to resign his kingdom to the church; and he persuaded him, that he could no wise so effectually disappoint the French invasion, as by thus putting himself under the immediate protection of the apostolic see. John, lying under the agonies of present terror, made no scruple of submitting to this condition. He passed a charter, in which he said, that not constrained by fear, but of his own free will, and by the common advice and consent of his barons, he had, for remission of his own sins, and those of his family, resigned England and Ireland to God, to St. Peter and St. Paul, and to pope Innocent and his successors in the apostolic chair: He agreed to hold these dominions as feudatory of the church of Rome, by the annual payment of a thousand

CHAP. XI.

1213.
15th May.
The king's submission to the pope.

[e] M. West. p. 271.
Annal. Burt. p. 268.
[h] Rymer, vol. I. p. 166. M. Paris, p. 163.
[i] Rymer, vol. I. p. 170. M. Paris, p. 163.

CHAP.
XI.
1213.

marks; seven hundred for England, three hundred for Ireland: And he stipulated, that, if he or his successors should ever presume to revoke or infringe this charter, they should instantly, except upon admonition they repented of their offence, forfeit all right to their dominions [u].

15th May.

IN consequence of this agreement, John did homage to Pandolf as the pope's legate, with all the submissive rites which the feudal law required of vassals before their liege-lord and superior. He came disarmed into the legate's presence, who was seated on a throne; he flung himself on his knees before him; he lifted up his joined hands, and put them within those of Pandolf; he swore fealty to the pope; and he paid part of the tribute which he owed for his kingdom as the patrimony of St. Peter. The legate, elated by this supreme triumph of sacerdotal power, could not forbear discovering extravagant symptoms of joy and exultation: He trampled on the money, which was laid at his feet, as an earnest of the subjection of the kingdom: An insolence, of which, however offensive to all the English, no one present, except the archbishop of Dublin, dared to take any notice. But though Pandolf had brought the king to submit to these base conditions, he still refused to free him from the excommunication and interdict, till an estimation should be taken of the losses of the ecclesiastics, and full compensation and restitution should be made them.

JOHN, reduced to this abject situation under a foreign power, still showed the same disposition to tyrannize over his subjects, which had been the chief cause of all his misfortunes. One Peter of Pomfret, a hermit, had foretold, that the king, this very year, should lose his crown; and for that rash prophecy, he had been thrown into prison in Corfe-castle. John now determined to

[u] Rymer, vol. I. p. 176. M. Paris, p. 165.

bring

bring him to punishment as an impostor; and though the man pleaded, that his prophecy was fulfilled, and that the king had lost the royal and independent crown which he formerly wore, the defence was supposed to aggravate his guilt: He was dragged at horses tails, to the town of Warham, and there hanged on a gibbet with his son [1].

When Pandolf, after receiving the homage of John, returned to France, he congratulated Philip on the success of his pious enterprize; and informed him, that John, moved by the terror of the French arms, had now come to a just sense of his guilt, had returned to obedience under the apostolic see; and even consented to do homage to the pope for his dominions; and having thus made his kingdom a part of St. Peter's patrimony, had rendered it impossible for any Christian prince, without the most manifest and most flagrant impiety, to attack him [m]. Philip was enraged on receiving this intelligence: He exclaimed, that having, at the pope's instigation, undertaken an expedition, which had cost him above 60,000 pounds sterling, he was frustrated of his purpose, at the time when its success was become infallible: He complained, that all the expence had fallen upon him; all the advantages had accrued to Innocent: He threatened to be no longer the dupe of these hypocritical pretences: And assembling his vassals, he laid before them the ill-treatment which he had received, exposed the interested and fraudulent conduct of the pope, and required their assistance to execute his enterprize against England, in which, he told them, that, notwithstanding the inhibitions and menaces of the legate, he was determined to persevere. The French barons were, in that age, little less ignorant and superstitious than the English: Yet, so

[1] M. Paris, p. 165. Chron. Dunst. vol. I. p. 56.
[m] Trivet, p. 169.

much

much does the influence of those religious principles depend on the present dispositions of men! they all vowed to follow their prince on his intended expedition, and were resolute not to be disappointed of that glory and those riches which they had long expected from this enterprize. The earl of Flanders alone, who had previously formed a secret treaty with John, declaring against the injustice and impiety of the undertaking, retired with his forces [*]; and Philip, that he might not leave so dangerous an enemy behind him, first turned his arms against the dominions of that prince. Meanwhile, the English fleet was assembled under the earl of Salisbury, the king's natural brother; and, though inferior in number, received orders to attack the French in their harbours. Salisbury performed this service with so much success, that he took three hundred ships; destroyed a hundred more [*]: And Philip, finding it impossible to prevent the rest from falling into the hands of the enemy, set fire to them himself, and thereby rendered it impossible for him to proceed any farther in his enterprize.

JOHN, exulting in his present security, insensible to his past disgrace, was so elated with his success, that he thought of no less than invading France in his turn, and recovering all those provinces which the prosperous arms of Philip had formerly ravished from him. He proposed this expedition to the barons, who were already assembled for the defence of the kingdom. But the English nobles both hated and despised their prince: They prognosticated no success to any enterprize conducted by such a leader: And pretending that their time of service was elapsed, and all their provisions exhausted, they refused to second his undertaking [p]. The king, however, resolute in his purpose, embarked with a few followers, and sailed to

[*] M. Paris, p. 166. p. 59. Tilvet, p. 157.
[*] M. Paris, p. 166. Chron. Dunst. vol. I.
[p] M. Paris, p. 166.

Jersey,

Jerfey, in the foolifh expectation, that the barons would at laft be afhamed to ftay behind⁹. But finding himfelf difappointed, he returned to England; and raifing fome troops, threatened to take vengeance on all his nobles for their defertion and difobedience. The archbifhop of Canterbury, who was in a confederacy with the barons, here interpofed; ftrictly inhibited the king from thinking of fuch an attempt; and threatened him with a renewal of the fentence of excommunication, if he pretended to levy war upon any of his fubjects, before the kingdom were freed from the fentence of interdict'.

THE church had recalled the feveral anathemas pronounced againft John, by the fame gradual progrefs with which fhe had at firft iffued them. By receiving his homage, and admitting him to the rank of a vaffal, his depofition had been virtually annulled, and his fubjects were again bound by their oaths of allegiance. The exiled prelates had then returned in great triumph, with Langton at their head; and the king, hearing of their approach, went forth to meet them, and throwing himfelf on the ground before them, he entreated them, with tears, to have compaffion on him and the kingdom of England'. The primate, feeing thefe marks of fincere penitence, led him to the chapter-houfe of Winchefter, and there adminiftered an oath to him, by which he again fwore fealty and obedience to pope Innocent and his fucceffors; promifed to love, maintain, and defend holy church and the clergy; engaged that he would re-eftablifh the good laws of his predeceffors, particularly thofe of St. Edward, and would abolifh the wicked ones; and expreffed his refolution of maintaining juftice and right in all his dominions'. The primate next gave him abfolution in the requifite forms, and admitted him to dine with him, to the great joy of

CHAP. XL.

1213.

20th July.

q M. Paris, p. 166. r M. Paris, p. 167. s M. Paris, p. 166. Ann. Waverl. p. 172. t M. Par. p. 166.

CHAP. XI.
1213.

all the people. The sentence of interdict, however, was still upheld against the kingdom. A new legate, Nicholas, bishop of Frescati, came into England, in the room of Pandolf; and he declared it to be the pope's intentions never to loosen that sentence till full restitution were made to the clergy of every thing taken from them, and ample reparation for all damages which they had sustained. He only permitted mass to be said with a low voice in the churches, till those losses and damages could be estimated to the satisfaction of the parties. Certain barons were appointed to take an account of the claims; and John was astonished at the greatness of the sums to which the clergy made their losses to amount. No less than twenty thousand marks were demanded by the monks of Canterbury alone; twenty-three thousand for the see of Lincoln; and the king, finding these pretensions to be exorbitant and endless, offered the clergy the sum of a hundred thousand marks for a final acquittal. The clergy rejected the offer with disdain; but the pope, willing to favour his new vassal, whom he found zealous in his declarations of fealty, and regular in paying the stipulated tribute to Rome, directed his legate to accept of forty thousand. The issue of the whole was, that the bishops and considerable abbots got reparation beyond what they had any title to demand: The inferior clergy were obliged to sit down contented with their losses: And the king, after the interdict was taken off, renewed, in the most solemn manner, and by a new charter, sealed with gold, his professions of homage and obedience to the see of Rome.

1214.

WHEN this vexatious affair was at last brought to a conclusion, the king, as if he had nothing farther to attend to but triumphs and victories, went over to Poictou, which still acknowledged his authority*; and he carried

* Queen Eleanor died in 1203 or 1204.

war into Philip's dominions. He besieged a castle near Angiers; but the approach of Prince Lewis, Philip's son, obliged him to raise the siege with such precipitation, that he left his tents, machines, and baggage behind him; and he returned to England with disgrace. About the same time, he heard of the great and decisive victory gained by the king of France at Bovines over the emperor Otho, who had entered France at the head of 150,000 Germans; a victory which established for ever the glory of Philip, and gave full security to all his dominions. John could, therefore, think henceforth of nothing farther, than of ruling peaceably his own kingdom; and his close connexions with the pope, which he was determined at any price to maintain, ensured him, as he imagined, the certain attainment of that object. But the last and most grievous scene of this prince's misfortunes still awaited him; and he was destined to pass through a series of more humiliating circumstances than had ever yet fallen to the lot of any other monarch.

Discontents of the barons.

THE introduction of the feudal law into England by William the Conqueror had much infringed the liberties, however imperfect, enjoyed by the Anglo-Saxons in their ancient government, and had reduced the whole people to a state of vassalage under the king or barons, and even the greater part of them to a state of real slavery. The necessity also of entrusting great power in the hands of a prince, who was to maintain military dominion over a vanquished nation, had engaged the Norman barons to submit to a more severe and absolute prerogative, than that to which men of their rank, in other feudal governments, were commonly subjected. The power of the crown, once raised to a high pitch, was not easily reduced; and the nation, during the course of a hundred and fifty years, was governed by an authority unknown, in the same degree, to all the kingdoms founded by the northern conquerors.

CHAP.
XI.

1214.

querors. Henry I. that he might allure the people to give an exclusion to his elder brother Robert, had granted them a charter, favourable in many particulars to their liberties; Stephen had renewed the grant; Henry II. had confirmed it: But the concessions of all these princes had still remained without effect; and the same unlimited, at least irregular authority, continued to be exercised both by them and their successors. The only happiness was, that arms were never yet ravished from the hands of the barons and people: The nation, by a great confederacy, might still vindicate its liberties: And nothing was more likely, than the character, conduct and fortunes of the reigning prince, to produce such a general combination against him. Equally odious and contemptible, both in public and private life, he affronted the barons by his insolence, dishonoured their families by his gallantries, enraged them by his tyranny, and gave discontent to all ranks of men by his endless exactions and impositions [v]. The effect of these lawless practices had already appeared in the general demand made by the barons of a restoration of their privileges; and after he had reconciled himself to the pope, by abandoning the independence of the kingdom, he appeared to all his subjects in so mean a light, that they universally thought they might with safety and honour insist upon their pretensions.

But nothing forwarded this confederacy so much as the concurrence of Langton, archbishop of Canterbury; a man, whose memory, though he was obtruded on the nation by a palpable encroachment of the see of Rome, ought always to be respected by the English. This prelate, whether he was moved by the generosity of his nature, and his affection to public good; or had entertained

[v] Chron. Mailr. p. 188. T. Wykes, p. 36. Ann. Waverl. p. 181. W. Heming. p. 557.

an animosity against John, on account of the long opposition made by that prince to his election; or thought that an acquisition of liberty to the people would serve to encrease and secure the privileges of the church; had formed the plan of reforming the government, and had prepared the way for that great innovation, by inserting those singular clauses above mentioned, in the oath which he administered to the king, before he would absolve him from the sentence of excommunication. Soon after, in a private meeting of some principal barons at London, he showed them a copy of Henry I.'s charter, which, he said, he had happily found in a monastery; and he exhorted them to insist on the renewal and observance of it: The barons swore, that they would sooner lose their lives than depart from so reasonable a demand [w]. The confederacy began now to spread wider, and to comprehend almost all the barons in England; and a new and more numerous meeting was summoned by Langton at St. Edmondsbury, under colour of devotion. He again produced to the assembly the old charter of Henry; renewed his exhortations of unanimity and vigour in the prosecution of their purpose; and represented in the strongest colours the tyranny to which they had so long been subjected, and from which it now behoved them to free themselves and their posterity [x]. The barons, inflamed by his eloquence, incited by the sense of their own wrongs, and encouraged by the appearance of their power and numbers, solemnly took an oath, before the high altar, to adhere to each other, to insist on their demands, and to make endless war on the king, till he should submit to grant them [y]. They agreed, that, after the festival of Christmas, they would prefer in a body their common petition; and, in the mean time, they separated, after mutually engaging, that they would put themselves in a posture of defence, would inlist

CHAP. XI.

1814.

November.

[w] M. Paris, p. 167.   [x] Ibid. p. 175.   [y] Ibid. p. 176.

men

CHAP. XL

men and purchase arms, and would supply their castles with the necessary provisions.

1215.
5th January.

THE barons appeared in London on the day appointed; and demanded of the king, that, in consequence of his own oath before the primate, as well as in deference to their just rights, he should grant them a renewal of Henry's charter, and a confirmation of the laws of St. Edward. The king, alarmed with their zeal and unanimity, as well as with their power, required a delay; promised that, at the festival of Easter, he would give them a positive answer to their petition; and offered them the archbishop of Canterbury, the bishop of Ely, and the earl of Pembroke, the Mareschal, as sureties for his fulfilling this engagement[a]. The barons accepted of the terms, and peaceably returned to their castles.

15th Jan.

DURING this interval, John, in order to break or subdue the league of his barons, endeavoured to avail himself of the ecclesiastical power, of whose influence he had, from his own recent misfortunes, had such fatal experience. He granted to the clergy a charter, relinquishing for ever that important prerogative, for which his father and all his ancestors had zealously contended; yielding to them the free election on all vacancies; reserving only the power to issue a congé d'elire, and to subjoin a confirmation of the election; and declaring that, if either of these were withheld, the choice should nevertheless be deemed just and valid[a]. He made a vow to lead an army into Palestine against the infidels, and he took on him the cross; in hopes, that he should receive from the church that protection, which he tendered to every one that had entered into this sacred and meritorious engagement[b].

[a] M. Paris, p. 176. W. Web. p. 173.   [a] Rymer, vol. I. p. 197.
[b] Rymer, vol. I. p. 200. Trivet, p. 162. T. Wykes, p. 37. M. West. p. 273.

And

JOHN.

And he sent to Rome his agent, William de Mauclerc, in order to appeal to the pope against the violence of his barons, and procure him a favourable sentence from that powerful tribunal [c]. The barons also were not negligent on their part in endeavouring to engage the pope in their interests: They dispatched Eustace de Vescie to Rome; laid their case before Innocent as their feudal lord; and petitioned him to interpose his authority with the king, and oblige him to restore and confirm all their just and undoubted privileges [d].

INNOCENT beheld with regret the disturbances which had arisen in England, and was much inclined to favour John in his pretensions. He had no hopes of retaining and extending his newly acquired superiority over that kingdom, but by supporting so base and degenerate a prince, who was willing to sacrifice every consideration to his present safety: And he foresaw, that, if the administration should fall into the hands of those gallant and high-spirited barons, they would vindicate the honour, liberty, and independence of the nation, with the same ardour which they now exerted in defence of their own. He wrote letters therefore to the prelates, to the nobility, and to the king himself. He exhorted the first to employ their good offices in conciliating peace between the contending parties, and putting an end to civil discord: To the second, he expressed his disapprobation of their conduct in employing force to extort concessions from their reluctant sovereign: The last, he advised to treat his nobles with grace and indulgence, and to grant them such of their demands as should appear just and reasonable [e].

THE barons easily saw, from the tenor of these letters, that they must reckon on having the pope, as well as the king, for their adversary; but they had already advanced

[c] Rymer, vol. i. p. 184.   [d] Ibid.   [e] Ibid. p. 196, 197.

CHAP. XI.

1215.

too far to recede from their pretensions, and their passions were so deeply engaged, that it exceeded even the power of superstition itself any longer to controul them. They also foresaw, that the thunders of Rome, when not seconded by the efforts of the English ecclesiastics, would be of small avail against them; and they perceived, that the most considerable of the prelates, as well as all the inferior clergy, professed the highest approbation of their cause. Besides, that these men were seized with the national passion for laws and liberty; blessings, of which they themselves expected to partake; there concurred very powerful causes to loosen their devoted attachment to the apostolic see. It appeared, from the late usurpations of the Roman pontiff, that he pretended to reap alone all the advantages accruing from that victory, which, under his banners, though at their own peril, they had every where obtained over the civil magistrate. The pope assumed a despotic power over all the churches: Their particular customs, privileges, and immunities, were treated with disdain: Even the canons of general councils were set aside by his dispensing power: The whole administration of the church was centered in the court of Rome: All preferments ran of course in the same channel: And the provincial clergy saw, at least felt, that there was a necessity for limiting these pretensions. The legate, Nicholas, in filling those numerous vacancies which had fallen in England during an interdict of six years, had proceeded in the most arbitrary manner; and had paid no regard, in conferring dignities, to personal merit, to rank, to the inclination of the electors, or to the customs of the country. The English church was universally disgusted; and Langton himself, though he owed his elevation to an incroachment of the Romish see, was no sooner established in his high office, than he became jealous of the privileges annexed to it, and formed ed attachments with the country subjected to his jurisdiction. These causes, though they opened slowly the eyes of men, failed not to produce their effect: They set bounds to the usurpations of the papacy: The tide first stopped, and then turned against the sovereign pontiff: And it is otherwise inconceivable, how that age, so prone to superstition, and so sunk in ignorance, or rather so devoted to a spurious erudition, could have escaped falling into an absolute and total slavery under the court of Rome.

ABOUT the time that the pope's letters arrived in England, the malcontent barons, on the approach of the festival of Easter, when they were to expect the king's answer to their petition, met by agreement at Stamford; and they assembled a force, consisting of above 2000 knights, besides their retainers and inferior persons without number. Elated with their power, they advanced in a body to Brackley, within fifteen miles of Oxford, the place where the court then resided; and they there received a message from the king, by the archbishop of Canterbury and the earl of Pembroke, desiring to know what those liberties were which they so zealously challenged from their sovereign. They delivered to these messengers a schedule, containing the chief articles of their demands; which was no sooner shown to the king, than he burst into a furious passion, and asked, why the barons did not also demand of him his kingdom? swearing, that he would never grant them such liberties as must reduce himself to slavery[f].

No sooner were the confederated nobles informed of John's reply, than they chose Robert Fitz-Walter their general, whom they called *the mareschal of the army of God and of holy church*; and they proceeded without farther ceremony to levy war upon the king. They be-

CHAP. XI.

1215.

Insurrection of the barons.

17th April.

[f] M. Paris, p. 176.

sieged

CHAP. XI.

1215.
24th May.

sieged the castle of Northampton during fifteen days, though without success [f]: The gates of Bedford castle were willingly opened to them by William Beauchamp, its owner: They advanced to Ware in their way to London, where they held a correspondence with the principal citizens: They were received without opposition into that capital: And finding now the great superiority of their force, they issued proclamations, requiring the other barons to join them; and menacing them, in case of refusal or delay, with committing devastation on their houses and estates [g]. In order to show what might be expected from their prosperous arms, they made incursions from London, and laid waste the king's parks and palaces; and all the barons, who had hitherto carried the semblance of supporting the royal party, were glad of this pretence for openly joining a cause, which they always had secretly favoured. The king was left at Odiham in Hampshire, with a poor retinue of only seven knights; and after trying several expedients to elude the blow, after offering to refer all differences to the pope alone, or to eight barons, four to be chosen by himself, and four by the confederates [h], he found himself at last obliged to submit at discretion.

Magna Charta.
15th June.

A CONFERENCE between the king and the barons was appointed at Runnemede, between Windsor and Staines; a place which has ever since been extremely celebrated, on account of this great event. The two parties encamped apart, like open enemies; and after a debate of a few days, the king, with a facility somewhat suspicious,

19th June.

signed and sealed the charter which was required of him. This famous deed, commonly called the GREAT CHARTER, either granted or secured very important liberties

[f] M. Paris, p. 177. Chron. Dunst. vol. I. p. 71. [g] M. Paris, p. 177. [h] Rymer, vol. I. p. 200.

and

and privileges to every order of men in the kingdom; to the clergy, to the barons, and to the people.

THE freedom of elections was secured to the clergy: The former charter of the king was confirmed, by which the necessity of a royal congé d'elire and confirmation was superseded: All check upon appeals to Rome was removed, by the allowance granted every man to depart the kingdom at pleasure: And the fines to be imposed on the clergy, for any offence, were ordained to be proportional to their lay estates, not to their ecclesiastical benefices.

THE privileges granted to the barons were either abatements in the rigour of the feudal law, or determinations in points which had been left by that law, or had become by practice, arbitrary and ambiguous. The reliefs of heirs succeeding to a military fee were ascertained; an earl's and baron's at a hundred marks, a knight's at a hundred shillings. It was ordained by the charter, that, if the heir be a minor, he shall, immediately upon his majority, enter upon his estate, without paying any relief: The king shall not sell his wardship: he shall levy only reasonable profits upon the estate, without committing waste, or hurting the property: He shall uphold the castles, houses, mills, parks, and ponds: And if he commit the guardianship of the estate to the sheriff or any other, he shall previously oblige them to find surety to the same purpose. During the minority of a baron, while his lands are in wardship, and are not in his own possession, no debt which he owes to the Jews shall bear any interest. Heirs shall be married without disparagement; and before the marriage be contracted, the nearest relations of the person shall be informed of it. A widow, without paying any relief, shall enter upon her dower, the third part of her husband's rents: She shall not be compelled to marry, so long as she chuses to continue single; she shall only give security never to marry without her lord's consent.

consent. The king shall not claim the wardship of any minor, who holds lands by military tenure of a baron, on pretence that he also holds lands of the crown, by soccage or any other tenure. Scutages shall be estimated at the same rate as in the time of Henry I.; and no scutage or aid, except in the three general feudal cases, the king's captivity, the knighting of his eldest son, and the marrying of his eldest daughter, shall be imposed but by the great council of the kingdom; the prelates, earls, and great barons, shall be called to this great council, each by a particular writ; the lesser barons by a general summons of the sheriff. The king shall not seize any baron's land for a debt to the crown, if the baron possesses as many goods and chattels as are sufficient to discharge the debt. No man shall be obliged to perform more service for his fee than he is bound to by his tenure. No governor or constable of a castle shall oblige any knight to give money for castle-guard, if the knight be willing to perform the service in person, or by another able-bodied man; and if the knight be in the field himself, by the king's command, he shall be exempted from all other service of this nature. No vassal shall be allowed to sell so much of his land as to incapacitate himself from performing his service to his lord.

These were the principal articles, calculated for the interest of the barons; and had the charter contained nothing farther, national happiness and liberty had been very little promoted by it, as it would only have tended to encrease the power and independence of an order of men, who were already too powerful, and whose yoke might have become more heavy on the people than even that of an absolute monarch. But the barons, who alone drew and imposed on the prince this memorable charter, were necessitated to insert in it other clauses of a more extensive and more beneficent nature: They could not expect the concurrence of the people, without comprehending, together

ther with their own, the interests of inferior ranks of men; and all provisions, which the barons, for their own sake, were obliged to make, in order to ensure the free and equitable administration of justice, tended directly to the benefit of the whole community. The following were the principal clauses of this nature.

It was ordained, that all the privileges and immunities above mentioned, granted to the barons against the king, should be extended by the barons to their inferior vassals. The king bound himself not to grant any writ, empowering a baron to levy aids from his vassals, except in the three feudal cases. One weight and one measure shall be established throughout the kingdom. Merchants shall be allowed to transact all business, without being exposed to any arbitrary tolls and impositions: They and all free men shall be allowed to go out of the kingdom and return to it at pleasure: London, and all cities and burghs, shall preserve their ancient liberties, immunities, and free customs: Aids shall not be required of them but by the consent of the great council: No towns or individuals shall be obliged to make or support bridges but by ancient custom: The goods of every freeman shall be disposed of according to his will: If he die intestate, his heirs shall succeed to them. No officer of the crown shall take any horses, carts, or wood, without the consent of the owner. The king's courts of justice shall be stationary, and shall no longer follow his person: They shall be open to every one; and justice shall no longer be sold, refused, or delayed by them. Circuits shall be regularly held every year: The inferior tribunals of justice, the county court, sheriff's turn, and court-leet, shall meet at their appointed time and place: The sheriffs shall be incapacitated to hold pleas of the crown: and shall not put any person upon his trial, from rumour or suspicion alone, but upon the evidence of lawful witnesses. No freeman shall be taken or imprisoned, or dispossessed of his free tenement and liberties, or outlawed, or banished, or any wise hurt or injured, unless by the legal judgment of his peers, or by the law of the land; and all who suffered otherwise, in this or the two former reigns, shall be restored to their rights and possessions. Every freeman shall be fined in proportion to his fault; and no fine shall be levied on him to his utter ruin: Even a villain or rustic shall not, by any fine, be bereaved of his carts, ploughs, and implements of husbandry. This was the only article calculated for the interests of this body of men, probably at that time the most numerous in the kingdom.

It must be confessed, that the former articles of the Great Charter contain such mitigations and explanations of the feudal law as are reasonable and equitable; and that the latter involve all the chief outlines of a legal government, and provide for the equal distribution of justice, and free enjoyment of property; the great objects for which political society was at first founded by men, which the people have a perpetual and unalienable right to recal, and which no time, nor precedent, nor statute, nor positive institution, ought to deter them from keeping ever uppermost in their thoughts and attention. Though the provisions made by this charter might, conformably to the genius of the age, be esteemed too concise, and too bare of circumstances, to maintain the execution of its articles, in opposition to the chicanery of lawyers, supported by the violence of power; time gradually ascertained the sense of all the ambiguous expressions; and those generous barons, who first extorted this concession, still held their swords in their hands, and could turn them against those who dared, on any pretence, to depart from the original spirit and meaning of the grant. We may, now, from the tenor of this charter, conjecture what those laws were of king Edward, which the English nation,

JOHN.

tion, during so many generations, still desired, with such an obstinate perseverance, to have recalled and established. They were chiefly these latter articles of *Magna Charta*; and the barons, who, at the beginning of these commotions, demanded the revival of the Saxon laws, undoubtedly thought that they had sufficiently satisfied the people by procuring them this concession, which comprehended the principal objects to which they had so long aspired. But what we are most to admire, is the prudence and moderation of those haughty nobles themselves, who were enraged by injuries, inflamed by opposition, and elated by a total victory over their sovereign. They were content, even in this plenitude of power, to depart from some articles of Henry I.'s charter, which they made the foundation of their demands, particularly from the abolition of wardships, a matter of the greatest importance; and they seem to have been sufficiently careful not to diminish too far the power and revenue of the crown. If they appear, therefore, to have carried other demands to too great a height, it can be ascribed only to the faithless and tyrannical character of the king himself, of which they had long had experience, and which, they foresaw, would, if they provided no farther security, lead him soon to infringe their new liberties, and revoke his own concessions. This alone gave birth to those other articles, seemingly exorbitant, which were added as a rampart for the safeguard of the Great Charter.

THE barons obliged the king to agree that London should remain in their hands, and the Tower be consigned to the custody of the primate, till the 15th of August ensuing, or till the execution of the several articles of the Great Charter [k]. The better to ensure the same end, he allowed them to chuse five-and-twenty

[k] Rymer, vol. i. p. 201. Chron. Dunst. vol. i. p. 73.

members

members from their own body, as conservators of the public liberties; and no bounds were set to the authority of these men either in extent or duration. If any complaint were made of a violation of the charter, whether attempted by the king, justiciaries, sheriffs, or foresters, any four of these barons might admonish the king to redress the grievance: If satisfaction were not obtained, they could assemble the whole council of twenty-five; who, in conjunction with the great council, were empowered to compel him to observe the charter; and, in case of resistance, might levy war against him, attack his castles, and employ every kind of violence, except against his royal person, and that of his queen and children. All men throughout the kingdom were bound, under the penalty of confiscation, to swear obedience to the twenty-five barons; and the freeholders of each county were to chuse twelve knights, who were to make report of such evil customs as required redress, conformably to the tenor of the Great Charter [1]. The names of those conservators were, the earls of Clare, Albemarle, Gloucester, Winchester, Hereford, Roger Bigod, earl of Norfolk, Robert de Vere, earl of Oxford, William Mareschal the younger, Robert Fitz-Walter, Gilbert de Clare, Eustace de Vescey, Gilbert Delaval, William de Moubray, Geoffrey de Say, Roger de Mombezon, William de Huntingfield, Robert de Ros, the constable of Chester, William de Aubenie, Richard de Perci, William Malet, John Fitz-Robert, William de Lanvalay, Hugh de Bigod, and Roger de Montfichet [m]. These men were, by this convention, really invested with the sovereignty of the kingdom: They were rendered co-ordinate with the king, or rather superior to

---

[1] This seems a very strong proof that the house of commons was not then in being; otherwise the knights and burgesses from the several counties would have given into the lords a bill of grievances, without so unusual an election.
[m] M. Paris, p. 181.

him, in the exercife of the executive power: And as there was no circumftance of government which, either directly or indirectly, might not bear a relation to the fecurity or obfervance of the Great Charter, there could fcarcely occur any incident in which they might not lawfully interpofe their authority.

JOHN feemed to fubmit paffively to all thefe regulations, however injurious to majefty: He fent writs to all the fheriffs, ordering them to conftrain every one to fwear obedience to the twenty-five barons[n]: He difmiffed all his foreign forces: He pretended that his government was thenceforth to run in a new tenor, and be more indulgent to the liberty and independence of his people. But he only diffembled, till he fhould find a favourable opportunity for annulling all his conceffions. The injuries and indignities which he had formerly fuffered from the pope and the king of France, as they came from equals or fuperiors, feemed to make but fmall impreffion on him: But the fenfe of this perpetual and total fubjection, under his own rebellious vaffals, funk deep in his mind, and he was determined, at all hazards, to throw off fo ignominious a flavery[o]. He grew fullen, filent, and referved: He fhunned the fociety of his courtiers and nobles: He retired into the Ifle of Wight, as if defirous of hiding his fhame and confufion; but in this retreat he meditated the moft fatal vengeance againft all his enemies[p]. He fecretly fent abroad his emiffaries to inlift foreign foldiers, and to invite the rapacious Brabançons into his fervice, by the profpect of fharing the fpoils of England, and reaping the forfeitures of fo many opulent barons, who had incurred the guilt of rebellion by rifing in arms againft him[q]: And he difpatched a meffenger to Rome, in order to lay before the pope the Great Charter, which he had been compelled to fign, and

[n] M. Paris, p. 184. [o] Ibid. p. 185. [p] Ibid. [q] M. Paris, p. 253. Chron. Dunft. vol. I. p. 72. Chron. Mailr. p. 188.

CHAP. XI.

1215.

to complain, before that tribunal, of the violence which had been imposed upon him[*].

INNOCENT, considering himself as feudal lord of the kingdom, was incensed at the temerity of the barons, who, though they pretended to appeal to his authority, had dared, without waiting for his consent, to impose such terms on a prince, who, by resigning to the Roman pontiff his crown and independence, had placed himself immediately under the papal protection. He issued, therefore, a bull, in which, from the plenitude of his apostolic power, and from the authority which God had committed to him, to build and destroy kingdoms, to plant and overthrow, he annulled and abrogated the whole charter, as unjust in itself, as obtained by compulsion, and as derogatory to the dignity of the apostolic see. He prohibited the barons from exacting the observance of it: He even prohibited the king himself from paying any regard to it: He absolved him and his subjects from all oaths which they had been constrained to take to that purpose: And he pronounced a general sentence of excommunication against every one who should persevere in maintaining such treasonable and iniquitous pretensions[*].

Renewal of the civil wars.

THE king, as his foreign forces arrived along with this bull, now ventured to take off the mask; and, under sanction of the pope's decree, recalled all the liberties which he had granted to his subjects, and which he had solemnly sworn to observe. But the spiritual weapon was found upon trial to carry less force with it than he had reason, from his own experience, to apprehend. The primate refused to obey the pope in publishing the sentence of excommunication against the barons; and though he was cited to Rome, that he might attend a general council, there assembled, and was suspended, on account

[*] M. Paris, p. 183. Chron. Dunst. vol. l. p. 73.   [*] Rymer, vol. i. p. 203, 204, 205, 208. M. Paris, p. 184, 185, 187.

of his disobedience to the pope, and his secret correspondence with the king's enemies [1]. Though a new and particular sentence of excommunication was pronounced by name against the principal barons [2], John still found that his nobility and people, and even his clergy, adhered to the defence of their liberties, and to their combination against him: The sword of his foreign mercenaries was all he had to trust to for restoring his authority.

The barons, after obtaining the Great Charter, seem to have been lulled into a fatal security, and to have taken no rational measures, in case of the introduction of a foreign force, for re-assembling their armies. The king was, from the first, master of the field; and immediately laid siege to the castle of Rochester, which was obstinately defended by William de Albiney, at the head of a hundred and forty knights with their retainers, but was at last reduced by famine. John, irritated with the resistance, intended to have hanged the governor and all the garrison; but, on the representation of William de Mauleon, who suggested to him the danger of reprizals, he was content to sacrifice, in this barbarous manner, the inferior prisoners only [3]. The captivity of William de Albiney, the best officer among the confederated barons, was an irreparable loss to their cause; and no regular opposition was thenceforth made to the progress of the royal arms. The ravenous and barbarous mercenaries, incited by a cruel and enraged prince, were let loose against the estates, tenants, manors, houses, parks of the barons, and spread devastation over the face of the kingdom. Nothing was to be seen, but the flames of villages and castles reduced to ashes, the consternation and misery of the inhabitants, tortures exercised by the soldiery to make them reveal their concealed treasures, and reprizals no less barbarous, committed by the barons and their partizans on the

[1] M. Paris, p. 189. [2] Rymer, vol. i. p. 212. M. Paris, p. 191.
[3] M. Paris, p. 187.

CHAP. XI.
1215.

royal demesnes, and on the estates of such as still adhered to the crown. The king, marching through the whole extent of England, from Dover to Berwic, laid the provinces waste on each side of him; and considered every state, which was not his immediate property, as entirely hostile, and the object of military execution. The nobility of the north, in particular, who had shewn greatest violence in the recovery of their liberties, and who, acting in a separate body, had expressed their discontent even at the concessions made by the Great Charter, as they could expect no mercy, fled before him with their wives and families, and purchased the friendship of Alexander, the young king of Scots, by doing homage to him.

Prince Lewis called over.

THE barons, reduced to this desperate extremity, and menaced with the total loss of their liberties, their properties, and their lives, employed a remedy no less desperate; and making applications to the court of France, they offered to acknowledge Lewis, the eldest son of Philip, for their sovereign, on condition that he would afford them protection from the violence of their enraged prince. Though the sense of the common rights of mankind, the only rights that are entirely indefeasible, might have justified them in the deposition of their king, they declined insisting before Philip on a pretension which is commonly so disagreeable to sovereigns, and which sounds harshly in their royal ears. They affirmed, that John was incapable of succeeding to the crown, by reason of the attainder passed upon him during his brother's reign; though that attainder had been reversed, and Richard had even, by his last will, declared him his successor. They pretended that he was already legally deposed by sentence of the peers of France, on account of the murder of his nephew; though that sentence could not possibly regard any thing but his transmarine dominions,

dominions, which alone he held in vassalage to that crown. On more plausible grounds, they affirmed, that he had already deposed himself by doing homage to the pope, changing the nature of his sovereignty, and resigning an independent crown for a fee under a foreign power. And as Blanche of Castile, the wife of Lewis, was descended by her mother from Henry II. they maintained, though many other princes stood before her in the order of succession, that they had not shaken off the royal family, in chusing her husband for their sovereign.

PHILIP was strongly tempted to lay hold on the rich prize which was offered to him. The legate menaced him with interdicts and excommunications, if he invaded the patrimony of St. Peter, or attacked a prince who was under the immediate protection of the holy see[e]: But as Philip was assured of the obedience of his own vassals, his principles were changed with the times, and he now undervalued as much all papal censures, as he formerly pretended to pay respect to them. His chief scruple was with regard to the fidelity which he might expect from the English barons in their new engagements, and the danger of entrusting his son and heir into the hands of men, who might, on any caprice or necessity, make peace with their native sovereign, by sacrificing a pledge of so much value. He therefore exacted from the barons twenty-five hostages of the most noble birth in the kingdom[f]; and having obtained this security, he sent over first a small army to the relief of the confederates; then more numerous forces, which arrived with Lewis himself at their head.

THE first effect of the young prince's appearance in England was the desertion of John's foreign troops, who, being mostly levied in Flanders, and other provinces of

[e] M. Paris, p. 194. M. West, p. 275. Chron. Dunst. vol. i. p. 74. [f] M. Paris, p. 194.

HISTORY OF ENGLAND.

CHAP. XI.
1216.

France, refused to serve against the heir of their monarchy[a]. The Gascons and Poictevins alone, who were still John's subjects, adhered to his cause; but they were too weak to maintain that superiority in the field, which they had hitherto supported against the confederated barons. Many considerable noblemen deserted John's party, the earls of Salisbury, Arundel, Warrene, Oxford, Albemarle, and William Mareschal the younger: His castles fell daily into the hands of the enemy; Dover was the only place which, from the valour and fidelity of Hubert de Burgh, the governor, made resistance to the progress of Lewis[a]: And the barons had the melancholy prospect of finally succeeding in their purpose, and of escaping the tyranny of their own king, by imposing on themselves and the nation a foreign yoke. But this union was of short duration between the French and English nobles; and the imprudence of Lewis, who, on every occasion, showed too visible a preference to the former, encreased that jealousy which it was so natural for the latter to entertain in their present situation[b]. The viscount of Melun, too, it is said, one of his courtiers, fell sick at London, and finding the approaches of death, he sent for some of his friends among the English barons, and warning them of their danger, revealed Lewis's secret intentions of exterminating them and their families, as traitors to their prince, and of bestowing their estates and dignities on his native subjects, in whose fidelity he could more reasonably place confidence[c]: This story, whether true or false, was universally reported and believed; and concurring with other circumstances, which rendered it credible, did great prejudice to the cause of Lewis. The earl of Salisbury, and other noblemen, deserted again to John's party[d]; and as men easily changed sides in a civil war, especially

[a] M. Paris, p. 195. [a] Ibid. p. 198. Chron. Dunst. vol. I. p. 76, 78. [b] W. Heming. p. 559. [c] M. Paris, p. 199. M. West. p. 277. [d] Chron. Dunst. vol. I. p. 78.

where

where their power is founded on an hereditary and inde- CHAP.
pendent authority, and is not derived from the opinion and XI.
favour of the people, the French prince had reason to
dread a sudden reverse of fortune. The king was assem- 1216.
bling a considerable army, with a view of fighting one
great battle for his crown; but passing from Lynne to
Lincolnshire, his road lay along the sea-shore, which was
overflowed at high water; and not chusing the proper
time for his journey, he lost in the inundation all his car-
riages, treasure, baggage, and regalia. The affliction for
this disaster, and vexation from the distracted state of his
affairs, encreased the sickness under which he then laboured; and though he reached the castle of Newark, he
was obliged to halt there, and his distemper soon after
put an end to his life, in the forty-ninth year of his age, 17th Octob.
and eighteenth of his reign; and freed the nation from Death
the dangers, to which it was equally exposed by his
success or by his misfortunes.

THE character of this prince is nothing but a compli- and charac-
cation of vices, equally mean and odious; ruinous to ter of the
himself, and destructive to his people. Cowardice, inactivity, folly, levity, licentiousness, ingratitude, treachery, tyranny, and cruelty; all these qualities appear too
evidently in the several incidents of his life, to give us
room to suspect, that the disagreeable picture has been
anywise overcharged by the prejudices of the ancient
historians. It is hard to say, whether his conduct to his
father, his brother, his nephew, or his subjects, was most
culpable; or whether his crimes, in these respects, were
not even exceeded by the baseness which appeared in his
transactions with the king of France, the pope, and the
barons. His European dominions, when they devolved to
him by the death of his brother, were more extensive than
have ever, since his time, been ruled by any English monarch: But he first lost by his misconduct the flourishing
provinces in France, the ancient patrimony of his family:

VOL. II.   H   He

CHAP. XI.
1216.

He subjected his kingdom to a shameful vassalage under the see of Rome: He saw the prerogatives of his crown diminished by law, and still more reduced by faction: And he died at last, when in danger of being totally expelled by a foreign power, and of either ending his life miserably in prison, or seeking shelter as a fugitive from the pursuit of his enemies.

THE prejudices against this prince were so violent, that he was believed to have sent an embassy to the Miramoulin or emperor of Morocco, and to have offered to change his religion and become Mahometan, in order to purchase the protection of that monarch. But though this story is told us, on plausible authority, by Matthew Paris[*], it is in itself utterly improbable; except, that there is nothing so incredible but may be believed to proceed from the folly and wickedness of John.

THE monks throw great reproaches on this prince for his impiety and even infidelity; and as an instance of it, they tell us, that, having one day caught a very fat stag, he exclaimed, *How plump and well fed is this animal! and yet, I dare swear, he never heard mass*[†]. This sally of wit, upon the usual corpulency of the priests, more than all his enormous crimes and iniquities, made him pass with them for an atheist.

JOHN left two legitimate sons behind him, Henry, born on the first of October, 1207, and now nine years of age; and Richard, born on the sixth of January, 1209; and three daughters, Jane afterwards married to Alexander king of Scots; Eleanor married first to William Marefchal the younger, earl of Pembroke, and then to Simon Mountfort, earl of Leicester; and Isabella married to the emperor Frederic II. All these children were born to him by Isabella of Angoulesme, his second wife.

[*] P. 163. [†] M. Paris, 170.

His

JOHN.

His illegitimate children were numerous; but none of them were anywife diftinguifhed.

IT was this king, who, in the ninth year of his reign, firft gave by charter to the city of London, the right of electing annually a mayor out of its own body, an office which was till now held for life. He gave the city alfo power to elect and remove its fheriffs at pleafure, and its common-council-men annually. London bridge was finifhed in this reign: The former bridge was of wood. Maud the emprefs was the firft that built a ftone bridge in England.

CHAP. XI.

1214.

APPENDIX

APPENDIX II.

The FEUDAL and ANGLO-NORMAN GOVERNMENT and MANNERS.

Origin of the feudal law——Its progress——Feudal government of England——The feudal parliament ——The commons——Judicial power——Revenue of the crown——Commerce——The church ——Civil laws——Manners.

THE feudal law is the chief foundation, both of the political government and of the jurisprudence, established by the Normans in England. Our subject therefore requires, that we should form a just idea of this law, in order to explain the state, as well of that kingdom, as of all other kingdoms of Europe, which, during those ages, were governed by similar institutions. And though I am sensible, that I must here repeat many observation and reflections which have been communicated by others [a]; yet, as every book, agreeably to the observation of a great historian [b], should be as complete as possible within itself, and should never refer, for any thing material, to other books, it will be necessary, in this place, to deliver a short plan of that prodigious fabric, which, for several centuries, preserved such a mixture of liberty and oppression, order and anarchy, stabi-

[a] L'Esprit de Loix. Dr. Robertson's History of Scotland.
[b] Padre Paolo Hist. Conc. Trid.

HISTORY OF ENGLAND.

Appendix II.

Origin of the feudal law.

lity and revolution, as was never experienced in any other age, or any other part of the world.

AFTER the northern nations had subdued the provinces of the Roman empire, they were obliged to establish a system of government, which might secure their conquests, as well against the revolt of their numerous subjects who remained in the provinces, as from the inroads of other tribes, who might be tempted to ravish from them their new acquisitions. The great change of circumstances made them here depart from those institutions which prevailed among them, while they remained in the forests of Germany; yet was it still natural for them to retain, in their present settlement, as much of their ancient customs as was compatible with their new situation.

THE German governments, being more a confederacy of independent warriors, than a civil subjection, derived their principal force from many inferior and voluntary associations, which individuals formed under a particular head or chieftain, and which it became the highest point of honour to maintain with inviolable fidelity. The glory of the chief consisted in the number, the bravery, and the zealous attachment of his retainers: The duty of the retainers required, that they should accompany their chief in all wars and dangers, that they should fight and perish by his side, and that they should esteem his renown or his favour a sufficient recompence for all their services[1]. The prince himself was nothing but a great chieftain, who was chosen from among the rest, on account of his superior valour or nobility; and who derived his power from the voluntary association or attachment of the other chieftains.

WHEN a tribe, governed by these ideas, and actuated by these principles, subdued a large territory, they found,

[1] Tacit. de Mor. Germ.

that

APPENDIX II.

that, though it was neceſſary to keep themſelves in a military poſture, they could neither remain united in a body, nor take up their quarters in ſeveral garriſons, and that their manners and inſtitutions debarred them from uſing theſe expedients; the obvious ones, which, in a like ſituation, would have been employed by a more civilized nation. Their ignorance in the art of finances, and perhaps the devaſtations inſeparable from ſuch violent conqueſts, rendered it impracticable for them to levy taxes ſufficient for the pay of numerous armies; and their repugnance to ſubordination, with their attachment to rural pleaſures, made the life of the camp or garriſon, if perpetuated during peaceful times, extremely odious and diſguſtful to them. They ſeized, therefore, ſuch a portion of the conquered lands as appeared neceſſary; they aſſigned a ſhare for ſupporting the dignity of their prince and government; they diſtributed other parts, under the title of fiefs, to the chiefs; theſe made a new partition among their retainers; the expreſs condition of all theſe grants was, that they might be reſumed at pleaſure, and that the poſſeſſor, ſo long as he enjoyed them, ſhould ſtill remain in readineſs to take the field for the defence of the nation. And though the conquerors immediately ſeparated, in order to enjoy their new acquiſitions, their martial diſpoſition made them readily fulfil the terms of their engagement: They aſſembled on the firſt alarm; their habitual attachment to the chieftain made them willingly ſubmit to his command; and thus a regular military force, though concealed, was always ready to defend, on any emergence, the intereſt and honour of the community.

We are not to imagine, that all the conquered lands were ſeized by the northern conquerors; or that the whole of the land thus ſeized was ſubjected to thoſe military ſervices. This ſuppoſition is confuted by the hiſtory

Appendix II.

tory of all the nations on the continent. Even the idea, given us of the German manners by the Roman historian, may convince us, that that bold people would never have been content with so precarious a subsistence, or have fought to procure establishments, which were only to continue during the good pleasure of their sovereign. Though the northern chieftains accepted of lands, which, being considered as a kind of military pay, might be resumed at the will of the king or general; they also took possession of estates, which, being hereditary and independent, enabled them to maintain their native liberty, and support, without court-favour, the honour of their rank and family.

Progress of the feudal law.

BUT there is a great difference, in the consequences, between the distribution of a pecuniary subsistence, and the assignment of lands burthened with the condition of military service. The delivery of the former, at the weekly, monthly, or annual terms of payment, still recalls the idea of a voluntary gratuity from the prince, and reminds the soldier of the precarious tenure by which he holds his commission. But the attachment, naturally formed with a fixed portion of land, gradually begets the idea of something like property, and makes the possessor forget his dependant situation, and the condition which was at first annexed to the grant. It seemed equitable, that one who had cultivated and sowed a field, should reap the harvest: Hence fiefs, which were at first entirely precarious, were soon made annual. A man, who had employed his money in building, planting, or other improvements, expected to reap the fruits of his labour or expence: Hence they were next granted during a term of years. It would be thought hard to expel a man from his possessions, who had always done his duty, and performed the conditions on which he originally received them: Hence the chieftains, in a subsequent period, thought themselves

APPENDIX II.

themselves entitled to demand the enjoyment of their feudal lands during life. It was found, that a man would more willingly expose himself in battle, if assured, that his family should inherit his possessions, and should not be left by his death in want and poverty: Hence fiefs were made hereditary in families, and descended, during one age, to the son, then to the grandson, next to the brothers, and afterwards to more distant relations [b]. The idea of property stole in gradually upon that of military pay; and each century made some sensible addition to the stability of fiefs and tenures.

In all these successive acquisitions, the chief was supported by his vassals; who, having originally a strong connexion with him, augmented by the constant intercourse of good offices, and by the friendship arising from vicinity and dependance, were inclined to follow their leader against all his enemies, and voluntarily, in his private quarrels, paid him the same obedience to which, by their tenure, they were bound in foreign wars. While he daily advanced new pretensions to secure the possession of his superior fief, they expected to find the same advantage, in acquiring stability to their subordinate ones; and they zealously opposed the intrusion of a new lord, who would be inclined, as he was fully intitled, to bestow the possession of their lands on his own favourites and retainers. Thus the authority of the sovereign gradually decayed; and each noble, fortified in his own territory by the attachment of his vassals, became too powerful to be expelled by an order from the throne; and he secured by law what he had at first acquired by usurpation.

During this precarious state of the supreme power, a difference would immediately be experienced between those portions of territory which were subjected to the feudal tenures, and those which were possessed by an allo-

[b] Lib. Feud. lib. i. tit. 1.

dial

dial or free title. Though the latter possessions had at first been esteemed much preferable, they were soon found, by the progressive changes introduced into public and private law, to be of an inferior condition to the former. The possessors of a feudal territory, united by a regular subordination under one chief, and by the mutual attachments of the vassals, had the same advantages over the proprietors of the other, that a disciplined army enjoys over a dispersed multitude; and were enabled to commit with impunity all injuries on their defenceless neighbours. Every one, therefore, hastened to seek that protection which he found so necessary; and each allodial proprietor, resigning his possessions into the hands of the king, or of some nobleman respected for power or valour, received them back with the condition of feudal services [1], which, though a burden somewhat grievous, brought him ample compensation, by connecting him with the neighbouring proprietors, and placing him under the guardianship of a potent chieftain. The decay of the political government thus necessarily occasioned the extension of the feudal: The kingdoms of Europe were universally divided into baronies, and these into inferior fiefs: And the attachment of vassals to their chief, which was at first an essential part of the German manners, was still supported by the same causes from which it at first arose; the necessity of mutual protection, and the continued intercourse, between the head and the members, of benefits and services.

But there was another circumstance which corroborated these feudal dependencies, and tended to connect the vassals with their superior lord by an indissoluble bond of union. The northern conquerors, as well as the more early Greeks and Romans, embraced a policy, which is unavoidable to all nations that have made slender advances

[1] Marculf. Form. 47. apud Lindenbr. p. 1258.

APPENDIX II.

in refinement: They every where united the civil jurisdiction with the military power. Law, in its commencement, was not an intricate science, and was more governed by maxims of equity, which seem obvious to common sense, than by numerous and subtile principles, applied to a variety of cases by profound reasonings from analogy. An officer, though he had passed his life in the field, was able to determine all legal controversies which could occur within the district committed to his charge; and his decisions were the most likely to meet with a prompt and ready obedience, from men who respected his person, and were accustomed to act under his command. The profit arising from punishments, which were then chiefly pecuniary, was another reason for his desiring to retain the judicial power; and when his fief became hereditary, this authority, which was essential to it, was also transmitted to his posterity. The counts and other magistrates, whose power was merely official, were tempted, in imitation of the feudal lords, whom they resembled in so many particulars, to render their dignity perpetual and hereditary; and in the decline of the regal power, they found no difficulty in making good their pretensions. After this manner the vast fabric of feudal subordination became quite solid and comprehensive; it formed every where an essential part of the political constitution; and the Norman and other barons, who followed the fortunes of William, were so accustomed to it, that they could scarcely form an idea of any other species of civil government [m].

The Saxons, who conquered England, as they exterminated the ancient inhabitants, and thought themselves secured by the sea against new invaders, found it less re-

[m] The ideas of the feudal government were so rooted, that even lawyers, in those ages, could not form a notion of any other constitution. *Regnum*, (says Bracton, lib. 1. cap. 34.) *quod ex comitatibus & baronibus dicitur esse constitutum*.

Appendix II.

quisite to maintain themselves in a military posture: The quantity of land, which they annexed to offices, seems to have been of small value; and for that reason continued the longer in its original situation, and was always possessed during pleasure by those who were intrusted with the command. These conditions were too precarious to satisfy the Norman barons, who enjoyed more independent possessions and jurisdictions in their own country; and William was obliged, in the new distribution of land, to copy the tenures, which were now become universal on the continent. England of a sudden became a feudal kingdom [a]; and received all the advantages, and was exposed to all the inconveniences, incident to that species of civil polity.

The feudal government of England.

ACCORDING to the principles of the feudal law, the king was the supreme lord of the landed property: All possessors, who enjoyed the fruits or revenue of any part of it, held those privileges, either mediately or immediately, of him; and their property was conceived to be, in some degree, conditional [b]. The land was still apprehended to be a species of *benefice*, which was the original conception of a feudal property; and the vassal owed, in return for it, stated services to his baron, as the baron himself did for his land to the crown. The vassal was obliged to defend his baron in war; and the baron, at the head of his vassals, was bound to fight in defence of the king and kingdom. But besides these military services, which were casual, there were others imposed of a civil nature, which were more constant and durable.

THE northern nations had no idea, that any man, trained up to honour, and enured to arms, was ever to be governed, without his own consent, by the absolute will of another; or that the administration of justice was ever

[a] Coke Comm. on Lit. p. 1, n. ad sect. 1. p. 109. Smith de Rep. lib. 3. cap. 10.
[b] Seldon of Titles.

to be exercised by the private opinion of any one magistrate, without the concurrence of some other persons, whose interest might induce them to check his arbitrary and iniquitous decisions. The king, therefore, when he found it necessary to demand any service of his barons or chief tenants, beyond what was due by their tenures, was obliged to assemble them, in order to obtain their *consent*: And when it was necessary to determine any controversy which might arise among the barons themselves, the question must be discussed in their presence, and be decided according to their opinion or *advice*. In these two circumstances of consent and advice, consisted chiefly the civil services of the ancient barons; and these implied all the considerable incidents of government. In one view, the barons regarded this attendance as their principal *privilege*; in another, as a grievous *burden*. That no momentous affairs could be transacted without their consent and advice, was in *general* esteemed the great security of their possessions and dignities: But as they reaped no immediate profit from their attendance at court, and were exposed to great inconvenience and charge by an absence from their own estates, every one was glad to exempt himself from each *particular* exertion of this power; and was pleased both that the call for that duty should seldom return upon him, and that others should undergo the burden in his stead. The king, on the other hand, was usually anxious, for several reasons, that the assembly of the barons should be full at every stated or casual meeting: This attendance was the chief badge of their subordination to his crown, and drew them from that independence which they were apt to affect in their own castles and manors; and where the meeting was thin or ill attended, its determinations had less authority, and commanded not so ready an obedience from the whole community.

THE

Appendix II.

The case was the same with the barons in their courts, as with the king in the supreme council of the nation. It was requisite to assemble the vassals, in order to determine by their vote any question which regarded the barony; and they sat along with the chief in all trials, whether civil or criminal, which occurred within the limits of their jurisdiction. They were bound to pay suit and service at the court of their baron; and as their tenure was military, and consequently honourable, they were admitted into his society, and partook of his friendship. Thus, a kingdom was considered only as a great barony, and a barony as a small kingdom. The barons were peers to each other in the national council, and, in some degree, companions to the king: The vassals were peers to each other in the court of barony, and companions to their baron [p].

But though this resemblance so far took place, the vassals, by the natural course of things, universally, in the feudal constitutions, fell into a greater subordination under the baron, than the baron himself under his sovereign; and these governments had a necessary and infallible tendency to augment the power of the nobles. The great chief, residing in his country-seat, which he was commonly allowed to fortify, lost, in a great measure, his connexion or acquaintance with the prince; and added every day new force to his authority over the vassals of the barony. They received from him education in all military exercises: His hospitality invited them to live and enjoy society in his hall: Their leisure, which was great, made them perpetual retainers on his person, and partakers of his country sports and amusements: They had no means of gratifying their ambition but by making a figure in his train: His favour and countenance was their greatest honour: His displeasure exposed them to contempt and ignominy: And they felt every

[p] Du Cange Gloss. in verb. Par. Cujac. Commun. in Lib. Feud. li. i. tit. p. 13. Spelm. Gloss. in verb.

moment

moment the necessity of his protection, both in the controversies which occurred with other vassals, and, what was more material, in the daily inroads and injuries which were committed by the neighbouring barons. During the time of general war, the sovereign, who marched at the head of his armies, and was the great protector of the state, always acquired some accession to his authority, which he lost during the intervals of peace and tranquillity: But the loose police, incident to the feudal constitutions, maintained a perpetual, though secret hostility, between the several members of the state; and the vassals found no means of securing themselves against the injuries to which they were continually exposed, but by closely adhering to their chief, and falling into a submissive dependence upon him.

If the feudal government was so little favourable to the true liberty even of the military vassal, it was still more destructive of the independence and security of the other members of the state, or what, in a proper sense, we call the people. A great part of them were *serfs*, and lived in a state of absolute slavery or villainage: The other inhabitants of the country paid their rent in services, which were in a great measure arbitrary; and they could expect no redress of injuries, in a court of barony, from men who thought they had a right to oppress and tyrannize over them: The towns were situated either within the demesnes of the king, or the lands of the great barons, and were almost entirely subjected to the absolute will of their master. The languishing state of commerce kept the inhabitants poor and contemptible; and the political institutions were calculated to render that poverty perpetual. The barons and gentry, living in rustic plenty and hospitality, gave no encouragement to the arts, and had no demand for any of the more elaborate manufactures: Every profession was held in contempt but that of arms: And if any merchant or manufacturer rose by industry and

and frugality to a degree of opulence, he found himself but the more exposed to injuries, from the envy and avidity of the military nobles.

These concurring causes gave the feudal governments so strong a bias towards aristocracy, that the royal authority was extremely eclipsed in all the European states; and, instead of dreading the growth of monarchical power, we might rather expect that the community would every where crumble into so many independent baronies, and lose the political union by which they were cemented. In elective monarchies, the event was commonly answerable to this expectation; and the barons, gaining ground on every vacancy of the throne, raised themselves almost to a state of sovereignty, and sacrificed to their power both the rights of the crown and the liberties of the people. But hereditary monarchies had a principle of authority which was not so easily subverted; and there were several causes which still maintained a degree of influence in the hands of the sovereign.

The greatest baron could never lose view entirely of those principles of the feudal constitution which bound him, as a vassal, to submission and fealty towards his prince; because he was every moment obliged to have recourse to those principles, in exacting fealty and submission from his own vassals. The lesser barons, finding that the annihilation of royal authority left them exposed, without protection, to the insults and injuries of more potent neighbours, naturally adhered to the crown, and promoted the execution of general and equal laws. The people had still a stronger interest to desire the grandeur of the sovereign; and the king, being the legal magistrate, who suffered by every internal convulsion or oppression, and who regarded the great nobles as his immediate rivals, assumed the salutary office of general guardian or protector of the commons. Besides the prerogatives with which the

APPENDIX II.

the law invested him; his large demesnes and numerous retainers rendered him, in one sense, the greatest baron in his kingdom; and where he was possessed of personal vigour and abilities (for his situation required these advantages), he was commonly able to preserve his authority, and maintain his station as head of the community, and the chief fountain of law and justice.

THE first kings of the Norman race were favoured by another circumstance, which preserved them from the encroachments of their barons. They were generals of a conquering army, which was obliged to continue in a military posture, and to maintain great subordination under their leader, in order to secure themselves from the revolt of the numerous natives, whom they had bereaved of all their properties and privileges. But though this circumstance supported the authority of William and his immediate successors, and rendered them extremely absolute, it was lost as soon as the Norman barons began to incorporate with the nation, to acquire a security in their possessions, and to fix their influence over their vassals, tenants, and slaves. And the immense fortunes, which the Conqueror had bestowed on his chief captains, served to support their independence, and make them formidable to the sovereign.

HE gave, for instance, to Hugh de Abrincis, his sister's son, the whole county of Chester, which he erected into a palatinate, and rendered by his grant almost independent of the crown[q]. Robert, earl of Mortaigne, had 973 manors and lordships: Allan, earl of Britanny and Richmond, 442: Odo, bishop of Baieux, 439[r]: Geoffrey, bishop of Coutance, 280[s]: Walter Giffard, earl of Buckingham, 107: William, earl Warrenne, 298, besides 28 towns or hamlets in Yorkshire: Todenei, 81: Roger

[q] Camd. in Chesh. Spel. Gloss. in verb. Comes Palatinus.
[r] Brady's Hist. p. 198. 200.   [s] Order. Vital.

Bigod,

114   HISTORY OF ENGLAND.

<small>Appendix II.</small>

Bigod, 123: Robert, earl of Eu, 119: Roger Mortimer, 132, besides several hamlets: Robert de Stafford 130: Walter de Eurus, earl of Salisbury, 46: Geoffrey de Mandeville, 118: Richard de Clare, 171: Hugh de Beauchamp, 47: Baldwin de Ridvers, 164: Henry de Ferrers, 222: William de Percy, 119': Norman d'Arcy, 33'. Sir Henry Spelman computes, that, in the large county of Norfolk, there were not, in the Conqueror's time, above sixty-six proprietors of land ". Men, possessed of such princely revenues and jurisdictions, could not long be retained in the rank of subjects. The great earl Warrenne, in a subsequent reign, when he was questioned concerning his right to the lands which he possessed, drew his sword, which he produced as his title; adding, that William the Bastard did not conquer the kingdom himself; but that the barons, and his ancestor among the rest, were joint adventurers in the enterprize".

<small>The feudal parliament.</small>

THE supreme legislative power of England was lodged in the king and great council, or what was afterwards called the parliament. It is not doubted but the archbishops, bishops, and most considerable abbots were constituent members of this council. They sat by a double title: By prescription, as having always possessed that privilege, through the whole Saxon period, from the first establishment of Christianity; and by their right of baronage, as holding of the king *in capite* by military service. These two titles of the prelates were never accurately distinguished. When the usurpations of the church had risen to such a height, as to make the bishops affect a separate dominion, and regard their seat in parliament

---

<small>' Dugdale's Baronage, from Domesday Book, vol. I. p. 60. 74. lii. 812. 113. 136. 138. 156. 174. 200. 207. 223. 256. 257. 269.

" Ibid. p. 369. It is remarkable that this family of d'Arcy seems to be the only male descendant of any of the Conqueror's barons now remaining among the peers. Lord Holderness is the heir of that family.

" Spel. Gloss. in verb. *Domesday*.   2 Dug. Bar. vol. I. p. 78. Ibid. Originum Juridicialium, p. 13.</small>

APPENDIX II.

as a degradation of their episcopal dignity; the king insisted that they were barons, and, on that account, obliged, by the general principles of the feudal law, to attend on him in his great councils [y]. Yet there still remained some practices, which supposed their title to be derived merely from ancient possession: When a bishop was elected, he sat in parliament before the king had made him restitution of his temporalities; and during the vacancy of a see, the guardian of the spiritualities was summoned to attend along with the bishops.

THE barons were another constituent part of the great council of the nation. These held immediately of the crown by a military tenure: They were the most honourable members of the state, and had a *right* to be consulted in all public deliberations: They were the immediate vassals of the crown, and owed as a *service* their attendance in the court of their supreme lord. A resolution, taken without their consent, was likely to be but ill executed: And no determination of any cause or controversy among them had any validity, where the vote and advice of the body did not concur. The dignity of earl or count was official and territorial, as well as hereditary; and as all the earls were also barons, they were considered as military vassals of the crown, were admitted in that capacity into the general council, and formed the most honourable and powerful branch of it.

BUT there was another class of the immediate military tenants of the crown, no less, or probably more, numerous than the barons, the tenants *in capite* by knights service; and these, however inferior in power or property, held by a tenure which was equally honourable with that of the others. A barony was commonly composed of several knights fees: And though the number seems not to have been exactly defined, seldom consisted of less than fifty

[y] Spel. Gloss. In verb. *Baro.*

hyde

Appendix II.

hydes of land [a]: But where a man held of the king only one or two knights fees, he was still an immediate vassal of the crown, and as such had a title to have a seat in the general councils. But as this attendance was usually esteemed a burthen, and one too great for a man of slender fortune to bear constantly, it is probable that, though he had a title, if he pleased, to be admitted, he was not obliged, by any penalty, like the barons, to pay a regular attendance. All the immediate military tenants of the crown amounted not fully to 700, when Domesday-book was framed; and as the members were well pleased, on any pretext, to excuse themselves from attendance, the assembly was never likely to become too numerous for the dispatch of public business.

The commons.

So far the nature of a general council, or ancient parliament, is determined without any doubt or controversy. The only question seems to be with regard to the commons, or the representatives of counties and boroughs; whether they were also, in more early times, constituent parts of parliament? This question was once disputed in England with great acrimony: But such is the force of time and evidence, that they can sometimes prevail even over faction; and the question seems, by general consent, and even by their own, to be at last determined against the ruling party. It is agreed, that the commons were no part of the great council, till some ages after the conquest; and that the military tenants alone of the crown composed that supreme and legislative assembly.

THE vassals of a baron were by their tenure immediately dependant on him, owed attendance at his court, and paid all their duty to the king, through that depend-

[a] Four hydes made one knight's fee: The relief of a barony was twelve times greater than that of a knight's fee; whence we may conjecture his usual value. Spelm. Gloss. in verb. Feudum. There were 243,600 hydes in England, and 60,215 knights fees; whence it is evident that there were a little more than four hydes in each knight's fee.

ance

APPENDIX II.

ance which their lord was obliged by *his* tenure to acknowledge to his sovereign and superior. Their land, comprehended in the barony, was represented in parliament by the baron himself, who was supposed, according to the fictions of the feudal law, to possess the direct property of it, and it would have been deemed incongruous to give it any other representation. They stood in the same capacity to him, that he and the other barons did to the king: The former were peers of the barony; the latter were peers of the realm: The vassals possessed a subordinate rank within their district; the baron enjoyed a superior dignity in the great assembly: They were in some degree his companions at home; he the king's companion at court: And nothing can be more evidently repugnant to all feudal ideas, and to that gradual subordination, which was essential to those ancient institutions, than to imagine that the king would apply either for the advice or consent of men, who were of a rank so much inferior, and whose duty was immediately paid to the *mesne* lord, that was interposed between them and the throne [a].

If it be unreasonable to think that the vassals of a barony, though their tenure was military and noble and honourable, were ever summoned to give their opinion in national councils, much less can it be supposed, that the tradesmen or inhabitants of boroughs, whose condition was so much inferior, would be admitted to that privilege. It appears from Domesday, that the greatest boroughs were, at the time of the conquest, scarcely more than country villages; and that the inhabitants lived in entire dependance on the king or great lords, and were of a station little better than servile [b]. They were not then so much as incorporated; they formed no community; were

[a] Spelm. Gloss. in verb. *Baro*.
[b] *Liber homo* anciently signified a gentleman; for scarce any one besides was entirely free. Spelm. Gloss. in verbo.

not regarded as a body politic; and being really nothing but a number of low dependant tradesmen, living, without any particular civil tie, in neighbourhood together, they were incapable of being represented in the states of the kingdom. Even in France, a country which made more early advances in arts and civility than England, the first corporation is sixty years posterior to the conquest under the duke of Normandy; and the erecting of these communities was an invention of Lewis the Gross, in order to free the people from slavery under the lords, and to give them protection, by means of certain privileges and a separate jurisdiction [c]. An ancient French writer calls them a new and wicked device, to procure liberty to slaves, and encourage them in shaking off the dominion of their masters [d]. The famous charter, as it is called, of the conqueror to the city of London, though granted at a time when he assumed the appearance of gentleness and lenity, is nothing but a letter of protection, and a declaration that the citizens should not be treated as slaves [e]. By the English feudal law, the superior lord was prohibited from marrying his female ward to a burgess or a villain [f]; so near were these two ranks esteemed to each other, and so much inferior to the nobility and gentry. Besides possessing the advantages of birth, riches, civil powers and privileges, the nobles and gentlemen alone were armed, a circumstance which gave them a mighty superiority, in an age when nothing but the military profession was honourable, and when the loose execution of laws gave so much encouragement to open violence, and rendered it so decisive in all disputes and controversies [g].

THE great similarity among the feudal governments of Europe is well known to every man that has any

[c] Du Cange's Gloss. in verb. communia, communitas.
[d] Holingshed, vol. iii. p. 15.
[e] Stat. of Marton, 1235, cap. 6.
[f] Gelberius de vita sua, lib. 3. cap. 7.
[g] Madox's Baron. Angl. p. 19.

acquaintance

APPENDIX II.

acquaintance with ancient history; and the antiquaries of all foreign countries, where the question was never embarrassed by party disputes, have allowed, that the commons came very late to be admitted to a share in the legislative power. In Normandy particularly, whose constitution was most likely to be William's model in raising his new fabric of English government, the states were entirely composed of the clergy and nobility; and the first incorporated boroughs or communities of that dutchy were Rouen and Falaise, which enjoyed their privileges by a grant of Philip Augustus in the year 1207 [b]. All the ancient English historians, when they mention the great council of the nation, call it an assembly of the baronage, nobility, or great men; and none of their expressions, though several hundred passages might be produced, can, without the utmost violence, be tortured to a meaning, which will admit the commons to be constituent members of that body [l]. If in the long period of 200 years, which elapsed between the Conquest and the latter end of Henry III. and which abounded in factions, revolutions, and convulsions of all kinds, the house of commons never performed one single legislative act, so considerable as to be once mentioned by any of the numerous historians of that age, they must have been totally

---

[b] Norman. De Chesail, p. 1066. Du Cange Gloss. in verb. *communia*.

[l] Sometimes the historians mention the people, *populus*, as a part of the parliament: but they always mean the laity, in opposition to the clergy. Sometimes the word *communitas* is found; but it always means *communitas baronagii*. These points are clearly proved by Dr. Brady. There is also mention sometimes made of a crowd or multitude that thronged into the great council on particular interesting occasions; but as deputies from boroughs are never once spoke of, the proof, that they had not then any existence, becomes the more certain and undeniable. These never could make a crowd, as they must have had a regular place assigned them, if they had made a regular part of the legislative body. There were only 130 boroughs who received writs of summons from Edward I. It is expressly said in Gesta Reg. Steph. p. 930, that it was usual for the populace, *vulgus*, to crowd into the great councils; where they were plainly mere spectators, and could only gratify their curiosity.

insignificant: And in that case, what reason can be assigned for their ever being assembled? Can it be supposed, that men of so little weight or importance possessed a negative voice against the king and the barons? Every page of the subsequent histories discovers their existence; though these histories are not written with greater accuracy than the preceding ones, and indeed scarcely equal them in that particular. The *Magna Charta* of king John provides, that no scutage or aid should be imposed, either on the land or towns, but by consent of the great council; and for more security, it enumerates the persons entitled to a seat in that assembly, the prelates and immediate tenants of the crown, without any mention of the commons: An authority so full, certain, and explicit, that nothing but the zeal of party could ever have procured credit to any contrary hypothesis.

It was probably the example of the French barons, which first emboldened the English to require greater independence from their sovereign: It is also probable, that the boroughs and corporations of England were established in imitation of those of France. It may, therefore, be proposed as no unlikely conjecture, that both the chief privileges of the peers in England and the liberty of the commons were originally the growth of that foreign country.

In ancient times, men were little solicitous to obtain a place in the legislative assemblies; and rather regarded their attendance as a burden, which was not compensated by any return of profit or honour, proportionate to the trouble and expence. The only reason for instituting those public councils, was, on the part of the subject, that they desired some security from the attempts of arbitrary power; and on the part of the sovereign, that he despaired of governing men of such independent spirits without their own consent and concurrence. But the commons,

APPENDIX II.

commons, or the inhabitants of boroughs, had not as yet reached such a degree of consideration, as to desire *security* against their prince, or to imagine that, even if they were assembled in a representative body, they had power or rank sufficient to enforce it. The only protection, which they aspired to, was against the immediate violence and injustice of their fellow-citizens; and this advantage each of them looked for, from the courts of justice, or from the authority of some great lord, to whom, by law, or his own choice, he was attached. On the other hand, the sovereign was sufficiently assured of obedience in the whole community, if he procured the concurrence of the nobles; nor had he reason to apprehend, that any order of the state could resist his and their united authority. The military sub-vassals could entertain no idea of opposing both their prince and their superiors: The burgesses and tradesmen could much less aspire to such a thought: And thus, even if history were silent on the head, we have reason to conclude, from the known situation of society during those ages, that the commons were never admitted as members of the legislative body.

The *executive* power of the Anglo-Norman government was lodged in the king. Besides the stated meetings of the national council at the three great festivals of Christmas, Easter, and Whitsuntide [1], he was accustomed, on any sudden exigence, to summon them together. He could, at his pleasure, command the attendance of his barons and their vassals, in which consisted the military force of the kingdom; and could employ them, during forty days, either in resisting a foreign enemy, or reducing his rebellious subjects. And, what was of great importance, the whole *judicial* power was ultimately in his hands, and was exercised by officers and ministers of his appointment.

[1] Dugd. Orig. Jurid. p. 15. Spelm. Gloss. in verbo *parliamentum*.

Appendix II.

Judicial power.

THE general plan of the Anglo-Norman government was, that the court of barony was appointed to decide such controversies as arose between the several vassals or subjects of the same barony; the hundred-court and county-court, which were still continued as during the Saxon times [n], to judge between the subjects of different baronies [o]; and the *curia Regis*, or king's court, to give sentence among the barons themselves [p]. But this plan, though simple, was attended with some circumstances, which, being derived from a very extensive authority, assumed by the Conqueror, contributed to increase the royal prerogative; and as long as the state was not disturbed by arms, reduced every order of the community to some degree of dependance and subordination.

THE king himself often sat in his court, which always attended his person [q]: He there heard causes and pronounced judgment [r]; and though he was assisted by the advice of the other members, it is not to be imagined that a decision could easily be obtained contrary to his inclination or opinion. In his absence the chief justiciary presided, who was the first magistrate in the state, and a kind of viceroy, on whom depended all the civil affairs

---

[n] Ang. Sacra. vol. i. p. 314, &c. Dugd. Orig. Jurid. p. 27. 29. Madox Hist. of Exch. p. 75, 76. Spelm. Gloss. in verbo *Hundred*.

[o] None of the feudal governments in Europe had such institutions as the county courts, which the great authority of the Conqueror still retained from the Saxon customs. All the freeholders of the county, even the greatest barons, were obliged to attend the Sheriff in these courts, not to shift them in the administration of justice. By this means, they received frequent and sensible admonitions of their dependance on the king or supreme magistrate: They formed a kind of community with their fellow-barons and freeholders: They were often drawn from their individual and independent state, peculiar to the feudal system; and were made members of a political body. And, perhaps, this institution of county-courts in England has had greater effects on the government, than has yet been distinctly pointed out by historians, or traced by antiquaries. The barons were never able to free themselves from this attendance on the sheriffs and itinerant justices till the reign of Henry III.

[q] Brady Pref. p. 143. [r] Madox Hist. of Exch. p. 103. [s] Brady, lib. 3. cap. 9. § 3. cap. 10. § 1.

APPENDIX II.

of the kingdom¹. The other chief officers of the crown, the conſtable, mareſchal, ſeneſchal, chamberlain, treaſurer and ᵗchancellor ᵘ, were members, together with ſuch feudal barons as thought proper to attend, and the barons of the Exchequer, who at firſt were alſo feudal barons, appointed by the king'. This court, which was ſometimes called the king's court, ſometimes the court of Exchequer, judged in all cauſes, civil and criminal, and comprehended the whole buſineſs which is now ſhared out among four courts, the Chancery, the King's Bench, the Common Pleas, and the Exchequer ⁿ.

SUCH an accumulation of powers was itſelf a great ſource of authority, and rendered the juriſdiction of the court formidable to all the ſubjects; but the turn, which judicial trials took ſoon after the Conqueſt, ſerved ſtill more to increaſe its authority, and to augment the royal prerogatives. William, among the other violent changes which he attempted and effected, had introduced the Norman law into England ʷ, had ordered all the pleadings to be in that tongue, and had interwoven, with the Engliſh juriſprudence, all the maxims and principles which the Normans, more advanced in cultivation, and naturally litigious, were accuſtomed to obſerve in the diſtribution of juſtice. Law now became a ſcience, which at firſt fell entirely into the hands of the Normans; and which, even after it was communicated to the Engliſh, required ſo much ſtudy and application, that the laity, in thoſe ignorant ages, were incapable of attaining it, and it was a myſtery almoſt ſolely confined to the clergy, and chiefly to the monks ˣ. The great

---

ᵗ Spelm. Gloſſ. in verbo *juſticiarii*.   ᵘ Madox Hiſt. Exch. p. 27. 29. 33. 38. 40. 56. The Normans introduced the practice of ſealing charters; and the chancellor's office was to keep the Great Seal. Joſelph. Dugd. p. 33, 34.   ᵛ Madox Hiſt. of the Exch. p. 134, 135. Gerv. Dorob. p. 1387.   ᵘ Madox Hiſt. of the Exch. p. 36, 70.   ʷ Dial. de Scac. p. 30. apud Madox Hiſt. of the Exchequer.   ˣ Malmſf. lib. 4. p. 153.

officers

Appendix II

officers of the crown and the feudal barons, who were military men, found themselves unfit to penetrate into those obscurities; and though they were entitled to a seat in the supreme judicature, the business of the court was wholly managed by the chief justiciary and the law barons, who were men appointed by the king, and entirely at his disposal [y]. This natural course of things was forwarded by the multiplicity of business, which flowed into that court, and which daily augmented by the appeals from all the subordinate judicatures of the kingdom.

In the Saxon times, no appeal was received in the king's court, except upon the denial or delay of justice by the inferior courts; and the same practice was still observed in most of the feudal kingdoms of Europe. But the great power of the Conqueror established at first in England an authority, which the monarchs in France were not able to attain till the reign of St. Lewis, who lived near two centuries after: He empowered his court to receive appeals both from the courts of barony and the county-courts, and by that means brought the administration of justice ultimately into the hands of the sovereign [z]. And lest the expence or trouble of a journey to court should discourage suitors, and make them acquiesce in the decision of the inferior judicatures, itinerant judges were afterwards established, who made their circuits throughout the kingdom, and tried all causes that were brought before them [a]. By this expedient, the courts of barony were kept in awe; and if they still pre-

---

[y] Dureé. Orig. Jurid. p. 25. [z] Madox. Hist. of the Exch. p. 65. Glanv. lib. 12. cap. 1. 7. LL. Hen. I. § 31. apud Wilkins, p. 248. Fitz-Stephens, p. 36. Coke's Comment. on the statute of Malbridge, cap. 20.

[a] Madox H'st. of the Exch. p. 83, 84. 100. Gerv. Dorob. p. 1410. What made the Anglo-Norman barons more readily submit to appeals from their court to the King's Court of Exchequer, was, their being accustomed in like appeals in Normandy to the ducal court of Exchequer. See Gilbert's History of the Exchequer, p. 1, 2; though the author thinks it doubtful, whether the Norman court was not rather copied from the English, p. 6.

served

APPENDIX II.

ferved fome influence, it was only from the apprehenfions, which the vaffals might entertain, of difobliging their fuperior by appealing from his jurifdiction. But the county-courts were much difcredited; and as the freeholders were found ignorant of the intricate principles and forms of the new law, the lawyers gradually brought all bufinefs before the king's judges, and abandoned the ancient fimple and popular judicature. After this manner, the formalities of juftice, which, though they appear tedious aud cumberfome, are found requifite to the fupport of liberty in all monarchical governments, proved at firft, by a combination of caufes, very advantageous to royal authority in England.

THE power of the Norman kings was alfo much fupported by a great revenue; and by a revenue, that was fixed, perpetual, and independent of the fubject. The people, without betaking themfelves to arms, had no check upon the king, and no regular fecurity for the due adminiftration of juftice. In thofe days of violence, many inftances of oppreffion paffed unheeded; and foon after were openly pleaded as precedents, which it was unlawful to difpute or controul. Princes and minifters were too ignorant to be themfelves fenfible of the advantages attending an equitable adminiftration; and there was no eftablifhed council or affembly which could protect the people, and, by withdrawing fupplies, regularly and peaceably admonifh the king of his duty, and enfure the execution of the laws.

THE firft branch of the king's ftated revenue was the royal demefnes or crown lands, which were very extenfive, and comprehended, befide a great number of manors, moft of the chief cities of the kingdom. It was eftablifhed by law, that the king could alienate no part of his demefne, and that he himfelf, or his fucceffor, could, at any time, refume fuch donations[b]: But this law was

[b] Fleta, lib. 1 cap. 8. § 17. lib. 3. cap. 6. § 3. Bracton, lib. 2. cap. 5.

Appendix II.

never regularly observed; which happily rendered in time the crown somewhat more dependant. The rent of the crown-lands, considered merely as so much riches, was a source of power: The influence of the king over his tenants and the inhabitants of his towns, encreased this power: But the other numerous branches of his revenue, besides supplying his treasury, gave, by their very nature, a great latitude to arbitrary authority, and were a support of the prerogative; as will appear from an enumeration of them.

THE king was never content with the stated rents, but levied heavy talliages at pleasure on the inhabitants both of town and country, who lived within his demesne. All bargains of sale, in order to prevent theft, being prohibited, except in boroughs and public markets [c], he pretended to exact tolls on all goods which were there sold [d]. He seized two hogsheads, one before and one behind the mast, from every vessel that imported wine. All goods paid to his customs a proportional part of their value [e]: Passage over bridges and on rivers was loaded with tolls at pleasure [f]: And though the boroughs by degrees brought the liberty of farming these impositions, yet the revenue profited by these bargains; new sums were often exacted for the renewal and confirmation of their charters [g], and the people were thus held in perpetual dependance.

SUCH was the situation of the inhabitants within the royal demesnes. But the possessors of land, or the military tenants, though they were better protected, both by law, and by the great privilege of carrying arms, were, from the nature of their tenures, much exposed to the inroads of power, and possessed not what we should

[c] LL. Will. 1. cap. 61. [d] Madox, p. 530. [e] Ibid. p. 529. This author says a Esloamb. But it is not easy to reconcile this account to other authorities. [f] Madox. p. 529. [g] Madox's Hist. of the Exch. p. 275, 276, 277, &c.

esteem

APPENDIX II.

esteem, in our age, a very durable security. The Conqueror ordained, that the barons should be obliged to pay nothing beyond their stated services [g], except a reasonable aid to ransom his person if he were taken in war, to make his eldest son a knight, and to marry his eldest daughter. What should, on these occasions, be deemed a reasonable aid, was not determined; and the demands of the crown were so far discretionary.

THE king could require in war the personal attendance of his vassals, that is, of almost all the landed proprietors; and if they declined the service, they were obliged to pay him a composition in money, which was called a scutage. The sum was, during some reigns, precarious and uncertain; it was sometimes levied without allowing the vassal the liberty of personal service [h]; and it was a usual artifice of the king's to pretend an expedition, that he might be entitled to levy the scutage from his military tenants. Danegelt was another species of land-tax levied by the early Norman kings, arbitrarily, and contrary to the laws of the Conqueror [i]. Moneyage was also a general land-tax of the same nature, levied by the two first Norman kings, and abolished by the charter of Henry I. [k]. It was a shilling paid every three years by each hearth, to induce the king not to use his prerogative in debasing the coin. Indeed, it appears from that charter, that, though the Conqueror had granted his military tenants an immunity from all taxes and tallages; he and his son William had never thought themselves bound to observe that rule, but had levied impositions at pleasure on all the landed estates of the kingdom. The utmost that Henry grants is, that the land cultivated by the military tenant himself shall not be so burdened; but he reserves the power of taxing the farmers: And as it is

[g] LL. Will. Conq. § 55.
[i] Madox's Hist. of the Exch. p. 475.
[h] Gervase de Tilbury, p. 25.
[k] Matth. Paris, p. 38.

known,

known, that Henry's charter was never observed in any one article, we may be assured, that this prince and his successors retracted even this small indulgence, and levied arbitrary impositions on all the lands of all their subjects. These taxes were sometimes very heavy; since Malmesbury tells us, that, in the reign of William Rufus, the farmers, on account of them, abandoned tillage, and a famine ensued [l].

THE escheats were a great branch both of power and of revenue, especially during the first reigns after the conquest. In default of posterity from the first baron, his land reverted to the crown, and continually augmented the king's possessions. The prince had indeed by law a power of alienating these escheats; but by this means he had an opportunity of establishing the fortunes of his friends and servants, and thereby enlarging his authority. Sometimes he retained them in his own hands; and they were gradually confounded with the royal demesnes, and became difficult to be distinguished from them. This confusion is probably the reason why the king acquired the right of alienating his demesnes.

BUT besides escheats from default of heirs, those which ensued from crimes or breach of duty towards the superior lord, were frequent in ancient times. If the vassal, being thrice summoned to attend his superior's court, and do fealty, neglected or refused obedience, he forfeited all title to his land [m]. If he denied his tenure, or refused his service, he was exposed to the same penalty [n]. If he sold his estate without licence from his lord [o], or if he sold it upon any other tenure or title than that by which he himself held it [p], he lost all right to it. The adhering

[l] So also Chron. Abb. St. Petri de Burgo, p. 55. Knyghton, p. 2366.
[m] Hoveden. de Feud. Disp. cap. 38. col. 836. [n] Lib. Feud. lib. 3. tit. 1. 4. tit. lib. 21. 39. [o] Lib. Feud. lib. 1. tit. 21.
[p] Id. lib. 4. tit. 44.

APPENDIX II.

to his lord's enemies, deserting him in war, betraying his secrets, debauching his wife or his near relations, or even using indecent freedoms with them, might be punished by forfeiture. The higher crimes, rapes, robbery, murder, arson, &c. were called felony; and being interpreted want of fidelity to his lord, made him lose his fief. Even where the felon was vassal to a baron, though his immediate lord enjoyed the forfeiture, the king might retain possession of his estate during a twelvemonth, and had the right of spoiling and destroying it, unless the baron paid him a reasonable composition. We have not here enumerated all the species of felonies, or of crimes by which forfeiture was incurred: We have said enough to prove, that the possession of feudal property was anciently somewhat precarious, and that the primary idea was never lost, of its being a kind of *fee* or *benefice*.

WHEN a baron died, the king immediately took possession of the estate; and the heir, before he recovered his right, was obliged to make application to the crown, and desire that he might be admitted to do homage for his land, and pay a composition to the king. This composition was not at first fixed by law, at least by practice: The king was often exorbitant in his demands, and kept possession of the land till they were complied with.

If the heir were a minor, the king retained the whole profit of the estate till his majority; and might grant what sum he thought proper for the education and maintenance of the young baron. This practice was also founded on the notion, that a fief was a benefice, and that, while the heir could not perform his military services, the revenue devolved to the superior, who employed another in his stead. It is obvious, that a great proportion of the landed property must, by means of this device, be continually in the hands of the prince, and that all the noble families were thereby held in perpetual dependance. When the king granted the wardship of a rich heir to any one, he had the opportunity of enriching a favourite or minister: If he sold it, he thereby levied a considerable sum of money. Simon de Mountfort paid Henry III. 10,000 marks, an immense sum in those days, for the wardship of Gilbert de Umfreville [f]. Geoffrey de Mandeville paid to the same prince the sum of 20,000 marks, that he might marry Isabel countess of Glocester, and possess all her lands and knights fees. This sum would be equivalent to 300,000, perhaps 400,000 pounds in our time [g].

If the heir were a female, the king was entitled to offer her any husband of her rank he thought proper; and if she refused him, she forfeited her land. Even a male heir could not marry without the royal consent; and it was usual for men to pay large sums for the liberty of making their own choice in marriage [h]. No man could dispose of his land, either by sale or will, without the consent of his superior. The possessor was never considered as full proprietor: He was still a kind of beneficiary; and could not oblige his superior to accept of any vassal that was not agreeable to him.

Fines, amerciaments, and oblatas, as they were called, were another considerable branch of the royal power and revenue. The ancient records of the exchequer, which are still preserved, give surprizing accounts of the numerous fines and amerciaments levied in those days [b], and of the strange inventions fallen upon to exact money from

[f] Madox's Hist. of the Exch. p. 223.   [g] Id. p. 322.
[a] Id. p. 310.   [b] Id. p. 272.

the

APPENDIX II.

the subject. It appears, that the ancient kings of England put themselves entirely on the foot of the barbarous eastern princes, whom no man must approach without a present, who sell all their good offices, and who intrude themselves into every business that they may have a pretence for extorting money. Even justice was avowedly bought and sold; the king's court itself, though the supreme judicature of the kingdom, was open to none that brought not presents to the king; the bribes given for the expedition, delay^c, suspension, and, doubtless, for the perversion of justice, were entered in the public registers of the royal revenue, and remain as monuments of the perpetual iniquity and tyranny of the times. The barons of the exchequer, for instance, the first nobility of the kingdom, were not ashamed to insert, as an article in their records, that the county of Norfolk paid a sum, that they might be fairly dealt with^d; the borough of Yarmouth, that the king's charters, which they have for their liberties, might not be violated^e; Richard, son of Gilbert, for the king's helping him to recover his debt from the Jews^f; Serlo, son of Terlavaston, that he might be permitted to make his defence, in case he were accused of a certain homicide^g; Walter de Burton for free law, if accused of wounding another^h; Robert de Essart, for having an inquest to find whether Roger, the butcher, and Wace and Humphrey, accused him of robbery and theft out of envy and ill-will, or notⁱ; William Buhurst, for having an inquest to find whether he were accused of the death of one Godwin out of ill-will or for just cause^k. I have selected these few instances from a great number of a like kind, which Madox had selected from a still greater number, preserved in the ancient rolls of the exchequer^l.

^c Madox's Hist. of Exch. p. 274. 309. ^d Id. p. 295.
^e Id. ibid. ^f Id. p. 296. He paid 100 marks, a great sum in those days. ^g Id. p. 296. ^h Id. ibid. ⁱ Id. p. 298.
^k Id. p. 302. ^l Chap. xii.

SOMETIMES

Sometimes the party litigant offered the king a certain portion, a half, a third, a fourth, payable out of the debts, which he, as the executor of justice, should assist him in recovering[n]. Theophania de Westland agreed to pay the half of 212 marks, that she might recover that sum against James de Fughleston[o]; Solomon the Jew engaged to pay one mark out of every seven that he should recover against Hugh de la Hose[p]; Nicholas Morrel promised to pay sixty pounds, that the earl of Flanders might be distrained to pay him 343 pounds, which the earl had taken from him; and these sixty pounds were to be paid out of the first money that Nicholas should recover from the earl[r].

As the king assumed the entire power over trade, he was to be paid for a permission to exercise commerce or industry of any kind[s]. Hugh Oisel paid 400 marks for liberty to trade in England[t]: Nigel de Havene gave fifty marks for the partnership in merchandize which he had with Gervase de Hanton[u]: The men of Worcester paid 100 shillings, that they might have the liberty of selling and buying dyed cloth, as formerly[v]: Several other towns paid for a like liberty[w]. The commerce indeed of the kingdom was so much under the controul of the king, that he erected gilds, corporations, and monopolies, wherever he pleased; and levied sums for these exclusive privileges[x].

There were no profits so small as to be below the king's attention. Henry, son of Arthur, gave ten dogs, to have a recognition against the countess of Copland for one knight's fee[y]. Roger, son of Nicholas, gave twenty lampreys and twenty shads for an inquest to find, whether

[n] Madox's Hist. of Exch. p. 311, 312. [o] Id. p. 312. [p] Id. p. 314. [q] Id. p. 298. [r] Id. ibid. [s] Id. p. 303. [t] Id. ibid. [u] Id. p. 79. [v] Id. ibid. [w] Id. p. 232, 233, &c. [x] Id. ibid.

Gilbert,

APPENDIX II.

Gilbert, son of Alured, gave to Roger 200 muttons to obtain his confirmation for certain lands, or whether Roger took them from him by violence [r]: Geoffrey Fitz-Pierre, the chief justiciary, gave two good Norway hawks, that Walter le Madine might have leave to export a hundred weight of cheese out of the king's dominions [a].

It is really amusing to remark the strange business in which the king sometimes interfered, and never without a present: The wife of Hugh de Neville gave the king 200 hens, that she might lie with her husband one night [b]; and she brought with her two sureties, who answered each for a hundred hens. It is probable that her husband was a prisoner, which debarred her from having access to him. The abbot of Rucford paid ten marks, for leave to erect houses and place men upon his land near Welhang, in order to secure his wood there from being stolen [b]: Hugh archdeacon of Wells, gave one tun of wine for leave to carry 600 summs of corn whither he would [c]: Peter de Peraris gave twenty marks for leave to salt fishes, as Peter Chevalier used to do [d].

It was usual to pay high fines, in order to gain the king's good-will, or mitigate his anger. In the reign of Henry II. Gilbert, the son of Fergus, fines in 919 pounds 9 shillings to obtain that prince's favour; William de Chataignes a thousand marks, that he would remit his displeasure. In the reign of Henry III. the city of London fines in no less a sum than 20,000 pounds on the same account [e].

The king's protection and good offices of every kind were bought and sold. Robert Grislet paid twenty marks of silver, that the king would help him against the earl of Mortaigne in a certain plea [f]: Robert de Cundet gave

[r] Madox's Hist. of Exch. p. 305.   [a] Id. p. 325.   [b] Id. p. 326.   [b] Id. ibid.   [c] Id. p. 320.   [d] Id. p. 326.   [e] Id. p. 327, 319.   [f] Id. p. 329.

thirty marks of silver, that the king would bring him to an accord with the bishop of Lincoln [g]: Ralph de Breckham gave a hawk, that the king would protect him [h]; and this is a very frequent reason for payments: John, son of Ordgar, gave a Norway hawk, to have the king's request to the king of Norway to let him have his brother Godard's chattels [i]: Richard de Neville gave twenty palfreys to obtain the king's request to Isolda Bisset, that she should take him for a husband [k]: Roger Fitz-Walter gave three good palfreys to have the king's letter to Roger Bertram's mother, that she should marry him [l]: Eling, the dean, paid 100 marks, that his whore and his children might be let out upon bail [m]: The bishop of Winchester gave one tun of good wine for his not putting the king in mind to give a girdle to the countess of Albemarle [n]: Robert de Veaux gave five of the best palfreys, that the king would hold his tongue about Henry Pinal's wife [o]. There are, in the records of exchequer, many other singular instances of a like nature [p]. It will however

---

[g] Madox's Hist. of Exch. p. 332.   [h] Id. p. 332.
[i] Id. ibid.   [k] Id. p. 333.   [l] Id. ibid.   [m] Id. p. 342. *Pro habenda amica sua & filiis,* &c.   [n] Id. p. 352.
[o] Id. ibid. *Ut rex taceret de uxore Henrici Pinel.*

[p] *We shall gratify the reader's curiosity by subjoining a few more instances from Madox,* p. 352. Hugh Oisel was to give the king two robes of a good green colour, to have the king's letters patent to the merchants of Flanders, with a request to render him 1000 marks, which he lost in Flanders. The abbot of Hyde paid thirty marks, to have the king's letters of request to the archbishop of Canterbury, to remove certain monks that were against the abbot. Roger de Trihanton paid twenty marks and a palfrey, to have the king's request to Richard de Umfreville to give him his sister to wife, and to the sister that she would accept of him for a husband: William de Chevaringworth paid five marks, to have the king's letter to the abbot of Persora, to let him enjoy peaceably his tythes as formerly; Matthew de Hereford, clerk, paid ten marks for a letter of request to the bishop of Landaff, to let him enjoy peaceably his church of Sebeofrith; Andrew Nuulun gave three Flemish caps, for the king's request to the prior of Chikesand, for performance of an agreement made between them; Henry de Fonibus gave a Lombardy horse of value.

APPENDIX II.

ever be juſt to remark, that the ſame ridiculous practices and dangerous abuſes prevailed in Normandy, and probably in all the other ſtates of Europe. England was not, in this reſpect, more barbarous than its neighbours.

THESE iniquitous practices of the Norman kings were ſo well known, that, on the death of Hugh Bigod, in the reign of Henry II. the beſt and moſt juſt of theſe princes, the eldeſt ſon and the widow of this nobleman came to court, and ſtrove, by offering large preſents to the king, each of them to acquire poſſeſſion of that rich inheritance. The king was ſo equitable as to order the cauſe to be tried by the great council: But, in the mean time, he ſeized all the money and treaſure of the deceaſed. Peter of Blois, a judicious, and even an elegant writer for that age, gives a pathetic deſcription of the venality of juſtice, and the oppreſſions of the poor, under the reign of Henry: And he ſcruples not to complain to the king himſelf of theſe abuſes. We may judge what the caſe would be under the government of worſe princes. The articles of enquiry concerning the conduct of ſheriffs, which Henry promulgated in 1170, ſhow the great power, as well as the licentiouſneſs, of theſe officers.

AMERCIAMENTS or fines for crimes and treſpaſſes were another conſiderable branch of the royal revenue. Moſt

value, to have the king's requeſt to Henry Fitz-Harvey, that he would give him his daughter to wife: Roger, ſon of Nicholas, promiſed all the lampreys he could get, to have the king's requeſt to earl William Marſhal, that he would grant him the manor of Langeford at Firm. The burgeſſes of Gloceſter promiſed 300 lampreys, that they might not be diſtrained to find the pilſoners of Poictou with neceſſaries, unleſs they pleaſed. Id. p. 352. Jordan, ſon of Reginald, paid twenty marks to have the king's requeſt to William Paulel, that he would grant him the land of Mill Niereanir, and the cuſtody of his heirs; and if Jordan obtained the ſame, he was to pay the twenty marks, otherwiſe not. Id. p. 353.

§ Madox's Hiſt. of Exch. p. 359.
‡ Benet. Abb. p. 130, 181.
ᵉ Petri Bleſ. Epiſt. 95. apud Bibl. Patrum, tom. 24. p. 2014.
ᶠ Hoveden, Chron. Gerv. p. 1410.
ᵃ Madox, chap. xiv.

crimes were atoned for by money; the fines impofed were not limited by any rule or ftatute; and frequently occafioned the total ruin of the perfon, even for the flighteft trefpaffes. The foreft-laws, particularly, were a great fource of oppreffion. The king poffeffed fixty-eight forefts, thirteen chaces, and feven hundred and eighty-one parks, in different parts of England*; and, confidering the extreme paffion of the Englifh and Normans for hunting, thefe were fo many fnares laid for the people, by which they were allured into trefpaffes, and brought within the reach of arbitrary and rigorous laws, which the king had thought proper to enact by his own authority.

But the moft barefaced acts of tyranny and oppreffion were practifed againft the Jews, who were entirely out of the protection of law, were extremely odious from the bigotry of the people, and were abandoned to the immeafurable rapacity of the king and his minifters. Befides many other indignities, to which they were continually expofed, it appears that they were once all thrown into prifon, and the fum of 66,000 marks exacted for their liberty[x]: At another time, Ifaac the Jew paid alone 5100 marks[y]; Brun, 3000 marks[z]; Jurnet, 2000; Bennet, 500: At another, Licorica, widow of David, the Jew of Oxford, was required to pay 6000 marks; and fhe was delivered over to fix of the richeft and difcreeteft Jews in England, who were to anfwer for the fum[a]. Henry III. borrowed 5000 marks from the earl of Cornwal; and for his repayment configned over to him all the Jews in England[b]. The revenue arifing from exactions upon this nation was fo confiderable, that there was a particular court of exchequer fet apart for managing it[c].

[w] Spelm. Gloff. in verbo Forefta. p. 151. This happened in the reign of king John. [x] Madox's Hift. of the Exch. p. 151. [y] Id. p. 153. [z] Id. p. 163. [a] Id. p. 156. [b] Id. chap. vii.

APPENDIX II.

We may judge concerning the low state of commerce among the English, when the Jews, notwithstanding these oppressions, could still find their account in trading among them, and lending them money. And as the improvements of agriculture were also much checked by the immense possessions of the nobility, by the disorders of the times, and by the precarious state of feudal property, it appears that industry of no kind could then have place in the kingdom [d].

It is asserted by Sir Harry Spelman [e], as an undoubted truth, that, during the reigns of the first Norman princes, every edict of the king, issued with the consent of his privy-council, had the full force of law. But the barons, surely, were not so passive as to entrust a power, entirely arbitrary and despotic, into the hands of the sovereign. It only appears, that the constitution had not fixed any precise boundaries to the royal power; that the right of issuing proclamations on any emergence, and of exacting obedience to them, a right which was always supposed inherent in the crown, is very difficult to be distinguished from a legislative authority; that the extreme imperfection of the ancient laws, and the sudden exigencies which often occurred in such turbulent governments, obliged the prince to exert frequently the latent powers of his prerogative; that he naturally proceeded, from the acquiescence of the people, to assume, in many particulars of moment, an authority from which

---

[d] We learn from the extracts given us of Domesday by Brady, in his Treatise of boroughs, that almost all the boroughs of England had suffered in the stock of the Conquest, and had extremely decayed between the death of the Confessor, and the time when Domesday was framed.

[e] Gloss. in verb. jurisdictio Dei. The author of the Mirror des justices complains, that ordinances are only made by the king and his clerks, and by aliens and others, who dare not contradict the king, but study to please him. Whence, he concludes, laws are oftener dictated by will, than founded on right.

he had excluded himself by express statutes, charters, or concessions, and which was, in the main, repugnant to the general genius of the constitution; and that the lives, the personal liberty, and the properties of all his subjects, were less secured by law against the exertion of his arbitrary authority, than by the independent power and private connexions of each individual. It appears from the Great Charter itself, that not only John, a tyrannical prince, and Richard, a violent one, but their father Henry, under whose reign the prevalence of gross abuses is the least to be suspected, were accustomed, from their sole authority, without process of law, to imprison, banish, and attaint the freemen of their kingdom.

A GREAT baron, in ancient times, considered himself as a kind of sovereign within his territory; and was attended by courtiers and dependants more zealously attached to him than the ministers of state and the great officers were commonly to *their* sovereign. He often maintained in his court the parade of royalty, by establishing a justiciary, constable, mareschal, chamberlain, seneschal, and chancellor, and assigning to each of these officers a separate province and command. He was usually very assiduous in exercising his jurisdiction; and took such delight in that image of sovereignty, that it was found necessary to restrain his activity, and prohibit him by law from holding courts too frequently [e]. It is not to be doubted, but the example set him by the prince, of a mercenary and sordid extortion, would be faithfully copied; and that all his good and bad offices, his justice and injustice, were equally put to sale. He had the power, with the king's consent, to exact talliages even from the free citizens who lived within his barony; and as his necessities made him rapacious, his authority was usually found to be more oppressive and tyrannical than that of the sovereign [f]. He

[e] Dugd. Jurid. Orig. p. 26. [f] Madox Hist. of Exch. p. 520.

APPENDIX II.

was ever engaged in hereditary or personal animosities or confederacies with his neighbours, and often gave protection to all desperate adventurers and criminals who could be useful in serving his violent purposes. He was able alone, in times of tranquillity, to obstruct the execution of justice within his territories; and by combining with a few malcontent barons of high rank and power, he could throw the state into convulsions. And, on the whole, though the royal authority was confined within bounds, and often within very narrow ones, yet the check was irregular, and frequently the source of great disorders; nor was it derived from the liberty of the people, but from the military power of many petty tyrants, who were equally dangerous to the prince, and oppressive to the subject.

THE power of the church was another rampart against royal authority; but this defence was also the cause of many mischiefs and inconveniencies. The dignified clergy, perhaps, were not so prone to immediate violence as the barons; but as they pretended to a total independence on the state, and could always cover themselves with the appearances of religion, they proved, in one respect, an obstruction to the settlement of the kingdom, and to the regular execution of the laws. The policy of the conqueror was in this particular liable to some exception. He augmented the superstitious veneration for Rome, to which that age was so much inclined; and he broke those bands of connexion, which, in the Saxon times, had preserved an union between the lay and the clerical orders. He prohibited the bishops from sitting in the county courts; he allowed ecclesiastical causes to be tried in spiritual courts only[s]; and he so much exalted the power of the clergy, that of 60,215 knights fees, into

[s] Char. Will. apud Wilkins, p. 230. Spel. Conc. vol. II. p. 14.

which he divided England, he placed no lefs than 28,015 under the church [h].

The right of primogeniture was introduced with the feudal law: An inftitution which is hurtful, by producing and maintaining an unequal divifion of private property; but is advantageous in another refpect, by accuftoming the people to a preference in favour of the eldeft fon, and thereby preventing a partition or difputed fucceffion in the monarchy. The Normans introduced the ufe of firnames, which tend to preferve the knowledge of families and pedigrees. They abolifhed none of the old abfurd methods of trial by the crofs or ordeal; and they added a new abfurdity, the trial by fingle combat [i], which became a regular part of jurifprudence, and was conducted with all the order, method, devotion, and folemnity imaginable [k]. The ideas of chivalry alfo feem to have been imported by the Normans: No traces of thofe fantaftic notions are to be found among the plain and ruftic Saxons. The feudal inftitutions, by raifing the military tenants to a kind of fovereign dignity, by rendering perfonal ftrength and valour requifite, and by making every knight and baron his own protector and avenger, begat that martial pride and fenfe of honour, which, being cultivated and embellifhed by the poets and romance-writers of the age, ended in chivalry. The virtuous knight fought not only in his own quarrel, but in that of the innocent, of the helplefs, and, above all, of the fair, whom he fuppofed to be for ever under the guardianfhip of his valiant arm. The uncourteous knight, who, from his caftle, exercifed

---

[h] Spel. Glff. in verb. *manus mortua*. We are not to imagine, as fome have done, that the church p:ffeffed lands in this proportion, but only that they and their vaffals enjoyed fuch a proportionable part of the landed property.
[i] LL. Will. cap. 68.
[k] Spel. Gloff. in verb. *campus*. The laft inftance of thefe duels was in the 15th of Eliz. So long did that abfurdity remain.

APPENDIX II.

robbery on travellers, and committed violence on virgins, was the object of his perpetual indignation; and he put him to death, without scruple, or trial, or appeal, wherever he met with him. The great independence of men made personal honour and fidelity the chief tie among them; and rendered it the capital virtue of every true knight, or genuine professor of chivalry. The solemnities of single combat, as established by law, banished the notion of every thing unfair or unequal in rencounters; and maintained an appearance of courtesy between the combatants, till the moment of their engagement. The credulity of the age grafted on this stock the notion of giants, enchanters, dragons, spells[1], and a thousand wonders, which still multiplied during the times of the Crusades; when men, returning from so great a distance, used the liberty of imposing every fiction on their believing audience. These ideas of chivalry infected the writings, conversation, and behaviour of men, during some ages; and even after they were, in a great measure, banished by the revival of learning, they left modern *gallantry* and the *point of honour*, which still maintain their influence, and are the genuine offspring of those ancient affectations.

The concession of the Great Charter, or rather its full establishment (for there was a considerable interval of time between the one and the other), gave rise, by degrees, to a new species of government, and introduced some order and justice into the administration. The ensuing scenes of our history are therefore somewhat different from the preceding. Yet the Great Charter contained no establishment of new courts, magistrates, or senates, nor abolition of the old. It introduced no new distribution of the powers of the commonwealth, and no innovation in the political or public law of the kingdom.

[1] In all legal single combats, it was part of the champion's oath, that he carried not about him any herb, spell, or inchantment, by which he might procure victory. Dugd. Orig. Jurid. p. 82.

It

Appendix II.

It only guarded, and that merely by verbal clauses, against such tyrannical practices as are incompatible with civilized government, and, if they become very frequent, are incompatible with all government. The barbarous licence of the kings, and perhaps of the nobles, was thenceforth somewhat more restrained: Men acquired some more security for their properties and their liberties: And government approached a little nearer to that end for which it was originally instituted, the distribution of justice, and the equal protection of the citizens. Acts of violence and iniquity in the crown, which before were only deemed injurious to individuals, and were hazardous chiefly in proportion to the number, power, and dignity of the persons affected by them, were now regarded, in some degree, as public injuries, and as infringements of a charter calculated for general security. And thus the establishment of the Great Charter, without seeming anywise to innovate in the distribution of political power, became a kind of epoch in the constitution.

CHAP. XII.

HENRY III.

Settlement of the government——General pacification——Death of the Protector——Some commotions——Hubert de Burgh displaced——The bishop of Winchester minister——King's partiality to foreigners——Grievances——Ecclesiastical grievances——Earl of Cornwal elected king of the Romans——Discontent of the barons——Simon de Mountfort earl of Leicester——Provisions of Oxford——Usurpation of the barons——Prince Edward——Civil wars of the barons——Reference to the king of France——Renewal of the civil wars——Battle of Lewes——House of commons——Battle of Evesham, and death of Leicester——Settlement of the government——Death——and character of the king——Miscellaneous transactions of this reign.

MOST sciences, in proportion as they encrease and improve, invent methods by which they facilitate their reasonings; and employing general theorems, are enabled to comprehend, in a few propositions, a great number of inferences and conclusions. History also, being a collection of facts which are multiplying without end, is obliged to adopt such arts of abridgment, to retain the more material events, and to drop all the minute circumstances, which are only interesting during the time, or to the

CHAP. XII.
1216.

the persons engaged in the transactions. This truth is no where more evident than with regard to the reign upon which we are going to enter. What mortal could have the patience to write or read a long detail of such frivolous events as those with which it is filled, or attend to a tedious narrative which would follow, through a series of fifty-six years, the caprices and weaknesses of so mean a prince as Henry ? The chief reason, why protestant writers have been so anxious to spread out the incidents of this reign, is in order to expose the rapacity, ambition, and artifices of the court of Rome, and to prove, that the great dignitaries of the catholic church, while they pretended to have nothing in view but the salvation of souls, had bent all their attention to the acquisition of riches, and were restrained by no sense of justice or of honour, in the pursuit of that great object[e]. But this conclusion would readily be allowed them, though it were not illustrated by such a detail of uninteresting incidents; and follows, indeed, by an evident necessity, from the very situation in which that church was placed with regard to the rest of Europe. For, besides that ecclesiastical power, as it can always cover its operations under a cloak of sanctity, and attacks men on the side where they dare not employ their reason, lies less under controul than civil government; besides this general cause, I say, the pope and his courtiers were foreigners to most of the churches which they governed; they could not possibly have any other object than to pillage the provinces for present gain; and as they lived at a distance, they would be little awed by shame or remorse, in employing every lucrative expedient which was suggested to them. England being one of the most remote provinces attached to the Romish hierarchy, as well as the most prone to superstition, felt severely, during this reign, while its patience

[e] M. Paris, p. 613.

was

HENRY III.

was not yet fully exhausted, the influence of these causes; and we shall often have occasion to touch cursorily upon such incidents. But we shall not attempt to comprehend every transaction transmitted to us; and till the end of the reign, when the events become more memorable, we shall not always observe an exact chronological order in our narration.

CHAP. XII.

1216.

The earl of Pembroke, who, at the time of John's death, was mareschal of England, was by his office at the head of the armies, and, consequently, during a state of civil wars and convulsions, at the head of the government; and it happened fortunately for the young monarch and for the nation, that the power could not have been intrusted into more able and more faithful hands. This nobleman, who had maintained his loyalty unshaken to John during the lowest fortune of that monarch, determined to support the authority of the infant prince; nor was he dismayed at the number and violence of his enemies. Sensible that Henry, agreeably to the prejudices of the times, would not be deemed a sovereign, till crowned and anointed by a churchman, he immediately carried the young prince to Glocester, where the ceremony of coronation was performed, in the presence of Gualo, the legate, and of a few noblemen, by the bishops of Winchester and Bath[a]. As the concurrence of the papal authority was requisite to support the tottering throne, Henry was obliged to swear fealty to the pope, and renew that homage, to which his father had already subjected the kingdom[b]: And in order to enlarge the authority of Pembroke, and to give him a more regular and legal title to it, a general council of the barons was soon after summoned at Bristol, where that nobleman was chosen protector of the realm.

Settlement of the government.

28th Oct.

11th Nov.

[a] M. Paris. p. 200. Hist. Croyl. Cont. p. 474. W. Heming. p. 561. Trivet, p. 168.   [b] M. Paris, p. 200.

Vol. II.   L   Pembroke,

PEMBROKE, that he might reconcile all men to the government of his pupil, made him grant a new charter of liberties, which, though mostly copied from the former concessions extorted from John, contains some alterations, which may be deemed remarkable[p]. The full privilege of elections in the clergy, granted by the late king, was not confirmed, nor the liberty of going out of the kingdom, without the royal consent: Whence we may conclude, that Pembroke and the barons, jealous of the ecclesiastical power, both were desirous of renewing the king's claim to issue a congè d'elire to the monks and chapters, and thought it requisite to put some check to the frequent appeals to Rome. But what may chiefly surprize us is, that the obligation to which John had subjected himself, of obtaining the consent of the great council before he levied any aids or scutages upon the nation, was omitted; and this article was even declared hard and severe, and was expresly left to future deliberation. But we must consider, that, though this limitation may perhaps appear to us the most momentous in the whole charter of John, it was not regarded in that light by the ancient barons, who were more jealous in guarding against particular acts of violence in the crown, than against such general impositions, which, unless they were evidently reasonable and necessary, could scarcely, without general consent, be levied upon men who had arms in their hands, and who could repel any act of oppression, by which they were all immediately affected. We accordingly find that Henry, in the course of his reign, while he gave frequent occasions for complaint, with regard to his violations of the Great Charter, never attempted, by his mere will, to levy any aids or scutages; though he was often reduced to great necessities, and was refused supply by his people. So much

[p] Rymer, vol. i. p. 215.

easier

easier was it for him to transgress the law, when individuals alone were affected, than even to exert his acknowledged prerogatives, where the interest of the whole body was concerned.

CHAP.
XII.

1216.

THIS charter was again confirmed by the king in the ensuing year, with the addition of some articles to prevent the oppressions by sheriffs: And also with an additional charter of forests, a circumstance of great moment in those ages, when hunting was so much the occupation of the nobility, and when the king comprehended so considerable a part of the kingdom within his forests, which he governed by peculiar and arbitrary laws. All the forests, which had been enclosed since the reign of Henry II. were disaforested; and new perambulations were appointed for that purpose: Offences in the forests were declared to be no longer capital; but punishable by fine, imprisonment, and more gentle penalties: And all the proprietors of land recovered the power of cutting and using their own wood at their pleasure.

THUS, these famous charters were brought nearly to the shape in which they have ever since stood; and they were, during many generations, the peculiar favourites of the English nation, and esteemed the most sacred rampart to national liberty and independence. As they secured the rights of all orders of men, they were anxiously defended by all, and became the basis, in a manner, of the English monarchy, and a kind of original contract, which both limited the authority of the king, and ensured the conditional allegiance of his subjects. Though often violated, they were still claimed by the nobility and people; and as no precedents were supposed valid that infringed them, they rather required, than lost authority, from the frequent attempts made against them in several ages, by regal and arbitrary power.

WHILE Pembroke, by renewing and confirming the Great Charter, gave so much satisfaction and security to

CHAP. XII.
1216.

the nation in general, he also applied himself successfully to individuals: He wrote letters, in the king's name, to all the malcontent barons; in which he represented to them, that, whatever jealousy and animosity they might have entertained against the late king, a young prince, the lineal heir of their ancient monarchs, had now succeeded to the throne, without succeeding either to the resentments or principles of his predecessor: That the desperate expedient, which they had employed, of calling in a foreign potentate, had, happily for them, as well as for the nation, failed of entire success; and it was still in their power, by a speedy return to their duty, to restore the independence of the kingdom, and to secure that liberty, for which they so zealously contended: That, as all past offences of the barons were now buried in oblivion, they ought, on their part, to forget their complaints against their late sovereign, who, if he had been anywise blameable in his conduct, had left to his son the salutary warning, to avoid the paths which had led to such fatal extremities: And that having now obtained a charter for their liberties, it was their interest to shew, by their conduct, that this acquisition was not incompatible with their allegiance, and that the rights of king and people, so far from being hostile and opposite, might mutually support and sustain each other[q].

THESE considerations, enforced by the character of honour and constancy, which Pembroke had ever maintained, had a mighty influence on the barons; and most of them began secretly to negotiate with him, and many of them openly returned to their duty. The diffidence which Lewis discovered of their fidelity, forwarded this general propension towards the king; and when the French prince refused the government of the castle of Hertford to Robert Fitz-Walter, who had been so active

[q] Rymer, vol. i, p. 215. Brady's App. N° 143.

against

against the late king, and who claimed that fortress as his property, they plainly saw, that the English were excluded from every trust, and that foreigners had engrossed all the confidence and affection of their new sovereign'. The excommunication too, denounced by the legate, against all the adherents of Lewis, failed not, in the turn which men's dispositions had taken, to produce a mighty effect upon them; and they were easily persuaded to consider a cause as impious, for which they had already entertained an unsurmountable aversion'. Though Lewis made a journey to France, and brought over succours from that kingdom', he found on his return, that his party was still more weakened by the desertion of his English confederates, and that the death of John had, contrary to his expectations, given an incurable wound to his cause. The earls of Salisbury, Arundel, and Warrenne, together with William Mareshal, eldest son of the protector, had embraced Henry's party; and every English nobleman was plainly watching for an opportunity of returning to his allegiance. Pembroke was so much strengthened by these accessions, that he ventured to invest Mount-forel; though upon the approach of the count of Perche with the French army, he desisted from his enterprize, and raised the siege". The count, elated with this success, marched to Lincoln; and being admitted into the town, he began to attack the castle, which he soon reduced to extremity. The protector summoned all his forces from every quarter in order to relieve a place of such importance; and he appeared so much superior to the French, that they shut themselves up within the city, and resolved to act upon the defensive". But the garrison of the castle, having received a strong reinforcement, made a vigorous sally

CHAP.
XII.
1216.

upon the besiegers; while the English army, by concert, assaulted them in the same instant from without, mounted the walls by scalade, and bearing down all resistance, entered the city sword in hand. Lincoln was delivered over to be pillaged; the French army was totally routed; the count of Perche, with only two persons more, was killed, but many of the chief commanders and about 400 knights were made prisoners by the English [x]. So little blood was shed in this important action, which decided the fate of one of the most powerful kingdoms in Europe; and such wretched soldiers were those ancient barons, who yet were unacquainted with every thing but arms!

PRINCE Lewis was informed of this fatal event, while employed in the siege of Dover, which was still valiantly defended against him by Hubert de Burgh. He immediately retreated to London, the centre and life of his party; and he there received intelligence of a new disaster, which put an end to all his hopes. A French fleet, bringing over a strong reinforcement, had appeared on the coast of Kent, where they were attacked by the English under the command of Philip d'Albiney, and were routed with considerable loss. D'Albiney employed a stratagem against them, which is said to have contributed to the victory: 'Having gained the wind of the French, he came down upon them with violence; and throwing in their faces a great quantity of quicklime, which he purposely carried on board, he so blinded them, that they were disabled from defending themselves [y].

AFTER this second misfortune of the French, the English barons hastened every where to make peace with the protector, and, by an early submission, to prevent those attainders, to which they were exposed on account

[x] M. Paris, p. 204, 205. Chron. de Mailr. p. 195.
[y] M. Paris, p. 206. Ann. Waverl. p. 183. W. Heming. p. 563. Trivet, p. 169. M. West. p. 277. Knyghton, p. 2428.

of

of their rebellion. Lewis, whose cause was now totally desperate, began to be anxious for the safety of his person, and was glad, on any honourable conditions, to make his escape from a country, where, he found, every thing was now become hostile to him. He concluded a peace with Pembroke, promised to evacuate the kingdom, and only stipulated, in return, an indemnity to his adherents, and a restitution of their honours and fortunes, together with the free and equal enjoyment of those liberties, which had been granted to the rest of the nation [a]. Thus was happily ended a civil war, which seemed to be founded on the most incurable hatred and jealousy, and had threatened the kingdom with the most fatal consequences.

THE precautions, which the king of France used in the conduct of this whole affair, are remarkable. He pretended, that his son had accepted of the offer from the English barons, without his advice, and contrary to his inclination: The armies sent to England were levied in Lewis's name: When that prince came over to France for aid, his father publicly refused to grant him any assistance, and would not so much as admit him to his presence: Even after Henry's party acquired the ascendant, and Lewis was in danger of falling into the hands of his enemies, it was Blanche of Castile his wife, not the king his father, who raised armies and equipped fleets for his succour [b]. All these artifices were employed, not to satisfy the pope; for he had too much penetration to be so easily imposed on: Nor yet to deceive the people; for they were too gross even for that purpose: They only served for a colouring to Philip's cause; and in public affairs, men are often better pleased, that the truth, though known to every body, should be wrapped up under a decent co-

[a] Rymer, vol. I. p. 221. M. Paris, p. 307. Chron. Dunst. vol. I. p. 83. M. West. p. 278. Knyghton, p. 2429.
[b] M. Paris, p. 256. Chron. Dunst. vol. I. p. 82.

CHAP. XII.

1216.

ver, than if it were exposed in open day-light to the eyes of all the world.

AFTER the expulsion of the French, the prudence and equity of the protector's subsequent conduct contributed to cure entirely those wounds which had been made by intestine discord. He received the rebellious barons into favour; observed strictly the terms of peace which he had granted them; restored them to their possessions; and endeavoured, by an equal behaviour, to bury all past animosities in perpetual oblivion. The clergy alone, who had adhered to Lewis, were sufferers in this revolution. As they had rebelled against their spiritual sovereign, by disregarding the interdict and excommunication, it was not in Pembroke's power to make any stipulations in their favour; and Gualo, the legate, prepared to take vengeance on them for their disobedience [b]. Many of them were deposed; many suspended; some banished; and all who escaped punishment, made atonement for their offence, by paying large sums to the legate, who amassed an immense treasure by this expedient.

Death of the protector.

THE earl of Pembroke did not long survive the pacification, which had been chiefly owing to his wisdom and valour [c]; and he was succeeded in the government by Peter des Roches, bishop of Winchester, and Hubert de Burgh, the justiciary. The councils of the latter were chiefly followed; and had he possessed equal authority in the kingdom with Pembroke, he seemed to be every way worthy of filling the place of that virtuous nobleman. But the licentious and powerful barons, who had once broken the reins of subjection to their prince, and had obtained by violence an enlargement of their liberties and independence, could ill be restrained by laws under a minority; and the people, no less than the king, suffered from their outrages and disorders. They

Some commotions.

[b] Brady's App. N° 144. Chron. Dunst. vol. I. p. 83.   [c] M. Paris, p. 210.

retained

retained by force the royal caftles, which they had feized during the paft convulfions, or which had been committed to their cuftody by the protector[d]: They ufurped the king's demefnes[e]: They oppreffed their vaffals: They infefted their weaker neighbours: They invited all diforderly people to enter in their retinue, and to live upon their lands: And they gave them protection in all their robberies and extortions.

No one was more infamous for thefe violent and illegal practices than the earl of Albemarle; who, though he had early returned to his duty, and had been ferviceable in expelling the French, augmented to the utmoft the general diforder, and committed outrages in all the counties of the North. In order to reduce him to obedience, Hubert feized an opportunity of getting poffeffion of Rockingham caftle, which Albemarle had garrifoned with his licentious retinue: But this nobleman, inftead of fubmitting, entered into a fecret confederacy with Fawkes de Breauté, Peter de Mauleon, and other barons, and both fortified the caftle of Biham for his defence, and made himfelf mafter by furprize of that of Fotheringay. Pandulf, who was reftored to his legatefhip, was active in fuppreffing this rebellion; and, with the concurrence of eleven bifhops, he pronounced the fentence of excommunication againft Albemarle and his adherents[f]: An army was levied: A fcutage of ten fhillings a knight's fee was impofed on all the military tenants: Albemarle's affociates gradually deferted him: And he himfelf was obliged at laft to fue for mercy. He received a pardon, and was reftored to his whole eftate.

This impolitic lenity, too frequent in thofe times, was probably the refult of a fecret combination among the barons, who never could endure to fee the total ruin

CHAP. XII.

1216.

of one of their own order: But it encouraged Fawkes de Breauté, a man whom king John had raised from a low origin, to persevere in the course of violence, to which he had owed his fortune, and to set at naught all law and justice. When thirty-five verdicts were at one time found against him, on account of his violent expulsion of so many freeholders from their possessions; he came to the court of justice with an armed force, seized the judge who had pronounced the verdicts, and imprisoned him in Bedford castle. He then levied open war against the king; but being subdued, and taken prisoner, his life was granted him: but his estate was confiscated, and he was banished the kingdom [1].

1222.

JUSTICE was executed with greater severity against disorders less premeditated, which broke out in London. A frivolous emulation in a match of wrestling, between the Londoners on the one hand, and the inhabitants of Westminster and those of the neighbouring villages on the other, occasioned this commotion. The former rose in a body, and pulled down some houses belonging to the abbot of Westminster: But this riot, which, considering the tumultuous disposition familiar to that capital, would have been little regarded, seemed to become more serious by the symptoms which then appeared, of the former attachment of the citizens to the French interest. The populace, in the tumult, made use of the cry of war commonly employed by the French troops; *Mountjoy, mountjoy, God help us and our Lord Lewis.* The justiciary made enquiry into the disorder; and finding one Constantine Fitz Arnulf to have been the ringleader, an insolent man, who justified his crime in Hubert's presence, he proceeded against him by martial law, and ordered him immediately to be hanged, without trial or

[1] Rymer, vol. i. p. 198. M. Paris, p. 222. 214. Ann. Waverl. p. 189. Chron. Dunst. vol. i. p. 141. 146. M. West. p. 283.

form

form of procefs. He alfo cut off the feet of fome of Con-
ftantine's accomplices [b].

THIS act of power was complained of as an infringement of the Great Charter: Yet the jufticiary, in a parliament fummoned at Oxford (for the great councils about this time began to receive that appellation), made no fcruple to grant in the king's name a renewal and confirmation of that charter. When the affembly made application to the crown for this favour, as a law in thofe times feemed to lofe its validity, if not frequently renewed, William de Briewere, one of the council of regency, was fo bold as to fay openly, that thofe liberties were extorted by force, and ought not to be obferved: But he was reprimanded by the archbifhop of Canterbury, and was not countenanced by the king or his chief minifters [i]. A new confirmation was demanded and granted two years after; and an aid, amounting to a fifteenth of all moveables, was given by the parliament, in return for this indulgence. The king iffued writs anew to the fheriffs, enjoining the obfervance of the charter; but he inferted a remarkable claufe in the writs, that thofe, who payed not the fifteenth, fhould not for the future be entitled to the benefit of thofe liberties [k].

THE low ftate, into which the crown was fallen, made it requifite for a good minifter to be attentive to the prefervation of the royal prerogatives, as well as to the fecurity of public liberty. Hubert applied to the pope, who had always great authority in the kingdom, and was now confidered as its fuperior lord; and defired him to iffue a bull, declaring the king to be of full age, and entitled to exercife in perfon all the acts of royalty [l]. In confequence of this declaration, the jufticiary refigned into Henry's hands the two important fortreffes of the

[b] M. Paris, p. 217, 218, 259. Ann. Waverl. p. 287. Chron. Dunft. vol. I. p. 119. [i] M. Weft. p. 282. [k] Clauf. 9 H. 3. m. 9. and m. 6. d. [l] M. Paris, p. 220.

Tower

CHAP. XII.
1222.

Tower and Dover castle, which had been entrusted to his custody; and he required the other barons to imitate his example. They refused compliance: The earls of Chester and Albemarle, John Constable of Chester, John de Lacy, Brian de l'Isle, and William de Cantel, with some others, even formed a conspiracy to surprize London, and met in arms at Waltham with that intention: But finding the king prepared for defence, they desisted from their enterprize. When summoned to court, in order to answer for their conduct, they scrupled not to appear, and to confess the design: But they told the king, that they had no bad intentions against his person, but only against Hubert de Burgh, whom they were determined to remove from his office[m]. They appeared too formidable to be chastised; and they were so little discouraged by the failure of their first enterprize, that they again met in arms at Leicester, in order to seize the king, who then resided at Northampton: But Henry, informed of their purpose, took care to be so well armed and attended, that the barons found it dangerous to make the attempt; and they sat down and kept Christmas in his neighbourhood[n]. The archbishop and the prelates, finding every thing tend towards a civil war, interposed with their authority, and threatened the barons with the sentence of excommunication, if they persisted in detaining the king's castles. This menace at last prevailed: Most of the fortresses were surrendered; though the barons complained, that Hubert's castles were soon after restored to him, while the king still kept theirs in his own custody. There are said to have been 1115 castles at that time in England[o].

It must be acknowledged, that the influence of the prelates and the clergy was often of great service to the

[m] Chron. Dunst. vol. i. p. 137.   [n] M. Paris, p. 221. Chron. Dunst. vol. i. p. 138.   [o] Coke's Comment. on Magna Charta, chap. 17.

public.

public. Though the religion of that age can merit no
better name than that of superstition, it served to unite
together a body of men who had great sway over the
people, and who kept the community from falling to
pieces, by the factions and independent power of the
nobles. And what was of great importance, it threw
a mighty authority into the hands of men, who by their
profession were averse to arms and violence ; who tempered by their mediation the general disposition towards
military enterprizes ; and who still maintained, even
amidst the shock of arms, those secret links, without
which it is impossible for human society to subsist.

NOTWITHSTANDING these intestine commotions in
England, and the precarious authority of the crown,
Henry was obliged to carry on war in France ; and he
employed to that purpose the fifteenth which had been
granted him by parliament. Lewis VIII. who had succeeded to his father Philip, instead of complying with
Henry's claim, who demanded the restitution of Normandy and the other provinces wrested from England,
made an irruption into Poictou, took Rochelle [P], after a
long siege, and seemed determined to expel the English
from the few provinces which still remained to them.
Henry sent over his uncle, the earl of Salisbury ; together with his brother prince Richard, to whom he had
granted the earldom of Cornwal, which had escheated
to the crown. Salisbury stopped the progress of Lewis's
arms, and retained the Poictevin and Gascon vassals in
their allegiance : But no military action of any moment
was performed on either side. The earl of Cornwal,
after two years' stay in Guienne, returned to England.

THIS prince was no wise turbulent or factious in his
disposition : His ruling passion was to amass money, in

[P] Rymer, vol. I. p. 269. Trivet, p. 179.

which

CHAP. XII.

1237.

which he succeeded so well as to become the richest subject in Christendom: Yet his attention to gain threw him sometimes into acts of violence, and gave disturbance to the government. There was a manor, which had formerly belonged to the earldom of Cornwal, but had been granted to Waleran de Ties, before Richard had been invested with that dignity, and while the earldom remained in the crown. Richard claimed this manor, and expelled the proprietor by force: Waleran complained: The king ordered his brother to do justice to the man, and restore him to his rights: The earl said that he would not submit to these orders, till the cause should be decided against him by the judgment of his peers: Henry replied, that it was first necessary to re-instate Waleran in possession, before the cause could be tried; and he re-iterated his orders to the earl [q]. We may judge of the state of the government, when this affair had nearly produced a civil war. The earl of Cornwal, finding Henry peremptory in his commands, associated himself with the young earl of Pembroke, who had married his sister, and who was displeased on account of the king's requiring him to deliver up some royal castles which were in his custody. These two malcontents took into the confederacy the earls of Chester, Warenne, Glocester, Hereford, Warwic, and Ferrers, who were all disgusted on a like account [r]. They assembled an army, which the king had not the power or courage to resist; and he was obliged to give his brother satisfaction, by grants of much greater importance than the manor, which had been the first ground of the quarrel [s].

THE character of the king, as he grew to man's estate, became every day better known; and he was found in every respect unqualified for maintaining a proper sway among those turbulent barons, whom the

[q] M. Paris, p. 233. [r] Ibid. [s] Ibid.

feudal

feudal conftitution fubjected to his authority. Gentle, humane, and merciful even to a fault, he feems to have been fteady in no other circumftance of his character; but to have received every impreffion from thofe who furrounded him, and whom he loved, for the time, with the moft imprudent and moft unreferved affection. Without activity or vigour, he was unfit to conduct war; without policy or art, he was ill-fitted to maintain peace: His refentments, though hafty and violent, were not dreaded, while he was found to drop them with fuch facility; his friendfhips were little valued, becaufe they were neither derived from choice, nor maintained with conftancy. A proper pageant of ftate in a regular monarchy, where his minifters could have conducted all affairs in his name and by his authority; but too feeble in thofe diforderly times to fway a fceptre, whofe weight depended entirely on the firmnefs and dexterity of the hand which held it.

CHAP. XII.

1217.

THE ableft and moft virtuous minifter that Henry ever poffeffed, was Hubert de Burgh [1]; a man who had been fteady to the crown in the moft difficult and dangerous times, and who yet fhewed no difpofition, in the height of his power, to enflave or opprefs the people. The only exceptionable part of his conduct is that which is mentioned by Matthew Paris [2]; if the fact be really true, and proceeded from Hubert's advice, namely, the recalling publicly and the annulling of the charter of forefts, a conceffion fo reafonable in itfelf, and fo paffionately claimed both by the nobility and people: But it muft be confeffed that this meafure is fo unlikely, both from the circumftances of the times and character of the minifter, that there is reafon to doubt of its reality, efpecially as it is mentioned by no other hiftorian. Hu-

Hubert de Burgh difplaced.

[1] Ypod Neuftriæ, p. 464. [2] P. 132. M. Weft. p. 218. afcribes this counfel to Peter bifhop of Winchefter.

bert,

CHAP.
XII.
1227.

'1231.

Bishop of
Winchester
minister.

bert, while he enjoyed his authority, had an entire ascendant over Henry, and was loaded with honours and favours beyond any other subject. Besides acquiring the property of many castles and manors, he married the eldest sister of the king of Scots, was created earl of Kent, and by an unusual concession, was made chief justiciary of England for life: Yet Henry, in a sudden caprice, threw off this faithful minister, and exposed him to the violent persecutions of his enemies. Among other frivolous crimes objected to him, he was accused of gaining the king's affections by enchantment, and of purloining from the royal treasury a gem, which had the virtue to render the wearer invulnerable, and of sending this valuable curiosity to the prince of Wales *. The nobility, who hated Hubert on account of his zeal in resuming the rights and possessions of the crown, no sooner saw the opportunity favourable, than they inflamed the king's animosity against him, and pushed him to seek the total ruin of his minister. Hubert took sanctuary in a church: The king ordered him to be dragged from thence: He recalled those orders: He afterwards renewed them: He was obliged by the clergy to restore him to the sanctuary: He constrained him soon after to surrender himself prisoner, and he confined him in the castle of the Devises. Hubert made his escape, was expelled the kingdom, was again received into favour, recovered a great share of the king's confidence, but never showed any inclination to reinstate himself in power and authority ª.

THE man, who succeeded him in the government of the king and kingdom, was Peter, bishop of Winchester, a Poictevin by birth, who had been raised by the late king, and who was no less distinguished by his arbitrary

* M. Paris, p. 259. ª Ibid. p. 259, 260, 261. 266. Chron. T. Wykes, p. 40, 41. Chron. Dunst. vol. i. p. 220, 221. M. West. p. 291. 301.

principles

principles and violent conduct, than by his courage and abilities. This prelate had been left by king John justiciary and regent of the kingdom during an expedition which that prince made into France; and his illegal administration was one chief cause of that great combination among the barons, which finally extorted from the crown the charter of liberties, and laid the foundations of the English constitution. Henry, though incapable, from his character, of pursuing the same violent maxims which had governed his father, had imbibed the same arbitrary principles; and in prosecution of Peter's advice, he invited over a great number of Poictevins and other foreigners, who, he believed, could more safely be trusted than the English, and who seemed useful to counterbalance the great and independent power of the nobility [y]. Every office and command was bestowed on these strangers; they exhausted the revenues of the crown, already too much impoverished [z]; they invaded the rights of the people; and their insolence, still more provoking than their power, drew on them the hatred and envy of all orders of men in the kingdom [a].

THE barons formed a combination against this odious ministry, and withdrew from parliament; on pretence of the danger to which they were exposed from the machinations of the Poictevins. When again summoned to attend, they gave for answer, that the king should dismiss his foreigners, otherwise they would drive both him and them out of the kingdom, and put the crown on another head, more worthy to wear it [b]: Such was the style they used to their sovereign! They at last came to parliament, but so well attended, that they seemed in a condition to prescribe laws to the king and ministry. Peter des Roches, however, had in the interval found means of

[y] M. Paris, p. 263.
[z] M. Paris, p. 252.
[a] Chron. Dunst. vol. I. p. 151.
[b] Ibid. p. 265.

CHAP. XII.
1233.

sowing diffention among them, and of bringing over to his party the earl of Cornwal, as well as the earls of Lincoln and Chester. The confederates were difconcerted in their measures: Richard, earl Marischal, who had succeeded to that dignity on the death of his brother, William, was chafed into Wales; he thence withdrew into Ireland; where he was treacherously murdered by the contrivance of the bishop of Winchester[c]. The estates of the more obnoxious barons were confiscated, without legal sentence or trial by their peers[d]; and were bestowed with a profuse liberality on the Poictevins. Peter even carried his infolence so far as to declare publickly, that the barons of England must not pretend to put themselves on the same foot with those of France, or assume the same liberties and privileges: The monarch in the former country had a more absolute power than in the latter. It had been more justifiable for him to have said, that men, so unwilling to submit to the authority of laws, could with the worse grace claim any shelter or protection from them.

WHEN the king at any time was checked in his illegal practices, and when the authority of the Great Charter was objected to him, he was wont to reply; "Why should I observe this charter, which is neglected by all my grandees, both prelates and nobility?" It was very reasonably said to him: "You ought, sir, to set them the example[e]."

So violent a ministry, as that of the bishop of Winchester, could not be of long duration; but its fall proceeded at last from the influence of the church, not from the efforts of the nobles. Edmond, the primate, came to court, attended by many of the other prelates, and represented to the king the pernicious measures embraced by Peter des Roches, the discontents of his people,

[c] Chron. Dunst. vol. I. p. 219. [d] M. Paris, p. 265. [e] Ibid. p. 609.

the ruin of his affairs; and, after requiring the dismission of the minister and his associates, threatened him with excommunication, in case of his refusal. Henry, who knew that an excommunication, so agreeable to the sense of the people, could not fail of producing the most dangerous effects, was obliged to submit: Foreigners were banished: The natives were restored to their place in council [f]: The primate, who was a man of prudence, and who took care to execute the laws, and observe the charter of liberties, bore the chief sway in the government.

But the English in vain flattered themselves that they should be long free from the dominion of foreigners. The king, having married Eleanor, daughter of the count of Provence [g], was surrounded by a great number of strangers from that country, whom he caressed with the fondest affection, and enriched by an imprudent generosity [h]. The bishop of Valence, a prelate of the house of Savoy, and maternal uncle to the queen, was his chief minister, and employed every art to amass wealth for himself and his relations. Peter of Savoy, a brother of the same family, was invested in the honour of Richmond, and received the rich wardship of earl Warrenne: Boniface of Savoy was promoted to the see of Canterbury: Many young ladies were invited over from Provence, and married to the chief noblemen in England, who were the king's wards [i]: And as the source of Henry's bounty began to fail, his Savoyard ministry applied to Rome, and obtained a bull, permitting him to resume all past grants; absolving him from the oath which he had taken to maintain them; even enjoining him to make such a resumption, and representing those

[f] M. Paris, p. 271, 272. [g] Rymer, vol. I. p. 448. [h] M. Paris, p. 286. [h] M. Paris, p. 236. 301. 303. 316. 341. M. West. p. 302. 304. [i] M. Paris, p. 424. M. West. p. 338.

164   HISTORY OF ENGLAND.

CHAP.
XII.

1236.

grants as invalid, on account of the prejudice which ensued from them to the Roman pontiff, in whom the superiority of the kingdom was vested [h]. The opposition, made to the intended refumption, prevented it from taking place; but the nation faw the indignities to which the king was willing to fubmit, in order to gratify the avidity of his foreign favourites. About the fame time, he publifhed in England the fentence of excommunication, pronounced againft the emperor Frederic, his brother-in-law [i]; and faid in excufe, that, being the pope's vaffal, he was obliged by his allegiance to obey all the commands of his holinefs. In this weak reign, when any neighbouring potentate infulted the king's dominions, inftead of taking revenge for the injury, he complained to the pope as his fuperior lord, and begged him to give protection to his vaffal [m].

Grievances.

1247.

THE refentment of the Englifh barons rofe high, at the preference given to foreigners; but no remonftrance or complaint could ever prevail on the king to abandon them, or even to moderate his attachment towards them. After the Provençals and Savoyards might have been fuppofed pretty well fatiated with the dignities and riches which they had acquired, a new fet of hungry foreigners were invited over, and fhared among them thofe favours, which the king ought in policy to have conferred on the Englifh nobility, by whom his government could have been fupported and defended. His mother, Ifabella, who had been unjuftly taken by the late king from the count de la Marche, to whom fhe was betrothed, was no fooner miftrefs of herfelf by the death of her hufband, than fhe married that nobleman [n]; and fhe had born him four fons; Guy, William, Geoffrey, and Aymer, whom fhe fent over to England, in order to pay a vifit to their

[h] M. Paris, p. 295. 301. Dunft. vol. i. p. 150. [l] Rymer, vol. i. p. 383. [m] Chron.
[n] Trivet, p. 176.

brother.

brother. The good-natured and affectionate difpofition of Henry was moved at the fight of fuch near relations; and he confidered neither his own circumftances, nor the inclinations of his people, in the honours and riches which he conferred upon them [*]. Complaints rofe as high againft the credit of the Gafcon, as ever they had done againft that of the Poictevin and of the Savoyard favourites; and to a nation prejudiced againft them, all their meafures appeared exceptionable and criminal. Violations of the Great Charter were frequently mentioned; and it is indeed more than probable, that foreigners, ignorant of the laws, and relying on the boundlefs affections of a weak prince, would, in an age when a regular adminiftration was not any where known, pay more attention to their prefent intereft than to the liberties of the people. It is reported, that the Poictevins and other ftrangers, when the laws were at any time appealed to, in oppofition to their oppreffions, fcrupled not to reply, *What did the Englifh laws fignify to them? They minded them not.* And as words are often more offenfive than actions, this open contempt of the Englifh tended much to aggravate the general difcontent, and made every act of violence, committed by the foreigners, appear not only an injury, but an affront to them [*].

I reckon not among the violations of the Great Charter fome arbitrary exertions of prerogative to which Henry's neceffities pufhed him, and which, without producing any difcontent, were uniformly continued by all his fucceffors, till the laft century. As the parliament often refufed him fupplies, and that in a manner fomewhat rude and indecent [*], he obliged his opulent fubjects, particularly the citizens of London, to grant him loans of money; and it is natural to imagine, that the fame

[*] M. Paris, p. 491. M. Weft. p. 338. Knyghton, p. 2436.
[*] M. Paris, p. 566. 666. Ann. Waverl. p. 214. Chron. Dunft. vol. I. p. 331.   [*] M. Paris, p. 301.

CHAP. XII.
1247.

want of œconomy, which reduced him to the neceſſity of borrowing, would prevent him from being very punctual in the repayment [r]. He demanded benevolences, or pretended voluntary contributions, from his nobility and prelates [s]. He was the firſt king of England ſince the conqueſt, that could fairly be ſaid to lie under the reſtraint of law; and he was alſo the firſt that practiſed the diſpenſing power, and employed the clauſe of *non obſtante* in his grants and patents. When objections were made to this novelty, he replied, that the pope exerciſed that authority; and why might not he imitate the example? But the abuſe which the pope made of his diſpenſing power, in violating the canons of general councils, in invading the privileges and cuſtoms of all particular churches, and in uſurping on the rights of patrons, was more likely to excite the jealouſy of the people, than to reconcile them to a ſimilar practice in their civil government. Roger de Thurkeſby, one of the king's Juſtices, was ſo diſpleaſed with the precedent, that he exclaimed, *Alas! what times are we fallen into? Behold, the civil court is corrupted in imitation of the eccleſiaſtical, and the river is poiſoned from that fountain.*

THE king's partiality and profuſe bounty to his foreign relations, and to their friends and favourites, would have appeared more tolerable to the Engliſh, had any thing been done mean-while for the honour of the nation, or had Henry's enterprizes in foreign countries been attended with any ſucceſs or glory to himſelf or to the public: At leaſt, ſuch military talents in the king would have ſerved to keep his barons in awe, and have given weight and authority to his government. But though he declared war againſt Lewis IX. in 1242, and made an expedition into Guienne, upon the invitation of his father-in-law, the count de la Marche, who promiſed to join

[r] M. Paris, p. 496. [s] M. Paris, p. 907.

him

HENRY III.

him with all his forces; he was unsuccessful in his attempts against that great monarch, was worsted at Taillebourg, was deserted by his allies, lost what remained to him of Poictou, and was obliged to return, with loss of honour, into England[t]. The Gascon nobility were attached to the English government; because the distance of their sovereign allowed them to remain in a state of almost total independence: And they claimed, some time after, Henry's protection against an invasion which the king of Castile made upon that territory. Henry returned into Guienne, and was more successful in this expedition; but he thereby involved himself and his nobility in an enormous debt, which both encreased their discontents, and exposed him to greater danger from their enterprizes[u].

WANT of œconomy, and an ill-judged liberality, were Henry's great defects; and his debts, even before this expedition, had become so troublesome, that he sold all his plate and jewels, in order to discharge them. When this expedient was first proposed to him, he asked, where he should find purchasers? It was replied, the citizens of London. *On my word*, said he, *if the treasury of Augustus were brought to sale, the citizens are able to be the purchasers: These clowns, who assume to themselves the name of barons, abound in every thing, while we are reduced to necessities*[w]. And he was thenceforth observed to be more forward and greedy in his exactions upon the citizens[x].

BUT the grievances, which the English during this reign had reason to complain of in the civil government, seem to have been still less burthensome than those which they suffered from the usurpations and exactions of the court of Rome. On the death of Langton in 1228, the monks of Christ-church elected Walter de Hemesham,

CHAP.
XII.

1247.

1253.

Ecclesiastical grievances.

[t] M. Paris, p. 393. 394. 398. 399. 405. W. Heming. p. 574. Chron. Dunst. vol. I. p. 153. [u] M. Paris, p. 614. [w] M. Paris, p. 501. [x] M. Paris, p. 501. 507. 518 578. 606. 625. 648.

M 4   one

CHAP. XII.

1231.

one of their own body, for his succeffor: But as Henry refufed to confirm the election, the pope, at his defire, annulled it [f]; and immediately appointed Richard, chancellor of Lincoln, for archbifhop, without waiting for a new election. On the death of Richard in 1231, the monks elected Ralph de Neville bifhop of Chichefter; and though Henry was much pleafed with the election, the pope, who thought that prelate too much attached to the crown, affumed the power of annulling his election [g]. He rejected two clergymen more, whom the monks had fucceffively chofen; and he at laft told them, that, if they would elect Edmond, treafurer of the church of Salifbury, he would confirm their choice; and his nomination was complied with. The pope had the prudence to appoint both times very worthy primates; but men could not forbear obferving his intention of thus drawing gradually to himfelf the right of beftowing that important dignity.

THE avarice, however, more than the ambition of the fee of Rome, feems to have been in this age the ground of general complaint. The papal minifters, finding a vaft ftock of power amaffed by their predeceffors, were defirous of turning it to immediate profit, which they enjoyed at home, rather than of enlarging their authority in diftant countries, where they never intended to refide. Every thing was become venal in the Romifh tribunals; fimony was openly practifed; no favours, and even no juftice could be obtained without a bribe; the higheft bidder was fure to have the preference, without regard either to the merits of the perfon or of the caufe; and befides the ufual perverfions of right in the decifion of controverfies, the pope openly affumed an abfolute and uncontroled authority of fetting afide, by the plenitude of his apoftolic power, all particular rules, and all privileges of patrons, churches, and convents,

[f] M. Paris, p. 244. [g] Ibid. p. 254.

On

On pretence of remedying these abuses, pope Honorius, in 1216, complaining of the poverty of his see as the source of all grievances, demanded from every cathedral two of the best prebends, and from every convent two monks portions, to be set apart as a perpetual and settled revenue of the papal crown: But all men being sensible that the revenue would continue for ever, the abuses immediately return, his demand was unanimously rejected. About three years after, the pope demanded and obtained the tenth of all ecclesiastical revenues, which he levied in a very oppressive manner; requiring payment before the clergy had drawn their rents or tythes, and sending about usurers, who advanced them the money at exorbitant interest. In the year 1240, Otho, the legate, having in vain attempted the clergy in a body, obtained separately, by intrigues and menaces, large sums from the prelates and convents, and on his departure is said to have carried more money out of the kingdom than he left in it. This experiment was renewed four years after with success by Martin the nuncio, who brought from Rome powers of suspending and excommunicating all clergymen that refused to comply with his demands. The king, who relied on the pope for the support of his tottering authority, never failed to countenance those exactions.

MEANWHILE, all the chief benefices of the kingdom were conferred on Italians; great numbers of that nation were sent over at one time to be provided for; non-residence and pluralities were carried to an enormous height; Mansel, the king's chaplain, is computed to have held at once seven hundred ecclesiastical livings; and the abuses became so evident as to be palpable to the blindness of superstition itself. The people, entering into associations, rose against the Italian clergy; pillaged their barns; wasted their lands; insulted the persons of such of them as they found in the kingdom [a]; and when the jus-

CHAP.
XII.

1231.

[a] Rymer, vol. I. p. 323. M. Paris, p. 253. 257.

tices

tices made enquiry into the authors of this disorder, the guilt was found to involve so many, and those of such high rank, that it passed unpunished. At last, when Innocent IV. in 1245, called a general council at Lyons, in order to excommunicate the emperor Frederic, the king and nobility sent over agents to complain before the council of the rapacity of the Romish church. They represented, among many other grievances, that the benefices of the Italian clergy in England had been estimated, and were found to amount to 60,000 marks [b] a year, a sum which exceeded the annual revenue of the crown itself [c]. They obtained only an evasive answer from the pope; but as mention had been made before the council, of the feudal subjection of England to the see of Rome, the English agents, at whose head was Roger Bigod earl of Norfolk, exclaimed against the pretension, and insisted, that king John had no right, without the consent of his barons, to subject the kingdom to so ignominious a servitude [d]. The popes indeed, afraid of carrying matters too far against England, seem thenceforth to have little insisted on that pretension.

This check, received at the council of Lyons, was not able to stop the court of Rome in its rapacity: Innocent exacted the revenues of all vacant benefices, the twentieth of all ecclesiastical revenues without exception; the third of such as exceeded a hundred marks a year, and the half of such as were possessed by non-residents [e]. He claimed the goods of all intestate clergymen [f]; he pretended a title to inherit all money gotten by usury; he le-

[b] Innocent's bull in Rymer, vol. I. p. 471, says only 50,000 marks a year.
[c] M. Paris, p. 451. The customs were part of Henry's revenue, and amounted to 6000 pounds a year: They were at first small sums paid by the merchants for the use of the king's warehouses, measures, weights, &c. See Gilbert's history of the Exch. p. 214.
[d] M. Paris, p. 460. [e] M. Paris, p. 480. Ann. Burt. p. 305.
373. [f] M. Paris, p. 474.

vied

vied benevolences upon the people; and when the king, contrary to his usual practice, prohibited these exactions, he threatened to pronounce against him the same censures, which he had emitted against the emperor Frederic [r].

But the most oppressive expedient employed by the pope, was the embarking of Henry in a project for the conquest of Naples, or Sicily on this side the Fare, as it was called; an enterprize, which threw much dishonour on the king, and involved him, during some years, in great trouble and expence. The Romish church, taking advantage of favourable incidents, had reduced the kingdom of Sicily to the same state of feudal vassalage which she pretended to extend over England, and which, by reason of the distance, as well as high spirit of this latter kingdom, she was not able to maintain. After the death of the emperor, Frederic II., the succession of Sicily devolved to Conradine, grandson of that monarch; and Mainfroy, his natural son, under pretence of governing the kingdom during the minority of the prince, had formed a scheme of establishing his own authority. Pope Innocent, who had carried on violent war against the emperor, Frederic, and had endeavoured to dispossess him of his Italian dominions, still continued hostilities against his grandson; but being disappointed in all his schemes by the activity and artifices of Mainfroy, he found, that his own force alone was not sufficient to bring to a happy issue so great an enterprize. He pretended to dispose of the Sicilian crown, both as superior lord of that particular kingdom, and as vicar of Christ, to whom all kingdoms of the earth were subjected; and he made a tender of it to Richard earl of Cornwal, whose immense riches, he flattered himself, would be able to support the military operations

[r] M. Paris, p. 476.

CHAP. XII.

1255.

against Mainfroy. As Richard had the prudence to refuse the present [b], he applied to the king, whose levity and thoughtless disposition gave Innocent more hopes of success; and he offered him the crown of Sicily for his second son, Edmond [i]. Henry, allured by so magnificent a present, without reflecting on the consequences, without consulting either with his brother or the parliament, accepted of the insidious proposal; and gave the pope unlimited credit to expend whatever sums he thought necessary for completing the conquest of Sicily. Innocent who was engaged by his own interests to wage war with Mainfroy, was glad to carry on his enterprizes at the expence of his ally: Alexander IV. who succeeded him in the papal throne, continued the same policy: And Henry was surprized to find himself on a sudden involved in an immense debt, which he had never been consulted in contracting. The sum already amounted to 135,541 marks beside interest [k]; and he had the prospect, if he answered this demand, of being soon loaded with more exorbitant expences; if he refused it, of both incurring the pope's displeasure, and losing the crown of Sicily, which he hoped soon to have the glory of fixing on the head of his son.

He applied to the parliament for supply; and that he might be sure not to meet with opposition, he sent no writs to the more refractory barons: But even those who were summoned, sensible of the ridiculous cheat imposed by the pope, determined not to lavish their money on such chimerical projects; and making a pretext of the absence of their brethren, they refused to take the king's demands into consideration [l]. In this extremity the clergy were his only resource; and as both their temporal and spiri-

[b] M. Paris, p. 650. p. 599. 613. p. 317.
[i] Rymer, vol. I. p. 502. 512. 530. M. Paris, p. 599. 613.
[k] Rymer, vol. I. p. 587. Chron. Dunst. vol. I.
[l] M. Paris, p. 624.

tual sovereign concurred in loading them, they were ill able to defend themselves against this united authority.

THE pope published a crusade for the conquest of Sicily; and required every one, who had taken the cross against the infidels, or had vowed to advance money for that service, to support the war against Mainfroy, a more terrible enemy, as he pretended, to the Christian faith than any Saracen [a]. He levied a tenth on all ecclesiastical benefices in England for three years; and gave orders to excommunicate all bishops who made not punctual payment. He granted to the king the goods of intestate clergymen; the revenues of vacant benefices; the revenues of all non-residents [b]. But these taxations, being levied by some rule, were deemed less grievous than another imposition, which arose from the suggestion of the bishop of Hereford, and which might have opened the door to endless and intolerable abuses.

THIS prelate, who resided at the court of Rome by a deputation from the English church, drew bills of different values, but amounting on the whole to 150,540 marks, on all the bishops and abbots of the kingdom; and granted these bills to Italian merchants, who, it was pretended, had advanced money for the service of the war against Mainfroy [c]. As there was no likelihood of the English prelates submitting, without compulsion, to such an extraordinary demand, Rustand, the legate, was charged with the commission of employing authority to that purpose; and he summoned an assembly of the bishops and abbots, whom he acquainted with the pleasure of the pope and of the king. Great were the surprize and indignation of the assembly: The bishop of Worcester exclaimed, that he would lose his life rather

[a] Rymer, vol. 1. p. 547, 548, &c. [b] Rymer, vol. 1. p. 597, 598.
[c] M. Paris, p. 612. 616. Chron. T. Wykes, p. 54.

than

than comply: The bishop of London said, that the pope and king were more powerful than he; but if his mitre were taken off his head, he would clap on a helmet in its place. The legate was no less violent on the other hand; and he told the assembly, in plain terms, that all ecclesiastical benefices were the property of the pope, and he might dispose of them, either in whole or in part, as he saw proper. In the end, the bishops and abbots, being threatened with excommunication, which made all their revenues fall into the king's hands, were obliged to submit to the exaction: And the only mitigation which the legate allowed them, was, that the tenths, already granted, should be accepted as a partial payment of the bills. But the money was still insufficient for the pope's purpose: The conquest of Sicily was as remote as ever: The demands which came from Rome were endless: Pope Alexander became so urgent a creditor, that he sent over a legate to England; threatening the kingdom with an interdict, and the king with excommunication, if the arrears, which he pretended to be due to him, were not instantly remitted: And at last, Henry, sensible of the cheat, began to think of breaking off the agreement, and of resigning into the pope's hands that crown, which it was not intended by Alexander that he or his family should never enjoy.

Earl of Cornwal elected king of the Romans.

THE earl of Cornwal had now reason to value himself on his foresight, in refusing the fraudulent bargain with Rome, and in preferring the solid honours of an opulent and powerful prince of the blood of England, to the empty and precarious glory of a foreign dignity. But he had not always firmness sufficient to adhere to this resolution: His vanity and ambition prevailed at last over his prudence and his avarice; and he was engaged in an enterprize

enterprize no less extensive and vexatious than that of his brother, and not attended with much greater probability of success. The immense opulence of Richard having made the German princes cast their eye on him as a candidate for the empire; he was tempted to expend vast sums of money on his election, and he succeeded so far as to be chosen king of the Romans, which seemed to render his succession infallible to the imperial throne. He went over to Germany, and carried out of the kingdom not less a sum than seven hundred thousand marks, if we may credit the account given by some ancient authors[a], which is probably much exaggerated[1]. His money, while it lasted, procured him friends and partizans: But it was soon drained from him by the avidity of the German princes; and having no personal or family connexions in that country, and no solid foundation of power, he found at last, that he had lavished away the frugality of a whole life, in order to procure a spendid title; and that his absence from England, joined to the weakness of his brother's government, gave reins to the factious and turbulent dispositions of the English barons, and involved his own country and family in great calamities.

THE successful revolt of the nobility from king John, and their imposing on him and his successors limitations of their royal power, had made them feel their own weight

[a] M. Paris, p. 638. The same author, a few pages before, makes Richard's transfers amount to little more than half the sum, p. 634. The king's dissipations and expences, throughout his whole reign, according to the same author, had amounted only to about 940,000 marks, p. 638.

[1] The sums mentioned by ancient authors, who were almost all monks, are often improbable, and never consistent. But we know, from an infallible authority, the public remonstrance to the council of Lyons, that the king's revenues were below 60,000 marks a year. His brother therefore could never have been master of 700,000 marks; especially as he did not sell his estates in England, as we learn from the same author: And we hear afterwards of his ordering all his woods to be cut, in order to satisfy the rapacity of the German princes: His son succeeded to the earldom of Cornwal and his other revenues.

CHAP. XII.

1244.

and importance, had set a dangerous precedent of resistance, and being followed by a long minority, had impoverished, as well as weakened that crown, which they were at last induced, from the fear of worse consequences, to replace on the head of young Henry. In the king's situation, either great abilities and vigour were requisite to overawe the barons, or great caution and reserve to give them no pretence for complaints; and it must be confessed, that this prince was possessed of neither of these talents. He had not prudence to chuse right measures; he wanted even that constancy which sometimes gives weight to wrong ones; he was entirely devoted to his favourites, who were always foreigners; he lavished on them without discretion his diminished revenue; and finding that his barons indulged their disposition towards tyranny, and observed not to their own vassals the same rules which they had imposed on the crown, he was apt, in his administration, to neglect all the salutary articles of the Great Charter: which he remarked to be so little regarded by his nobility. This conduct had extremely lessened his authority in the kingdom; had multiplied complaints against him; and had frequently exposed him to affronts, and even to dangerous attempts upon his prerogative. In the year 1244, when he desired a supply from parliament, the barons, complaining of the frequent breaches of the Great Charter, and of the many fruitless applications which they had formerly made for the redress of this and other grievances, demanded in return, that he should give them the nomination of the great justiciary and of the chancellor, to whose hands chiefly the administration of justice was committed: And, if we may credit the historian[*], they had formed the plan of other limitations, as well as of associations to maintain them, which would have reduced the king to be an absolute

[*] M. Paris, p. 431.

cypher,

cypher, and have held the crown in perpetual pupillage and dependance. The king, to satisfy them, would agree to nothing but a renewal of the charter, and a general permission to excommunicate all the violators of it: And he received no supply, except a scutage of twenty shillings on each knight's fee for the marriage of his eldest daughter to the king of Scotland; a burthen which was expresly annexed to their feudal tenures.

CHAP. XII.

1255.

FOUR years after, in a full parliament, when Henry demanded a new supply, he was openly reproached with a breach of his word, and the frequent violations of the charter. He was asked, whether he did not blush to desire any aid from his people, whom he professedly hated and despised, to whom on all occasions he preferred aliens and foreigners, and who groaned under the oppressions, which he either permitted or exercised over them. He was told that, besides disparaging his nobility by forcing them to contract unequal and mean marriages with strangers, no rank of men was so low as to escape vexations from him or his ministers; that even the victuals consumed in his houshold, the clothes which himself and his servants wore, still more the wine which they used, were all taken by violence from the lawful owners, and no compensation was ever made them for the injury; that foreign merchants, to the great prejudice and infamy of the kingdom, shunned the English harbours, as if they were possessed by pirates, and the commerce with all nations was thus cut off by these acts of violence; that loss was added to loss, and injury to injury, while the merchants, who had been despoiled of their goods, were also obliged to carry them at their own charge to whatever place the king was pleased to appoint them; that even the poor fishermen on the coast could not escape his oppressions and those of his courtiers; and finding that they had not full liberty to dispose of their commodities in the English market, were frequently constrained to carry them to foreign ports, and to hazard all the perils of the ocean, rather than those which awaited them from his oppressive emissaries; and that his very religion was a ground of complaint to his subjects, while they observed, that the waxen tapers and splendid silks, employed in so many useless processions, were the spoils which he had forcibly ravished from the true owners [w]. Throughout this remonstrance, in which the complaints, derived from an abuse of the ancient right of purveyance, may be supposed to be somewhat exaggerated, there appears a strange mixture of regal tyranny in the practices which gave rise to it, and of aristocratical liberty, or rather licentiousness, in the expressions employed by the parliament. But a mixture of this kind is observable in all the ancient feudal governments; and both of them proved equally hurtful to the people.

As the king, in answer to their remonstrance, gave the parliament only good words and fair promises, attended with the most humble submissions, which they had often found deceitful, he obtained at that time no supply; and therefore, in the year 1253, when he found himself again under the necessity of applying to parliament, he had provided a new pretence, which he deemed infallible, and taking the vow of a Crusade, he demanded their assistance in that pious enterprize [x]. The parliament, however, for some time hesitated to comply; and the ecclesiastical order sent a deputation, consisting of four prelates, the primate, and the bishops of Winchester, Salisbury, and Carlisle, in order to remonstrate with him on his frequent violations of their privileges, the oppressions with which he had loaded them and all his subjects [y], and the uncanonical

[w] M. Paris, p. 498. See farther, p. 578. M. West. p. 348.
[x] M. Paris, p. 518. 558. 568. Chron. Dunst. vol. I. p. 293.
[y] M. Paris, p. 568.

nonical and forced elections which were made to vacant dignities. "It is true," replied the king, "I have been somewhat faulty in this particular: I obtruded you, my lord of Canterbury, upon your fee: I was obliged to employ both entreaties and menaces, my lord of Winchester, to have you elected: My proceedings, I confess, were very irregular, my lords of Salisbury and Carlisle, when I raised you from the lowest stations to your present dignities: I am determined henceforth to correct these abuses; and it will also become you, in order to make a thorough reformation, to resign your present benefices; and try to enter again in a more regular and canonical manner *." The bishops, surprized at these unexpected sarcasms, replied, that the question was not at present how to correct past errors, but to avoid them for the future. The king promised redress both of ecclesiastical and civil grievances; and the parliament in return agreed to grant him a supply, a tenth of the ecclesiastical benefices, and a scutage of three marks on each knight's fee: But as they had experienced his frequent breach of promise, they required, that he should ratify the Great Charter in a manner still more authentic and more solemn than any which he had hitherto employed. All the prelates and abbots were assembled: They held burning tapers in their hands: The Great Charter was read before them: They denounced the sentence of excommunication against every one who should thenceforth violate that fundamental law: They threw their tapers on the ground, and exclaimed, *May the soul of every one, who incurs this sentence, so stink and corrupt in Hell!* The king bore a part in this ceremony; and subjoined: "So help me God, I will keep all these articles inviolate, as I am a man, as I am a christian, as I am a knight, and as I am a king crowned and anointed."

* M. Paris, p. 579.

CHAP.
XII.
1235.

"anointed[a]." Yet was the tremendous ceremony no sooner finished, than his favourites, abusing his weakness, made him return to the same arbitrary and irregular administration; and the reasonable expectations of his people were thus perpetually eluded and disappointed [b].

1252.
Simon de
Mountfort
earl of Leicester.

ALL these imprudent and illegal measures afforded a pretence to Simon de Mountfort, earl of Leicester, to attempt an innovation in the government, and to wrest the sceptre from the feeble and irresolute hand which held it. This nobleman was a younger son of that Simon de Mountfort, who had conducted with such valour and renown the Crusade against the Albigenses, and who, though he tarnished his famous exploits by cruelty and ambition, had left a name very precious to all the bigots of that age, particularly to the ecclesiastics. A large inheritance in England fell by succession to this family; but as the elder brother enjoyed still more opulent possessions in France, and could not perform fealty to two masters, he transferred his right to Simon, his younger brother, who came over to England, did homage for his lands, and was raised to the dignity of earl of Leicester. In the year 1238, he espoused Eleanor dowager of William earl of Pembroke, and sister to the king [c]; but the marriage of this princess with a subject and a foreigner, though contracted with Henry's consent, was loudly complained of by the earl of Cornwal, and all the barons of England; and Leicester was supported against their violence, by the king's favour and authority alone [d]. But he had no sooner established himself in his possessions and dignities, than he acquired, by infinuation and address, a strong

[a] M. Paris, p. 580. Ann. Burt. p. 323. Ann. Waverl. p. 810. W. Heming. p. 571. M. Well. p. 353.   [b] M. Paris, p. 597. 608.
[c] Ibid. p. 314.   [d] Ibid. p. 315.

interest

interest with the nation, and gained equally the affections of all orders of men. He lost, however, the friendship of Henry from the usual levity and fickleness of that prince; he was banished the court; he was recalled; he was entrusted with the command of Guienne [*], where he did good service and acquired honour; he was again disgraced by the king, and his banishment from court seemed now final and irrevocable. Henry called him traitor to his face; Leicester gave him the lie, and told him, that, if he were not his sovereign, he would soon make him repent of that insult. Yet was this quarrel accommodated either from the good-nature or timidity of the king; and Leicester was again admitted into some degree of favour and authority. But as this nobleman was become too great to preserve an entire complaisance to Henry's humours, and to act in subserviency to his other minions; he found more advantage in cultivating his interest with the public, and in inflaming the general discontents, which prevailed against the administration. He filled every place with complaints against the infringement of the Great Charter, the acts of violence committed on the people, the combination between the pope and the king in their tyranny and extortions, Henry's neglect of his native subjects and barons; and though himself a foreigner, he was more loud than any in representing the indignity of submitting to the dominion of foreigners. By his hypocritical pretensions to devotion, he gained the favour of the zealots and clergy: By his seeming concern for public good, he acquired the affections of the public: And besides the private friendships, which he had cultivated with the barons, his animosity against the favourites created an union of interests between him and that powerful order.

A RECENT quarrel, which broke out between Leicester and William de Valence, Henry's half-brother, and

[*] Rymer, vol. I. p. 459. 513.

chief favourite, brought matters to extremity [f], and determined the former to give full scope to his bold and unbounded ambition, which the laws and the king's authority had hitherto with difficulty restrained. He secretly called a meeting of the most considerable barons, particularly Humphrey de Bohun, high constable, Roger Bigod, earl Marefchal, and the earls of Warwic and Glocefter; men, who by their family and possessions stood in the first rank of the English nobility. He represented to this company the necessity of reforming the state, and of putting the execution of the laws into other hands than those which had hitherto appeared, from repeated experience, so unfit for the charge with which they were entrusted. He exaggerated the oppressions exercised against the lower orders of the state, the violations of the barons' privileges, the continued depredations made on the clergy; and in order to aggravate the enormity of his conduct, he appealed to the Great Charter, which Henry had so often ratified, and which was calculated to prevent for ever the return of those intolerable grievances. He magnified the generosity of their ancestors, who, at a great expence of blood, had extorted that famous concession from the crown; but lamented their own degeneracy, who allowed so important an advantage, once obtained, to be wrested from them by a weak prince and by infolent strangers. And he infifted, that the king's word, after so many submissions and fruitless promises on his part, could no longer be relied on; and that nothing but his absolute inability to violate national privileges could henceforth ensure the regular obfervance of them.

These topics, which were founded in truth, and suited so well the sentiments of the company, had the desired effect; and the barons embraced a resolution of redressing the public grievances, by taking into their own hands the

[f] M. Paris, p. 649.

administration

administration of government. Henry having summoned a parliament, In expectation of receiving supplies for his Sicilian project, the barons appeared in the hall, clad in complete armour, and with their swords by their side: The king, on his entry, struck with the unusual appearance, asked them what was their purpose, and whether they pretended to make him their prisoner [f]? Roger Bigod replied, in the name of the rest, that he was not their prisoner, but their sovereign; that they even intended to grant him large supplies, in order to fix his son on the throne of Sicily; that they only expected some return for this expence and service; and that, as he had frequently made submissions to the parliament, had acknowledged his past errors, and had still allowed himself to be carried into the same path, which gave them such just reason of complaint, he must now yield to more strict regulations, and confer authority on those who were able and willing to redress the national grievances. Henry, partly allured by the hopes of supply, partly intimidated by the union and martial appearance of the barons, agreed to their demand; and promised to summon another parliament at Oxford, in order to digest the new plan of government, and to elect the persons who were to be entrusted with the chief authority.

This parliament, which the royalists, and even the nation, from experience of the confusions that attended its measures, afterwards denominated the *mad parliament*, met on the day appointed; and as all the barons brought along with them their military vassals, and appeared with an armed force, the king, who had taken no precautions against them, was in reality a prisoner in their hands, and was obliged to submit to all the terms which they were pleased to impose upon him. Twelve barons were selected from among the king's ministers; twelve more were

[f] Annal. Theokesbury.

chosen by parliament: To these twenty-four, unlimited authority was granted to reform the state; and the king himself took an oath, that he would maintain whatever ordinances they should think proper to enact for that purpose [h]. Leicester was at the head of this supreme council, to which the legislative power was thus in reality transferred; and all their measures were taken by his secret influence and direction. Their first step bore a specious appearance, and seemed well calculated for the end which they professed to be the object of all these innovations: They ordered that four knights should be chosen by each county; that they should make enquiry into the grievances of which their neighbourhood had reason to complain, and should attend the ensuing parliament, in order to give information to that assembly of the state of their particular counties [i]: A nearer approach to our present constitution than had been made by the barons in the reign of king John, when the knights were only appointed to meet in their several counties, and there to draw up a detail of their grievances. Meanwhile the twenty-four barons proceeded to enact some regulations, as a redress of such grievances as were supposed to be sufficiently notorious. They ordered that three sessions of parliament should be regularly held every year, in the months of February, June, and October; that a new sheriff should be annually elected by the votes of the freeholders in each county [k]; that the sheriffs should have no power of fining the barons who did not attend their courts, or the circuits of the justiciaries; that no heirs should be committed to the wardship of foreigners, and no castles intrusted to their custody; and that no new warrens or forests should be created, nor the revenues of any counties or hundreds be let to farm. Such were the regulations

[h] Rymer, vol. I. p. 655. Chron. Dunst. vol. I. p. 334. Knyghton, p. 2415. [i] M. Paris, p. 657. Addit. p. 140. Ann. Burt. p. 412. [k] Chron. Dunst. vol. I. p. 336.

which

which the twenty-four barons established at Oxford, for the redress of public grievances.

But the earl of Leicester and his associates, having advanced so far to satisfy the nation, instead of continuing in this popular course, or granting the king that supply which they had promised him, immediately provided for the extension and continuance of their own authority. They rouzed anew the popular clamour which had long prevailed against foreigners; and they fell with the utmost violence on the king's half-brothers, who were supposed to be the authors of all national grievances, and whom Henry had no longer any power to protect. The four brothers, sensible of their danger, took to flight, with an intention of making their escape out of the kingdom; they were eagerly pursued by the barons; Aymer, one of the brothers, who had been elected to the see of Winchester, took shelter in his episcopal palace, and carried the others along with him; they were surrounded in that place, and threatened to be dragged out by force, and to be punished for their crimes and misdemeanors; and the king, pleading the sacredness of an ecclesiastical sanctuary, was glad to extricate them from this danger by banishing them the kingdom. In this act of violence, as well as in the former usurpations of the barons, the queen and her uncles were thought to have secretly concurred; being jealous of the credit acquired by the brothers, which, they found, had eclipsed and annihilated their own.

But the subsequent proceedings of the twenty-four barons were sufficient to open the eyes of the nation, and to prove their intention of reducing, for ever, both the king and the people under the arbitrary power of a very narrow aristocracy, which must at last have terminated either in anarchy, or in a violent usurpation and tyranny. They pretended that they had not yet digested all the regulations necessary for the reformation of the state, and for

HENRY III.

should chuse a committee of twelve persons, who should, in the intervals of the sessions, possess the authority of the whole parliament, and should attend, on a summons, the person of the king, in all his motions. But so powerful were these barons, that this regulation was also submitted to; the whole government was overthrown, or fixed on new foundations; and the monarchy was totally subverted, without its being possible for the king to strike a single stroke in defence of the constitution against the newly-erected oligarchy.

THE report that the king of the Romans intended to pay a visit to England, gave alarm to the ruling barons, who dreaded lest the extensive influence and established authority of that prince would be employed to restore the prerogatives of his family, and overturn their plan of government[a]. They sent over the bishop of Worcester, who met him at St. Omars; asked him, in the name of the barons, the reason of his journey, and how long he intended to stay in England; and insisted, that, before he entered the kingdom, he should swear to observe the regulations established at Oxford. On Richard's refusal to take this oath, they prepared to resist him as a public enemy; they fitted out a fleet, assembled an army, and exciting the inveterate prejudices of the people against foreigners, from whom they had suffered so many oppressions, spread the report, that Richard, attended by a number of strangers, meant to restore by force the authority of his exiled brothers, and to violate all the securities provided for public liberty. The king of the Romans was at last obliged to submit to the terms required of him[b].

BUT the barons, in proportion to their continuance in power, began gradually to lose that popularity which had assisted them in obtaining it; and men repined, that

[a] M. Paris, p. 661.   [b] Ibid. p. 661, 662. Chron. T. Wykes, p. 53.

them to do their duty, and would shed the last drop of his blood in promoting the interests, and satisfying the just wishes of the nation [r].

The barons, urged by so pressing a necessity, published at last a new code of ordinances for the reformation of the state [s]: but the expectations of the people were extremely disappointed, when they found that these consisted only of some trivial alterations in the municipal law; and still more, when the barons pretended that the task was not yet finished, and that they must farther prolong their authority, in order to bring the work of reformation to the desired period. The current of popularity was now much turned to the side of the crown; and the barons had little to rely on for their support, besides the private influence and power of their families, which, though exorbitant, was likely to prove inferior to the combination of king and people. Even this basis of power was daily weakened by their intestine jealousies and animosities; their ancient and inveterate quarrels broke out when they came to share the spoils of the crown; and the rivalship between the earls of Leicester and Glocester, the chief leaders among them, began to disjoint the whole confederacy. The latter, more moderate in his pretensions, was desirous of stopping or retarding the career of the barons' usurpations; but the former, enraged at the opposition which he met with in his own party, pretended to throw up all concern in English affairs; and he retired into France [t].

The kingdom of France, the only state with which England had any considerable intercourse, was at this time governed by Lewis IX. a prince of the most singular character that is to be met with in all records of history. This monarch united, to the mean and abject superstition of a monk, all the courage and magnanimity

[r] Annal. Burt. p. 427. Dunst. vol. i. p. 342.   [s] Ibid. p. 418. 419.   [t] Chron.

CHAP. XII.
1259.

of the greatest hero; and, what may be deemed more extraordinary, the justice and integrity of a disinterested patriot, the mildness and humanity of an accomplished philosopher. So far from taking advantage of the divisions among the English, or attempting to expel those dangerous rivals from the provinces, which they still possessed in France, he had entertained many scruples with regard to the sentence of attainder pronounced against the king's father, had even expressed some intention of restoring the other provinces, and was only prevented from taking that imprudent resolution by the united remonstrances of his own barons, who represented the extreme danger of such a measure[u], and, what had a greater influence on Lewis, the justice of punishing, by a legal sentence, the barbarity and felony of John. Whenever this prince interposed in English affairs, it was always with an intention of composing the differences between the king and his nobility; he recommended to both parties every peaceable and reconciling measure; and he used all his authority with the earl of Leicester, his native subject, to bend him to a compliance with Henry. He made a treaty with England, at a time when the distractions of that kingdom were at the greatest height, and when the king's authority was totally annihilated; and the terms which he granted might, even in a more prosperous state of their affairs, be deemed reasonable and advantageous to the English. He yielded up some territories which had been conquered from Poictou and Guienne; he ensured the peaceable possession of the latter province to Henry; he agreed to pay that prince a large sum of money; and he only required that the king should, in return, make a final cession of Normandy, and the other provinces, which he could never entertain any hopes of recovering by force of arms[w].

20th May.

[u] M. Paris, p. 604. [w] Rymer, vol. L p. 675. M. Paris, p. 566. Chron. T. Wykes, p. 53. Trivet, p. 208. M. West. p. 371.

This

HENRY III.

This cession was ratified by Henry, by his two sons and two daughters, and by the king of the Romans and his three sons: Leicester alone, either moved by a vain arrogance, or desirous to ingratiate himself with the English populace, protested against the deed, and insisted on the right, however distant, which might accrue to his consort[x]. Lewis saw, in this obstinacy, the unbounded ambition of the man; and as the barons insisted that the money due by treaty should be at their disposal, not at Henry's, he also saw, and probably with regret, the low condition to which this monarch, who had more erred from weakness than from any bad intentions, was reduced by the turbulence of his own subjects.

But the situation of Henry soon after wore a more favourable aspect. The twenty-four barons had now enjoyed the sovereign power near three years; and had visibly employed it, not for the reformation of the state, which was their first pretence, but for the aggrandizement of themselves and of their families. The breach of trust was apparent to all the world: Every order of men felt it, and murmured against it: The dissentions among the barons themselves, which encreased the evil, made also the remedy more obvious and easy: And the secret desertion, in particular, of the earl of Glocester to the crown, seemed to promise Henry certain success in any attempt to resume his authority. Yet durst he not take that step, so reconcilable both to justice and policy, without making a previous application to Rome, and desiring an absolution from his oaths and engagements[y].

The pope was at this time much dissatisfied with the conduct of the barons; who, in order to gain the favour of the people and clergy of England, had expelled all the Italian ecclesiastics, had confiscated their benefices, and

CHAP. XII.

1259.

1261.

---

[x] Chron. T. Wykes, p. 53. [y] Ann. Burt. p. 389.

seemed

CHAP. XII.
1261.

seemed determined to maintain the liberties and privileges of the English church, in which the rights of patronage, belonging to their own families, were included. The extreme animosity of the English clergy against the Italians was also a source of his disgust to this order; and an attempt which had been made by them for farther liberty, and greater independence on the civil power, was therefore less acceptable to the court of Rome [a]. About the same time that the barons at Oxford had annihilated the prerogatives of the monarchy, the clergy met in a synod at Merton, and passed several ordinances, which were no less calculated to promote their own grandeur at the expence of the crown. They decreed, that it was unlawful to try ecclesiastics by secular judges; that the clergy were not to regard any prohibitions from civil courts; that lay-patrons had no right to confer spiritual benefices; that the magistrate was obliged, without farther enquiry, to imprison all excommunicated persons; and that ancient usage, without any particular grant or charter, was a sufficient authority for any clerical possessions or privileges [b]. About a century before, these claims would have been supported by the court of Rome beyond the most fundamental articles of faith: They were the chief points maintained by the great martyr, Becket; and his resolution in defending them had exalted him to the high station which he held in the catalogue of Romish saints. But principles were changed with the times: The pope was become somewhat jealous of the great independence of the English clergy, which made them stand less in need of his protection, and even emboldened them to resist his authority, and to complain of the preference given to the Italian courtiers, whose interests, it is natural to imagine, were the chief object of his concern. He was ready, therefore, on the king's application, to

[a] Rymer, vol. 1. p. 755.   [b] Ann. Burt. p. 389.

annul

annul these new constitutions of the church of England[b]. And, at the same time, he absolved the king and all his subjects from the oath which they had taken to observe the provisions of Oxford[c].

CHAP. XII.

1261.

PRINCE Edward, whose liberal mind, though in such early youth, had taught him the great prejudice which his father had incurred, by his levity, inconstancy, and frequent breach of promise, refused for a long time to take advantage of this absolution; and declared that the provisions of Oxford, how unreasonable soever in themselves, and how much soever abused by the barons, ought still to be adhered to by those who had sworn to observe them[d]. He himself had been constrained by violence to take that oath; yet was he determined to keep it. By this scrupulous fidelity, the prince acquired the confidence of all parties, and was afterwards enabled to recover fully the royal authority, and to perform such great actions, both during his own reign and that of his father.

Prince Edward.

THE situation of England, during this period, as well as that of most European kingdoms, was somewhat peculiar. There was no regular military force maintained in the nation: The sword, however, was not, properly speaking, in the hands of the people: The barons were alone entrusted with the defence of the community; and after any effort which they made, either against their own prince or against foreigners, as the military retainers departed home, the armies were disbanded, and could not speedily be re-assembled at pleasure. It was easy therefore, for a few barons, by a combination, to get the start of the other party, to collect suddenly their troops, and to appear unexpectedly in the field with an army, which

[b] Rymer, vol. I. p. 735. [c] Rymer, vol. i. p. 722. M. Paris, p. 666. W. Heming. p. 580. Ypod. Neust. p. 463. Knyghton, p. 2446. [d] M. Paris, p. 667.

VOL. II. O their

CHAP. their antagonists, though equal, or even superior, in power
XII.   and interest, would not dare to encounter. Hence the
1261. sudden revolutions, which often took place in those governments: Hence the frequent victories obtained without a blow by one faction over the other: And hence it
happened, that the seeming prevalence of a party was
seldom a prognostic of its long continuance in power and
authority.

1262. THE king, as soon as he received the pope's absolution
from his oath, accompanied with menaces of excommunication against all opponents, trusting to the countenance of the church, to the support promised him by
many considerable barons, and to the returning favour
of the people, immediately took off the mask. After justifying his conduct by a proclamation, in which he set
forth the private ambition, and the breach of trust, con-
spicuous in Leicester and his associates, he declared, that
he had resumed the government, and was determined
thenceforth to exert the royal authority for the protection of his subjects. He removed Hugh le Despenser
and Nicholas de Ely, the justiciary and chancellor appointed by the barons; and put Philip Basset and Walter
de Merton in their place. He substituted new sheriffs in
all the counties, men of character and honour: He
placed new governors in most of the castles: He changed

23d April. all the officers of his houshold: He summoned a parliament, in which the resumption of his authority was ratified, with only five dissenting voices: And the barons,
after making one fruitless effort to take the king by surprize at Winchester, were obliged to acquiesce in those
new regulations*.

THE king, in order to cut off every objection to his
conduct, offered to refer all the differences between him

* M. Paris, p. 668. Chron. T. Wykes, p. 55.

and

and the earl of Leicester, to Margaret queen of France[f]. The celebrated integrity of Lewis gave a mighty influence to any decision which issued from his court; and Henry probably hoped that the gallantry, on which all barons, as true knights, valued themselves, would make them ashamed not to submit to the award of that princess. Lewis merited the confidence reposed in him. By an admirable conduct, probably as political as just, he continually interposed his good offices to allay the civil discords of the English: He forwarded all healing measures, which might give security to both parties: And he still endeavoured, though in vain, to sooth by persuasion the fierce ambition of the earl of Leicester, and to convince him how much it was his duty to submit peaceably to the authority of his sovereign.

CHAP. XII.

1264.

THAT bold and artful conspirator was nowise discouraged by the bad success of his past enterprizes. The death of Richard earl of Glocester, who was his chief rival in power, and who, before his decease, had joined the royal party, seemed to open a new field to his violence, and to expose the throne to fresh insults and injuries. It was in vain that the king professed his intentions of observing strictly the Great Charter, even of maintaining all the regulations made by the reforming barons at Oxford or afterwards, except those which entirely annihilated the royal authority: These powerful chieftains, now obnoxious to the court, could not peaceably resign the hopes of entire independence and uncontrouled power, with which they had flattered themselves, and which they had so long enjoyed. Many of them engaged in Leicester's views; and, among the rest, Gilbert the young earl of Glocester, who brought him a mighty accession of power, from the extensive authority possessed by that opu-

1265.

Civil wars of the barons.

[f] Rymer, vol. I. p. 744.

lent

CHAP. XII.
1246.

lent family. Even Henry, son of the king of the Romans, commonly called Henry d'Allmaine, though a prince of the blood, joined the party of the barons against the king, the head of his own family. Leicester himself, who still resided in France, secretly formed the links of this great conspiracy, and planned the whole scheme of operations.

The princes of Wales, notwithstanding the great power of the monarchs, both of the Saxon and Norman line, still preserved authority in their own country. Though they had often been constrained to pay tribute to the crown of England, they were with difficulty retained in subordination, or even in peace; and almost through every reign, since the conquest, they had infested the English frontiers with such petty incursions and sudden inroads, as seldom merit to have place in a general history. The English, still content with repelling their invasions, and chasing them back into their mountains, had never pursued the advantages obtained over them, nor been able, even under their greatest and most active princes, to fix a total, or so much as a feudal subjection on the country. This advantage was reserved to the present king, the weakest and most indolent. In the year 1237, Lewellyn, prince of Wales, declining in years and broken with infirmities, but still more harassed with the rebellion and undutiful behaviour of his younger son, Griffin, had recourse to the protection of Henry; and consenting to subject his principality, which had so long maintained, or soon recovered, its independence, to vassalage under the crown of England, had purchased security and tranquillity on these dishonourable terms. His eldest son and heir, David, renewed the homage to England; and having taken his brother prisoner, delivered him into Henry's hands, who committed him to custody in the Tower. That prince, endeavouring to make his escape, lost his

life

life in the attempt; and the prince of Wales, freed from the apprehensions of so dangerous a rival, paid thenceforth less regard to the English monarch, and even renewed those incursions, by which the Welsh, during so many ages, had been accustomed to infest the English borders. Lewellyn, however, the son of Griffin, who succeeded to his uncle, had been obliged to renew the homage, which was now claimed by England as an established right; but he was well pleased to inflame those civil discords, on which he rested his present security, and founded his hopes of future independence. He entered into a confederacy with the earl of Leicester, and collecting all the force of his principality, invaded England with an army of 30,000 men. He ravaged the lands of Roger de Mortimer, and of all the barons, who adhered to the crown [a]; he marched into Cheshire, and committed like depredations on prince Edward's territories; every place, where his disorderly troops appeared, was laid waste with fire and sword; and though Mortimer, a gallant and expert soldier, made stout resistance, it was found necessary that the prince himself should head the army against this invader. Edward repulsed prince Lewellyn, and obliged him to take shelter in the mountains of North Wales: But he was prevented from making farther progress against the enemy, by the disorders which soon after broke out in England.

The Welsh invasion was the appointed signal for the malcontent barons to rise in arms; and Leicester, coming over secretly from France, collected all the forces of his party, and commenced an open rebellion. He seized the person of the bishop of Hereford; a prelate obnoxious to all the inferior clergy, on account of his devoted attachment to the court of Rome [b]. Simon, bishop of Norwich, and

[a] Chron. Dunst. vol. I. p. 334. p. 382. 392. [b] Trivet, p. 211. M. West.

John Mansel, because they had published the pope's bull, absolving the king and kingdom from their oaths to observe the provisions of Oxford, were made prisoners, and exposed to the rage of the party. The king's demesnes were ravaged with unbounded fury[1]; and as it was Leicester's interest to allure to his side, by the hopes of plunder, all the disorderly ruffians in England, he gave them a general licence to pillage the barons of the opposite party, and even all neutral persons. But one of the principal resources of his faction was the populace of the cities, particularly of London; and as he had, by his hypocritical pretensions to sanctity, and his zeal against Rome, engaged the monks and lower ecclesiastics in his party, his dominion over the inferior ranks of men became uncontroulable. Thomas Fitz-Richard, mayor of London, a furious and licentious man, gave the countenance of authority to these disorders in the capital; and having declared war against the substantial citizens, he loosened all the bands of government, by which that turbulent city was commonly but ill restrained. On the approach of Easter, the zeal of superstition, the appetite for plunder, or what is often as prevalent with the populace as either of these motives, the pleasure of committing havoc and destruction, prompted them to attack the unhappy Jews, who were first pillaged without resistance, then massacred to the number of five hundred persons[2]. The Lombard bankers were next exposed to the rage of the people; and though, by taking sanctuary in the churches, they escaped with their lives, all their money and goods became a prey to the licentious multitude. Even the houses of the rich citizens, though English, were attacked by night; and way was made by sword and by fire to the pillage of their goods, and often to the destruction of their persons. The queen, who, though defended by the Tower, was

[1] Trivet, p. 217. M. West. p. 382. [2] Chron. T. Wykes, p. 59.

terrified

HENRY III.

terrified by the neighbourhood of such dangerous commotions, resolved to go by water to the castle of Windsor; but as she approached the bridge, the populace assembled against her: The cry ran, *drown the witch*; and besides abusing her with the most opprobrious language, and pelting her with rotten eggs and dirt, they had prepared large stones to sink her barge, when she should attempt to shoot the bridge; and she was so frightened, that she returned to the Tower[1].

The violence and fury of Leicester's faction had risen to such a height in all parts of England, that the king, unable to resist their power, was obliged to set on foot a treaty of peace; and to make an accommodation with the barons on the most disadvantageous terms[m]. He agreed to confirm anew the provisions of Oxford, even those which entirely annihilated the royal authority; and the barons were again re-instated in the sovereignty of the kingdom. They restored Hugh le Despenser to the office of chief justiciary; they appointed their own creatures sheriffs in every county of England; they took possession of all the royal castles and fortresses; they even named all the officers of the king's household; and they summoned a parliament to meet at Westminster, in order to settle more fully their plan of government. They here produced a new list of twenty-four barons, to whom they proposed that the administration should be entirely committed; and they insisted, that the authority of this junto should continue, not only during the reign of the king, but also during that of prince Edward.

This prince, the life and soul of the royal party, had unhappily, before the king's accommodation with the barons, been taken prisoner by Leicester in a parley at Windsor[n]; and that misfortune, more than any other

CHAP. XII.

1263.

18th July.

14th Oct.

[1] Chron. T. Wykes, p. 57. Trivet, p. 211.   [m] Chron. Dunst. vol. I. p. 335. [n] M. Paris, p. 669. Trivet, p. 213.

incident,

CHAP. XII.
1263.

incident, had determined Henry to submit to the ignominious conditions imposed upon him. But Edward having recovered his liberty by the treaty, employed his activity in defending the prerogatives of his family; and he gained a great party even among those who had at first adhered to the cause of the barons. His cousin, Henry d'Allmaine, Roger Bigod earl marefhal, earl Warrenne, Humphrey Bohun earl of Hereford, John lord Baffet, Ralph Baffet, Hamond l'Eftrange, Roger Mortimer, Henry de Piercy, Robert de Brus, Roger de Leybourne, with almoft all the Lords Marchers, as they were called, on the borders of Wales and of Scotland, the moft warlike parts of the kingdom, declared in favour of the royal caufe; and hoftilities, which were fcarcely well compofed, were again renewed in every part of England. But the near balance of the parties, joined to the univerfal clamour of the people, obliged the king and barons to open anew the negotiations for peace: and it was agreed by both fides to fubmit their differences to the arbitration of the king of France [o].

Reference to the king of France.

THIS virtuous prince, the only man who, in like circumftances, could fafely have been intrufted with such an authority by a neighbouring nation, had never ceafed to interpofe his good offices between the Englifh factions; and had even, during the fhort interval of peace, invited over to Paris both the king and the earl of Leicefter, in order to accommodate the differences between them; but found, that the fears and animofities on both fides, as well as the ambition of Leicefter, were fo violent, as to render all his endeavours ineffectual. But when this folemn appeal, ratified by the oaths and fubfcriptions of the leaders in both factions, was made to his judgment, he was not difcouraged from purfuing his

[o] M. Paris, p. 648. Chron. T. Wykes, p. 58. W. Heming. p. 580. Chron. Dunft. vol. I. p. 363.

honourable

honourable purpose: He summoned the states of France at Amiens; and there, in the presence of that assembly, as well as in that of the king of England and Peter de Montfort, Leicester's son, he brought this great cause to a trial and examination. It appeared to him, that the provisions of Oxford, even had they not been extorted by force, had they not been so exorbitant in their nature, and subversive of the ancient constitution, were expressly established as a temporary expedient, and could not, without breach of trust, be rendered perpetual by the barons. He therefore annulled these provisions; restored to the king the possession of his castles, and the power of nomination to the great offices; allowed him to retain what foreigners he pleased in his kingdom, and even to confer on them places of trust and dignity; and, in a word, re-established the royal power in the same condition on which it stood before the meeting of the parliament at Oxford. But while he thus suppressed dangerous innovations, and preserved unimpaired the prerogatives of the English crown, he was not negligent of the rights of the people; and besides ordering that a general amnesty should be granted for all past offences, he declared, that his award was not any wise meant to derogate from the privileges and liberties which the nation enjoyed by any former concessions or charters of the crown [p].

This equitable sentence was no sooner known in England, than Leicester and his confederates determined to reject it, and to have recourse to arms, in order to procure to themselves more safe and advantageous conditions [q]. Without regard to his oaths and subscriptions, that enterprising conspirator directed his two sons, Richard and Peter de Montfort, in conjunction with Robert de Ferrars, earl of Derby, to attack the city

[p] Rymer, vol. I. p. 776, 777. &c. Chron. T. Wykes, p. 58. Knyghton, p. 2446. [q] Chron. Dunst. vol. I. p. 363.

CHAP. XIII.
1264.

of Worcester; while Henry and Simon de Montfort, two others of his sons, assisted by the prince of Wales, were ordered to lay waste the estate of Roger de Mortimer. He himself resided at London; and employing as his instrument, Fitz-Richard, the seditious mayor, who had violently and illegally prolonged his authority, he wrought up that city to the highest ferment and agitation. The populace formed themselves into bands and companies; chose leaders; practised all military exercises; committed violence on the royalists: And, to give them greater countenance in their disorders, an association was entered into between the city and eighteen great barons, never to make peace with the king but by common consent and approbation. At the head of those who swore to maintain this association, were the earls of Leicester, Glocester, and Derby, with le Despenser, the chief justiciary; men who had all previously sworn to submit to the award of the French monarch. Their only pretence for this breach of faith was, that the latter part of Lewis's sentence was, as they affirmed, a contradiction to the former: He ratified the charter of liberties, yet annulled the provisions of Oxford; which were only calculated, as they maintained, to preserve that charter; and without which, in their estimation, they had no security for its observance.

THE king and prince, finding a civil war inevitable, prepared themselves for defence; and summoning the military vassals from all quarters, and being reinforced by Baliol lord of Galloway, Brus lord of Annandale, Henry Piercy, John Comyn [r], and other barons of the north, they composed an army, formidable, as well from its numbers as its military prowess and experience. The first enterprize of the royalists was the attack of Northampton, which was defended by Simon de Montfort, with many of the principal barons of that party: And a breach being

[r] Rymer, vol. I. p. 772. M. West. p. 385. Ypod. Neust. p. 469.

made

made in the walls by Philip Baffet, the place was carried by affault, and both the governor and the garrifon were made prifoners. The royalifts marched thence to Leicefter and Nottingham; both which places having opened their gates to them, prince Edward proceeded with a detachment into the county of Derby, in order to ravage with fire and fword the lands of the earl of that name, and take revenge on him for his difloyalty. Like maxims of war prevailed with both parties throughout England; and the kingdom was thus expofed in a moment to greater devaftation, from the animofities of the rival barons, than it would have fuffered from many years of foreign or even domeftic hoftilities, conducted by more humane and more generous principles.

The earl of Leicefter, mafter of London, and of the counties in the fouth-eaft of England, formed the fiege of Rochefter, which alone declared for the king in thofe parts, and which, befides earl Warrenne, the governor, was garrifoned by many noble and powerful barons of the royal party. The king and prince haftened from Nottingham, where they were then quartered, to the relief of the place; and on their approach, Leicefter raifed the fiege, and retreated to London, which, being the centre of his power, he was afraid might, in his abfence, fall into the king's hands, either by force, or by a correfpondence with the principal citizens, who were all fecretly inclined to the royal caufe. Reinforced by a great body of Londoners, and having fummoned his partizans from all quarters, he thought himfelf ftrong enough to hazard a general battle with the royalifts, and to determine the fate of the nation in one great engagement; which, if it proved fuccefsful, muft be decifive againft the king, who had no retreat for his broken troops in thofe parts; while Leceifter himfelf, in cafe of any finifter accident, could eafily take fhelter in the city. To give the better colouring to his caufe, he previoufly fent

a meffage

instant; were chased off the field; and Edward, transported by his martial ardour, and eager to revenge the insolence of the Londoners against his mother[1], put them to the sword for the length of four miles, without giving them any quarter, and without reflecting on the fate, which in the mean time attended the rest of the army. The earl of Leicester, seeing the royalists thrown into confusion by their eagerness in the pursuit, led on his remaining troops against the bodies commanded by the two royal brothers: He defeated with great slaughter the forces headed by the king of the Romans; and that prince was obliged to yield himself prisoner to the earl of Glocester: He penetrated to the body, where the king himself was placed, threw it into disorder, pursued his advantage, chased it into the town of Lewes, and obliged Henry to surrender himself prisoner[2].

PRINCE Edward, returning to the field of battle from his precipitate pursuit of the Londoners, was astonished to find it covered with the dead bodies of his friends, and still more to hear, that his father and uncle were defeated and taken prisoners, and that Arundel, Comyn, Brus, Hamon l'Estrange, Roger Leybourne, and many considerable barons of his party, were in the hands of the victorious enemy. Earl Warrenne, Hugh Bigod, and William de Valence, struck with despair at this event, immediately took to flight, hurried to Pevencey, and made their escape beyond sea[w]: But the prince, intrepid amidst the greatest disasters, exhorted his troops to revenge the death of their friends, to relieve the royal captives, and to snatch an easy conquest from an enemy, disordered by their own victory[x]. He found his followers intimidated by their situation; while Leicester, afraid of a sud-

[1] M. Paris, p. 670. Chron. T. Wykes, p. 61. W. Heming. p. 593. M. West p. 387. Ypod. Neust. p. 459. H. Knyghton, p. 2450.
[2] M. Paris, p. 670. M. West. p. 387. [w] Chron. T. Wykes, p. 63. [x] W. Heming. p. 584.

CHAP. XII.

1264.

den and violent blow from the prince, amused him by a feigned negotiation, till he was able to recal his troops from the pursuit, and bring them into order [r]. There now appeared no farther resource to the royal party; surrounded by the armies and garrisons of the enemy, destitute of forage and provisions, and deprived of their sovereign, as well as of their principal leaders, who could alone inspirit them to an obstinate resistance. The prince, therefore, was obliged to submit to Leicester's terms, which were short and severe, agreeably to the suddenness and necessity of the situation: He stipulated, that he and Henry d'Allmaine should surrender themselves prisoners as pledges in lieu of the two kings; that all other prisoners on both sides should be released[s]; and that, in order to settle fully the terms of agreement, application should be made to the king of France, that he should name six Frenchmen, three prelates, and three noblemen: These six to chuse two others of their own country: And these two to chuse one Englishman, who, in conjunction with themselves, were to be invested by both parties with full powers to make what regulations they thought proper for the settlement of the kingdom. The prince and young Henry accordingly delivered themselves into Leicester's hands, who sent them under a guard to Dover castle. Such are the terms of agreement, commonly called the *Mise* of Lewes, from an obsolete French term of that meaning: For it appears, that all the gentry and nobility of England, who valued themselves on their Norman extraction, and who disdained the language of their native country, made familiar use of the French tongue, till this period, and for some time after.

LEICESTER had no sooner obtained this great advantage, and gotten the whole royal family in his power,

[r] W. Heming. p. 584. [s] M. Paris, p. 671. Knyghton, p. 2451.

HENRY III.

than he openly violated every article of the treaty, and acted as sole master, and even tyrant of the kingdom. He still detained the king in effect a prisoner, and made use of that prince's authority to purposes the most prejudicial to his interests, and the most oppressive of his people[a]. He every where disarmed the royalists, and kept all his own partizans in a military posture[b]: He observed the same partial conduct in the deliverance of the captives, and even threw many of the royalists into prison, besides those who were taken in the battle of Lewes: He carried the king from place to place, and obliged all the royal castles, on pretence of Henry's commands, to receive a governor and garrison of his own appointment : All the officers of the crown and of the household were named by him ; and the whole authority, as well as arms of the state, was lodged in his hands : He instituted in the counties a new kind of magistracy, endowed with new and arbitrary powers, that of conservators of the peace[c]: His avarice appeared barefaced, and might induce us to question the greatness of his ambition, at least the largeness of his mind, if we had not reason to think, that he intended to employ his acquisitions as the instruments for attaining farther power and grandeur. He seized the estates of no less than eighteen barons, as his share of the spoil gained in the battle of Lewes: He engrossed to himself the ransom of all the prisoners; and told his barons, with a wanton insolence, that it was sufficient for them, that he had saved them by that victory from the forfeitures and attainders which hung over them[d]: He even treated the earl of Glocester in the same injurious manner, and applied to his own use the ransom of the king of the Romans, who in the field of battle had yielded himself pri-

[a] Rymer, vol. I. p. 790, 791, &c. [b] Ibid. p. 795. Brady's Append, No. 211, 212. Chron. T. Wykes. p. 63. [c] Rymer, vol. I. p. 791. [d] Knyghton, p. 2453.

soner to that nobleman. Henry, his eldest son, made a monopoly of all the wool in the kingdom, the only valuable commodity for foreign markets which it at that time produced. The inhabitants of the cinque-ports, during the present dissolution of government, betook themselves to the most licentious piracy, preyed on the ships of all nations, threw the mariners into the sea, and by these practices soon banished all merchants from the English coasts and harbours. Every foreign commodity rose to an exorbitant price; and woollen cloth, which the English had not then the art of dying, was worn by them white, and without receiving the last hand of the manufacturer. In answer to the complaints which arose on this occasion, Leicester replied, that the kingdom could well enough subsist within itself, and needed no intercourse with foreigners. And it was found, that he even combined with the pirates of the cinque-ports, and received as his share the third of their prizes [f].

No farther mention was made of the reference to the king of France, so essential an article in the agreement of Lewes; and Leicester summoned a parliament, composed altogether of his own partizans, in order to rivet, by their authority, that power, which he had acquired by so much violence, and which he used with so much tyranny and injustice. An ordinance was there passed, to which the king's consent had been previously extorted, that every act of royal power should be exercised by a council of nine persons, who were to be chosen and removed by the majority of three, Leicester himself, the earl of Glocester, and the bishop of Chichester [g]. By this intricate plan of government, the sceptre was really put into Leicester's hands; as he had the entire direction of the bishop of Chichester, and thereby commanded all the resolutions of the council of three, who could appoint or discard at pleasure every member of the supreme council.

CHAP. XII.

1264.

But it was impossible that things could long remain in this strange situation. It behoved Leicester either to descend with some peril into the rank of a subject, or to mount up with no less into that of a sovereign; and his ambition, unrestrained either by fear or by principle, gave too much reason to suspect him of the latter intention. Mean while, he was exposed to anxiety from every quarter; and felt that the smallest incident was capable of overturning that immense and ill-cemented fabric, which he had reared. The queen, whom her husband had left abroad, had collected in foreign parts an army of desperate adventurers, and had assembled a great number of ships, with a view of invading the kingdom, and of bringing relief to her unfortunate family. Lewis, detesting Leicester's usurpations and perjuries, and disgusted at the English barons, who had refused to submit to his award, secretly favoured all her enterprizes, and was generally believe to be making preparations for the same purpose. An English army, by the pretended authority of the captive king, was assembled on the sea-coast to oppose this projected invasion [b]; but Leicester owed his safety more to cross winds, which long detained and at last dispersed and ruined the queen's fleet, than to any resistance, which, in their present situation, could have been expected from the English.

Leicester found himself better able to resist the spiritual thunders, which were levelled against him. The pope, still adhering to the king's cause against the barons, dispatched cardinal Guido as his legate into England, with orders to excommunicate, by name, the three earls, Leicester, Glocester, and Norfolk, and all others in general, who concurred in the oppression and captivity of

[b] Brady's App. N° 216, 217. Chron. Dunst. vol. L. p. 373. M. West. p. 385.

Vol. II. P their

CHAP.
XII.

1264.

their sovereign[j]. Leicester menaced the legate with death, if he set foot within the kingdom; but Guido, meeting in France the bishops of Winchester, London, and Worcester, who had been sent thither on a negotiation, commanded them, under the penalty of ecclesiastical censures, to carry his bull into England, and to publish it against the barons. When the prelates arrived off the coast, they were boarded by the piratical mariners of the cinque-ports, to whom probably they gave a hint of the cargo, which they brought along with them: The bull was torn and thrown into the sea; which furnished the artful prelates with a plausible excuse for not obeying the orders of the legate. Leicester appealed from Guido to the pope in person; but before the ambassadors, appointed to defend his cause, could reach Rome, the pope was dead; and they found the legate himself, from whom they had appealed, seated on the papal throne, by the name of Urban IV. That daring leader was no wise dismayed with this incident; and as he found that a great part of his popularity in England was founded on his opposition to the court of Rome, which was now become odious, he persisted with the more obstinacy in the prosecution of his measures.

1265.
20th Jan.

House of Commons.

THAT he might both encrease, and turn to advantage his popularity, Leicester summoned a new parliament in London, where, he knew, his power was uncontrolable; and he fixed this assembly on a more democratical basis, than any which had ever been summoned since the foundation of the monarchy. Besides the barons of his own party, and several ecclesiastics, who were not immediate tenants of the crown; he ordered returns to be made of two knights from each shire, and, what is more remarkable, of deputies from the boroughs, an order of men which,

[j] Rymer, vol. L. p. 758. Chron. Dunst. vol. I. p. 373.

in former ages, had always been regarded as too mean to
enjoy a place in the national councils [k]. This period is
commonly esteemed the epoch of the house of commons
in England; and it is certainly the first time that historians speak of any representatives sent to parliament by
the boroughs. In all the general accounts given in preceding times of those assemblies, the prelates and barons
only are mentioned as the constituent members; and even
in the most particular narratives delivered of parliamentary
transactions, as in the trial of Thomas a Becket, where
the events of each day, and almost of each hour, are
carefully recorded by contemporary authors [l], there is not,
throughout the whole, the least appearance of a house of
commons. But though that house derived its existence
from so precarious, and even so invidious, an origin as Leicester's usurpation, it soon proved, when summoned by
the legal princes, one of the most useful, and, in process of time, one of the most powerful members of
the national constitution; and gradually rescued the kingdom from aristocratical as well as from regal tyranny.
But Leicester's policy, if we must ascribe to him so great
a blessing, only forwarded by some years an institution,
for which the general state of things had already prepared
the nation; and it is otherwise inconceivable, that a
plant, set by so inauspicious a hand, could have attained
to so vigorous a growth, and have flourished in the midst
of such tempests and convulsions. The feudal system,
with which the liberty, much more the power, of the
commons was totally incompatible, began gradually to
decline; and both the king and the commonalty, who
felt its inconveniencies, contributed to favour this new
power, which was more submissive than the barons to the
regular authority of the crown, and at the same time
afforded protection to the inferior orders of the state.

[k] Rymer, vol. I. p. 802. Brady, Matthew Paris, Knyghton, Hoveden, &c.
[l] Fitz-Stephen, Hist. Quadrip.

LEICESTER,

CHAP. XII.

1265.

LEICESTER, having thus assembled a parliament of his own model, and trusting to the attachment of the populace of London, seized the opportunity of crushing his rivals among the powerful barons. Robert de Ferrars, earl of Derby, was accused in the king's name, seized, and committed to custody, without being brought to any legal trial [m]. John Gifford, menaced with the same fate, fled from London, and took shelter in the borders of Wales. Even the earl of Glocester, whose power and influence had so much contributed to the success of the barons, but who of late was extremely disgusted with Leicester's arbitrary conduct, found himself in danger from the prevailing authority of his ancient confederate; and he retired from parliament [n]. This known dissention gave courage to all Leicester's enemies and to the king's friends, who were now sure of protection from so potent a leader. Though Roger Mortimer, Hamon L'Estrange, and other powerful marchers of Wales, had been obliged to leave the kingdom, their authority still remained over the territories subjected to their jurisdiction; and there were many others who were disposed to give disturbance to the new government. The animosities, inseparable from the feudal aristocracy, broke out with fresh violence, and threatened the kingdom with new convulsions and disorders.

THE earl of Leicester, surrounded with these difficulties, embraced a measure, from which he hoped to reap some present advantages, but which proved in the end the source of all his future calamities. The active and intrepid prince Edward had languished in prison ever since the fatal battle of Lewes; and as he was extremely popular in the kingdom, there arose a general desire of seeing him again restored to liberty [o]. Leicester, finding

[m] Chron. T. Wykes, p. 66. Ann. Waverl. p. 216. [n] M. Paris, p. 671. Ann. Waverl. p. 216. [o] Knyghton, p. 2451.

that

HENRY III.

that he could with difficulty oppose the concurring wishes of the nation, stipulated with the prince, that, in return, he should order his adherents to deliver up to the barons all their castles, particularly those on the borders of Wales; and should swear neither to depart the kingdom during three years, nor introduce into it any foreign forces [p]. The king took an oath to the same effect, and he also passed a charter, in which he confirmed the agreement or *Mise* of Lewes; and even permitted his subjects to rise in arms against him, if he should ever attempt to infringe it [q]. So little care did Leicester take, though he constantly made use of the authority of this captive prince, to preserve to him any appearance of royalty or kingly prerogatives!

IN consequence of this treaty, prince Edward was brought into Westminster-hall, and was declared free by the barons: But instead of really recovering his liberty, as he had vainly expected, he found, that the whole transaction was a fraud on the part of Leicester; that he himself still continued a prisoner at large, and was guarded by the emissaries of that nobleman; and that, while the faction reaped all the benefit from the performance of his part of the treaty, care was taken that he should enjoy no advantage by it. As Glocester, on his rupture with the barons, had retired for safety to his estates on the borders of Wales; Leicester followed him with an army to Hereford [r], continued still to menace and negotiate; and that he might add authority to his cause, he carried both the king and prince along with him. The earl of Glocester here concerted with young Edward the manner of that prince's escape. He found means to convey to him a horse of extraordinary swiftness; and appointed Roger Mortimer, who had returned

CHAP. XII.

1265.

11thMarch.

[p] Ann. Waverl. p. 216. Dunst. vol. i. p. 378.
[q] Blackstone's Mag. Charta. Chron. W. Hemingf. p. 585.
[r] Chron. T. Wykes, p. 67. Ann. Waverl. Chron. Dunst. vol. i. p. 383, 384.

into

into the kingdom, to be ready at hand with a small party to receive the prince, and to guard him to a place of safety. Edward pretended to take the air with some of Leicester's retinue, who were his guards; and making matches between their horses, after he thought he had tired and blown them sufficiently, he suddenly mounted Glocester's horse, and called to his attendants, that he had long enough enjoyed the pleasure of their company, and now bid them adieu. They followed him for some time, without being able to overtake him; and the appearance of Mortimer with his company put an end to their pursuit.

THE royalists, secretly prepared for this event, immediately flew to arms; and the joy of this gallant prince's deliverance, the oppressions under which the nation laboured, the expectation of a new scene of affairs, and the countenance of the earl of Glocester, procured Edward an army which Leicester was utterly unable to withstand. This nobleman found himself in a remote quarter of the kingdom; surrounded by his enemies; barred from all communication with his friends by the Severne, whose bridges Edward had broken down; and obliged to fight the cause of his party under these multiplied disadvantages. In this extremity he wrote to his son, Simon de Montfort, to hasten from London with an army for his relief; and Simon had advanced to Kenilworth with that view, where, fancying that all Edward's force and attention were directed against his father, he lay secure and unguarded. But the prince, making a sudden and forced march, surprized him in his camp, dispersed his army, and took the earl of Oxford, and many other noblemen prisoners, almost without resistance. Leicester, ignorant of his son's fate, passed the Severne in boats during Edward's absence, and lay at Evesham, in expectation of being every hour joined by his friends from London: When the prince, who availed himself of every

every favourable moment, appeared in the field before him. Edward made a body of his troops advance from the road which led to Kenilworth, and ordered them to carry the banners taken from Simon's army; while he himself, making a circuit with the rest of his forces, purposed to attack the enemy on the other quarter. Leicester was long deceived by this stratagem, and took one division of Edward's army for his friends; but at last, perceiving his mistake, and observing the great superiority and excellent disposition of the royalists, he exclaimed, that they had learned from him the art of war; adding, "The Lord have mercy on our souls, for I see "our bodies are the prince's!" The battle immediately began, though on very unequal terms. Leicester's army, by living on the mountains of Wales without bread, which was not then much used among the inhabitants, had been extremely weakened by sickness and desertion, and was soon broken by the victorious royalists; while his Welsh allies, accustomed only to a desultory kind of war, immediately took to flight, and were pursued with great slaughter. Leicester himself, asking for quarter, was slain in the heat of the action, with his eldest son Henry, Hugh le Despenser, and about an hundred and sixty knights, and many other gentlemen of his party. The old king had been purposely placed by the rebels in the front of the battle; and being clad in armour, and thereby not known by his friends, he received a wound, and was in danger of his life: But crying out, *I am Henry of Winchester, your king,* he was saved; and put in a place of safety by his son, who flew to his rescue.

CHAP. XII.

1265.
Battle of Evesham, and death of Leicester. 4th August.

THE violence, ingratitude, tyranny, rapacity, and treachery of the earl of Leicester, gave a very bad idea of his moral character, and make us regard his death as the most fortunate event, which, in this conjuncture, could have happened to the English nation: Yet must we

P 4   allow

CHAP. XII.
1265.

allow the man to have possessed great abilities, and the appearance of great virtues, who, though a stranger, could, at a time when strangers were the most odious, and the most universally decried, have acquired so extensive an interest in the kingdom, and have so nearly paved his way to the throne itself. His military capacity, and his political craft, were equally eminent: He possessed the talents both of governing men and conducting business: And though his ambition was boundless, it seems neither to have exceeded his courage nor his genius; and he had the happiness of making the low populace, as well as the haughty barons, co-operate towards the success of his selfish and dangerous purposes. A prince of greater abilities and vigour than Henry might have directed the talents of this nobleman either to the exaltation of his throne, or to the good of his people: But the advantages given to Leicester, by the weak and variable administration of the king, brought on the ruin of royal authority, and produced great confusions in the kingdom, which, however, in the end preserved and extremely improved national liberty, and the constitution. His popularity, even after his death, continued so great, that, though he was excommunicated by Rome, the people believed him to be a saint; and many miracles were said to be wrought upon his tomb [a].

Settlement of the government.

THE victory of Evesham, with the death of Leicester, proved decisive in favour of the royalists, and made an equal, though an opposite, impression on friends and enemies in every part of England. The king of the Romans recovered his liberty: The other prisoners of the royal party were not only freed, but courted, by their keepers: Fitz-Richard, the seditious mayor of London, who had marked out forty of the most wealthy citizens for slaughter, immediately stopped his hand on receiving

[a] Chron. de Mailr. p. 232.

intelligence

intelligence of this great event: And almost all the castles, garrisoned by the barons, hastened to make their submissions, and to open their gates to the king. The isle of Axholme alone, and that of Ely, trusting to the strength of their situation, ventured to make resistance; but were at last reduced, as well as the castle of Dover, by the valour and activity of prince Edward [t]. Adam de Gourdon, a courageous baron, maintained himself during some time in the forests of Hampshire, committed depredations in the neighbourhood, and obliged the prince to lead a body of troops into that country against him. Edward attacked the camp of the rebels; and being transported by the ardour of battle, leaped over the trench with a few followers, and encountered Gourdon in single combat. The victory was long disputed between these valiant combatants; but ended at last in the prince's favour, who wounded his antagonist, threw him from his horse, and took him prisoner. He not only gave him his life; but introduced him that very night to the queen at Guilford, procured him his pardon, restored him to his estate, received him into favour, and was ever after faithfully served by him [u].

A TOTAL victory of the sovereign over so extensive a rebellion commonly produces a revolution of government, and strengthens, as well as enlarges, for some time, the prerogatives of the crown: Yet no sacrifices of national liberty were made on this occasion; the Great Charter remained still inviolate; and the king, sensible that his own barons, by whose assistance alone he had prevailed, were no less jealous of their independence than the other party, seems thenceforth to have more carefully abstained from all those exertions of power, which had afforded so plausible a pretence to the rebels. The clemency of this victory is also remarkable: No blood was shed on the

[t] M. Paris, p. 676. W. Heming. p. 582. [u] M Paris, p. 675.

scaffold:

218   HISTORY OF ENGLAND.

CHAP. scaffold: No attainders, except of the Mountfort family,
XII. were carried into execution: And though a parliament,
1266. assembled at Winchester, attainted all those who had
borne arms against the king, easy compositions were
made with them for their lands *; and the highest sum,
levied on the most obnoxious offenders, exceeded not five
years rent of their estate. Even the earl of Derby, who
again rebelled, after having been pardoned and restored
to his fortune, was obliged to pay only seven years rent,
and was a second time restored. The mild disposition of
the king, and the prudence of the prince, tempered the
insolence of victory, and gradually restored order to the
several members of the state, disjointed by so long a continuance of civil wars and commotions.

THE city of London, which had carried farthest the
rage and animosity against the king, and which seemed
determined to stand upon its defence after almost all the
kingdom had submitted, was, after some interval, restored
to most of its liberties and privileges; and Fitz-Richard,
the mayor, who had been guilty of so much illegal violence, was only punished by fine and imprisonment. The
countess of Leicester, the king's sister, who had been
extremely forward in all attacks on the royal family,
was dismissed the kingdom with her two sons, Simon
and Guy, who proved very ungrateful for this lenity.
Five years afterwards they assassinated, at Viterbo in
Italy, their cousin Henry d'Allmaine, who at that very
time was endeavouring to make their peace with the
king; and by taking sanctuary in the church of the Fran-
ciscans, they escaped the punishment due to so great an
enormity º.

1267. THE merits of the earl of Glocester, after he returned
to his allegiance, had been so great in restoring the

* M. Paris, p. 675.   º Rymer, vol. I. p. 879. vol. II. p. 4, 5.
Chron. T. Wykes, p. 54. W. Hemingf. p. 589. Trivet, p. 240.

prince

prince to his liberty, and assisting him in his victories against the rebellious barons, that it was almost impossible to content him in his demands; and his youth and temerity, as well as his great power, tempted him, on some new disgust, to raise again the flames of rebellion in the kingdom. The mutinous populace of London, at his instigation, took to arms; and the prince was obliged to levy an army of 30,000 men, in order to suppress them. Even this second rebellion did not provoke the king to any act of cruelty; and the earl of Glocester himself escaped with total impunity. He was only obliged to enter into a bond of 20,000 marks, that he should never again be guilty of rebellion: A strange method of enforcing the laws, and a proof of the dangerous independence of the barons in those ages! These potent nobles were, from the danger of the precedent, averse to the execution of the laws of forfeiture and felony against any of their fellows; though they could not, with a good grace, refuse to concur in obliging them to fulfil any voluntary contract and engagement into which they had entered.

THE prince finding the state of the kingdom tolerably composed, was seduced, by his avidity for glory, and by the prejudices of the age, as well as by the earnest solicitations of the king of France, to undertake an expedition against the infidels in the Holy Land *y*; and he endeavoured previously to settle the state in such a manner, as to dread no bad effects from his absence. As the formidable power and turbulent disposition of the earl of Glocester gave him apprehensions, he insisted on carrying him along with him, in consequence of a vow, which that nobleman had made to undertake the same voyage: In the mean time, he obliged him to resign some

y M. Paris, p. 677.

CHAP. XII.
1270.

of his castles, and to enter into a new bond not to disturb the peace of the kingdom[a]. He sailed from England with an army, and arrived in Lewis's camp before Tunis in Africa, where he found that monarch already dead, from the intemperance of the climate and the fatigues of his enterprize. The great, if not only weakness of this prince in his government, was the imprudent passion for crusades; but it was his zeal chiefly that procured him from the clergy the title of St. Lewis, by which he is known in the French history; and if that appellation had not been so extremely prostituted, as to become rather a term of reproach, he seems, by his uniform probity and goodness, as well as his piety, to have fully merited the title. He was succeeded by his son, Philip, denominated the Hardy; a prince of some merit, though much inferior to that of his father.

1271.

PRINCE Edward, not discouraged by this event, continued his voyage to the Holy Land, where he signalized himself by acts of valour; revived the glory of the English name in those parts; and struck such terror into the Saracens, that they employed an assassin to murder him, who wounded him in the arm, but perished in the attempt[b]. Meanwhile, his absence from England was attended with many of those pernicious consequences which had been dreaded from it. The laws were not executed: The barons oppressed the common people with impunity[c]: They gave shelter on their estates to bands of robbers, whom they employed in committing ravages on the estates of their enemies: The populace of London returned to their usual licentiousness: And the old king, unequal to the burthen of public affairs, called aloud for his gallant son to return[d], and to assist him in

[a] Chron. T. Wykes, p. 92. [b] M. Paris, p. 678, 679. W. Heming. p. 510. [c] Chron. Dunst. vol. L. p. 404. [d] Rymer, vol. L p. 889. M. Paris, p. 678.

swaying

HENRY III.

swaying that sceptre, which was ready to drop from his feeble and irresolute hands. At last, overcome by the cares of government, and the infirmities of age, he visibly declined, and he expired at St. Edmondsbury in the 64th year of his age, and 56th of his reign; the longest reign that is to be met with in the English annals. His brother, the king of the Romans (for he never attained the title of emperor), died about seven months before him.

THE most obvious circumstance of Henry's character is his incapacity for government, which rendered him as much a prisoner in the hands of his own ministers and favourites, and as little at his own disposal, as when detained a captive in the hands of his enemies. From this source, rather than from insincerity or treachery, arose his negligence in observing his promises; and he was too easily induced, for the sake of present convenience, to sacrifice the lasting advantages arising from the trust and confidence of his people. Hence too were derived his profusion to favourites, his attachment to strangers, the variableness of his conduct, his hasty resentments, and his sudden forgiveness and return of affection. Instead of reducing the dangerous power of his nobles, by obliging them to observe the laws towards their inferiors, and setting them the salutary example in his own government; he was seduced to imitate their conduct, and to make his arbitrary will, or rather that of his ministers, the rule of his actions. Instead of accommodating himself, by a strict frugality, to the embarrassed situation in which his revenue had been left, by the military expeditions of his uncle, the dissipations of his father, and the usurpations of the barons; he was tempted to levy money by irregular exactions, which, without enriching himself, impoverished, at least disgusted his people. Of all men, nature seemed least to have fitted him for being a tyrant; yet are there instances of oppres-

sion

CHAP. XII.

1272.

sion in his reign, which, though derived from the precedents left him by his predecessors, had been carefully guarded against by the Great Charter, and are inconsistent with all rules of good government. And on the whole we may say, that greater abilities, with his good dispositions, would have prevented him from falling into his faults; or with worse dispositions, would have enabled him to maintain and defend them.

This prince was noted for his piety and devotion, and his regular attendance on public worship; and a saying of his on that head is much celebrated by ancient writers. He was engaged in a dispute with Lewis IX. of France, concerning the preference between sermons and masses: He maintained the superiority of the latter, and affirmed, that he would rather have one hour's conversation with a friend, than hear twenty the most elaborate discourses pronounced in his praise [*].

Henry left two sons, Edward his successor, and Edmond earl of Lancaster; and two daughters, Margaret queen of Scotland, and Beatrix dutchess of Britanny. He had five other children, who died in their infancy.

Miscellaneous transactions of this reign.

The following are the most remarkable laws enacted during this reign. There had been great disputes between the civil and ecclesiastical courts concerning bastardy. The common law had deemed all those to be bastards who were born before wedlock: By the canon law they were legitimate: And when any dispute of inheritance arose, it had formerly been usual for the civil courts to issue writs to the spiritual, directing them to enquire into the legitimacy of the person. The bishop always returned an answer agreeable to the canon law, though contrary to the municipal law of the kingdom. For this reason, the civil courts had changed the terms of their writ; and instead of requiring the spiritual courts to make inquisition

[*] Walsing. Edw. I. p. 43.

concerning

concerning the legitimacy of the person, they only proposed the simple question of fact, whether he were born before or after wedlock? The prelates complained of this practice to the parliament assembled at Merton in the twentieth of this king, and desired that the municipal law might be rendered conformable to the canon: But received from all the nobility the memorable reply, *Nolumus leges Angliæ mutare*, We will not change the laws of England [f].

AFTER the civil wars, the parliament, summoned at Marlebridge, gave their approbation to most of the ordinances which had been established by the reforming barons, and which, though advantageous to the security of the people, had not received the sanction of a legal authority. Among other laws, it was there enacted, that all appeals from the courts of inferior lords should be carried directly to the king's courts, without passing through the courts of the lords immediately superior [g]. It was ordained, that money should bear no interest during the minority of the debtor [h]. This law was reasonable, as the estates of minors were always in the hands of their lords, and the debtors could not pay interest where they had no revenue. The charter of king John had granted this indulgence: It was omitted in that of Henry III. for what reason is not known; but it was renewed by the statute of Marlebridge. Most of the other articles of this statute are calculated to restrain the oppressions of sheriffs, and the violence and iniquities committed in distraining cattle and other goods. Cattle, and the instruments of husbandry, formed at that time the chief riches of the people.

IN the 35th year of this king an assize was fixed of bread, the price of which was settled, according to the

[f] Statute of Merton, chap. 9.   [g] Statute of Marleb. chap. 20.
[h] Ibid. chap. 16.

different

CHAP.
XII.

1070.

different prices of corn, from one shilling a quarter to seven shillings and sixpence [1], money of that age. These great variations are alone a proof of bad tillage [k]: Yet did the prices often rise much higher, than any taken notice of by the statute. The chronicle of Dunstable tells us, that, in this reign, wheat was once sold for a mark, nay, for a pound a quarter; that is, three pounds of our present money [l]. The same law affords us a proof of the little communication between the parts of the kingdom, from the very different prices which the same commodity bore at the same time. A brewer, says the statute, may sell two gallons of ale for a penny in cities, and three or four gallons for the same price in the country. At present, such commodities, by the great consumption of the people, and the great flocks of the brewers, are rather cheapest in cities. The Chronicle above-mentioned observes, that wheat one year was sold in many places for eight shillings a quarter, but never rose in Dunstable above a crown.

Though commerce was still very low, it seems rather to have encreased since the Conquest; at least, if we may judge of the increase of money by the price of corn. The medium between the highest and lowest prices of wheat, assigned by the statute, is four shillings and three pence a quarter, that is, twelve shillings and nine pence of our present money. This is near half of the middling price in our time. Yet the middling price of cattle, so late as the reign of king Richard, we found to be above eight, near ten times lower than the present. Is not this the true inference, from comparing these facts, that, in all

[1] Statutes at large, p. 6. [k] We learn from Cicero's orations against Verres, lib. iii. cap. 84. 92. that the price of corn in Sicily was, during the praetorship of Saturdus, five Denarii a Modius; during that of Verres, which immediately succeeded, only two Sesterces: That is, ten times lower; a presumption, or rather a proof, of the very bad state of tillage in antient times. [l] So also Knyghton, p. 2444.

uncivilized

uncivilized nations, cattle, which propagate of themselves, bear always a lower price than corn, which requires more art and stock to render it plentiful, than those nations are possessed of? It is to be remarked, that Henry's assize of corn was copied from a preceding assize established by king John; consequently, the prices which we have here compared of corn and cattle may be looked on as contemporary; and they were drawn, not from one particular year, but from an estimation of the middling prices for a series of years. It is true, the prices, assigned by the assize of Richard, were meant as a standard for the accompts of sheriffs and escheators; and as considerable profits were allowed to these ministers, we may naturally suppose, that the common value of cattle was somewhat higher: Yet still, so great a difference between the prices of corn and cattle as that of four to one, compared to the present rates, affords important reflections concerning the very different state of industry and tillage in the two periods.

INTEREST had in that age mounted to an enormous height, as might be expected from the barbarism of the times and men's ignorance of commerce. Instances occur of fifty per cent. payed for money [m]. There is an edict of Philip Augustus near this period, limiting the Jews in France to 48 per cent. [n] Such profits tempted the Jews to remain in the kingdom, notwithstanding the grievous oppressions to which, from the prevalent bigotry and rapine of the age, they were continually exposed. It is easy to imagine how precarious their state must have been under an indigent prince, somewhat restrained in his tyranny over his native subjects, but who possessed an unlimited authority over the Jews, the sole proprietors of money in the kingdom, and hated, on account of their riches, their religion, and their usury: Yet will our ideas scarcely come up to the extortions which, in fact, we find

[m] M. Paris, p. 586. [n] Brussel Traité des Fiefs, vol. I. p. 576.

CHAP. to have been practised upon them. In the year 1241,
XII. 20,000 marks were exacted from them [o]: Two years
1272. after, money was again extorted; and one Jew alone,
Aaron of York, was obliged to pay above 4000 marks [p]:
In 1250, Henry renewed his oppressions; and the same
Aaron was condemned to pay him 30,000 marks upon an
accusation of forgery [q]: The high penalty imposed upon
him, and which, it seems, he was thought able to pay, is
rather a presumption of his innocence than of his guilt.
In 1255, the king demanded 8000 marks from the Jews,
and threatened to hang them if they refused compliance.
They now lost all patience, and desired leave to retire
with their effects out of the kingdom. But the king replied: "How can I remedy the oppressions you complain
"of? I am myself a beggar. I am spoiled, I am strip-
"ped of all my revenues: I owe above 200,000 marks;
"and if I had said 300,000, I should not exceed the
"truth: I am obliged to pay my son, prince Edward,
"15,000 marks a year: I have not a farthing; and I
"must have money, from any hand, from any quarter,
"or by any means." He then delivered over the Jews
to the earl of Cornwal, that those whom the one brother
had flayed, the other might embowel, to make use of the
words of the historian [r]. King John, his father, once demanded 10,000 marks from a Jew of Bristol; and on his
refusal, ordered one of his teeth to be drawn every day
till he should comply. The Jew lost seven teeth; and
then paid the sum required of him [s]. One talliage laid
upon the Jews in 1243 amounted to 60,000 marks [t]; a
sum equal to the whole yearly revenue of the crown.

To give a better pretence for extortions, the improbable
and absurd accusation, which has been at different times
advanced against that nation, was revived in England,

[o] M. Paris, p. 371.   [p] Ibid. p. 410.   [q] Ibid. p. 525.
[r] Ibid. p. 606.   [s] Ibid. p. 160.   [t] Madox, p. 151.

that they had crucified a child in derision of the sufferings
of Christ. Eighteen of them were hanged at once for
this crime [o]: Though it is no wise credible, that even the
antipathy born them by the Christians, and the oppressions under which they laboured, would ever have pushed
them to be guilty of that dangerous enormity. But it is
natural to imagine, that a race, exposed to such insults
and indignities, both from king and people, and who had
so uncertain an enjoyment of their riches, would carry
usury to the utmost extremity, and by their great profits
make themselves some compensation for their continual
perils.

Though these acts of violence against the Jews proceeded much from bigotry, they were still more derived from
avidity and rapine. So far from desiring in that age to
convert them, it was enacted by law in France, that, if
any Jew embraced Christianity, he forfeited all his goods,
without exception, to the king or his superior lord.
These plunderers were careful, lest the profits accruing
from their dominion over that unhappy race, should be
diminished by their conversion [p].

Commerce must be in a wretched condition, where
interest was so high, and where the sole proprietors of
money employed it in usury only, and were exposed to
such extortion and injustice. But the bad police of the
country was another obstacle to improvements; and rendered all communication dangerous, and all property precarious. The Chronicle of Dunstable says [q], that men
were never secure in their houses, and that whole villages
were often plundered by bands of robbers, though no civil
wars at that time prevailed in the kingdom. In 1249,
some years before the insurrection of the barons, two
merchants of Brabant came to the king at Winchester,

[o] M. Paris, p. 613. [p] Brussel, vol. i. p. 622. Du Cange verbo
Judæi. [q] Vol. i. p. 155.

CHAP. XII.

1172.

and told him, that they had been spoiled of all their goods by certain robbers, whom they knew, because they saw their faces every day in his court; that like practices prevailed all over England, and travellers were continually exposed to the danger of being robbed, bound, wounded, and murdered; that these crimes escaped with impunity, because the ministers of justice themselves were in a confederacy with the robbers; and that they, for their part, instead of bringing matters to a fruitless trial by law, were willing, though merchants, to decide their cause with the robbers by arms and a duel. The king, provoked at these abuses, ordered a jury to be inclosed, and to try the robbers: The jury, though consisting of twelve men of property in Hampshire, were found to be also in a confederacy with the felons, and acquitted them. Henry, in a rage, committed the jury to prison, threatened them with severe punishment, and ordered a new jury to be inclosed, who, dreading the fate of their fellows, at last found a verdict against the criminals. Many of the king's own houshold were discovered to have participated in the guilt; and they said, for their excuse, that they received no wages from him, and were obliged to rob for a maintenance [y]. *Knights and esquires,* says the Dictum of Kenelworth, *who were robbers, if they have no land, shall pay the half of their goods, and find sufficient security to keep henceforth the peace of the kingdom.* Such were the manners of the times!

ONE can the less repine, during the prevalence of such manners, at the frauds and forgeries of the clergy; as it gives less disturbance to society, to take men's money from them with their own consent, though by deceits and lies, than to ravish it by open force and violence. During this reign the papal power was at its summit, and was

[y] M. Paris, p. 504.

even

HENRY III.

even beginning infenfibly to decline, by reafon of the immeafurable avarice and extortions of the court of Rome, which difgufted the clergy as well as laity, in every kingdom of Europe. England itfelf, though funk in the deepeft abyfs of ignorance and fuperftition, had ferioufly entertained thoughts of fhaking off the papal yoke*; and the Roman pontiff was obliged to think of new expedients for rivetting it fafter upon the Chriftian world. For this purpofe, Gregory IX. publifhed his decretals *, which are a collection of forgeries, favourable to the court of Rome, and confift of the fuppofed decrees of popes in the firft centuries. But thefe forgeries are fo grofs, and confound fo palpably all language, hiftory, chronology, and antiquities; matters more ftubborn than any fpeculative truths whatfoever; that even that church, which is not ftartled at the moft monftrous contradictions and abfurdities, has been obliged to abandon them to the critics. But in the dark period of the thirteenth century, they paffed for undifputed and authentic; and men, entangled in the mazes of this falfe literature, joined to the philofophy, equally falfe, of the times, had nothing wherewithal to defend themfelves, but fome fmall remains of common fenfe, which paffed for profanenefs and impiety, and the indelible regard to felf-intereft, which, as it was the fole motive in the priefts for framing thefe impoftures, ferved alfo, in fome degree, to protect the laity againft them.

ANOTHER expedient, devifed by the church of Rome, in this period, for fecuring her power, was the inftitution of new religious orders, chiefly the Dominicans and Francifcans, who proceeded with all the zeal and fuccefs that attend novelties; were better qualified to gain the populace than the old orders, now become rich and indolent;

CHAP. XII.

1272.

* M. Paris, p. 421. * Trivet, p. 191.

CHAP. XII.

1172.

dolent; maintained a perpetual rivalship with each other in promoting their gainful superstitions; and acquired a great dominion over the minds, and consequently over the purses of men, by pretending a desire of poverty and a contempt for riches. The quarrels which arose between these orders, lying still under the controul of the sovereign pontiff, never disturbed the peace of the church, and served only as a spur to their industry in promoting the common cause; and though the Dominicans lost some popularity by their denial of the immaculate conception, a point in which they unwarily engaged too far to be able to recede with honour, they counterbalanced this disadvantage by acquiring more solid establishments, by gaining the confidence of kings and princes, and by exercising the jurisdiction assigned them, of ultimate judges and punishers of heresy. Thus, the several orders of monks became a kind of regular troops or garrisons of the Romish church; and though the temporal interests of society, still more the cause of true piety, were hurt, by their various devices to captivate the populace, they proved the chief supports of that mighty fabric of superstition, and, till the revival of true learning, secured it from any dangerous invasion.

THE trial by ordeal was abolished in this reign by order of council: A faint mark of improvement in the age [b].

HENRY granted a charter to the town of Newcastle, in which he gave the inhabitants a licence to dig coal. This is the first mention of coal in England.

WE learn from Madox [c], that this king gave at one time 100 shillings to master Henry, his poet; Also the same year he orders this poet ten pounds.

[b] Rymer, vol. I. p. 228. Spelman, p. 326.
[c] Page 268.

IT

It appears from Selden, that in the 47th of this reign, a hundred and fifty temporal, and fifty spiritual barons were summoned to perform the service, due by their tenures[d]. In the 35th of the subsequent reign, eighty-six temporal barons, twenty bishops, and forty-eight abbots, were summoned to a parliament convened at Carlisle[e].

[d] Titles of honour, part 2. chap. 3.
[e] Parliamentary Hist. vol. I. p. 151.

CHAP. XIII.

EDWARD I.

Civil administration of the king——Conquest of Wales ——Affairs of Scotland——Competitors for the crown of Scotland——Reference to Edward—— Homage of Scotland——Award of Edward in favour of Baliol——War with France——Digression concerning the constitution of parliament ——War with Scotland——Scotland subdued—— War with France——Dissentions with the clergy ——Arbitrary measures——Peace with France ——Revolt of Scotland——That kingdom again subdued——again revolts——is again subdued—— Robert Bruce——Third revolt of Scotland—— Death and character of the king——Miscellaneous transactions of this reign.

THE English were as yet so little enured to obedience under a regular government, that the death of almost every king, since the conquest, had been attended with disorders; and the council, reflecting on the recent civil wars, and on the animosities which naturally remain after these great convulsions, had reason to apprehend dangerous consequences from the absence of the son and successor of Henry. They therefore hastened to proclaim prince Edward, to swear allegiance to him, and to summon the states of the kingdom, in order to provide for the public peace in this important conjuncture[f]. Walter

[f] Rymer, vol. II. p. 1. Walsing. p. 43. Trivet, p. 239.

Giffard,

EDWARD I.

Giffard, archbishop of York, the earl of Cornwal, son of Richard, king of the Romans, and the earl of Glocester, were appointed guardians of the realm, and proceeded peaceably to the exercise of their authority, without either meeting with opposition from any of the people, or being disturbed with emulation and faction among themselves. The high character acquired by Edward during the late commotions, his military genius, his success in subduing the rebels, his moderation in settling the kingdom, had procured him great esteem, mixed with affection, among all orders of men; and no one could reasonably entertain hopes of making any advantage of his absence, or of raising disturbance in the nation. The earl of Glocester himself, whose great power and turbulent spirit had excited most jealousy, was forward to give proofs of his allegiance; and the other malcontents, being destitute of a leader, were obliged to remain in submission to the government.

PRINCE Edward had reached Sicily in his return from the Holy Land, when he received intelligence of the death of his father; and he discovered a deep concern on the occasion. At the same time he learned the death of an infant son, John, whom his princess, Eleanor of Castile, had born him at Acre in Palestine; and as he appeared much less affected with that misfortune, the king of Sicily expressed a surprize at this difference of sentiment: But was told by Edward, that the death of a son was a loss which he might hope to repair; the death of a father was a loss irreparable[e].

EDWARD proceeded homeward; but as he soon learned the quiet settlement of the kingdom, he was in no hurry to take possession of the throne, but spent near a year in France, before he made his appearance in England. In his passage by Chalons in Burgundy, he was challenged

[e] Walsing. p. 44. Trivet. p. 240.

CHAP. XIII.

1273.

by the prince of the country to a tournament which he was preparing; and as Edward excelled in those martial and dangerous exercises, the true image of war, he declined not the opportunity of acquiring honour in that great assembly of the neighbouring nobles. But the image of war was here unfortunately turned into the thing itself. Edward and his retinue were so successful in the joust, that the French knights, provoked at their superiority, made a serious attack upon them, which was repulsed, and much blood was idly shed in the quarrel [b]. This rencounter received the name of the petty battle of Chalons.

EDWARD went from Chalons to Paris, and did homage to Philip for the dominions which he held in France [i].

1274. He thence returned to Guienne, and settled that province, which was in some confusion. He made his journey to London through France; in his passage he accommodated at Montreuil a difference with Margaret, countess of Flanders, heiress of that territory [k]; he was received with joyful acclamations by his people, and was solemnly 19th August. crowned at Westminster by Robert, archbishop of Canterbury.

Civil administration of the king.

THE king immediately applied himself to the re-establishment of his kingdom, and to the correcting of those disorders, which the civil commotions, and the loose administration of his father, had introduced into every part of government. The plan of his policy was equally generous and prudent. He considered the great barons both as the immediate rivals of the crown, and oppressors of the people; and he purposed, by an exact distribution of justice, and a rigid execution of the laws, to give at once protection to the inferior orders of the state, and to diminish the arbitrary power of the great, on which their

[a] Walsing. p. 44. Trivet, p. 241. M. West. p. 404.
[i] Walsing. p. 45. [k] Rymer, vol. II. p. 30, 33.

2 dangerous

dangerous authority was chiefly founded. Making it a rule in his own conduct to observe, except on extraordinary occasions, the privileges secured to them by the Great Charter, he acquired a right to insist upon their observance of the same charter towards their vassals and inferiors; and he made the crown be regarded by all the gentry and commonalty of the kingdom, as the fountain of justice, and the general asylum against oppression. Besides enacting several useful statutes, in a parliament which he summoned at Westminster, he took care to inspect the conduct of all his magistrates and judges, to displace such as were either negligent or corrupt, to provide them with sufficient force for the execution of justice, to extirpate all bands and confederacies of robbers, and to repress those more silent robberies, which were committed either by the power of the nobles, or under the countenance of public authority. By this rigid administration, the face of the kingdom was soon changed; and order and justice took place of violence and oppression: But amidst the excellent institutions and public-spirited plans of Edward, there still appears somewhat both of the severity of his personal character, and of the prejudices of the times.

As the various kinds of malefactors, the murderers, robbers, incendiaries, ravishers, and plunderers, had become so numerous and powerful, that the ordinary ministers of justice, especially in the western counties, were afraid to execute the laws against them, the king found it necessary to provide an extraordinary remedy for the evil; and he erected a new tribunal, which, however useful, would have been deemed, in times of more regular liberty, a great stretch of illegal and arbitrary power. It consisted of commissioners, who were empowered to enquire into disorders and crimes of all kinds, and to inflict the proper punishments upon them. The officers, charged

with

CHAP. XIII.

1275.

with this unusual commission, made their circuits throughout the counties of England most infested with this evil, and carried terror into all those parts of the kingdom. In their zeal to punish crimes, they did not sufficiently distinguish between the innocent and guilty; the smallest suspicion became a ground of accusation and trial; the slightest evidence was received against criminals; prisons were crowded with malefactors, real or pretended; severe fines were levied for small offences; and the king, though his exhausted exchequer was supplied by this expedient, found it necessary to stop the course of so great rigour, and after terrifying and dissipating, by this tribunal, the gangs of disorderly people in England, he prudently annulled the commission[l]; and never afterwards renewed it.

AMONG the various disorders to which the kingdom was subject, no one was more universally complained of than the adulteration of the coin; and as this crime required more art than the English of that age, who chiefly employed force and violence in their iniquities, were possessed of, the imputation fell upon the Jews[m]. Edward also seems to have indulged a strong prepossession against that nation; and this ill-judged zeal for Christianity being naturally augmented by an expedition to the Holy Land, he let loose the whole rigour of his justice against that unhappy people. Two hundred and eighty of them were hanged at once for this crime in London alone, besides those who suffered in other parts of the kingdom[n]. The houses and lands (for the Jews had of late ventured to make purchases of that kind), as well as the goods of great multitudes, were sold and confiscated: And the

[l] Spelman's Gloss. in verbo *Trailbaston*. But Spelman was either mistaken in placing this commission in the 6th year of the king, or it was renewed in 1305. See Rymer, vol. ii. p. 960. Trivet, p. 338. M. West. p. 452. [m] Walsing. p. 48. Heming. vol. I. p. 6.
[n] T. Wykes, p. 107.

king,

EDWARD I.

king, lest it should be suspected that the riches of the sufferers were the chief part of their guilt, ordered a moiety of the money, raised by these confiscations, to be set apart, and bestowed upon such as were willing to be converted to Christianity. But resentment was more prevalent with them, than any temptation from their poverty; and very few of them could be induced by interest to embrace the religion of their persecutors. The miseries of this people did not here terminate. Though the arbitrary talliages and exactions, levied upon them, had yielded a constant and considerable revenue to the crown; Edward, prompted by his zeal and his rapacity, resolved some time after* to purge the kingdom entirely of that hated race, and to seize to himself at once their whole property as the reward of his labour^p. He left them only money sufficient to bear their charges into foreign countries, where new persecutions and extortions awaited them: But the inhabitants of the cinque-ports, imitating the bigotry and avidity of their sovereign, despoiled most of them of this small pittance, and even threw many of them into the sea: A crime for which the king, who was determined to be the sole plunderer in his dominions, inflicted a capital punishment upon them. No less than fifteen thousand Jews were at this time robbed of their effects and banished the kingdom: Very few of that nation have since lived in England: And as it is impossible for a nation to subsist without lenders of money, and none will lend without a compensation, the practice of usury, as it was then called, was thenceforth exercised by the English themselves upon their fellow-citizens, or by Lombards and other foreigners. It is very much to be questioned, whether the dealings of these new usurers were equally open and unexceptionable with those of the

CHAP. XIII.

1275.

* In the year 1290.   p Walsing. p. 54. Heming. vol. I. p. 20. Tyrrel, p. 166.

old. By a law of Richard, it was enacted, that three copies should be made of every bond given to a Jew; one to be put into the hands of a public magistrate, another into those of a man of credit, and a third to remain with the Jew himself [q]. But as the canon law, seconded by the municipal, permitted no Christian to take interest, all transactions of this kind must, after the banishment of the Jews, have become more secret and clandestine; and the lender, of consequence, be paid both for the use of his money, and for the infamy and danger which he incurred by lending it.

THE great poverty of the crown, though no excuse, was probably the cause of this egregious tyranny exercised against the Jews; but Edward also practised other more honourable means of remedying that evil. He employed a strict frugality in the management and distribution of his revenue: He engaged the parliament to vote him a fifteenth of all moveables; the pope to grant him the tenth of all ecclesiastical revenues for three years; and the merchants to consent to a perpetual imposition of half a mark on every sack of wool exported, and a mark on three hundred skins. He also issued commissions to enquire into all encroachments on the royal demesne; into the value of escheats, forfeitures, and wardships; and into the means of repairing or improving every branch of the revenue [r]. The commissioners in the execution of their office, began to carry matters too far against the nobility, and to question titles to estates which had been transmitted from father to son for several generations. Earl Warrenne, who had done such eminent service in the late reign, being required to show his titles, drew his sword; and subjoined, that William, the Bastard, had not conquered the kingdom for himself alone: His ancestor was a joint adventurer in the enterprize; and he himself was

q Trivet, p. 128.   r Ann. Waverl. p. 235.

determined

EDWARD I.

determined to maintain what had from that period remained unquestioned in his family. The king, sensible of the danger, desisted from making farther enquiries of this nature.

But the active spirit of Edward could not long remain without employment. He soon after undertook an enterprize more prudent for himself, and more advantageous to his people. Lewellyn, prince of Wales, had been deeply engaged with the Mountfort faction; had entered into all their conspiracies against the crown; had frequently fought on their side; and till the battle of Evesham, so fatal to that party, had employed every expedient to depress the royal cause, and to promote the success of the barons. In the general accommodation, made with the vanquished, Lewellyn had also obtained his pardon; but as he was the most powerful, and therefore the most obnoxious vassal of the crown, he had reason to entertain anxiety about his situation, and to dread the future effects of resentment and jealousy in the English monarch. For this reason, he determined to provide for his security by maintaining a secret correspondence with his former associates; and he even made his addresses to a daughter of the earl of Leicester, who was sent to him from beyond sea, but being intercepted in her passage near the isles of Scilly, was detained in the court of England[a]. This incident increasing the mutual jealousy between Edward and Lewellyn, the latter, when required to come to England, and do homage to the new king, scrupled to put himself in the hands of an enemy, desired a safe-conduct from Edward, insisted upon having the king's son and other noblemen delivered to him as hostages, and demanded, that his consort should previously be set at liberty.

CHAP. XIII.

1275.

1276. Conquest of Wales.

[a] Walsing. p. 46, 47. Heming. vol. I. p. 5. Trivet, p. 248.

CHAP. XIII.

1276.

1277.

liberty¹. The king, having now brought the state to a full settlement, was not displeased with this occasion of exercising his authority, and subduing entirely the principality of Wales. He refused all Lewellyn's demands, except that of a safe-conduct; sent him repeated summons to perform the duty of a vassal; levied an army to reduce him to obedience; obtained a new aid of a fifteenth from parliament; and marched out with certain assurance of success against the enemy. Besides the great disproportion of force between the kingdom and the principality, the circumstances of the two states were entirely reversed; and the same intestine dissentions, which had formerly weakened England, now prevailed in Wales, and had even taken place in the reigning family. David and Roderic, brothers to Lewellyn, dispossessed of their inheritance by that prince, had been obliged to have recourse to the protection of Edward, and they seconded with all their interest, which was extensive, his attempts to enslave their native country. The Welsh prince had no resource but in the inaccessible situation of his mountains, which had hitherto, through many ages, defended his forefathers against all attempts of the Saxon and Norman conquerors; and he retired among the hills of Snowdun, resolved to defend himself to the last extremity. But Edward, equally vigorous and cautious, entering by the north with a formidable army, pierced into the heart of the country; and having carefully explored every road before him, and secured every pass behind him, approached the Welsh army in its last retreat. He here avoided the putting to trial the valour of a nation, proud of its ancient independence, and inflamed with animosity against its hereditary enemies; and he trusted to the slow, but sure effects of famine, for reducing that people to subjection. The rude and simple manners of the natives,

¹ Rymer, vol. ii. p. 63. Walsing. p. 46. Trivet, p. 247.

EDWARD I.

as well as the mountainous situation of their country, had made them entirely neglect tillage, and trust to pasturage alone for their subsistence: A method of life which had hitherto secured them against the irregular attempts of the English, but exposed them to certain ruin, when the conquest of the country was steddily pursued, and prudently planned by Edward. Destitute of magazines, cooped up in a narrow corner, they, as well as their cattle, suffered all the rigors of famine; and Lewellyn, without being able to strike a stroke for his independence, was at last obliged to submit at discretion, and receive the terms imposed upon him by the victor [u]. He bound himself to pay to Edward 50,000 pounds, as a reparation of damages; to do homage to the crown of England; to permit all the other barons of Wales, except four near Snowdun, to swear fealty to the same crown; to relinquish the country between Cheshire and the river Conway; to settle on his brother Roderic a thousand marks a year, and on David five hundred; and to deliver ten hostages as security for his future submission [w].

CHAP. XIII.
1277.
19th Nov.

EDWARD, on the performance of the other articles, remitted to the prince of Wales the payment of the 50,000 pounds [x], which were stipulated by treaty, and which, it is probable, the poverty of the country made it absolutely impossible for him to levy. But notwithstanding this indulgence, complaints of iniquities soon arose on the side of the vanquished: The English, insolent on their easy and bloodless victory, oppressed the inhabitants of the districts which were yielded to them: The lords marchers committed with impunity all kinds of violence on their Welsh neighbours: New and more severe terms were imposed on Lewellyn himself; and Edward, when the prince attended him at Worcester, exacted a promise that he would retain

[u] T. Wykes, p. 105.   [w] Rymer, vol. II. p. 88. Walsing. p. 7. Trivet, p. 251. T. Wykes, p. 106.   [x] Rymer, p. 92.

CHAP. XIII.
1277.

no perſon in his principality who ſhould be obnoxious to the Engliſh monarch[y]. There were other perſonal inſults which raiſed the indignation of the Welſh, and made them determine rather to encounter a force, which they had already experienced to be ſo much ſuperior, than to bear oppreſſion from the haughty victors. Prince David, ſeized with the national ſpirit, made peace with his brother, and promiſed to concur in the defence of public liberty. The Welſh flew to arms; and Edward, not diſpleaſed with the occaſion of making his conqueſt final and abſolute, aſſembled all his military tenants, and advanced into Wales with an army, which the inhabitants could not reaſonably hope to reſiſt. The ſituation of the country gave the Welſh at firſt ſome advantage over Luke de Tany, one of Edward's captains, who had paſſed the Menau with a detachment[z]: But Lewellyn, being ſurprized by Mortimer, was defeated and ſlain in an action, and 2000 of his followers were put to the ſword[a]. David, who ſucceeded him in the principality, could never collect an army ſufficient to face the Engliſh; and being chaced from hill to hill, and hunted from one retreat to another, was obliged to conceal himſelf under various diſguiſes, and was at laſt betrayed in his lurking-place to the enemy. Edward ſent him in chains to Shrewſbury; and bringing him to a formal trial before all the peers of England, ordered this ſovereign prince to be hanged, drawn, and quartered, as a traitor, for defending by arms the liberties of his native country, together with his own hereditary authority[b]. All the Welſh nobility ſubmitted to the conqueror; the laws of England, with the ſheriffs and other miniſters of juſtice, were

[y] Dr. Powell's Hiſt. of Wales, p. 344, 345. [z] Walſing. p. 50. Heming. vol. 1. p. 9. Trivet, p. 238. T. Wykes, p. 110.
[a] Heming. vol. i. p. 11. Trivet, p. 257. Ann. Waverl. p. 235.
[b] Heming. vol. I. p. 12. Trivet, p. 259. Ann. Waverl. p. 238. T. Wykes, p. 111. M. Weſt. p. 411.

eſtabliſhed

EDWARD I.

established in that principality; and though it was long before national antipathies were extinguished, and a thorough union attained between the people; yet this important conquest, which it had required eight hundred years fully to effect, was, at last, through the abilities of Edward, completed by the English.

CHAP. XIII.

1283.

THE king, sensible that nothing kept alive the ideas of military valour and of ancient glory, so much as the traditional poetry of the people, which, assisted by the power of music, and the jollity of festivals, made deep impression on the minds of the youth, gathered together all the Welsh bards, and, from a barbarous, though not absurd policy, ordered them to be put to death[c].

1284.

THERE prevails a vulgar story, which, as it well suits the capacity of the monkish writers, is carefully recorded by them: That Edward, assembling the Welsh, promised to give them a prince of unexceptionable manners, a Welshman by birth, and one who could speak no other language. On their acclamations of joy, and promise of obedience, he invested in the principality his second son Edward, then an infant, who had been born at Carnarvon. The death of his eldest son Alfonso, soon after, made young Edward heir of the monarchy: The principality of Wales was fully annexed to the crown; and henceforth gives a title to the eldest son of the kings of England.

THE settlement of Wales appeared so complete to Edward, that, in less than two years after, he went abroad, in order to make peace between Alphonso, king of Arragon, and Philip the Fair; who had lately succeeded his father Philip the Hardy on the throne of France[d]. The difference between these two princes had arisen about the

1286.

[c] Sir J. Wynne, p. 15.   [d] Rymer, vol. ii. p. 149, 152, 174.

CHAP.
XIII.

1286.

kingdom of Sicily, which the pope, after his hopes from England failed him, had bestowed on Charles, brother to St. Lewis, and which was claimed upon other titles, by Peter king of Arragon, father to Alphonso. Edward had powers from both princes to settle the terms of peace, and he succeeded in his endeavours; but as the controversy nowise regards England, we shall not enter into a detail of it. He stayed abroad above three years; and on his return, found many disorders to have prevailed, both from open violence, and from the corruption of justice.

THOMAS CHAMBERLAIN, a gentleman of some note, had assembled several of his associates at Boston, in Lincolnshire, under pretence of holding a tournament, an exercise practised by the gentry only; but in reality with a view of plundering the rich fair of Boston, and robbing the merchants. To facilitate his purpose, he privately set fire to the town; and while the inhabitants were employed in quenching the flames, the conspirators broke into the booths, and carried off the goods. Chamberlain himself was detected and hanged; but maintained so steddily the point of honour to his accomplices, that he could not be prevailed on, by offers or promises, to discover any of them. Many other instances of robbery and violence broke out in all parts of England; though the singular circumstances attending this conspiracy have made it alone be particularly recorded by historians [*].

1289.

BUT the corruption of the judges, by which the fountains of justice were poisoned, seemed of still more dangerous consequence. Edward, in order to remedy this prevailing abuse, summoned a parliament, and brought the judges to a trial; where all of them, except two, who were clergymen, were convicted of this flagrant iniquity, were fined, and deposed. The amount of the

[*] Heming. vol. I. p. 16, 17.

fines,

fives, levied upon them, is alone a sufficient proof of their guilt; being above one hundred thousand marks, an immense sum in those days, and sufficient to defray the charges of an expensive war between two great kingdoms. The king afterwards made all the new judges swear, that they would take no bribes; but his expedient, of deposing and fining the old ones, was the more effectual remedy.

WE now come to give an account of the state of affairs in Scotland, which gave rise to the most interesting transactions of this reign, and of some of the subsequent; though the intercourse of that kingdom with England, either in peace or war, had hitherto produced so few events of moment, that, to avoid tediousness, we have omitted many of them, and have been very concise in relating the rest. If the Scots had, before this period, any real history, worthy of the name, except what they glean from scattered passages in the English historians, those events, 'however minute, yet, being the only foreign transactions of the nation, might deserve a place in it.

THOUGH the government of Scotland had been continually exposed to those factions and convulsions which are incident to all barbarous, and to many civilized nations; and though the successions of their kings, the only part of their history which deserves any credit, had often been disordered by irregularities and usurpations, the true heir of the royal family had still in the end prevailed, and Alexander III. who had espoused the sister of Edward, probably inherited, after a period of about eight hundred years, and through a succession of males, the sceptre of all the Scottish princes, who had governed the nation since its first establishment in the island. This prince died, in 1286, by a fall from his horse at Kinghorn^f, without leaving any male issue, and without any descend-

^f Heming. vol. i. p. 29. Triver, p. 267.

ant, except Margaret, born of Eric, king of Norway, and of Margaret, daughter of the Scottish monarch. This princeis, commonly called the maid of Norway, though a female, and an infant, and a foreigner, yet being the lawful heir of the kingdom, had, through her grandfather's care, been recognized succeffor by the states of Scotland*; and on Alexander's death, the difpofitions which had been previoufly made againft that event, appeared fo juft and prudent, that no diforders, as might naturally be apprehended, enfued in the kingdom. Margaret was acknowledged queen of Scotland; five guardians, the bishops of St. Andrews and Glafgow, the earls of File and Buchan, and James, fteward of Scotland, entered peaceably upon the adminiftration; and the infant princess, under the protection of Edward, her great uncle, and Eric, her father, who exerted themfelves on this occafion, feemed firmly feated on the throne of Scotland. The Englifh monarch was naturally led to build mighty projects on this incident; and having lately, by force of arms, brought Wales under fubjection, he attempted, by the marriage of Margaret with his eldeft fon Edward, to unite the whole island into one monarchy, and thereby to give it fecurity both againft domeftic convulfions and foreign invafions. The amity which had of late prevailed between the two nations, and which, even in former times, had never been interrupted by any violent wars or injuries, facilitated extremely the execution of this project, fo favourable to the happinefs and grandeur of both kingdoms; and the ftates of Scotland readily gave their affent to the Englifh propofals, and even agreed, that their young fovereign fhould be educated in the court of Edward. Anxious, however, for the liberty and independency of their country, they took care to ftipulate very equitable conditions, ere they

* Rymer, vol. II. p. 266.

entrufted

entrusted themselves into the hands of so great and so ambitious a monarch. It was agreed, that they should enjoy all their ancient laws, liberties, and customs; that in case young Edward and Margaret should die without issue, the crown of Scotland should revert to the next heir, and should be inherited by him free and independent; that the military tenants of the crown should never be obliged to go out of Scotland, in order to do homage to the sovereign of the united kingdoms, nor the chapters of cathedral, collegiate, or conventual churches, in order to make elections; that the parliaments, summoned for Scottish affairs, should always be held within the bounds of that kingdom; and that Edward should bind himself, under the penalty of 100,000 marks, payable to the pope for the use of the holy wars, to observe all these articles [b]. It is not easy to conceive, that two nations could have treated more on a foot of equality than Scotland and England maintained during the whole course of this transaction: And though Edward gave his assent to the article concerning the future independency of the Scottish crown, with a *saving of his former rights*; this reserve gave no alarm to the nobility of Scotland, both because these rights, having hitherto been little heard of, had occasioned no disturbance, and because the Scots had so near a prospect of seeing them entirely absorbed in the rights of their sovereignty.

But this project, so happily formed and so amicably conducted, failed of success, by the sudden death of the Norvegian princess, who expired on her passage to Scotland [i], and left a very dismal prospect to the kingdom. Though disorders were for the present obviated by the authority of the regency formerly established, the suc-

[b] Rymer, vol. II. p. 482. [i] Heming. vol. I. p. 30. Tirrel, p. 268.

cession

cession itself of the crown was now become an object of dispute; and the regents could not expect, that a controversy, which is not usually decided by reason and argument alone, would be peaceably settled by them, or even by the states of the kingdom, amidst so many powerful pretenders. The posterity of William, king of Scotland, the prince taken prisoner by Henry II. being all extinct by the death of Margaret of Norway; the right to the crown devolved on the issue of David, earl of Huntingdon, brother to William, whose male line being also extinct, left the succession open to the posterity of his daughters. The earl of Huntingdon had three daughters; Margaret, married to Alan lord of Galloway, Isabella, wife of Robert Brus or Bruce, lord of Annandale, and Adama, who espoused Henry lord Hastings. Margaret, the eldest of the sisters, left one daughter, Devergilda, married to John Baliol, by whom she had a son of the same name, one of the present competitors for the crown: Isabella, the second, bore a son, Robert Bruce, who was now alive, and who also insisted on his claim: Adama, the third, left a son, John Hastings, who pretended that the kingdom of Scotland, like many other inheritances, was divisible among the three daughters of the earl of Huntingdon, and that he, in right of his mother, had a title to a third of it. Baliol and Bruce united against Hastings, in maintaining that the kingdom was indivisible; but each of them, supported by plausible reasons, asserted the preference of his own title. Baliol was sprung from the elder branch: Bruce was one degree nearer the common stock: If the principle of representation was regarded, the former had the better claim; If propinquity was considered, the latter was entitled to the preference [b]: The sentiments of men were divided: All the nobility had taken part on one side or the other:

[b] Heming. vol. I. p. 56.

EDWARD I.

The people followed implicitly their leaders: The two claimants themselves had great power and numerous retainers in Scotland: And it is no wonder that, among a rude people, more accustomed to arms than enured to laws, a controversy of this nature, which could not be decided by any former precedent among them, and which is capable of exciting commotions in the most legal and best established governments, should threaten the state with the most fatal convulsions.

EACH century has its peculiar mode in conducting business; and men, guided more by custom than by reason, follow, without enquiry, the manners, which are prevalent in their own time. The practice of that age, in controversies between states and princes, seems to have been to chuse a foreign prince, as an equal arbiter, by whom the question was decided, and whose sentence prevented those dismal confusions and disorders, inseparable at all times from war, but which were multiplied a hundred fold, and dispersed into every corner, by the nature of the feudal governments. It was thus that the English king and barons, in the preceding reign, had endeavoured to compose their dissentions by a reference to the king of France; and the celebrated integrity of that monarch had prevented all the bad effects, which might naturally have been dreaded from so perilous an expedient. It was thus that the kings of France and Arragon, and afterwards other princes, had submitted their controversies to Edward's judgment; and the remoteness of their states, the great power of the princes, and the little interest which he had on either side, had induced him to acquit himself with honour in his decisions. The parliament of Scotland, therefore, threatened with a furious civil war, and allured by the great reputation of the English monarch, as well as by the present amiable correspondence between the kingdoms, agreed in making a

reference

CHAP.
XIII.

1291.
Reference
to Edward.

reference to Edward; and Frafer, bifhop of St. Andrews, with other deputies, was fent to notify to him their refolution, and to claim his good offices in the prefent dangers to which they were expofed[1]. His inclination, they flattered themfelves, led him to prevent their diffentions, and to interpofe with a power, which none of the competitors would dare to withftand: When this expedient was propofed by one party, the other deemed it dangerous to object to it: Indifferent perfons thought that the imminent perils of a civil war would thereby be prevented: And no one reflected on the ambitious character of Edward, and the almoft certain ruin which muft attend a fmall ftate, divided by faction, when it thus implicitly fubmits itfelf to the will of fo powerful and encroaching a neighbour.

Homage of
Scotland.

THE temptation was too ftrong for the virtue of the Englifh monarch to refift. He purpofed to lay hold of the prefent favourable opportunity, and if not to create, at leaft to revive, his claim of a feudal fuperiority over Scotland; a claim which had hitherto lain in the deepeft obfcurity, and which, if ever it had been an object of attention, or had been fo much as fufpected, would have effectually prevented the Scottifh barons from chufing him for an umpire. He well knew, that, if this pretenfion were once fubmitted to, as it feemed difficult, in the prefent fituation of Scotland, to oppofe it, the abfolute fovereignty of that kingdom (which had been the cafe with Wales) would foon follow; and that one great vaffal, cooped up in an ifland with his liege lord, without refource from foreign powers, without aid from any fellow vaffals, could not long maintain his dominions againft the efforts of a mighty kingdom, affifted by all the cavils which the feudal law afforded his fuperior againft him. In purfuit of this great object, very advan-

[1] Heming. vol. i. p. 32.

tageous

tageous to England, perhaps in the end no less beneficial to Scotland, but extremely unjust and iniquitous in itself, Edward busied himself in searching for proofs of his pretended superiority; and instead of looking into his own archives, which, if his claim had been real, must have afforded him numerous records of the homages done by the Scottish princes, and could alone yield him any authentic testimony, he made all the monasteries be ransacked for old chronicles and histories written by Englishmen, and he collected all the passages which seemed anywise to favour his pretensions [m]. Yet even in this method of proceeding, which must have discovered to himself the injustice of his claim, he was far from being fortunate. He began his proofs from the time of Edward the elder, and continued them through all the subsequent Saxon and Norman times; but produced nothing to his purpose [n]. The whole amount of his authorities during the Saxon period, when stripped of the bombast and inaccurate style of the monkish historians, is, that the Scots had sometimes been defeated by the English, had received peace on disadvantageous terms, had made submissions to the English monarch, and had even perhaps fallen into some dependance on a power, which was so much superior, and which they had not at that time sufficient force to resist. His authorities from the Norman period were, if possible, still less conclusive: The historians indeed make frequent mention of homage done by the northern potentate; but no one of them says that it was done for his kingdom; and several of them declare, in express terms, that it was relative only to the fiefs which he enjoyed south of the Tweed [o]; in the same manner, as the king of England himself swore fealty to the French monarch, for the fiefs which he inherited in France. And to such

[m] Walsing. p. 35. [n] Rymer, vol. ii. p. 559. [o] Hoveden, p. 492. 662. M. Paris. p. 109. M. West. p. 356.

scandalous

scandalous shifts was Edward reduced, that he quotes a passage from Hoveden [p], where it is asserted, that a Scottish king had done homage to England; but he purposely omits the latter part of the sentence, which expresses that this prince did homage for the lands which he held in England.

When William, king of Scotland, was taken prisoner in the battle of Alnwic, he was obliged, for the recovery of his liberty, to swear fealty to the victor for his crown itself. The deed was performed according to all the rites of the feudal law: The record was preserved in the English archives, and is mentioned by all the historians: But as it is the only one of the kind, and as historians speak of this superiority as a great acquisition gained by the fortunate arms of Henry II. [q], there can remain no doubt, that the kingdom of Scotland was, in all former periods, entirely free and independent. Its subjection continued a very few years: King Richard desirous, before his departure for the Holy Land, to conciliate the friendship of William, renounced that homage, which, he says in express terms, had been extorted by his father; and he only retained the usual homage which had been done by the Scottish princes for the lands which they held in England.

But though this transaction rendered the independence of Scotland still more unquestionable, than if no fealty had ever been sworn to the English crown; the Scottish kings, apprized of the point aimed at by their powerful neighbours, seem for a long time to have retained some jealousy on that head, and in doing homage, to have anxiously obviated all such pretensions. When William in 1200 did homage to John at Lincoln, he was careful to insert a salvo for his royal dignity [r]: When Alexander III. sent assistance to his father-in-law, Henry III. during

[p] P. 662. [q] Neubr. lib. ii. cap. 4. Knyghton, p. 2394.
[r] Hoveden, p. 811.

the wars of the barons, he previously procured an acknowledgment, that this aid was granted only from friendship, not from any right claimed by the English monarch [s]: And when the same prince was invited to assist at the coronation of this very Edward, he declined attendance, till he received a like acknowledgment [t].

But as all these reasons (and stronger could not be produced) were but a feeble rampart against the power of the sword, Edward, carrying with him a great army, which was to enforce his proofs, advanced to the frontiers, and invited the Scottish parliament, and all the competitors, to attend him in the castle of Norham, a place situated on the southern banks of the Tweed, in order to determine that cause, which had been referred to his arbitration. But though this deference seemed due to so great a monarch, and was no more than what his father and the English barons had, in similar circumstances, paid to Lewis IX., the king, careful not to give umbrage, and determined never to produce his claim, till it should be too late to think of opposition, sent the Scottish barons an acknowledgment, that, though at that time they passed the frontiers, this step should never be drawn into precedent, or afford the English kings a pretence for exacting a like submission in any future transaction [v]. When the whole Scottish nation had thus unwarily put themselves in his power, Edward opened the conferences at Norham: He informed the parliament, by the mouth of Roger le Brabancon, his chief justiciary, that he was come thither to determine the right among the competitors to their crown; that he was determined to do strict justice to all parties; and that he was intitled to this authority, not in virtue of the reference made to him, but in quality of superior and liege lord of the kingdom [w].

[s] Rymer, vol. II. p. 844. [t] See note [B] at the end of the volume.
[u] Rymer, vol. II. p. 539. 845. Walsing. p. 56. [w] Rymer, vol. II. p. 543. See note [C] at the end of the volume.

He

He then produced his proofs of this superiority, which he pretended to be unquestionable, and he required of them an acknowledgment of it; a demand, which was superfluous if the fact were already known and avowed, and which plainly betrays Edward's consciousness of his lame and defective title. The Scottish parliament was astonished at so new a pretension, and answered only by their silence. But the king, in order to maintain the appearance of free and regular proceedings, desired them to remove into their own country, to deliberate upon his claim, to examine his proofs, to propose all their objections, and to inform him of their resolution: And he appointed a plain at Up-settleton, on the northern banks of the Tweed, for that purpose.

WHEN the Scottish barons assembled in this place, though moved with indignation at the injustice of this unexpected claim, and at the fraud with which it had been conducted, they found themselves betrayed into a situation, in which it was impossible for them to make any defence for the ancient liberty and independence of their country. The king of England, a martial and politic prince, at the head of a powerful army, lay at a very small distance, and was only separated from them by a river fordable in many places. Though by a sudden flight some of them might themselves be able to make their escape; what hopes could they entertain of securing the kingdom against his future enterprizes? Without a head, without union among themselves, attached all of them to different competitors, whose title they had rashly submitted to the decision of this foreign usurper, and who were thereby reduced to an absolute dependence upon him; they could only expect, by resistance, to entail on themselves and their posterity a more grievous and more destructive servitude. Yet even, in this desperate state of their affairs, the Scottish barons, as we learn from Walsingham,

EDWARD I.

CHAP.
XIII.

1291.

fingham [w], one of the beft hiftorians of that period, had the courage to reply, that, till they had a king, they could take no refolution on fo momentous a point: The journal of king Edward fays, that they made no anfwer at all.[x]: That is, perhaps, no *particular* anfwer or objection to Edward's claim: And by this folution it is poffible to reconcile the journal with the hiftorian. The king, therefore, interpreting their filence as confent, addreffed himfelf to the feveral competitors, and previoufly to his pronouncing fentence, required their acknowledgment of his fuperiority.

It is evident from the genealogy of the royal family of Scotland, that there could only be two queftions about the fucceffion, that between Baliol and Bruce on the one hand, and lord Haftings on the other, concerning the partition of the crown; and that between Baliol and Bruce themfelves, concerning the preference of their refpective titles, fuppofing the kingdom indivifible: Yet there appeared on this occafion no lefs than nine claimants befides; John Comyn or Cummin lord of Badenoch, Florence earl of Holland, Patric Dunbar earl of March, William de Vefcey, Robert de Pynkeni, Nicholas de Soules, Patric Galythly, Roger de Maudeville, Robert de Rofs; not to mention the king of Norway, who claimed as heir to his daughter Margaret [y]... Some of thefe competitors were defcended from more remote branches of the royal family; others were even fprung from illegitimate children; and as none of them had the leaft pretence of right, it is natural to conjecture, that Edward had fecretly encouraged them to appear in the lift of claimants, that he might fow the more divifion among the Scottifh nobility, make

[w] Page 58. M. Weft. p. 436. It is faid by Hemingford, vol. i. p. 31. that the king menaced violently the Scotch barons, and forced them to compliance, 'at laft' to filence. [x] Rymer, vol. ii. p. 558.
[y] Walfing. p. 58.

the

the cause appear the more intricate, and be able to chuse, among a great number, the most obsequious candidate.

But he found them all equally obsequious on this occasion [a]. Robert Bruce was the first that acknowledged Edward's right of superiority over Scotland; and he had so far foreseen the king's pretensions, that even in his petition, where he set forth his claim to the crown, he had previously applied to him as liege lord of the kingdom; a step which was not taken by any of the other competitors [a]. They all, however, with seeming willingness, made a like acknowledgment when required; though Baliol, lest he should give offence to the Scottish nation, had taken care to be absent during the first days; and he was the last that recognized the king's title [b]. Edward next deliberated concerning the method of proceeding in the discussion of this great controversy. He gave orders, that Baliol, and such of the competitors as adhered to him, should chuse forty commissioners; Bruce and his adherents forty more: To these the king added twenty-four Englishmen: He ordered these hundred and four commissioners to examine the cause deliberately among themselves, and make their report to him [c]: And he promised in the ensuing year to give his determination. Mean while, he pretended, that it was requisite to have all the fortresses of Scotland delivered into his hands, in order to enable him, without opposition, to put the true heir in possession of the crown; and this exorbitant demand was complied with, both by the states and by the claimants [d]. The governors also of all the castles immediately resigned their command; except Umfreville earl of Angus, who refused, without a formal and particular acquittal from the parliament and the several claimants,

[a] Rymer, vol. ii. p. 529. 545. Walsing. p. 55. Heming. vol. i. p. 33, 34. Trivet, p. 260. M. West. p. 413. [a] Rymer, vol. ii. p. 577, 578, 579. [b] Ibid. p. 546. [c] Ibid. p. 555, 556. [d] Ibid. p. 529. Walsing. p. 56, 57.

EDWARD I.

to surrender his fortresses to so domineering an arbiter, who had given to Scotland so many just reasons of suspicion[e]. Before this assembly broke up, which had fixed such a mark of dishonour on the nation, all the prelates and barons there present swore fealty to Edward; and that prince appointed commissioners to receive a like oath from all the other barons and persons of distinction in Scotland[f].

CHAP. XIII.
1291.

THE king having finally made, as he imagined, this important acquisition, left the commissioners to sit at Berwic, and examine the titles of the several competitors who claimed the precarious crown, which Edward was willing for some time to allow the lawful heir to enjoy. He went southwards, both in order to assist at the funeral of his mother, queen Eleanor, who died about this time, and to compose some differences which had arisen among his principal nobility. Gilbert earl of Glocester, the greatest baron of the kingdom, had espoused the king's daughter; and being elated by that alliance, and still more by his own power, which, he thought, set him above the laws, he permitted his bailiffs and vassals to commit violence on the lands of Humphrey Bohun earl of Hereford, who retaliated the injury by like violence. But this was not a reign in which such illegal proceedings could pass with impunity. Edward procured a sentence against the two earls, committed them both to prison, and would not restore them to their liberty till he exacted a fine of 1000 marks from Hereford, and one of 10,000 from his son-in-law.

DURING this interval, the titles of John Baliol and of Robert Bruce, whose claims appeared to be the best founded among the competitors for the crown of Scot-

1291.

[e] Rymer, vol. II. p. 531.   [f] Ibid. p. 573.

VOL. II.   S   land,

CHAP. XII.

1292.

Award of Edward in favour of Baliol.

1293.

land, were the subject of general disquisition, as well as of debate among the commissioners. Edward, in order to give greater authority to his intended decision, proposed this general question, both to the commissioners, and to all the celebrated lawyers in Europe; Whether a person descended from the elder sister, but farther removed by one degree, were preferable, in the succession of kingdoms, fiefs, and other indivisible inheritances, to one descended from the younger sister, but one degree nearer to the common stock? This was the true state of the case; and the principle of representation had now gained such ground every where, that a uniform answer was returned to the king in the affirmative. He therefore pronounced sentence in favour of Baliol; and when Bruce, upon this disappointment, joined afterwards lord Hastings, and claimed a third of the kingdom, which he now pretended to be divisible, Edward, though his interests seemed more to require the partition of Scotland, again pronounced sentence in favour of Baliol. That competitor, upon renewing his oath of fealty to England, was put in possession of the kingdom [f]; all his fortresses were restored to him [g]; and the conduct of Edward, both in the deliberate solemnity of the proceedings, and in the justice of the award, was so far unexceptionable.

HAD the king entertained no other view than that of establishing his superiority over Scotland, though the iniquity of that claim was apparent, and was aggravated by the most egregious breach of trust, he might have fixed his pretensions, and have left that important acquisition to his posterity: But he immediately proceeded in such a manner, as made it evident, that, not content with this usurpation, he aimed also at the absolute sovereignty and

[f] Rymer, vol. ii. p. 590, 591. 593, &c.   [g] Rymer, vol. ii. p. 590.

dominion

EDWARD I.

dominion of the kingdom. Instead of gradually enuring the Scots to the yoke, and exerting his rights of superiority with moderation, he encouraged all appeals to England; required king John himself, by six different summons on trivial occasions, to come to London[1]; refused him the privilege of defending his cause by a procurator; and obliged him to appear at the bar of his parliament as a private person[k]. These humiliating demands were hitherto quite unknown to a king of Scotland: They are, however, the necessary consequence of vassalage by the feudal law; and as there was no preceding instance of such treatment submitted to by a prince of that country, Edward must, from that circumstance alone, had there remained any doubt, have been himself convinced that his claim was altogether an usurpation[*]. But his intention plainly was, to enrage Baliol by these indignities, to engage him in rebellion, and to assume the dominion of the state, as the punishment of his treason and felony. Accordingly Baliol, though a prince of a soft and gentle spirit, returned into Scotland highly provoked at this usage, and determined at all hazards, to vindicate his liberty; and the war, which soon after broke out between France and England, gave him a favourable opportunity of executing his purpose.

THE violence, robberies, and disorders, to which that age was so subject, were not confined to the licentious barons and their retainers at land: The sea was equally infested with piracy: The feeble execution of the laws had given licence to all orders of men: And a general appetite for rapine and revenge, supported by a false point of honour, had also infected the merchants and mariners; and it pushed them, on any provocation, to seek redress by immediate retaliation upon the aggressors. A Norman

[1] Rymer, vol. ii. p. 603. 605, 606, 608, 615, 616. [k] Ryley's Placit. Parl. p. 152, 153. [*] See note [D] at the end of this volume.

CHAP. XIII.

1193.
War with
France.

and an English vessel met off the coast near Bayonne; and both of them having occasion for water, they sent their boats to land, and the several crews came at the same time to the same spring: There ensued a quarrel for the preference: A Norman, drawing his dagger, attempted to stab an Englishman; who, grappling with him, threw his adversary on the ground, and the Norman, as was pretended, falling on his own dagger, was slain[l]. This scuffle between two seamen about water, soon kindled a bloody war between the two nations, and involved a great part of Europe in the quarrel. The mariners of the Norman ship carried their complaints to the French king: Philip, without enquiring into the fact, without demanding redress, bade them take revenge, and trouble him no more about the matter[m]. The Normans, who had been more regular than usual in applying to the crown, needed but this hint to proceed to immediate violence. They seized an English ship in the channel; and hanging, along with some dogs, several of the crew on the yard-arm, in presence of their companions, dismissed the vessel[n]; and bade the mariners inform their countrymen, that vengeance was now taken for the blood of the Norman killed at Bayonne. This injury, accompanied with so general and deliberate an insult, was resented by the mariners of the cinque-ports, who, without carrying any complaint to the king, or waiting for redress, retaliated, by committing like barbarities on all French vessels without distinction. The French, provoked by their losses, preyed on the ships of all Edward's subjects, whether English or Gascon: The sea became a scene of piracy between the nations: The sovereigns, without either seconding or repressing the violence of their subjects, seemed to remain indifferent spectators: The English made pri-

[l] Walsing. p. 58. Hemingf. vol. i. p. 39.   [m] Walsing. p. 58.
[n] Heming. vol. i. p. 40. M. West. p. 419.

vate

vate associations with the Irish and Dutch seamen; the French with the Flemish and Genoese[*]: And the animosities of the people on both sides became every day more violent and barbarous. A fleet of two hundred Norman vessels set sail to the south for wine and other commodities; and in their passage seized all the English ships which they met with; hanged the seamen, and seized the goods. The inhabitants of the English sea-ports, informed of this incident, fitted out a fleet of sixty sail, stronger and better manned than the others, and awaited the enemy on their return. After an obstinate battle, they put them to rout, and sunk, destroyed, or took the greater part of them[p]. No quarter was given; and it is pretended that the loss of the French amounted to 15,000 men: Which is accounted for by this circumstance, that the Norman fleet was employed in transporting a considerable body of soldiers from the south.

The affair was now become too important to be any longer overlooked by the sovereigns. On Philip's sending an envoy to demand reparation and restitution, the king dispatched the bishop of London to the French court, in order to accommodate the quarrel. He first said, that the English courts of justice were open to all men; and if any Frenchman were injured, he might seek reparation by course of law[q]. He next offered to adjust the matter by private arbiters, or by a personal interview with the king of France, or by a reference either to the pope or the college of cardinals, or any particular cardinals agreed on by both parties[r]. The French, probably the more disgusted as they were hitherto losers in the quarrel, refused all these expedients: The vessels and the goods of merchants were confiscated on both sides: Depredations were continued by the Gascons on the western coast of

[*] Heming. vol. 1. p. 42. Chron. Dunst. vol. ii. p. 609.
[p] Walsing. p. 60. [q] Triv. p. 275. [r] Trivet, p. 274. Ibid.

HISTORY OF ENGLAND.

CHAP. XIII.

1293.

France, as well as by the English in the channel: Philip cited the king, as duke of Guienne, to appear in his court at Paris, and answer for these offences: And Edward, apprehensive of danger to that province, sent John St. John, an experienced soldier, to Bourdeaux, and gave him directions to put Guienne in a posture of defence [a].

1294.

THAT he might, however, prevent a final rupture between the nations, the king dispatched his brother, Edmond earl of Lancaster, to Paris; and as this prince had espoused the queen of Navarre, mother to Jane, queen of France, he seemed, on account of that alliance, the most proper person for finding expedients to accommodate the difference. Jane pretended to interpose with her good offices: Mary, the queen-dowager, feigned the same amicable disposition: And these two princesses told Edmond, that the circumstance the most difficult to adjust was the point of honour with Philip, who thought himself affronted by the injuries committed against him by his sub-vassals in Guienne: But if Edward would once consent to give him seizin and possession of that province, he would think his honour fully repaired, would engage to restore Guienne immediately, and would accept of a very easy satisfaction for all the other injuries. The king was consulted on the occasion; and as he then found himself in immediate danger of war with the Scots, which he regarded as the more important concern, this politic prince, blinded by his favourite passion for subduing that nation, allowed himself to be deceived by so gross an artifice [b]. He sent his brother orders to sign and execute the treaty with the two queens; Philip solemnly promised to execute his part of it; and the king's citation to appear in the court of France was accordingly recalled:

[a] Trivet, p. 276. Heming. vol. i. p. 42, 43. [b] Rymer, vol. II. p. 619, 620. Walsing. p. 61. Trivet, p. 277.

But

But the French monarch was no sooner put in possession of Guienne, than the citation was renewed; Edward was condemned for non-appearance; and Guienne, by a formal sentence, was declared to be forfeited and annexed to the crown [u].

EDWARD, fallen into a like snare with that which he himself had spread for the Scots, was enraged; and the more so, as he was justly ashamed of his own conduct, in being so egregiously over-reached by the court of France. Sensible of the extreme difficulties which he should encounter in the recovery of Gascony, where he had not retained a single place in his hands, he endeavoured to compensate that loss, by forming alliances with several princes, who, he projected, should attack France on all quarters, and make a diversion of her forces. Adolphus de Nassau, king of the Romans, entered into a treaty with him for that purpose [w]; as did also Amadæus, count of Savoy, the archbishop of Cologne, the counts of Gueldre and Luxembourg, the duke of Brabant and count of Barre, who had married his two daughters, Margaret and Eleanor: But these alliances were extremely burdensome to his narrow revenues, and proved in the issue entirely ineffectual. More impression was made on Guienne by an English army, which he completed by emptying the jails of many thousand thieves and robbers, who had been confined there for their crimes. So low had the profession of arms fallen, and so much had it degenerated from the estimation in which it stood during the vigour of the feudal system!

THE king himself was detained in England, first by contrary winds [x], then by his apprehensions of a Scottish invasion, and by a rebellion of the Welsh, whom he re-

[u] Rymer, vol. II. p. 610. 612. Walsing. p. 61. Trivet, p. 278.
[w] Heming. vol. I. p. 51. [x] Chron. Dunst. vol. II. p. 622.

pressed and brought again under subjection [y]. The army, which he sent to Guienne, was commanded by his nephew, John de Bretagne, earl of Richmond, and under him by St. John, Tibetot, de Vere, and other officers of reputation [z]; who made themselves masters of the town of Bayonne, as well as of Bourg, Blaye, Reole, St. Severe, and other places, which straitened Bourdeaux, and cut off its communication both by sea and land. The favour, which the Gascon nobility bore to the English government, facilitated these conquests, and seemed to promise still greater successes; but this advantage was soon lost by the misconduct of some of the officers. Philip's brother, Charles de Valois, who commanded the French armies, having laid siege to Podensac, a small fortress near Reole, obliged Giffard, the governor, to capitulate; and the articles, though favourable to the English, left all the Gascons prisoners at discretion, of whom about fifty were hanged by Charles as rebels: A policy, by which he both intimidated that people, and produced an irreparable breach between them and the English [a]. That prince immediately attacked Reole, where the earl of Richmond himself commanded; and as the place seemed not tenable, the English general drew his troops to the water side, with an intention of embarking with the greater part of the army. The enraged Gascons fell upon his rear, and at the same time opened their gates to the French, who, besides making themselves masters of the place, took many prisoners of distinction. St. Severe was more vigorously defended by Hugh de Vere, son of the earl of Oxford; but was at last obliged to capitulate. The French king, not content with these successes in Gascony, threatened England with an invasion;

[y] Walsing. p. 61. Heming. vol. I. p. 55. Trivet, p. 281. Chron.
Dunst. vol. II. p. 622.   [z] Tilet, p. 278.   [a] Heming.
vol. I. p. 49.

and

and, by a sudden attempt, his troops took and burnt Dover[b], but were obliged soon after to retire. And in order to make a greater diversion of the English force, and engage Edward in dangerous and important wars, he formed a secret alliance with John Baliol, king of Scotland; the commencement of that strict union, which, during so many centuries, was maintained by mutual interests and necessities, between the French and Scottish nations. John confirmed this alliance by stipulating a marriage between his eldest son and the daughter of Charles de Valois[c].

Digression concerning the constitution of parliament.

THE expences attending these multiplied wars of Edward, and his preparations for war, joined to alterations which had insensibly taken place in the general state of affairs, obliged him to have frequent recourse to parliamentary supplies, introduced the lower orders of the state into the public councils, and laid the foundations of great and important changes in the government.

THOUGH nothing could be worse calculated for cultivating the arts of peace, or maintaining peace itself, than the long subordination of vassalage from the king to the meanest gentleman, and the consequent slavery of the lower people, evils inseparable from the feudal system; that system was never able to fix the state in a proper warlike posture, or give it the full exertion of its power for defence, and still less for offence, against a public enemy. The military tenants, unacquainted with obedience, unexperienced in war, held a rank in the troops by their birth, not by their merits or services; composed a disorderly, and consequently a feeble army; and during the few days, which they were obliged by their tenures to remain in the field, were often more formidable to their own prince than to foreign powers, against whom they were assembled. The sovereigns came gradually to disuse

[b] Trivet, p. 284. Chron. Dunst. vol. II. p. 642. [c] Rymer, vol. II. p. 680, 631. 695. 697. Heming. vol. I. p. 76. Trivet, p. 285.

this

this cumberfome and dangerous machine, fo apt to recoil upon the hand which held it; and exchanging the military fervice for pecuniary fupplies, inlifted forces by means of a contract with particular officers (fuch as thofe the Italians denominate *Condottieri*), whom they difmiffed at the end of the war [d]. The barons and knights themfelves often entered into thefe engagements with the prince; and were enabled to fill their bands, both by the authority which they poffeffed over their vaffals and tenants, and from the great numbers of loofe, diforderly people, whom they found on their eftates, and who willingly embraced an opportunity of gratifying their appetite for war and rapine.

MEANWHILE, the old Gothic fabric, being neglected, went gradually to decay. Though the Conqueror had divided all the lands of England into fixty thoufand knights' fees, the number of thefe was infenfibly diminifhed by various artifices; and the king at laft found, that, by putting the law in execution, he could affemble a fmall part only of the ancient force of the kingdom. It was a ufual expedient for men, who held of the king or great barons by military tenure, to transfer their land to the church, and receive it back by another tenure, called frankalmoigne, by which they were not bound to perform any fervice [e]. A law was made againft this practice; but the abufe had probably gone far before it was attended to, and probably was not entirely corrected by the new ftatute, which, like moft laws of that age, we may conjecture to have been but feebly executed by the magiftrate againft the perpetual intereft of fo many individuals. The conftable and marefchal, when they muftered the armies, often, in a hurry, and for want of better information, received the fervice of a baron for fewer knights' fees than were due by him; and one precedent of this

[d] Cotton's Abr. p. 11. [e] Madox's Baronia Anglica, p. 114.

kind

kind was held good against the king, and became ever after a reason for diminishing the service [f]. The rolls of knights' fees were inaccurately kept; no care was taken to correct them before the armies were summoned into the field [g]; it was then too late to think of examining records and charters; and the service was accepted on the footing which the vassal himself was pleased to acknowledge, after all the various subdivisions and conjunctions of property had thrown an obscurity on the nature and extent of his tenure [h]. It is easy to judge of the intricacies which would attend disputes of this kind with individuals; when even the number of military fees, belonging to the church, whose property was fixed and unalienable, became the subject of controversy; and we find in particular, that, when the bishop of Durham was charged with seventy knights' fees for the aid levied on occasion of the marriage of Henry II.'s daughter to the duke of Saxony, the prelate acknowledged ten, and disowned the other sixty [i]. It is not known in what manner this difference was terminated; but had the question been concerning an armament to defend the kingdom, the bishop's service would probably have been received without opposition for ten fees; and this rate must also have fixed all his future payments. Pecuniary scutages, therefore, diminished as much as military services [k]: Other methods of filling the exchequer, as well as the armies, must be devised: New situations

[f] Madox's Baronia Anglica, p. 115.
[g] We hear only of one king, Henry II. who took this pains; and the record, called Liber niger Scaccarii, was the result of it.
[h] Madox, Bar. Ang. p. 116. [i] Ibid. p. 116. H. B. of Exch. p. 404.
[k] In order to pay the sum of 100,000 marks, at king Richard's ransom, twenty shillings were imposed on each knight's fee. Had the fees remained on the original footing, as settled by the Conqueror, this scutage would have amounted to 90,000 marks, which was nearly the sum required: But we find, that other grievous taxes were imposed to complete it: A certain proof, that many frauds and abuses had prevailed in the roll of knights' fees.

produced

produced new laws and inflitutions: And the great alterations in the finances and military power of the crown, as well as in private property, were the fource of equal innovations in every part of the legiflature or civil government.

The exorbitant eftates, conferred by the Norman on his barons and chieftains, remained not long entire and unimpaired. The landed property was gradually fhared out into more hands; and thofe immenfe baronies were divided, either by provifions to younger children, by partitions among co-heirs, by fale, or by efcheating to the king, who gratified a great number of his courtiers, by dealing them out among them in fmaller portions. Such moderate eftates, as they required œconomy, and confined the proprietors to live at home, were better calculated for duration; and the order of knights and fmall barons grew daily more numerous, and began to form a very refpectable rank or order in the ftate. As they were all immediate vaffals of the crown by military tenure, they were, by the principles of the feudal law, equally intitled with the greateft barons to a feat in the national or general councils; and this right, though regarded as a privilege, which the owners would not entirely relinquifh, was alfo confidered as a burthen, which they defired to be fubjected to on extraordinary occafions only. Hence it was provided in the charter of king John, that, while the great barons were fummoned to the national council by a particular writ, the fmall barons, under which appellation the knights were alfo comprehended, 'fhould only be called by a general fummons of the fheriff. The diftinction between great and fmall barons, like that between rich and poor, was not exactly defined; but, agreeably to the inaccuracy genius of that age, and to the fimplicity of ancient government, was left very much to be determined by the difcretion of the king and his minifters. It

EDWARD I.

was ufual for the prince to require, by a particular fummons, the attendance of a baron in one parliament, and to neglect him in future parliaments[1]; nor was this uncertainty ever complained of as an injury. He attended when required: He was better pleafed, on other occafions, to be exempted from the burthen: And as he was acknowledged to be of the fame order with the greateft barons, it gave them no furprize to fee him take his feat in the great council, whether he appeared of his own accord, or by a particular fummons from the king. The barons by *Writ*, therefore, began gradually to intermix themfelves with the barons by *Tenure*; and, as Camden tells us[m], from an ancient manufcript, now loft, that, after the battle of Evefham, a pofitive law was enacted, prohibiting every baron from appearing in parliament who was not invited thither by a particular fummons, the whole baronage of England held thenceforward their feat by writ, and this important privilege of their tenures was in effect abolifhed. Only, where writs had been regularly continued for fome time in one great family, the omiffion of them would have been regarded as an affront, and even as an injury.

A LIKE alteration gradually took place in the order of earls, who were the higheft rank of barons. The dignity of an earl, like that of a baron, was anciently territorial and official[n]: He exercifed jurifdiction within his county: He levied the third of the fines to his own profit: He was at once a civil and a military magiftrate: And though his authority, from the time of the Norman conqueft, was hereditary in England, the title was fo much connected with the office, that, where the king intended to create a new earl, he had no other expedient than to erect a certain territory into a county or earldom,

[1] Chancellor Weft's Enquiry into the Manner of creating Peers, p. 43, 46, 47, 55.   [m] In Britann. p. 122.   [n] Spelm. Gloff. in voce Comes.

CHAP. XIII.

1135.

and to bestow it upon the person and his family [a]. But as the sheriffs, who were the vicegerents of the earls, were named by the king, and removeable at pleasure, he found them more dependant upon him; and endeavoured to throw the whole authority and jurisdiction of the office into their hands. This magistrate was at the head of the finances, and levied all the king's rents within the county: He assessed at pleasure the talliages of the inhabitants in royal demesne: He had usually committed to him the management of wards, and often of escheats: He presided in the lower courts of judicature: And thus, though inferior to the earl in dignity, he was soon considered, by this union of the judicial and fiscal powers, and by the confidence reposed in him by the king, as much superior to him in authority, and undermined his influence within his own jurisdiction [b]. It became usual, in creating an earl, to give him a fixed salary, commonly about twenty pounds a year, in lieu of his third of the fines: The diminution of his power kept pace with the retrenchment of his profit: And the dignity of earl, instead of being territorial and official, dwindled into personal and titular. Such were the mighty alterations which already had fully taken place, or were gradually advancing, in the house of peers; that is, in the parliament: For there seems anciently to have been no other house.

BUT though the introduction of barons by writ, and of titular earls, had given some encrease to royal authority, there were other causes which counterbalanced those innovations, and tended, in a higher degree, to diminish the power of the sovereign. The disuse into which the feudal militia had in a great measure fallen,

[a] Essays on British Antiquities. This practice, however, seems to have been more familiar in Scotland, and the kingdoms on the continent, than in England.
[b] There are instances of princes of the blood who accepted of the office of sheriff. Spelman in voce Vicecomes.

made

made the barons almoſt entirely forget their dependance on the crown: By the diminution of the number of knights' fees, the king had no reaſonable compenſation when he levied ſcutages, and exchanged their ſervice for money: The alienations of the crown lands had reduced him to poverty: And, above all, the conceſſion of the Great Charter had ſet bounds to royal power, and had rendered it more difficult and dangerous for the prince to exert any extraordinary act of arbitrary authority. In this ſituation, it was natural for the king to court the friendſhip of the leſſer barons and knights, whoſe influence was no ways dangerous to him, and who, being expoſed to oppreſſion from their powerful neighbours, ſought a legal protection under the ſhadow of the throne. He deſired, therefore, to have their preſence in parliament, where they ſerved to controul the turbulent reſolutions of the great. To exact a regular attendance of the whole body would have produced confuſion, and would have impoſed too heavy a burden upon them. To ſummon only a few by writ, though is was practiſed, and had a good effect, ſerved not entirely the king's purpoſe; becauſe theſe members had no farther authority than attended their perſonal character, and were eclipſed by the appearance of the more powerful nobility. He therefore diſpenſed with the attendance of moſt of the leſſer barons in parliament; and in return for this indulgence (for ſuch it was then eſteemed), required them to chuſe in each county a certain number of their own body, whoſe charges they bore, and who, having gained the confidence, carried with them, of courſe, the authority of the whole order. This expedient had been practiſed at different times, in the reign of Henry III.ᵃ, and regularly during that of the preſent king. The numbers ſent up

ᵃ Rot. Clauſ. 38 Hen. III. m. 7. and 18 d. 1 As alſo Rot. Clauſ. 42 Hen. III. m. 1. 4. Prynne's Pref. to Cotten's Abridgment.

by each county varied at the will of the prince': They took their seat among the other peers; becaufe by their tenure they belonged to that order': The introducing of them into that houfe fcarcely appeared an innovation: And though it was eafily in the king's power, by varying their number, to command the refolutions of the whole parliament, this circumftance was little attended to in an age when force was more prevalent than laws, and when a refolution, though taken by the majority of a legal affembly, could not be executed if it oppofed the will of the more powerful minority.

But there were other important confequences which followed the diminution and confequent difufe of the ancient feudal militia. The king's expence in levying and maintaining a military force for every enterprize, was encreafed beyond what his narrow revenues were able to bear: As the fcutages of his military tenants, which were accepted in lieu of their perfonal fervice, had fallen to nothing, there were no means of fupply but from voluntary aids granted him by the parliament and clergy; or from the talliages which he might levy upon the towns and inhabitants in royal demefne. In the preceding year, Edward had been obliged to exact no lefs than the fixth of all moveables from the laity, and a moiety of all ecclefiaftical benefices' for his expedition into Poictou, and the fuppreffion of the Welfh: And this diftrefsful fituation, which was likely often to return upon him and his fucceffors, made him think of a new device, and fummon the reprefentatives of all the boroughs to parliament. This period, which is the twenty-third of his reign, feems to be the real and true epoch of the houfe of commons, and the faint dawn of popular government in England.

* Brady's Anfwer to Petit, from the records, p. 151.   * Brady's Treatife of Boroughs, App. N° 13.   * Ibid. p. 31. from the records. Heming. vol. i. p. 51. M. Weft. p. 412. Ryley, p. 462.

For

For the reprefentatives of the counties were only depu- CHAP. ties from the fmaller barons and leffer nobility: And the XIII. former precedent of reprefentatives from the boroughs, 1295. who were fummoned by the earl of Leicefter, was regarded as the act of a violent ufurpation, had been difcontinued in all the fubfequent parliaments, and if fuch a meafure had not become neceffary on other accounts, that precedent was more likely to blaft, than give credit to it.

DURING the courfe of feveral years, the kings of England, in imitation of other European princes, had embraced the falutary policy of encouraging and protecting the lower and more induftrious orders of the ftate; whom they found well difpofed to obey the laws and civil magiftrate, and whofe ingenuity and labour furnifhed commodities, requifite for the ornament of peace and fupport of war. Though the inhabitants of the country were ftill left at the difpofal of their imperious lords; many attempts were made to give more fecurity and liberty to citizens, and make them enjoy, unmolefted, the fruits of their induftry. Boroughs were erected by royal patent within the demefne lands: Liberty of trade was conferred upon them: The inhabitants were allowed to farm at a fixed rent their own tolls and cuftoms[u]: They were permitted to elect their own magiftrates: Juftice was adminiftered to them by thefe magiftrates, without obliging them to attend the fheriff or county court: And fome fhadow of independence, by means of thefe equitable privileges, was gradually acquired by the people[w]. The king, however, retained ftill the power of levying talliages or taxes upon them at pleafure[x]; and though their

[u] Madox, Firma Burgi, p. 21. [w] Brady of Boroughs, App. No. 1, 2, 3.
[x] The king had not only the power of talliating the inhabitants within his own demefnes, but that of granting to particular barons the power of talliating the inhabitants within theirs. See Brady's Anfwer to Petyt, p 118. Madox's Hift. of the Exchequer, p. 518.

VOL. II. T poverty,

274   HISTORY OF ENGLAND.

CHAP.   poverty, and the customs of the age, made these demands
XIII.   neither frequent nor exorbitant, such unlimited authority
1295.   in the sovereign was a sensible check upon commerce, and
was utterly incompatible with all the principles of a free
government. But when the multiplied necessities of the
crown produced a greater avidity for supply, the king,
whose prerogative entitled him to exact it, found that he
had not power sufficient to enforce his edicts, and that it
was necessary, before he imposed taxes, to smooth the way
for his demand, and to obtain the previous consent of
the boroughs, by solicitations, remonstrances, and authority. The inconvenience of transacting this business
with every particular borough was soon felt; and Edward
became sensible, that the most expeditious way of obtaining supply, was to assemble the deputies of all the boroughs, to lay before them the necessities of the state, to
discuss the matter in their presence, and to require their
consent to the demands of their sovereign. For this reason, he issued writs to the sheriffs, enjoining them to send
to parliament, along with two knights of the shire, two
deputies from each borough within their county [y], and
these provided with sufficient powers from their community, to consent, in their name, to what he and his
council should require of them. *As it is a most equitable
rule*, says he, in his preamble to this writ, *that what concerns all should be approved of by all; and common dangers
be repelled by united efforts* [z]; a noble principle, which
may seem to indicate a liberal mind in the king, and

[y] Writs were issued to about 120 cities and boroughs.

[z] Brady of Boroughs, p. 25. 33. from the records. The writs of the parliament, immediately preceding, remains; and the return of knights is there required, but not a word of the boroughs: A demonstration, that this was the very year in which they commenced. In the year immediately pre-ceding, the taxes were levied by a forming free consent of each particular bo-rough, beginning with London. Id. p. 31, 32, 33. from the records. Also b.s aofort to Petyt, p. 40, 41.

which

EDWARD I.

which laid the foundation of a free and an equitable government.

AFTER the election of these deputies, by the aldermen and common council, they gave sureties for their attendance before the king and parliament: Their charges were respectively borne by the borough which sent them: And they had so little idea of appearing as legislators, a character extremely wide of their low rank and condition [a], that no intelligence could be more disagreeable to any borough, than to find that they must elect, or to any individual than that he was elected to a trust from which no profit or honour could possibly be derived [b]. They composed not, properly speaking, any essential part of the parliament: They sat apart both from the barons and knights [c], who disdained to mix with such mean personages: After they had given their consent to the taxes required of them, their business being then finished, they separated, even though the parliament still continued to sit, and to canvass the national business [d]: And as they all consisted of men, who were real burgesses of the place from which they were sent, the sheriff, when he found no person of abilities or wealth sufficient for the office, often used the freedom of omitting particular boroughs in his returns; and as he received the thanks of the people for this indulgence, he gave no displeasure to the court, who levied on all the boroughs, without distinction, the tax agreed to by the majority of deputies [e].

THE

[a] Reliquiæ Spelm. p. 64. Prynne's Pref. to Cotton's Abridg. and the Abridg. passim. [b] Brady of Boroughs, p. 59. 60. [c] Ibid. p. 17, 38. from the records, and Append. p. 15. Also his Append. to his Anf. to Pety', Record. And his Gloss. in verb. *Communitas Regni.* p. 15.
[d] Ryley's Plccit. Parl. p. 241, 242, &c. Cotton's Abridg. p. 14.
[e] Brady of Boroughs, p. 50. from the records. There is even an instance in the reign of Edward III. when the king named all the deputies. Id. Anf. to Petyt, p. 161. If he fairly named the most considerable and creditable burgesses, little exception would be taken; as their business was not to check

276   HISTORY OF ENGLAND.

CHAP.
XIII.

1295.

The union, however, of the representatives from the boroughs gave gradually more weight to the whole order; and it became customary for them, in return for the supplies which they granted, to prefer petitions to the crown for the redress of any particular grievance, of which they found reason to complain. The more the king's demands multiplied, the faster these petitions encreased both in number and authority; and the prince found it difficult to refuse men, whose grants had supported his throne, and to whose assistance he might so soon be again obliged to have recourse. The commons however were still much below the rank of legislators [f]. Their petitions, though they received a verbal assent from the throne, were only the rudiments of laws: The judges were afterwards entrusted with the power of putting them into form: And the king, by adding to them the sanction of his authority, and that sometimes without the assent of the nobles, bestowed validity upon them. The age did not refine so much as to perceive the danger of these irregularities. No man was displeased, that the sovereign, at the desire of any class of men, should issue an order, which appeared only to concern that class; and his predecessors were so near possessing the whole legislative power, that he gave no disgust by assuming it in this seemingly inoffensive manner. But time and farther experience gradually opened men's eyes, and corrected these abuses. It was found, that no laws could be fixed for one order of men, without affecting the whole; and that the force and efficacy of laws depended entirely on the terms employed in wording them. The house of peers, therefore, the most powerful order in the state, with reason expected, that their assent should be

the king, but to reason with him, and consent to his demands. It was not till the reign of Richard II. that the sheriffs were deprived of the power of omitting boroughs at pleasure. See Stat. at Large, 5th Richard II. cap. 4.

[f] See note [E] at the end of the volume.

expresly

expressly granted to all public ordinances [g]: And in the reign of Henry V. the commons required that no laws should be framed merely upon their petitions, unless the statutes were worded by themselves, and had passed their house in the form of a bill [h].

But as the same causes, which had produced a partition of property, continued still to operate; the number of knights and lesser barons, or what the English call the gentry, perpetually encreased, and they sunk into a rank still more inferior to the great nobility. The equality of tenure was lost in the great inferiority of power and property; and the house of representatives from the counties was gradually separated from that of the peers, and formed a distinct order in the state [i]. The growth of commerce, meanwhile, augmented the private wealth and consideration of the burgesses; the frequent demands of the crown encreased their public importance; and as they resembled the knights of shires in one material circumstance, that of representing particular bodies of men; it no longer appeared unsuitable to unite them together in the same house, and to confound their rights and privileges [k]. Thus the third estate, that of the commons, reached at last its present form; and as the country gentlemen made thenceforwards no scruple of appearing as deputies from the boroughs, the distinction between the members was entirely lost, and the lower house acquired thence a great accession of weight and importance in the kingdom. Still, however, the office of this estate was

[g] In those instances found in Cotton's Abridgement, where the king appears to answer of himself, the petitions of the commons, be probably exerted no more than that power, which was long inherent in the crown, of regulating matters by royal edicts or proclamations. But no durable or general statute seems ever to have been made by the king from the petition of the commons alone, without the assent of the peers. It is more likely that the peers alone, without the commons, would enact statutes.

[h] Brady's Answer to Petyt, p. 85. from the records. [i] Cotton's Abridgment, p. 13. [k] See note [F] at the end of the volume.

very

278   HISTORY OF ENGLAND.

CHAP. XIII.
1295.

very different from that which it has since exercised with so much advantage to the public. Instead of checking and controuling the authority of the king, they were naturally induced to adhere to him, as the great fountain of law and justice, and to support him against the power of the aristocracy, which at once was the source of oppression to themselves, and disturbed him in the execution of the laws. The king, in his turn, gave countenance to an order of men, so useful and so little dangerous: The peers also were obliged to pay them some consideration: And by this means the third estate, formerly so abject in England, as well as in all other European nations, rose by slow degrees to their present importance; and in their progress made arts and commerce, the necessary attendants of liberty and equality, flourish in the kingdom.[l]

WHAT sufficiently proves, that the commencement of the house of burgesses, who are the true commons, was not an affair of chance, but arose from the necessities of the present situation, is, that Edward, at the very same time, summoned deputies from the inferior clergy, the first that ever met in England[m], and he required them to impose taxes on their constituents for the public service. Formerly the ecclesiastical benefices bore no part of the burthens of the state: The pope indeed of late had often levied impositions upon them: He had sometimes granted this power to the sovereign[a]: The king himself had, in the preceding year, exacted, by menaces and violence, a very grievous tax of half the revenues of the clergy: But as this precedent was dangerous, and could not easily be repeated in a government which required the consent of the subject to any extraordinary resolution, Edward found it more prudent to assemble a lower house of con-

[l] See note [G] at the end of the volume. Brady of Boroughs, p. 34. Gilbert's Hist. of the Exch. p. 48. T. Wykes, p. 99, 120.
[m] Archbishop Wake's State of the Church of England, p. 235.
[a] Ann. Waverl. p. 117, 128.

vocation,

vocation, to lay before them his necessities, and to ask some supply. But on this occasion he met with difficulties. Whether that the clergy thought themselves the most independent body in the kingdom, or were disgusted by the former exorbitant impositions, they absolutely refused their assent to the king's demand of a fifth of their moveables; and it was not till a second meeting, that, on their persisting in this refusal, he was willing to accept of a tenth. The barons and knights granted him, without hesitation, an eleventh; the burgesses, a seventh. But the clergy still scrupled to meet on the king's writ; lest by such an instance of obedience they should seem to acknowledge the authority of the temporal power: And this compromise was at last fallen upon, that the king should issue his writ to the archbishop; and that the archbishop should, in consequence of it, summon the clergy, who, as they then appeared to obey their spiritual superior, no longer hesitated to meet in convocation. This expedient, however, was the cause, why the ecclesiastics were separated into two houses of convocation under their several archbishops, and formed not one estate, as in other countries of Europe; which was at first the king's intention [v]. We now return to the course of our narration.

EDWARD, conscious of the reasons of disgust which he had given to the king of Scots, informed of the dispositions of that people, and expecting the most violent effects of their resentment, which he knew he had so well merited; employed the supplies, granted him by his people, in making preparations against the hostilities of his northern neighbour. When in this situation, he received intelligence of the treaty secretly concluded between John and Philip; and though uneasy at this concurrence of a French and Scottish war, he resolved not

[v] Gilbert's Hist. of Exch. p. 51. 54.

CHAP. XIII.
1296.

to encourage his enemies by a pusillanimous behaviour, or by yielding to their united efforts. He summoned John to perform the duty of a vassal, and to send him a supply of forces against an invasion from France, with which he was then threatened: He next required, that the fortresses of Berwic, Jedborough, and Roxborough, should be put into his hands as a security during the war [p]: He cited John to appear in an English parliament to be held at Newcastle: And when none of these successive demands were complied with, he marched northward with numerous forces, 30,000 foot and 4000 horse, to chastise his rebellious vassal. The Scottish nation, who had little reliance on the vigour and abilities of their prince, assigned him a council of twelve noblemen, in whose hands the sovereignty was really lodged [q], and who put the country in the best posture of which the present distractions would admit. A great army, composed of 40,000 infantry, though supported only by 500 cavalry, advanced to the frontiers; and after a fruitless attempt upon Carlisle, marched eastwards to defend those provinces which Edward was preparing to attack. But some of the most considerable of the Scottish nobles, Robert Bruce the father and son, the earls of March and Angus, prognosticating the ruin of their country, from the concurrence of intestine divisions and a foreign invasion, endeavoured here to ingratiate themselves with Edward, by an early submission; and the king, encouraged by this favourable incident, led his army into the enemies country, and crossed the Tweed, without opposition, at Coldstream. He then received a message from John, by which that prince, having now procured, for himself and his nation, pope Celestine's dispensation from former oaths, renounced the homage which had been done to

28 March.

[p] Rymer, vol. ii. p. 691. Walsing. p. 64. Heming. vol. i. p. 84. Tyrrel, p. 186. [q] Heming. vol. i. p. 75.

England,

EDWARD I.

England, and set Edward at defiance[f]. This bravado was but ill supported by the military operations of the Scots. Berwic was already taken by assault: Sir William Douglas, the governor, was made prisoner: Above 7000 of the garrison were put to the sword: And Edward, elated by this great advantage, dispatched earl Warrenne with 12,000 men, to lay siege to Dunbar, which was defended by the flower of the Scottish nobility.

The Scots, sensible of the importance of this place, which, if taken, laid their whole country open to the enemy, advanced with their main army, under the command of the earls of Buchan, Lenox, and Marre, in order to relieve it. Warrenne, not dismayed at the great superiority of their number, marched out to give them battle. He attacked them with great vigour; and as undisciplined troops, when numerous, are but the more exposed to a panic upon any alarm, he soon threw them into confusion, and chased them off the field with great slaughter. The loss of the Scots is said to have amounted to 20,000 men: The castle of Dunbar, with all its garrison, surrendered next day to Edward, who, after the battle, had brought up the main body of the English, and who now proceeded with an assured confidence of success. The castle of Roxborough was yielded by James, steward of Scotland; and that nobleman, from whom is descended the royal family of Stuart, was again obliged to swear fealty to Edward. After a feeble resistance, the castles of Edinburgh and Stirling opened their gates to the enemy. All the southern parts were instantly subdued by the English; and, to enable them the better to reduce the northern, whose inaccessible situation seemed to give them some more security, Edward sent for a strong reinforcement of Welsh and Irish, who, being

CHAP. XIII.

1296.

27th April.

[f] Rymer, vol. ii. p. 607. Walsing. p. 66. Heming. vol. I. p. 92.

accustomed

accustomed to a desultory kind of war, were the best fitted to pursue the fugitive Scots into the recesses of their lakes and mountains. But the spirit of the nation was already broken by their misfortunes; and the feeble and timid Baliol, discontented with his own subjects, and over-awed by the English, abandoned all those resources, which his people might yet have possessed in this extremity. He hastened to make his submissions to Edward; he expressed the deepest penitence for his disloyalty to his liege lord, and he made a solemn and irrevocable resignation of his crown into the hands of that monarch[c]. Edward marched northwards to Aberdeen and Elgin, without meeting an enemy: No Scotchman approached him but to pay him submission and do him homage: Even the turbulent Highlanders, ever refractory to their own princes, and averse to the restraint of laws, endeavoured to prevent the devastation of their country, by giving him early proofs of obedience: And Edward, having brought the whole kingdom to a seeming state of tranquillity, returned to the south with his army. There was a stone, to which the popular superstition of the Scots paid the highest veneration: All their kings were seated on it, when they received the rite of inauguration: An ancient tradition assured them, that, wherever this stone was placed, their nation should always govern: And it was carefully preserved at Scone, as the true palladium of their monarchy, and their ultimate resource amidst all their misfortunes. Edward got possession of it; and carried it with him to England[d]. He gave orders to destroy the records, and all those monuments of antiquity, which might preserve the memory of the independence of the kingdom, and refute the English claims of superiority. The Scots pretend, that he also destroyed all the annals

[c] Rymer, vol. ii. p. 718. Walsing. p. 67. Heming. vol. I. p. 59. Trivet, p. 292.   [d] Walsing. p. 68. Trivet, p. 299.

preserved

preserved in their convents: But it is not probable, that a nation, so rude and unpolished, should be possessed of any history which deserves much to be regretted. The great seal of Baliol was broken; and that prince himself was carried prisoner to London, and committed to custody in the Tower. Two years after, he was restored to liberty, and submitted to a voluntary banishment in France; where, without making any farther attempts for the recovery of his royalty, he died in a private station. Earl Warrenne was left governor of Scotland [u]: Englishmen were entrusted with the chief offices: And Edward, flattering himself that he had attained the end of all his wishes, and that the numerous acts of fraud and violence, which he had practised against Scotland, had terminated in the final reduction of that kingdom, returned with his victorious army into England.

An attempt, which he made about the same time, for the recovery of Guienne, was not equally successful. He sent thither an army of 7000 men, under the command of his brother the earl of Lancaster. That prince gained at first some advantages over the French at Bourdeaux; but he was soon after seized with a distemper, of which he died at Bayonne. The command devolved on the earl of Lincoln, who was not able to perform any thing considerable during the rest of the campaign [w].

But the active and ambitious spirit of Edward, while his conquests brought such considerable accessions to the English monarchy, could not be satisfied, so long as Guienne, the ancient patrimony of his family, was wrested from him by the dishonest artifices of the French monarch. Finding, that the distance of that province rendered all his efforts against it feeble and uncertain, he purposed to attack France in a quarter where she appeared more vul-

[u] Rymer, vol. II. p. 716. Trivet, p. 295. [w] Heming. vol. I. p. 72, 73, 74.

nerable;

nerable; and with this view he married his daughter, Elizabeth, to John earl of Holland, and, at the same time, contracted an alliance with Guy earl of Flanders, stipulated to pay him the sum of 75,000 pounds, and projected an invasion, with their united forces, upon Philip, their common enemy [r]. He hoped that, when he himself, at the head of the English, Flemish, and Dutch armies, reinforced by his German allies, to whom he had promised or remitted considerable sums, should enter the frontiers of France, and threaten the capital itself, Philip would at last be obliged to relinquish his acquisitions, and purchase peace by the restitution of Guienne. But, in order to set this great machine in movement, considerable supplies were requisite from the parliament; and Edward, without much difficulty, obtained from the barons and knights a new grant of a twelfth of all their moveables, and from the boroughs, that of an eighth. The great, and almost unlimited, power of the king over the latter, enabled him to throw the heavier part of the burthen on them; and the prejudices which he seems always to have entertained against the church, on account of the former zeal of the clergy for the Mountfort faction, made him resolve to load them with still more considerable impositions, and he required of them a fifth of their moveables. But he here met with an opposition, which for some time disconcerted all his measures, and engaged him in enterprizes that were somewhat dangerous to *him*; and would have proved fatal to any of his predecessors.

Dissensions with the clergy.

BONIFACE VIII. who had succeeded Celestine in the papal throne, was a man of the most lofty and enterprizing spirit; and, though not endowed with that severity of manners which commonly accompanies ambition in men of his order, he was determined to carry the authority of the tiara, and his dominion over the temporal power, to

[r] Rymer, vol. II. p. 761. Walsing. p. 68.

as great a height as it had ever attained in any former period. Sensible that his immediate predecessors, by oppressing the church in every province of Christendom, had extremely alienated the affections of the clergy, and had afforded the civil magistrate a pretence for laying like impositions on ecclesiastical revenues, he attempted to resume the former station of the sovereign pontiff, and to establish himself as the common protector of the spiritual order against all invaders. For this purpose, he issued very early in his pontificate a general bull, prohibiting all princes from levying, without his consent, any taxes upon the clergy, and all clergymen from submitting to such impositions; and he threatened both of them with the penalties of excommunication in case of disobedience[r]. This important edict is said to have been procured by the solicitation of Robert de Winchelsey, archbishop of Canterbury, who intended to employ it as a rampart against the violent extortions which the church had felt from Edward, and the still greater, which that prince's multiplied necessities gave them reason to apprehend. When a demand, therefore, was made on the clergy of a fifth of their moveables, a tax which was probably much more grievous than a fifth of their revenue, as their lands were mostly stocked with their cattle, and cultivated by their villains; the clergy took shelter under the bull of pope Boniface, and pleaded conscience in refusing compliance[s]. The king came not immediately to extremities on this repulse; but, after locking up all their granaries and barns, and prohibiting all rent to be paid them, he appointed a new synod, to confer with him upon his demand. The primate, not dismayed by these proofs of Edward's resolution, here plainly told him, that the clergy owed obedience to two sovereigns, their spiritual and their tempo-

[r] Rymer, vol. ii. p. 706. Heming. vol. i. p. 104. [s] Heming. vol. i. p. 107. Trivet, p. 296. Chron. Dunst. vol. ii. p. 672.

ral;

286   HISTORY OF ENGLAND.

CHAP. XIII.

ral; but their duty bound them to a much stricter attachment to the former than to the latter: They could not comply with his commands (for such, in some measure, the requests of the crown were then deemed), in contradiction to the express prohibition of the sovereign pontiff [a].

1297.

The clergy had seen, in many instances, that Edward paid little regard to those numerous privileges, on which they set so high a value. He had formerly seized, in an arbitrary manner, all the money and plate belonging to the churches and convents, and had applied them to the public service [b]; and they could not but expect more violent treatment on this sharp refusal, grounded on such dangerous principles. Instead of applying to the pope for a relaxation of his bull, he resolved immediately to employ the power in his hands; and he told the ecclesiastics, that, since they refused to support the civil government, they were unworthy to receive any benefit from it; and he would accordingly put them out of the protection of the laws. This vigorous measure was immediately carried into execution [c]. Orders were issued to the judges to receive no cause brought before them by the clergy; to hear and decide all causes in which they were defendants: To do every man justice against them; to do them justice against no body [d]. The ecclesiastics soon found themselves in the most miserable situation imaginable. They could not remain in their own houses or convents for want of subsistence: If they went abroad in quest of maintenance, they were dismounted, robbed of their horses and cloaths, abused by every ruffian, and no redress could be obtained by them for the most violent injury. The primate himself was attacked on the highway,

[a] Heming. vol. I. p. 107.   [b] Walsing. p. 65. Heming. vol. I. p. 58.   [c] Walsing. p. 69. Heming. vol. I. p. 107.
[d] M. West. p. 429.

was

was stripped of his equipage and furniture, and was at last reduced to board himself, with a single servant, in the house of a country clergyman[f]. The king, mean while, remained an indifferent spectator of all these violences; and, without employing his officers in committing any immediate injury on the priests, which might have appeared invidious and oppressive, he took ample vengeance on them for their obstinate refusal of his demands. Though the archbishop issued a general sentence of excommunication against all who attacked the persons or property of ecclesiastics, it was not regarded: While Edward enjoyed the satisfaction of seeing the people become the voluntary instruments of his justice against them, and enure themselves to throw off that respect for the sacred order, by which they had so long been overawed and governed.

THE spirits of the clergy were at last broken by this harsh treatment. Besides, that the whole province of York, which lay nearest the danger that still hung over them from the Scots, voluntarily, from the first, voted a fifth of their moveables; the bishops of Salisbury, Ely, and some others, made a composition for the secular clergy within their dioceses; and they agreed not to pay the fifth, which would have been an act of disobedience to Boniface's bull, but to deposite a sum equivalent in some church appointed them; whence it was taken by the king's officers[g]. Many particular convents and clergymen made payment of a like sum, and received the king's protection[h]. Those who had not ready money, entered into recognizances for the payment. And there was scarcely found one ecclesiastic in the kingdom, who seemed willing to suffer, for the sake of religious privileges, this new species of martyrdom, the most tedious and languishing of any, the most mortifying to spiritual

[f] Hemsley. vol. l. p. 109. [g] Heming. vol. i. p. 108, 109. Chron. Dunst. p. 653. [h] Chron. Dunst. vol. ii. p. 654.

pride,

pride, and not rewarded by that crown of glory, which the church holds up, with such oftentation, to her devoted adherents.

But as the money, granted by parliament, though confiderable, was not fufficient to fupply the king's neceffities, and that levied by compofitions with the clergy came in flowly, Edward was obliged, for the obtaining of farther fupply, to exert his arbitrary power, and to lay an oppreffive hand on all orders of men in the kingdom. He limited the merchants in the quantity of wool allowed to be exported; and at the fame time forced them to pay him a duty of forty fhillings a fack, which was computed to be above the third of the value [1]. He feized all the reft of the wool, as well as all the leather of the kingdom, into his hands, and difpofed of thefe commodities for his own benefit [k]: He required the fheriffs of each county to fupply him with 2000 quarters of wheat, and as many of oats, which he permitted them to feize wherever they could find them: The cattle and other commodities, neceffary for fupplying his army, were laid hold of without the confent of the owners [l]: And though he promifed to pay afterwards the equivalent of all thefe goods, men faw but little probability that a prince, who fubmitted fo little to the limitations of law, could ever, amidft his multiplied neceffities, be reduced to a ftrict obfervance of his engagements. He fhowed, at the fame time, an equal difregard to the principles of the feudal law, by which all the lands of his kingdom were held: In order to encreafe his army, and enable him to fupport that great effort, which he intended to make againft France, he required the attendance of every proprietor of land poffeffed of twenty pounds a year, even though he held not of the

[1] Walfing. p. 69. Trivet, p. 295. [k] Heming. vol. 1. p. 52. 210.
[l] Heming. vol. i. p. 121.

crown, and was not obliged by his tenure to perform any such service [m].

THESE acts of violence and of arbitrary power, notwithstanding the great personal regard generally borne to the king, bred murmurs in every order of men; and it was not long ere some of the great nobility, jealous of their own privileges, as well as of national liberty, gave countenance and authority to these complaints. Edward assembled on the sea-coast an army, which he purposed to send over to Gascony, while he himself should in person make an impression on the side of Flanders; and he intended to put these forces under the command of Humphrey Bohun, earl of Hereford, the constable, and Roger Bigod, earl of Norfolk, the mareschal of England. But these two powerful earls refused to execute his commands, and affirmed, that they were only obliged by their office to attend his person in the wars. A violent altercation ensued; and the king, in the height of his passion, addressing himself to the constable, exclaimed, *Sir earl, by God, you shall either go or hang.* *By God, Sir King*, replied Hereford, *I will neither go nor hang* [n]. And he immediately departed, with the mareschal, and above thirty other considerable barons.

UPON this opposition, the king laid aside the project of an expedition against Guienne; and assembled the forces, which he himself purposed to transport into Flanders. But the two earls, irritated in the contest, and elated by impunity, pretending that none of their ancestors had ever served in that country, refused to perform the duty of their office in mustering the army [o]. The king, now finding it adviseable to proceed with moderation, instead of attainting the earls, who possessed their dignities by hereditary right, appointed Thomas de Berke-

[m] Walsing. p. 69.   [n] Heming. vol. I. p. 112.
[o] Rymer, vol. ii. p. 783. Walsing. p. 70.

CHAP. XIII.

1297.

ley, and Geoffrey de Geyneville, to act, in that emergence, as conſtable and marefchal [r]. He endeavoured to reconcile himſelf with the church; took the primate again into favour [q]; made him, in conjunction with Reginald de Grey, tutor to the prince, whom he intended to appoint guardian of the kingdom during his abſence; and he even aſſembled a great number of the nobility in Weſtminſter-hall, to whom he deigned to make an apology for his paſt conduct. He pleaded the urgent neceſſities of the crown; his extreme want of money; his engagements from honour as well as intereſt to ſupport his foreign allies: And he promiſed, if ever he returned in ſafety, to redreſs all their grievances, to reſtore the execution of the laws, and to make all his ſubjects compenſation for the loſſes which they had ſuſtained. Meanwhile, he begged them to ſuſpend their animoſities; to judge of him by his future conduct, of which, he hoped, he ſhould be more maſter; to remain faithful to his government, or if he periſhed in the preſent war, to preſerve their allegiance to his ſon and ſucceſſor [r].

There were certainly, from the concurrence of diſcontents among the great, and grievances of the people, materials ſufficient, in any other period, to have kindled a civil war in England: But the vigour and abilities of Edward kept every one in awe; and his dexterity, in ſtopping on the brink of danger, and retracting the meaſures to which he had been puſhed by his violent temper and arbitrary principles, ſaved the nation from ſo great a calamity. The two great earls dared not to break out into open violence: They proceeded no farther than framing a remonſtrance, which was delivered to the king at Winchelſea, when he was ready to embark for Flanders. They there complained of the violations of the great charter and

[p] M. Weſt. p. 430. [q] Heming. vol. I. p. 113.
[r] Heming. vol. I. p. 114. M. Weſt. p. 430.

that

EDWARD I.

that of forests; the violent seizures of corn, leather, cattle, and above all, of wool, a commodity, which they affirmed to be equal in value to half the lands of the kingdom; the arbitrary imposition of forty shillings a sack on the small quantity of wool allowed to be exported by the merchants; and they claimed an immediate redress of all these grievances [t]. The king told them, that the greater part of his council were now at a distance, and without their advice he could not deliberate on measures of so great importance [u].

CHAP. XIII.

1297.

But the constable and mareschal, with the barons of their party, resolved to take advantage of Edward's absence, and to obtain an explicite assent to their demands. When summoned to attend the parliament at London, they came with a great body of cavalry and infantry; and before they would enter the city, required that the gates should be put into their custody [w]. The primate, who secretly favoured all their pretensions, advised the council to comply; and thus they became masters both of the young prince and of the resolutions of parliament. Their demands, however, were moderate; and such as sufficiently justify the purity of their intentions in all their past measures: They only required, that the two charters should receive a solemn confirmation; that a clause should be added to secure the nation for ever against all impositions and taxes without consent of parliament; and that they themselves, and their adherents, who had refused to attend the king into Flanders, should be pardoned for the offence, and should be again received into favour [x]. The prince of Wales and his council assented to these terms; and the charters were sent over to the king in

Dissensions with the barons.

[t] Walsing. p. 71. Heming. vol. I. p. 115. Trivet, p. 302.
[u] Walsing. p. 71. Heming. vol. I. p. 117. Trivet. p. 104.
[w] Heming. vol. I. p. 138. [x] Walsing. p. 73. Heming. vol. I. p. 138, 139, 140, 141. Trivet, p. 305.

U 2   Flanders

Flanders to be there confirmed by him. Edward felt the utmost reluctance to this measure, which, he apprehended, would for the future impose fetters on his conduct, and set limits to his lawless authority. On various pretences, he delayed three days giving any answer to the deputies; and when the pernicious consequences of his refusal were represented to him, he was at last obliged, after many internal struggles, to affix his seal to the charters, as also to the clause that bereaved him of the power, which he had hitherto assumed, of imposing arbitrary taxes upon the people [n].

That we may finish at once this interesting transaction concerning the settlement of the charters, we shall briefly mention the subsequent events which relate to it. The constable and marefchal, informed of the king's compliance, were satisfied; and not only ceased from disturbing the government, but affifted the regency with their power againſt the Scots, who had rifen in arms, and had thrown off the yoke of England [r]. But being fenfible, that the fmalleft pretence would fuffice to make Edward retract thefe detefted laws, which, though they had often received the fanction both of king and parliament, and had been acknowledged during three reigns, were never yet deemed to have fufficient validity; they infifted, that he ſhould again confirm them on his return to England, and ſhould thereby renounce all plea which he might derive from his refiding in a foreign country, when he formerly affixed his feal to them [o]. It appeared, that they judged aright of Edward's character and intentions: He delayed this confirmation as long as poſſible; and when the fear of worfe confequences obliged him again to comply, he expreſsly added a falvo for his royal dignity or prerogative, which in effect enervated the whole

[n] Walfing. p. 74. Heming. vol. i. p. 143.
[o] p. 143. [s] Hemingf. vol. i. p. 139.
[r] Heming. vol. i.

force

force of the charters[a]. The two earls and their adherents left the parliament in difguft; and the king was conftrained, on a future occafion, to grant to the people, without any fubterfuge, a pure and abfolute confirmation of thofe laws[b], which were fo much the object of their paffionate affection. Even farther fecurities were then provided for the eftablifhment of national privileges. Three knights were appointed to be chofen in each county, and were invefted with the power of punifhing, by fine and imprifonment, every tranfgreffion or violation of the charters[c]: A precaution which, though it was foon difufed, as encroaching too much on royal prerogative, proves the attachment which the Englifh, in that age, bore to liberty, and their well-grounded jealoufy of the arbitrary difpofition of Edward.

THE work, however, was not yet entirely finifhed and complete. In order to execute the leffer charter, it was requifite, by new perambulations, to fet bounds to the royal forefts, and to difafforeft all land which former encroachments had comprehended within their limits. Edward difcovered the fame reluctance to comply with this equitable demand; and it was not till after many delays on his part, and many folicitations and requefts, and even menaces of war and violence[d] on the part of the barons, that the perambulations were made, and exact boundaries fixed, by a jury in each county, to the extent of his forefts[e]. Had not his ambitious and active temper raifed him fo many foreign enemies, and obliged him to have recourfe fo often to the affiftance of his fubjects, it

[a] Heming. vol. I. p. 167, 168. [b] Heming. vol. I. p. 168.
[c] Hemingford, vol. I. p. 170. [d] Walfing. p. 80. We are told by Tyrrel, vol. II. p. 245. from the Chronicle of St. Albans, that the barons, not content with the execution of the charter of forefts, demanded of Edward as high terms as had been impofed on his father by the earl of Leicefter: But no other hiftorian mentions this particular.
[e] Heming. vol. I. p. 171. M. Weft. p. 431, 433.

CHAP.
XIII.

1297.

is not likely that those concessions could ever have been extorted from him.

But while the people, after so many successful struggles, deemed themselves happy in the secure possession of their privileges, they were surprized in 1305 to find, that Edward had secretly applied to Rome, and had procured, from that mercenary court, an absolution from all the oaths and engagements, which he had so often reiterated, to observe both the charters. There are some historians [f] so credulous as to imagine, that this perilous step was taken by him for no other purpose, than to acquire the merit of granting a new confirmation of the charters, as he did soon after; and a confirmation so much the more unquestionable, as it could never after be invalidated by his successors, on pretence of any force or violence which had been imposed upon him. But besides, that this might have been done with a better grace, if he had never applied for any such absolution, the whole tenor of his conduct proves him to be little susceptible of such refinements in patriotism; and this very deed itself, in which he anew confirmed the charters, carries on the face of it a very opposite presumption. Though he ratified the charters in general, he still took advantage of the papal bull so far as to invalidate the late perambulations of the forests, which had been made with such care and attention, and to reserve to himself the power, in case of favourable incidents, to extend as much as formerly those arbitrary jurisdictions. If the power was not in fact made use of, we can only conclude, that the favourable incidents did not offer.

Thus, after the contests of near a whole century, and these ever accompanied with violent jealousies, often with public convulsions, the Great Charter was finally esta-

[f] Brady, vol. ii. p. 84. Carte, vol. ii. p. 292.

blished

blished; and the English nation have the honour of extorting, by their perseverance, this concession from the ablest, the most warlike, and the most ambitious of all their princes [1]. It is computed, that above thirty confirmations of the charter were at different times required of several kings, and granted by them, in full parliament; a precaution which, while it discovers some ignorance of the true nature of law and government, proves a laudable jealousy of national privileges in the people, and an extreme anxiety, lest contrary precedents should ever be pleaded as an authority for infringing them. Accordingly we find, that, though arbitrary practices often prevailed, and were even able to establish themselves into settled customs, the validity of the Great Charter was never afterwards formally disputed; and that grant was still regarded as the basis of English government, and the sure rule by which the authority of every custom was to be tried and canvassed. The jurisdiction of the Starchamber, martial law, imprisonment by warrants from the privy-council, and other practices of a like nature, though established for several centuries, were scarcely ever allowed by the English to be parts of their constitution: The affection of the nation for liberty still prevailed over all precedent, and even all political reasoning: The exercise of these powers, after being long the source of secret murmurs among the people, was, in fulness of time, solemnly abolished, as illegal, at least as oppressive, by the whole legislative authority.

To return to the period from which this account of the charters has led us: Though the king's impatience to appear at the head of his armies in Flanders made him

[1] It must however be remarked, that the king never forgave the chief actuary in this transaction; and he found means afterwards to oblige both the constable and mareschal to resign their offices into his hands. The former received a new grant of it: But the office of mareschal was given to Thomas of Brotherton, the king's second son.

CHAP.
XIII.

1297.

overlook all confiderations, either of domeftic difcontents or of commotions among the Scots; his embarkation had been fo long retarded by the various obftructions thrown in his way, that he loft the proper feafon for action, and after his arrival made no progrefs againft the enemy. The king of France, taking advantage of his abfence, had broken into the Low Countries; had defeated the Flemings in the battle of Furnes; had made himfelf mafter of Lille, St. Omer, Courtrai, and Ypres; and feemed in a fituation to take full vengeance on the earl of Flanders, his rebellious vaffal. But Edward, feconded by an Englifh army of 50,000 men (for this is the number affigned by hiftorians [k]), was able to flop the career of his victories; and Philip, finding all the weak refources of his kingdom already exhaufted, began to dread a reverfe of fortune, and to apprehend an invafion on France itfelf. The king of England, on the other hand, difappointed of affiftance from Adolph king of the Romans, which he had purchafed at a very high price, and finding many urgent calls for his prefence in England, was defirous of ending, on any honourable terms, a war, which ferved only to divert his force from the execution of more important projects. This difpofition in both monarchs foon produced a ceffation of hoftilities for two years; and engaged them to fubmit their differences to the arbitration of pope Boniface.

1298.

BONIFACE was among the laft of the fovereign pontiffs that exercifed an authority over the temporal jurifdiction of princes; and thefe exorbitant pretenfions, which he had been tempted to affume from the fuccefsful example of his predeceffors, but of which the feafon was now paft, involved him in fo many calamities, and were attended with fo unfortunate a cataftrophe, that they have been

[k] Heming, vol. l. p. 146.

fecretly

EDWARD I.

secretly abandoned, though never openly relinquished, by his successors in the apostolic chair. Edward and Philip, equally jealous of papal claims, took care to insert in their reference, that Boniface was made judge of the difference by their consent, as a private person, not by any right of his pontificate; and the pope, without seeming to be offended at this mortifying clause, proceeded to give a sentence between them, in which they both acquiesced[l]. He brought them to agree, that their union should be cemented by a double marriage; that of Edward himself, who was now a widower, with Margaret, Philip's sister, and that of the prince of Wales, with Isabella, daughter of that monarch[m]. Philip was likewise willing to restore Guienne to the English, which he had indeed no good pretence to detain; but he insisted, that the Scots and their king, John Baliol, should, as his allies, be comprehended in the treaty, and should be restored to their liberty. The difference, after several disputes, was compromised, by their making mutual sacrifices to each other. Edward agreed to abandon his ally the earl of Flanders, on condition that Philip should treat in like manner his ally the king of Scots. The prospect of conquering these two countries, whose situation made them so commodious an acquisition to the respective kingdoms, prevailed over all other considerations; and though they were both finally disappointed in their hopes, their conduct was very reconcilable to the principles of an interested policy. This was the first specimen which the Scots had of the French alliance, and which was exactly conformable to what a smaller power must always expect, when it blindly attaches itself to the will and fortunes of a greater. That unhappy people, now engaged in a brave, though unequal contest for their liberties, were

CHAP. XIII.

1298.

Peace with France.

[l] Rymer, vol. ii. p. 817. Heming. vol. i. p. 149. Trivet, p. 310.
[m] Rymer, vol. ii. p. 823.

totally

CHAP.
XIII.
1296.

Recon of Scotland.

totally abandoned by the ally in whom they repofed their final confidence, to the will of an imperious conqueror.

Though England, as well as other European countries, was, in its ancient ftate, very ill qualified for making, and ftill worfe for maintaining conquefts, Scotland was fo much inferior in its internal force, and was fo ill fituated for receiving foreign fuccours, that it is no wonder Edward, an ambitious monarch, fhould have caft his eye on fo tempting an acquifition, which brought both fecurity and greatnefs to his native country. But the inftruments, whom he employed to maintain his dominion over the northern kingdom, were not happily chofen; and acted not with the requifite prudence and moderation, in reconciling the Scottifh nation to a yoke, which they bore with fuch extreme reluctance. Warrenne, retiring into England on account of his bad ftate of health, left the adminiftration entirely in the hands of Ormefby, who was appointed jufticiary of Scotland, and Creffingham, who bore the office of treafurer; and a fmall military force remained to fecure the precarious authority of thofe minifters. The latter had no other object than the amaffing of money by rapine and injuftice: The former diftinguifhed himfelf by the rigour and feverity of his temper: And both of them, treating the Scots as a conquered people, made them fenfible, too early, of the grievous fervitude into which they had fallen. As Edward required that all the proprietors of land fhould fwear fealty to him; every one, who refufed or delayed giving this teftimony of fubmiffion, was outlawed and imprifoned, and punifhed without mercy; and the braveft and moft generous fpirits of the nation were thus exafperated to the higheft degree againft the Englifh government *.

* Walfing. p. 70. Heming. vol. l. p. 118. Trivet, p. 199.

There

There was one William Wallace, of a small fortune, but descended of an ancient family, in the west of Scotland, whose courage prompted him to undertake, and enabled him finally to accomplish, the desperate attempt of delivering his native country from the dominion of foreigners. This man, whose valorous exploits are the object of just admiration, but have been much exaggerated by the traditions of his countrymen, had been provoked by the insolence of an English officer to put him to death; and finding himself obnoxious on that account to the severity of the administration, he fled into the woods, and offered himself as a leader to all those whom their crimes, or bad fortune, or avowed hatred of the English, had reduced to a like necessity. He was endowed with gigantic force of body, with heroic courage of mind, with disinterested magnanimity, with incredible patience, and ability to bear hunger, fatigue, and all the severities of the seasons; and he soon acquired, among those desperate fugitives, that authority to which his virtues so justly intitled him. Beginning with small attempts, in which he was always successful, he gradually proceeded to more momentous enterprizes; and he discovered equal caution in securing his followers, and valour in annoying the enemy. By his knowledge of the country, he was enabled, when pursued, to ensure a retreat among the morasses or forests or mountains; and again, collecting his dispersed associates, he unexpectedly appeared in another quarter, and surprized, and routed, and put to the sword, the unwary English. Every day brought accounts of his great actions, which were received with no less favour by his countrymen than terror by the enemy: All those, who thirsted after military fame, were desirous to partake of his renown: His successful valour seemed to vindicate the nation from the ignominy, into which it had fallen, by its tame submission to the English: And though no nobleman of note ventured as yet to join his party,

CHAP.
XIII.
1298.

party, he had gained a general confidence and attachment, which birth and fortune are not alone able to confer.

WALLACE having, by many fortunate enterprizes, brought the valour of his followers to correspond to his own, resolved to strike a decisive blow against the English government; and he concerted the plan of attacking Ormesby at Scone, and of taking vengeance on him, for all the violence and tyranny of which he had been guilty. The justiciary, apprized of his intentions, fled hastily into England: All the other officers of that nation imitated his example: Their terror added alacrity and courage to the Scots, who betook themselves to arms in every quarter: Many of the principal barons, and among the rest Sir William Douglas [o], openly countenanced Wallace's party: Robert Bruce secretly favoured and promoted the same cause: And the Scots, shaking off their fetters, prepared themselves to defend, by an united effort, that liberty which they had so unexpectedly recovered from the hands of their oppressors.

BUT Warrenne, collecting an army of 40,000 men in the north of England, determined to re-establish his authority; and he endeavoured, by the celerity of his armament and of his march, to compensate for his past negligence, which had enabled the Scots to throw off the English government. He suddenly entered Annandale, and came up with the enemy at Irvine, before their forces were fully collected, and before they had put themselves in a posture of defence. Many of the Scottish nobles, alarmed with their dangerous situation, here submitted to the English, renewed their oaths of fealty, promised to deliver hostages for their good behaviour, and received a pardon for past offences [p]. Others who had not yet declared themselves, such as the steward of Scotland and the

[o] Walsing. p. 70. Heming. vol. i. p. 118. [p] Heming. vol. L. p. 121, 122.

earl

earl of Lenox, joined, though with reluctance, the English army; and waited a favourable opportunity for embracing the cause of their distressed countrymen. But Wallace, whose authority over his retainers was more fully confirmed by the absence of the great nobles, persevered obstinately in his purpose; and finding himself unable to give battle to the enemy, he marched northwards, with an intention of prolonging the war, and of turning to his advantage the situation of that mountainous and barren country. When Warrenne advanced to Stirling, he found Wallace encamped at Cambuskenneth, on the opposite banks of the Forth; and being continually urged by the impatient Cressingham, who was actuated both by personal and national animosities against the Scots [q], he prepared to attack them in that position, which Wallace, no less prudent than courageous, had chosen for his army [r]. In spite of the remonstrances of Sir Richard Lundy, a Scotchman of birth and family, who sincerely adhered to the English, he ordered his army to pass a bridge which lay over the Forth; but he was soon convinced, by fatal experience, of the error of his conduct. Wallace, allowing such numbers of the English to pass as he thought proper, attacked them before they were fully formed, put them to rout, pushed part of them into the river, destroyed the rest by the edge of the sword, and gained a complete victory over them [s]. Among the slain was Cressingham himself, whose memory was so extremely odious to the Scots, that they flayed his dead body, and made saddles and girths of his skin [t]. Warrenne, finding the remainder of his army much dismayed by this misfortune, was obliged again to evacuate the kingdom, and retire into England. The castles of

CHAP. XIII.

1298.

---

q Heming. vol. i. p. 117.   r On the 11th of September 1297.
s Walsing. p. 73. Heming. vol. i. p. 127, 128, 129. Trivet. p. 307.
t Heming. vol. i. p. 130.

Roxborough

Roxborough and Berwic, ill fortified and feebly defended, fell soon after into the hands of the Scots.

Wallace, univerfally revered as the deliverer of his country, now received from the hands of his followers, the dignity of regent or guardian under the captive Baliol; and finding that the diforders of war, as well as the unfavourable feafons, had produced a famine in Scotland, he urged his army to march into England, to fubfift at the expence of the enemy, and to revenge all paft injuries, by retaliating on that hoftile nation. The Scots, who deemed every thing poffible under fuch a leader, joyfully attended his call. Wallace, breaking into the northern counties during the winter feafon, laid every place wafte with fire and fword; and after extending on all fides, without oppofition, the fury of his ravages, as far as the bifhopric of Durham, he returned, loaded with fpoils, and crowned with glory, into his own country[x]. The diforders, which at that time prevailed in England, from the refractory behaviour of the conftable and marefchal, made it impoffible to collect an army fufficient to refift the enemy, and expofed the nation to this lofs and difhonour.

But Edward, who received in Flanders intelligence of thefe events, and had already concluded a truce with France, now haftened over to England, in certain hopes, by his activity and valour, not only of wiping off this difgrace, but of recovering the important conqueft of Scotland, which he always regarded as the chief glory and advantage of his reign. He appeafed the murmurs of his people by conceffions and promifes: He reftored to the citizens of London the election of their own magiftrates, of which they had been bereaved in the latter part of his father's reign: He ordered ftrict enquiry to be made concerning the corn and other goods, which had been

[x] Heming. vol. I. p. 131, 132, 133.

violently

violently seized before his departure, as if he intended to pay the value to the owners [v]: And making public professions of confirming and observing the charters, he regained the confidence of the discontented nobles. Having, by all these popular arts, rendered himself entirely master of his people, he collected the whole military force of England, Wales, and Ireland; and marched with an army of near a hundred thousand combatants to the northern frontiers.

NOTHING could have enabled the Scots to resist, but for one season, so mighty a power, except an entire union among themselves; but as they were deprived of their king, whose personal qualities, even when he was present, appeared so contemptible, and had left among his subjects no principle of attachment to him or his family; factions, jealousies, and animosities unavoidably arose among the great, and distracted all their councils. The elevation of Wallace, though purchased by so great merit, and such eminent services, was the object of envy to the nobility, who repined to see a private gentleman raised above them by his rank, and still more by his glory and reputation. Wallace himself, sensible of their jealousy, and dreading the ruin of his country from those intestine discords, voluntarily resigned his authority, and retained only the command over that body of his followers, who, being accustomed to victory under his standard, refused to follow into the field any other leader. The chief power devolved on the steward of Scotland, and Cummin of Badenoch; men of eminent birth, under whom the great chieftains were more willing to serve in defence of their country. The two Scottish commanders, collecting their several forces from every quarter, fixed their station at Falkirk, and purposed there to abide the assault of the English. Wallace was at the head of a third body,

[v] Rymer, vol. ii. p. 825.

CHAP. XIII.
1298.

which acted under his command. The Scottish army placed their pikemen along their front: Lined the intervals between the three bodies with archers: And dreading the great superiority of the English in cavalry, endeavoured to secure their front by pallisadoes, tied together by ropes [x]. In this disposition, they expected the approach of the enemy.

22d July. Battle of Falkirk.

THE king, when he arrived in sight of the Scots, was pleased with the prospect of being able, by one decisive stroke, to determine the fortune of the war; and dividing his army also into three bodies, he led them to the attack. The English archers, who began about this time to surpass those of other nations, first chased the Scottish bowmen off the field; then pouring in their arrows among the pikemen, who were cooped up within their intrenchments, threw them into disorder, and rendered the assault of the English pikemen and cavalry more easy and successful. The whole Scottish army was broken, and chased off the field with great slaughter; which the historians, attending more to the exaggerated relations of the populace, than to the probability of things, make amount to fifty or sixty thousand men [y]. It is only certain, that the Scots never suffered a greater loss in any action, nor one which seemed to threaten more inevitable ruin to their country.

IN this general rout of the army, Wallace's military skill and presence of mind enabled him to keep his troops entire; and retiring behind the Carron, he marched leisurely along the banks of that small river, which protected him from the enemy. Young Bruce, who had already given many proofs of his aspiring genius, but who served hitherto in the English army, appeared on the op-

[x] Walsing. p. 75. Heming. vol. I. p. 167.
[y] Walsing. p. 76. T. Wykes, p. 127. Heming. vol. I. p. 163, 164, 165. Trivet, p. 313, says only 20,000. M. West. p. 431, says 40,000.

posite

posite banks; and distinguishing the Scottish chief, as well by his majestic port, as by the intrepid activity of his behaviour, called out to him, and desired a short conference. He here represented to Wallace the fruitless and ruinous enterprize in which he was engaged; and endeavoured to bend his inflexible spirit to submission under superior power and superior fortune: He insisted on the unequal contest between a weak state, deprived of its head and agitated by intestine discord, and a mighty nation, conducted by the ablest and most martial monarch of the age, and possessed of every resource either for protracting the war, or for pushing it with vigour and activity: If the love of his country were his motive for perseverance, his obstinacy tended only to prolong her misery; if he carried his views to private grandeur and ambition, he might reflect that, even if Edward should withdraw his armies, it appeared from past experience, that so many haughty nobles, proud of the pre-eminence of their families, would never submit to personal merit, whose superiority they were less inclined to regard as an object of admiration, than as a reproach and injury to themselves. To these exhortations Wallace replied, that, if he had hitherto acted alone as the champion of his country, it was solely because no second or competitor, or what he rather wished, no leader had yet appeared to place himself in that honourable station: That the blame lay entirely on the nobility, and chiefly on Bruce himself, who, uniting personal merit to dignity of family, had deserted the post, which both nature and fortune, by such powerful calls, invited him to assume: That the Scots, possessed of such a head, would, by their unanimity and concord, have surmounted the chief difficulty under which they now laboured, and might hope, notwithstanding their present losses, to oppose successfully all the power and abilities of Edward: That Heaven itself

CHAP. XIII.

1298.

CHAP.
XIII.

1298.

could not set a more glorious prize before the eyes either of virtue or ambition, than to join in one object, the acquisition of royalty with the defence of national independence: And that as the interests of his country, more than those of a brave man, could never be sincerely cultivated by a sacrifice of liberty, he himself was determined, as far as possible, to prolong not her misery, but her freedom, and was desirous that his own life, as well as the existence of the nation, might terminate, when they could no otherwise be preserved than by receiving the chains of a haughty victor. The gallantry of these sentiments, though delivered by an armed enemy, struck the generous mind of Bruce: The flame was conveyed from the breast of one hero to that of another: He repented of his engagements with Edward; and opening his eyes to the honourable path pointed out to him by Wallace, secretly determined to seize the first opportunity of embracing the cause, however desperate, of his oppressed country [r].

1299.

THE subjection of Scotland, notwithstanding this great victory of Edward, was not yet entirely completed. The English army, after reducing the southern provinces, was obliged to retire for want of provisions; and left the northern counties in the hands of the natives. The Scots, no less enraged at their present defeat, than elated by their past victories, still maintained the contest for liberty; but being fully sensible of the great inferiority of their force, they endeavoured, by applications to foreign courts, to procure to themselves some assistance. The supplications of the Scottish ministers were rejected by Philip; but were more successful with the court of Rome. Boniface, pleased with an occasion of exerting

[r] This story is told by all the Scotch writers; though it must be owned that Trivet and Hemingford, authors of good credit, both agree that Bruce was not at that time in Edward's army.

his

EDWARD I.

his authority, wrote a letter to Edward, exhorting him to put a stop to his oppressions on Scotland, and displaying all the proofs, such as they had probably been furnished him by the Scots themselves, for the ancient independence of that kingdom [a]. Among other arguments, hinted at above, he mentioned the treaty conducted and finished by Edward himself, for the marriage of his son with the heiress of Scotland; a treaty which would have been absurd, had he been superior lord of the kingdom, and had possessed, by the feudal law, the right of disposing of his ward in marriage. He mentioned several other striking facts, which fell within the compass of Edward's own knowledge; particularly, that Alexander, when he did homage to the king, openly and expressly declared in his presence, that he swore fealty not for his crown, but for the lands which he held in England: And the pope's letter might have passed for a reasonable one, had he not subjoined his own claim to be liege lord of Scotland; a claim which had not once been heard of, but which, with a singular confidence, he asserted to be full, entire, and derived from the most remote antiquity. The affirmative style, which had been so successful with him and his predecessors in spiritual contests, was never before abused after a more egregious manner in any civil controversy.

THE reply, which Edward made to Boniface's letter, contains particulars no less singular and remarkable [b]. He there proves the superiority of England by historical facts, deduced from the period of Brutus, the Trojan, who, he said, founded the British monarchy in the age of Eli and Samuel: He supports his position by all the events which passed in the island before the arrival of the Romans: And after laying great stress on the extensive dominions

CHAP. XIII.

1300. Scotland again subdued.

1301.

[a] Rymer, vol. ii. p. 844.   [b] Ibid. p. 863.

and heroic victories of king Arthur, he vouchsafes at last to descend to the time of Edward the elder, with which, in his speech to the states of Scotland, he had chosen to begin his claim of superiority. He asserts it to be a fact, *notorious and confirmed by the records of antiquity*, that the English monarchs had often conferred the kingdom of Scotland on their own subjects; had dethroned these vassal kings when unfaithful to them; and had substituted others in their stead. He displays with great pomp the full and complete homage which William had done to Henry II.; without mentioning the formal abolition of that *extorted* deed by king Richard, and the renunciation of all future claims of the same nature. Yet this paper he begins with a solemn appeal to the Almighty, the searcher of hearts, for his own firm persuasion of the justice of his claim; and no less than a hundred and four barons, assembled in parliament at Lincoln, concur, in maintaining before the pope, under their seals, the validity of these pretensions[c]. At the same time, however, they take care to inform Boniface, that, though they had justified their cause before him, they did not acknowledge him for their judge: The crown of England was free and sovereign: They had sworn to maintain all its royal prerogatives, and would never permit the king himself, were he willing, to relinquish its independency.

That neglect, almost total, of truth and justice, which sovereign states discover in their transactions with each other, is an evil universal and inveterate; is one great source of the misery to which the human race is continually exposed; and it may be doubted whether, in many instances, it be found in the end to contribute to the interests of those princes themselves, who thus sacrifice

[c] Rymer, vol. II. p. 873. Walsing. p. 85. Hemling. vol. I. p. 186. Trivet, p. 310. M. West. p. 443.

their integrity to their politics. As few monarchs have
lain under stronger temptations to violate the principles
of equity, than Edward in his transactions with Scotland;
so never were they violated with less scruple and reserve:
Yet his advantages were hitherto precarious and uncertain;
and the Scots, once roused to arms and enured to
war, began to appear a formidable enemy, even to this
military and ambitious monarch. They chose John
Cummin for their regent; and not content with maintaining
their independence in the northern parts, they
made incursions into the southern counties, which Edward
imagined he had totally subdued. John de Segrave,
whom he had left guardian of Scotland, led an
army to oppose them; and lying at Roslin, near Edinburgh,
sent out his forces in three divisions, to provide
themselves with forage and subsistence from the neighbourhood.
One party was suddenly attacked by the regent
and Sir Simon Fraser; and being unprepared, was
immediately routed and pursued with great slaughter.
The few that escaped, flying to the second division, gave
warning of the approach of the enemy: The soldiers ran
to their arms; and were immediately led on to take
revenge for the death of their countrymen. The Scots,
elated with the advantage already obtained, made a vigorous
impression upon them: The English, animated with
a thirst of vengeance, maintained a stout resistance: The
victory was long undecided between them; but at last declared
itself entirely in favour of the former, who broke
the English, and chaced them to the third division, now
advancing with a hasty march to support their distressed
companions. Many of the Scots had fallen in the two
first actions; most of them were wounded; and all of
them extremely fatigued by the long continuance of the
combat: Yet were they so transported with success and

military

CHAP. XIII.

military rage, that, having suddenly recovered their order, and arming the followers of their camp with the spoils of the slaughtered enemy, they drove with fury upon the ranks of the dismayed English. The favourable moment decided the battle; which the Scots, had they met with a steady resistance, were not long able to maintain t The English were chaced off the field: Three victories were thus gained in one day [d]: And the renown of these great exploits, seconded by the favourable dispositions of the people, soon made the regent master of all the fortresses in the south; and it became necessary for Edward to begin anew the conquest of the kingdom.

The king prepared himself for this enterprize with his usual vigour and abilities. He assembled both a great fleet and a great army; and entering the frontiers of Scotland, appeared with a force, which the enemy could not think of resisting in the open field: The English navy, which sailed along the coast, secured the army from any danger of famine: Edward's vigilance preserved it from surprizes: And by this prudent disposition they marched victorious from one extremity of the kingdom to the other, ravaging the open country, reducing all the castles [e], and receiving the submissions of all the nobility, even those of Cummin the regent. The most obstinate resistance was made by the castle of Brechin, defended by Sir Thomas Maule; and the place opened not its gates, till the death of the governor, by discouraging the garrison, obliged them to submit to the fate, which had overwhelmed the rest of the kingdom. Wallace, though he attended the English army in their march, found but few opportunities of signalizing that valour, which had formerly made him so terrible to his enemies.

Scotland subdued.

[d] Heming. vol. i. p. 197.   [e] Ibid. p. 205.

EDWARD,

EDWARD I.

EDWARD, having completed his conquest, which employed him during the space of near two years, now undertook the more difficult work of settling the country, of establishing a new form of government, and of making his acquisition durable to the crown of England. He seems to have carried matters to extremity against the natives: He abrogated all the Scottish laws and customs[f]: He endeavoured to substitute the English in their place: He entirely razed or destroyed all the monuments of antiquity: Such records or histories as had escaped his former search were now burnt or dispersed: And he hastened, by too precipitate steps, to abolish entirely the Scottish name, and to sink it finally in the English.

EDWARD, however, still deemed his favourite conquest exposed to some danger, so long as Wallace was alive; and being prompted both by revenge and policy, he employed every art to discover his retreat, and become master of his person. At last, that hardy warrior, who was determined, amidst the universal slavery of his countrymen, still to maintain his independency, was betrayed into Edward's hands by Sir John Monteith, his friend, whom he had made acquainted with the place of his concealment. The king, whose natural bravery and magnanimity should have induced him to respect like qualities in an enemy, enraged at some acts of violence committed by Wallace during the fury of war, resolved to overawe the Scots by an example of severity: He ordered Wallace to be carried in chains to London; to be tried as a rebel and traitor, though he had never made submissions, or sworn fealty to England, and to be executed on Tower-hill. This was the unworthy fate of a hero, who, through a course of many years, had, with signal conduct, intrepidity, and perseverance, defended,

[f] Ryley, p. 506.

CHAP.
XIII.

against a public and oppressive enemy, the liberties of his native country.

1305.

But the barbarous policy of Edward failed of the purpose to which it was directed. The Scots, already disgusted at the great innovations introduced by the sword of a conqueror into their laws and government, were farther enraged at the injustice and cruelty exercised upon Wallace; and all the envy which, during his life-time, had attended that gallant chief, being now buried in his grave, he was universally regarded as the champion of Scotland, and the patron of her expiring independency. The people, inflamed with resentment, were every where disposed to rise against the English government; and it was not long ere a new and more fortunate leader presented himself, who conducted them to liberty, to victory, and to vengeance.

1306.
Robert
Bruce.

Robert Bruce, grandson of that Robert who had been one of the competitors for the crown, had succeeded, by his grandfather's and father's death, to all their rights; and the demise of John Baliol, together with the captivity of Edward, eldest son of that prince, seemed to open a full career to the genius and ambition of this young nobleman. He saw that the Scots, when the title to their crown had expired in the males of their ancient royal family, had been divided into parties nearly equal between the houses of Bruce and Baliol; and that every incident, which had since happened, had tended to wean them from any attachment to the latter. The slender capacity of John had proved unable to defend them against their enemies: He had meanly resigned his crown into the hands of the conqueror: He had, before his deliverance from captivity, reiterated that resignation in a manner seemingly voluntary; and had in that deed thrown out many reflections extremely

extremely dishonourable to his ancient subjects, whom he publicly called traitors, ruffians, and rebels, and with whom, he declared, he was determined to maintain no farther correspondence[b]: He had, during the time of his exile, adhered strictly to that resolution; and his son, being a prisoner, seemed ill qualified to revive the rights, now fully abandoned, of his family. Bruce, therefore, hoped that the Scots, so long exposed, from the want of a leader, to the oppressions of their enemies, would unanimously fly to his standard, and would seat him on the vacant throne, to which he brought such plausible pretensions. His aspiring spirit, inflamed by the fervor of youth, and buoyed up by his natural courage, saw the glory alone of the enterprize, or regarded the prodigious difficulties, which attended it, as the source only of farther glory. The miseries and oppressions which he had beheld his countrymen suffer in their unequal contest; the repeated defeats and misfortunes which they had undergone; proved to him so many incentives to bring them relief, and conduct them to vengeance against the haughty victor. The circumstances which attended Bruce's first declaration are variously related; but we shall rather follow the account given by the Scottish historians; not that their authority is in general any wise comparable to that of the English, but because they may be supposed sometimes better informed concerning facts which so nearly interested their own nation.

BRUCE, who had long harboured in his breast the design of freeing his enslaved country, ventured at last to open his mind to John Cummin, a powerful nobleman, with whom he lived in strict intimacy. He found his friend, as he imagined, fully possessed with the same sentiments; and he needed to employ no arts of persuasion to make him embrace the resolution of throwing off, on the first fa-

[b] Brady's hist. vol. ii. App. No. 57.

vourable

vourable opportunity, the usurped dominion of the English. But on the departure of Bruce, who attended Edward to London, Cummin, who either had all along dissembled with him, or began to reflect more coolly in his absence, on the desperate nature of his undertaking, resolved to atone for his crime in assenting to this rebellion, by the merit of revealing the secret to the king of England. Edward did not immediately commit Bruce to custody; because he intended, at the same time, to seize his three brothers, who resided in Scotland; and he contented himself with secretly setting spies upon him, and ordering all his motions to be strictly watched. A nobleman of Edward's court, Bruce's intimate friend, was apprized of his danger; but not daring, amidst so many jealous eyes, to hold any conversation with him, he fell on an expedient to give him warning, that it was full time he should make his escape. He sent him, by a servant, a pair of gilt spurs and a purse of gold, which he pretended to have borrowed from him; and left it to the sagacity of his friend to discover the meaning of the present. Bruce immediately contrived the means of his escape; and as the ground was at that time covered with snow, he had the precaution, it is said, to order his horses to be shod with their shoes inverted, that he might deceive those who should track his path over the open fields or cross roads, through which he purposed to travel. He arrived in a few days at Dumfries, in Annandale, the chief seat of his family interest; and he happily found a great number of the Scottish nobility there assembled, and, among the rest, John Cummin, his former associate.

10th Feb. THE noblemen were astonished at the appearance of Bruce among them; and still more when he discovered to them the object of his journey. He told them, that he was come to live or die with them in defence of the liberties

berties of his country, and hoped, with their affiftance, to redeem the Scottifh name from all the indignities which it had fo long fuffered from the tyranny of their imperious mafters: That the facrifice of the rights of his family was the firft injury which had prepared the way for their enfuing flavery; and by refuming them, which was his firm purpofe, he opened to them the joyful profpect of recovering from the fraudulent ufurper their ancient and hereditary independence: That all paft misfortunes had proceeded from their difunion; and they would foon appear no lefs formidable than of old to their enemies, if they now deigned to follow into the field their rightful prince, who knew no medium between death and victory: That their mountains, and their valour, which had, during fo many ages, protected their liberty from all the efforts of the Roman empire, would ftill be fufficient, were they worthy of their generous anceftors, to defend them againft the utmoft violence of the Englifh tyrant: That it was unbecoming men, born to the moft ancient independence known in Europe, to fubmit to the will of any mafters; but fatal to receive thofe who, being irritated by fuch perfevering refiftance, and inflamed with the higheft animofity, would never deem themfelves fecure in their ufurped dominion, but by exterminating all the ancient nobility, and even all the ancient inhabitants: And that, being reduced to this defperate extremity, it were better for them at once to perifh, like brave men, with fwords in their hands, than to dread long, and at laft undergo the fate of the unfortunate Wallace, whofe merits, in the brave and obftinate defence of his country, were finally rewarded by the hands of an Englifh executioner.

THE fpirit with which this difcourfe was delivered, the bold fentiments which it conveyed, the novelty of Bruce's declaration, affifted by the graces of his youth
and

and manly deportment, made deep impreffion on the minds of his audience, and rouzed all thofe principles of indignation and revenge, with which they had long been fecretly actuated. The Scottifh nobles declared their unanimous refolution to ufe the utmoft efforts in delivering their country from bondage, and to fecond the courage of Bruce, in afferting his and their undoubted rights, againft their common oppreffors. Cummin alone, who had fecretly taken his meafures with the king, oppofed this general determination; and by reprefenting the great power of England, governed by a prince of fuch uncommon vigour and abilities, he endeavoured to fet before them the certain deftruction which they muft expect, if they again violated their oaths of fealty, and fhook off their allegiance to the victorious Edward[1]. Bruce, already apprized of his treachery, and forefeeing the certain failure of all his own fchemes of ambition and glory from the oppofition of fo potent a leader, took immediately his refolution; and moved, partly by refentment, partly by policy, followed Cummin on the diffolution of the affembly, attacked him in the cloyfters of the Grey Friars, through which he paffed, and running him through the body, left him for dead. Sir Thomas Kirkpatric, one of Bruce's friends, afking him, foon after, if the traitor was flain; *I believe fo*, replied Bruce. *And is that a matter*, cried Kirkpatric, *to be left to conjecture? I will fecure him.* Upon which he drew his dagger, ran to Cummin, and ftabbed him to the heart. This deed of Bruce and his affociates, which contains circumftances juftly condemned by our prefent manners, was regarded, in that age, as an effort of manly vigour and juft policy. The family of Kirkpatric took for the creft of their arms, which they ftill wear, a hand with a bloody dagger; and chofe for their motto thefe words, *I will fecure*

[1] M. Weft. p. 453.

him;

him; the expression employed by their ancestor, when he executed that violent action.

CHAP. XIII.

1306. Third revolt of Scotland.

This murder of Cummin affixed the seal to the conspiracy of the Scottish nobles: They had now no resource left but to shake off the yoke of England, or to perish in the attempt: The genius of the nation rouzed itself from its present dejection: And Bruce, flying to different quarters, excited his partizans to arms, attacked with success the dispersed bodies of the English, got possession of many of the castles, and having made his authority be acknowledged in most parts of the kingdom, was solemnly crowned and inaugurated in the abbey of Scone, by the bishop of St. Andrews, who had zealously embraced his cause. The English were again chased out of the kingdom, except such as took shelter in the fortresses that still remained in their hands; and Edward found, that the Scots, twice conquered in his reign, and often defeated, must yet be anew subdued. Not discouraged with these unexpected difficulties, he sent Aymer de Valence with a considerable force into Scotland, to check the progress of the malcontents; and that nobleman falling unexpectedly upon Bruce at Methven in Perthshire, threw his army into such disorder, as ended in a total defeat[k]. Bruce fought with the most heroic courage, was thrice dismounted in the action, and as often recovered himself; but was at last obliged to yield to superior fortune, and take shelter, with a few followers, in the western isles. The earl of Athole, Sir Simon Frazer, and Sir Christopher Seton, who had been taken prisoners, were ordered by Edward to be executed as rebels and traitors[l]. Many other acts of rigour were exercised by him; and that prince, vowing revenge against the whole Scottish nation, whom he deemed incorrigible in their aversion to his government, assembled a great army, and

1307.

[k] Walsing. p. 91. Heming. vol. 1. p. 222, 223. Tyrrel. p. 344.
[l] Heming. vol. 1. p. 223. M. West. p. 456.

was

CHAP. XIII.

1107.
7th July.
Death

and character of the king.

was preparing to enter the frontiers, secure of success, and determined to make the defenceless Scots the victims of his severity; when he unexpectedly sickened and died near Carlisle; enjoining, with last breath, his son and successor to prosecute the enterprize, and never to desist till he had finally subdued the kingdom of Scotland. He expired in the sixty-ninth year of his age, and the thirty-fifth of his reign, hated by his neighbours, but extremely respected and revered by his own subjects.

THE enterprizes, finished by this prince, and the projects which he formed, and brought near to a conclusion, were more prudent, more regularly conducted, and more advantageous to the solid interests of his kingdom, than those which were undertaken in any reign, either of his ancestors or his successors. He restored authority to the government, disordered by the weakness of his father; he maintained the laws against all the efforts of his turbulent barons; he fully annexed to his crown the principality of Wales; he took many wise and vigorous measures for reducing Scotland to a like condition; and though the equity of this latter enterprize may reasonably be questioned, the circumstances of the two kingdoms promised such certain success, and the advantage was so visible of uniting the whole island under one head, that those who give great indulgence to reasons of state in the measures of princes, will not be apt to regard this part of his conduct with much severity. But Edward, however exceptionable his character may appear on the head of justice, is the model of a politic and warlike king: He possessed industry, penetration, courage, vigilance, and enterprize: He was frugal in all expences that were not necessary; he knew how to open the public treasures on a proper occasion; he punished criminals with severity; he was gracious and affable to his servants and courtiers; and being of a majestic figure, expert in

all

EDWARD I.

all military exercises, and, in the main, well-proportioned in his limbs, notwithstanding the great length and the smallness of his legs, he was as well qualified to captivate the populace by his exterior appearance, as to gain the approbation of men of sense by his more solid virtues.

But the chief advantage which the people of England reaped, and still continue to reap, from the reign of this great prince, was the correction, extension, amendment, and establishment of the laws, which Edward maintained in great vigour, and left much improved to posterity: For the acts of a wise legislator commonly remain, while the acquisitions of a conqueror often perish with him. This merit has justly gained to Edward the appellation of the English Justinian. Not only the numerous statutes, passed in his reign, touch the chief points of jurisprudence, and, according to Sir Edward Coke [m], truly deserve the name of establishments, because they were more constant, standing, and durable laws than any made since; but the regular order maintained in his administration, gave an opportunity to the common law to refine itself, and brought the judges to a certainty in their determinations, and the lawyers to a precision in their pleadings. Sir Matthew Hale has remarked the sudden improvement of English law during this reign; and ventures to assert, that, till his own time, it had never received any considerable encrease [n]. Edward settled the jurisdiction of the several courts; first established the office of justice of peace; abstained from the practice, too common before him, of interrupting justice by mandates from the privy-council [o]; repressed robberies and disorders;

Miscellaneous transactions of this reign.

---

[m] Institute, p. 156.   [n] History of the English law, p. 158. 163.
[o] Articuli super Cart. cap. 6. Edward enacted a law to this purpose; but it is doubtful, whether he ever observed it. We are sure that scarcely any of his

CHAP. XIII.

1307.

orders [p], encouraged trade, by giving merchants an easy method of recovering their debts [q]; and, in short, introduced a new face of things by the vigour and wisdom of his administration. As law began now to be well established, the abuse of that blessing began also to be remarked. Instead of their former associations for robbery and violence, men entered into formal combinations to support each other in law-suits; and it was found requisite to check this iniquity by act of parliament [r].

There happened in this reign a considerable alteration in the execution of the laws: The king abolished the office of chief justiciary, which, he thought, possessed too much power, and was dangerous to the crown [s]: He completed the division of the court of exchequer into four distinct courts, which managed, each, its several branch, without dependance on any one magistrate; and as the lawyers afterwards invented a method, by means of their fictions, of carrying business from one court to another, the several courts became rivals and checks to each other; a circumstance which tended much to improve the practice of the law in England.

But though Edward appeared thus, throughout his whole reign, a friend to law and justice, it cannot be said that he was an enemy to arbitrary power; and in a government more regular and legal than was that of England in his age, such practices, as those which may be remarked in his administration, would have given sufficient ground of complaint, and sometimes were, even in his age, the

his successors did. The multitude of these letters of protection were the ground of a complaint by the commons in 3 Edward II. See Ryley, p. 525. This practice is declared illegal by the statute of Northampton, passed in the second of Edward III. but it still continued, like many other abuses. There are instances of it so late as the reign of queen Elizabeth.

[p] Statute of Winton.   [q] Statute of Acton Burnell.
[r] Statute of Conspirators.   [s] Spelman Gloss. In verbo *justiciarius*.
Gilbert's Hist. of the Exchequer, p. 8.

object

object of general displeasure. The violent plunder and banishment of the Jews; the putting of the whole clergy, at once, and by an arbitrary edict, out of the protection of law; the seizing of all the wool and leather of the kingdom; the heightening of the impositions on the former valuable commodity; the new and illegal commission of Trailbaston; the taking of all the money and plate of monasteries and churches, even before he had any quarrel with the clergy; the subjecting of every man possessed of twenty pounds a year to military service, though not bound to it by his tenure; his visible reluctance to confirm the great charter, as if that concession had no validity from the deeds of his predecessors; the captious clause which he at last annexed to his confirmation; his procuring of the pope's dispensation from the oaths which he had taken to observe that charter; and his levying of talliages at discretion even after the statute, or rather charter, by which he had renounced that prerogative; these are so many demonstrations of his arbitrary disposition, and prove with what exception and reserve we ought to celebrate his love of justice. He took care that his subjects should do justice to each other; but he desired always to have his own hands free in all his transactions, both with them and with his neighbours.

THE chief obstacle to the execution of justice in those times was the power of the great barons; and Edward was perfectly qualified, by his character and abilities, for keeping these tyrants in awe, and restraining their illegal practices. This salutary purpose was accordingly the great object of his attention; yet was he imprudently led into a measure which tended to encrease and confirm their dangerous authority. He passed a statute, which, by allowing them to entail their estates, made it impracticable to diminish the property of the great families,

CHAP. XIII.

1307.

lies, and left them every means of encrease and acquisition[t].

EDWARD observed a contrary policy with regard to the church: He seems to have been the first Christian prince that passed a statute of mortmain; and prevented by law the clergy from making new acquisitions of lands, which by the ecclesiastical canons they were for ever prohibited from alienating. The opposition between his maxims with regard to the nobility and to the ecclesiastics, lead us to conjecture, that it was only by chance he passed the beneficial statute of mortmain, and that his sole object was, to maintain the number of knights' fees, and to prevent the superiors from being defrauded of the profits of wardship, marriage, livery, and other emoluments arising from the feudal tenures. This is indeed the reason assigned in the statute itself, and appears to have been his real object in enacting it. The author of the annals of Waverly ascribes this act chiefly to the king's anxiety for maintaining the military force of the kingdom; but adds that he was mistaken in his purpose; for that the Amalekites were overcome more by the prayers of Moses than by the sword of the Israelites[u]. The statute of mortmain was often evaded afterwards by the invention of *Uses*.

EDWARD was active in restraining the usurpations of the church; and excepting his ardour for Crusades, which adhered to him during his whole life, seems, in other respects, to have been little infected with superstition, the vice chiefly of weak minds. But the passion for Crusades was really in that age the passion for glory. As the pope now felt himself somewhat more restrained in his former practice of pillaging the several churches in Europe, by

[t] Brady of Boroughs, p. 15. from the Records.
[u] P. 234. See also M. West. p. 409.

laying

laying impositions upon them, he permitted the generals of particular orders, who refided at Rome, to levy taxes on the convents fubjected to their jurifdiction; and Edward was obliged to enact a law againſt this new abuſe. It was alſo become a practice of the court of Rome to provide ſucceſſors to benefices before they became vacant: Edward found it likewiſe neceſſary to prevent by law this ſpecies of injuſtice.

The tribute of 1000 marks a year, to which king John, in doing homage to the pope, had fubjected the kingdom, had been pretty regularly paid fince his time, though the vaſſalage was conſtantly denied, and indeed, for fear of giving offence, had been but little infifted on. The payment was called by a new name of *cenſus*, not by that of tribute. King Edward ſeems to have always paid this money with great reluctance, and he ſuffered the arrears, at one time, to run on for fix years [w], at another for eleven [x]. But as princes in that age ſtood continually in need of the pope's good offices, for difpenfations of marriage and for other conceſſions, the court of Rome always found means, ſooner or later, to catch the money. The levying of firſt-fruits was alſo a new device, begun in this reign, by which his holineſs thruſt his fingers very frequently into the purſes of the faithful; and the king ſeems to have unwarily given way to it.

In the former reign, the taxes had been partly ſcutages, partly ſuch a proportional part of the moveables, as was granted by parliament: In this, ſcutages were entirely dropped; and the aſſeſſment on moveables was the chief method of taxation. Edward in his fourth year had a fifteenth granted him; in his fifth year a twelfth; in his eleventh year a thirtieth from the laity, a twentieth from the clergy; in his eighteenth year a fifteenth; in

[w] Rymer, vol. ii. p. 77. 107.   [x] Id. p. 862.

his twenty-second year a tenth from the laity, a sixth from London and other corporate towns, half of their benefices from the clergy; in his twenty-third year an eleventh from the barons and others, a tenth from the clergy, a seventh from the burgesses; in his twenty-fourth year a twelfth from the barons and others, an eighth from the burgesses, from the clergy, nothing, because of the pope's inhibition; in his twenty-fifth year an eighth from the laity, a tenth from the clergy of Canterbury, a fifth from those of York; in his twenty-ninth year a fifteenth from the laity, on account of his confirming the perambulations of the forests; the clergy granted nothing; in his thirty-third year, first a thirtieth from the barons and others, and a twentieth from the burgesses, then a fifteenth from all his subjects; in his thirty-fourth year a thirtieth from all his subjects for knighting his eldest son.

These taxes were moderate; but the king had also duties upon exportation and importation granted him from time to time: The heaviest were commonly upon wool. Poundage, or a shilling a pound, was not regularly granted the kings for life till the reign of Henry V.

In 1296, the famous mercantile society, called the *Merchant Adventurers*, had its first origin: It was instituted for the improvement of the woollen manufacture, and the vending of the cloth abroad, particularly at Antwerp[y]. For the English at this time scarcely thought of any more distant commerce.

This king granted a charter or declaration of protection and privileges to foreign merchants, and also ascertained the customs or duties which those merchants were in return to pay on merchandize imported and exported. He promised them security; allowed them a jury on trials,

[y] Anderson's History of Commerce, vol. i. p. 137.

trials, confisting half of natives, half of foreigners; and appointed them a justiciary in London for their protection. But notwithstanding this seeming attention to foreign merchants, Edward did not free them from the cruel hardship of making one answerable for the debts, and even for the crimes of another, that came from the same country [a]. We read of such practices among the present barbarous nations. The king also imposed on them a duty of two shillings on each tun of wine imported, over and above the old duty; and forty pence on each sack of wool exported, besides half a mark, the former duty [c].

In the year 1303, the Exchequer was robbed, and of no less a sum than 100,000 pounds, as is pretended [b]. The abbot and monks of Westminster were indicted for this robbery, but acquitted. It does not appear that the king ever discovered the criminals with certainty; though his indignation fell on the society of Lombard merchants, particularly the Frescobaldi, very opulent Florentines.

The pope having in 1307 collected much money in England, the king enjoined the nuncio not to export it in specie, but in bills of exchange [c]. A proof that commerce was but ill understood at that time.

Edward had by his first wife, Eleanor of Castile, four sons; but Edward, his heir and successor, was the only one that survived him. She also bore him eleven daughters, most of whom died in their infancy: Of the surviving, Joan was married first to the earl of Glocester, and after his death, to Ralph de Monthermer: Margaret espoused John duke of Brabant: Elizabeth espoused first John earl of Holland; and afterwards the earl of Hereford: Mary

[a] Anderson's Hist. of Commerce, vol. I. p. 146. [b] Rymer, vol iv. p. 361. It is the charter of Edw. I. which is there confirmed by Edw III. [b] Rymer, vol. ii. p. 930. [c] Rymer, vol. ii. p. 1092.

CHAP. XIII.
1307.

was a nun at Ambresbury. He had by his second wife, Margaret of France, two sons and a daughter; Thomas created earl of Norfolk, and marefchal of England; and Edmond who was created earl of Kent by his brother when king. The princess died in her infancy.

CHAP. XIV.

EDWARD II.

Weakness of the king——His passion for favourites ——Piers Gavaston——Discontent of the barons ——Murder of Gavaston——War with Scotland ——Battle of Bannockburn——Hugh le Despenser——Civil commotions——Execution of the earl of Lancaster——Conspiracy against the king——Insurrection——The king dethroned——Murdered ——His character——Miscellaneous transactions in this reign.

THE prepossessions, entertained in favour of young Edward, kept the English from being fully sensible of the extreme loss, which they had sustained by the death of the great monarch who filled the throne; and all men hastened with alacrity to take the oath of allegiance to his son and successor. This prince was in the twenty-third year of his age, was of an agreeable figure, of a mild and gentle disposition, and having never discovered a propensity to any dangerous vice, it was natural to prognosticate tranquillity and happiness from his government. But the first act of his reign blasted all these hopes, and shewed him to be totally unqualified for that perilous situation, in which every English monarch, during those ages, had, from the unstable form of the constitution, and the turbulent dispositions of the people derived from it, the misfortune to be placed. The indefatigable Robert Bruce, though his army had been dispersed, and he himself had been obliged to take shelter in the western isles,

remained

CHAP.
XIV.
1307.

remained not long unactive; but before the death of the late king, had fallied from his retreat, had again collected his followers, had appeared in the field, and had obtained by surprize an important advantage over Aymer de Valence, who commanded the English forces [d]. He was now become so considerable as to have afforded the king of England sufficient glory in subduing him, without incurring any danger of seeing all those mighty preparations, made by his father, fail in the enterprize. But Edward, instead of pursuing his advantages, marched but a little way into Scotland; and having an utter incapacity, and equal aversion, for all application or serious business, he immediately returned upon his footsteps, and disbanded his army. His grandees perceived from this conduct, that the authority of the crown, fallen into such feeble hands, was no longer to be dreaded, and that every insolence might be practised by them with impunity.

His passion for favourites, Piers Gavaston.

THE next measure, taken by Edward, gave them an inclination to attack those prerogatives which no longer kept them in awe. There was one Piers Gavaston, son of a Gascon knight of some distinction, who had honourably served the late king, and who, in reward of his merits, had obtained an establishment for his son in the family of the prince of Wales. This young man soon insinuated himself into the affections of his master, by his agreeable behaviour, and by supplying him with all those innocent, though frivolous amusements, which suited his capacity and his inclinations. He was endowed with the utmost elegance of shape and person, was noted for a fine mien and easy carriage, distinguished himself in all warlike and genteel exercises, and was celebrated for those quick sallies of wit, in which his countrymen usually excel. By all these accomplishments he gained so entire an ascendant over young Edward, whose heart was strongly

[d] Trivet, p. 341.

disposed

EDWARD II.

disposed to friendship and confidence, that the late king, apprehensive of the consequences, had banished him the kingdom, and had, before he died, made his son promise never to recall him. But no sooner did he find himself master, as he vainly imagined, than he sent for Gavaston; and, even before his arrival at court, endowed him with the whole earldom of Cornwal, which had escheated to the crown by the death of Edmond, son of Richard king of the Romans [a]. Not content with conferring on him those possessions, which had sufficed as an appanage for a prince of the blood, he daily loaded him with new honours and riches; married him to his own niece, sister of the earl of Glocester; and seemed to enjoy no pleasure in his royal dignity, but as it enabled him to exalt to the highest splendor this object of his fond affections.

The haughty barons, offended at the superiority of a minion, whose birth, though reputable, they despised, as much inferior to their own, concealed not their discontent; and soon found reasons to justify their animosity in the character and conduct of the man they hated. Instead of disarming envy by the moderation and modesty of his behaviour, Gavaston displayed his power and influence with the utmost ostentation; and deemed no circumstance of his good fortune so agreeable as its enabling him to eclipse and mortify all his rivals. He was vain-glorious, profuse, rapacious; fond of exterior pomp and appearance, giddy with prosperity; and, as he imagined, that his fortune was now as strongly rooted in the kingdom, as his ascendant was uncontrouled over the weak monarch, he was negligent in engaging partizans, who might support his sudden and ill-established grandeur. At all tournaments, he took delight in foiling the English nobility by his superior address: In every conversation, he made

CHAP. XIV.
1307.

Discontent of the barons.

[a] Rymer, vol. iii. p. 1. Hemingf. vol. i. p. 243. Walsing. p. 96.

them

330   HISTORY OF ENGLAND.

CHAP.   them the object of his wit and raillery: Every day his
XIV.   enemies multiplied upon him; and naught was wanting
1307.   but a little time to cement their union, and render it fatal,
        both to him and to his master [f].

It behoved the king to take a journey to France, both in order to do homage for the dutchy of Guienne, and to espouse the princess Isabella, to whom he had long been affianced, though unexpected accidents had hitherto retarded the completion of the marriage [g]. Edward left Gavaston guardian of the realm [h], with more ample powers than had usually been conferred [i]; and, on his return with his young queen, renewed all the proofs of that fond attachment to the favourite, of which every one so loudly complained. This princess was of an imperious and intriguing spirit; and finding that her husband's capacity required, as his temper inclined, him to be governed, she thought herself best intitled, on every account, to perform the office; and she contracted a mortal hatred against the person who had disappointed her in these expectations. She was well pleased, therefore, to see a combination of the nobility forming against Gavaston, who, sensible of her hatred, had wantonly provoked her by new insults and injuries.

1308.   Thomas, earl of Lancaster, cousin-german to the king, and first prince of the blood, was by far the most opulent and powerful subject in England, and possessed in his own right, and soon after in that of his wife, heiress of the family of Lincoln, no less than six earldoms, with a proportionable estate in land, attended with all the jurisdictions and power which commonly, in that age, were annexed to landed property. He was turbulent and factious in his disposition; mortally hated the favourite, whose influence over the king exceeded his own; and he soon became the

[f] T. de la More, p. 593. Walsing. p. 97. [g] T. de la More, p. 593. Trivet, cont. p. 3. [h] Rymer, vol. III. p. 47. Ypod. Neust. p. 499. [i] Brady's App. N° 49.

head

EDWARD II.

head of that party among the barons, who defired the depreffion of this infolent ftranger. The confederated nobles bound themfelves by oath to expel Gavafton: Both fides began already to put themfelves in a warlike pofture: The licentioufnefs of the age broke out in robberies and other diforders, the ufual prelude of civil war: And the royal authority, defpifed in the king's own hands, and hated in thofe of Gavafton, became infufficient for the execution of the laws, and the maintenance of peace in the kingdom. A parliament being fummoned at Weftminfter, Lancafter and his party came thither with an armed retinue; and were there enabled to impofe their own terms on the fovereign. They required the banifhment of Gavafton, impofed an oath on him never to return, and engaged the bifhops, who never failed to interpofe in all civil concerns, to pronounce him excommunicated, if he remained any longer in the kingdom[1]. Edward was obliged to fubmit[k]; but even in his compliance, gave proofs of his fond attachment to his favourite. Inftead of removing all umbrage, by fending him to his own country, as was expected, he appointed him lord lieutenant of Ireland[l], attended him to Briftol on his journey thither, and before his departure conferred on him new lands and riches both in Gafcony and England[m]. Gavafton, who did not want bravery, and poffeffed talents for war[n], acted, during his government, with vigour againft fome Irifh rebels, whom he fubdued.

MEANWHILE the king, lefs fhocked with the illegal violence which had been impofed upon him, than unhappy in the abfence of his minion, employed every expedient to foften the oppofition of the barons to his return; as if fuccefs in that point were the chief object of his

CHAP.
XIV.

1308.

[1] Trivet, cont. p. 5. p. 92. Murimuth, p. 39.
[a] Heming. vol. 1. p. 248.
[k] Rymer, vol. III. p. 80.
[m] Rymer, vol. III. p. 87.
T. de la Mor, p. 593.
[l] Ibid.

government,

331

CHAP. XIV.
1308.
7th Feb.

government. The high office of hereditary steward was conferred on Lancaster: His father-in-law, the earl of Lincoln, was bought off by other concessions: Earl Warrenne was also mollified by civilities, grants, or promises: The insolence of Gavaston being no longer before men's eyes, was left the object of general indignation: And Edward, deeming matters sufficiently prepared for his purpose, applied to the court of Rome, and obtained for Gavaston a dispensation from that oath which the barons had compelled him to take, that he would for ever abjure the realm °. He went down to Chester, to receive him on his first landing from Ireland; flew into his arms with transports of joy; and having obtained the formal consent of the barons in parliament to his re-establishment, set no longer any bounds to his extravagant fondness and affection. Gavaston himself, forgetting his past misfortunes, and blind to their causes, resumed the same ostentation and insolence; and became more than ever the object of general detestation among the nobility.

THE barons first discovered their animosity by absenting themselves from parliament; and finding that this expedient had not been successful, they began to think of employing sharper and more effectual remedies. Though there had scarcely been any national ground of complaint, except some dissipation of the public treasure: Though all the acts of mal-administration, objected to the king and his favourite, seemed of a nature more proper to excite heart-burnings in a ball or assembly, than commotions in a great kingdom: Yet such was the situation of the times, that the barons were determined, and were able, to make them the reasons of a total alteration in the constitution and civil government. Having come to parliament, in defiance of the laws and the king's prohibition, with a numerous retinue of armed followers, they

° Rymer, vol. III. p. 167.

found

found themselves entirely masters; and they presented a petition, which was equivalent to a command, requiring Edward to devolve on a chosen junto the whole authority, both of the crown and of the parliament. The king was obliged to sign a commission, empowering the prelates and barons to elect twelve persons, who should, till the term of Michaelmas, in the year following, have authority to enact ordinances for the government of the kingdom, and regulation of the king's household; consenting that these ordinances should, thenceforth, and for ever, have the force of laws; allowing the ordainers to form associations among themselves and their friends, for their strict and regular observance, and all this for the greater glory of God, the security of the church, and the honour and advantage of the king and kingdom *p*. The barons in return signed a declaration, in which they acknowledged, that they owed these concessions merely to the king's free grace; promised that this commission should never be drawn into precedent; and engaged, that the power of the ordainers should expire at the time appointed *q*.

CHAP. XIV.

1308.

16th March.

The chosen junto accordingly framed their ordinances, and presented them to the king and parliament, for their confirmation in the ensuing year. Some of these ordinances were laudable, and tended to the regular execution of justice: Such as those, requiring sheriffs to be men of property, abolishing the practice of issuing privy seals for the suspension of justice, restraining the practice of purveyance, prohibiting the adulteration and alteration of the coin, excluding foreigners from the farms of the revenue, ordering all payments to be regularly made into the exchequer, revoking all late grants of the crown, and giving the parties damages in the case of vexatious prosecutions. But what

1311.

p Brady's App. N° 50. Hem'ng. vol. l. p. 247. W. 608. p. 97. Ryley, p. 516. *q* Brady's App. N° 51.

chiefly

chiefly grieved the king, was the ordinance for the removal of evil counsellors, by which a great number of persons were by name excluded from every office of power and profit; and Piers Gavaston himself was for ever banished the king's dominions, under the penalty, in case of disobedience, of being declared a public enemy. Other persons, more agreeable to the barons, were substituted in all the offices. And it was ordained, that, for the future, all the considerable dignities in the household, as well as in the law, revenue, and military governments, should be appointed by the *baronage* in parliament; and the power of making war, or assembling his military tenants, should no longer be vested solely in the king, nor be exercised without the consent of the nobility.

EDWARD, from the same weakness both in his temper and situation, which had engaged him to grant this unlimited commission to the barons, was led to give a parliamentary sanction to their ordinances: But as a consequence of the same character, he *secretly* made a protest against them, and declared, that, since the commission was granted only for the making of ordinances to the advantage of king and kingdom, such articles as should be found prejudicial to both, were to be held as not ratified and confirmed [r]. It is no wonder, indeed, that he retained a firm purpose to revoke ordinances, which had been imposed on him by violence, which entirely annihilated the royal authority, and above all which deprived him of the company and society of a person whom, by an unusual infatuation, he valued above all the world, and above every consideration of interest or tranquillity.

As soon, therefore, as Edward, removing to York, had freed himself from the immediate terror of the barons power, he invited back Gavaston from Flanders, which that favourite had made the place of his retreat; and declaring

[r] Ryley's Placit. Part. p. 530. 541.

claring his banishment to be illegal, and contrary to the laws and customs of the kingdom[s], openly re-instated him in his former credit and authority. The barons, highly provoked at this disappointment, and apprehensive of danger to themselves, from the declared animosity of so powerful a minion, saw, that either his or their ruin was now inevitable; and they renewed, with redoubled zeal, their former confederacy against him. The earl of Lancaster was a dangerous head of this alliance: Guy, earl of Warwic, entered into it with a furious and precipitate passion: Humphrey Bohun, earl of Hereford, the constable, and Aymer de Valence, earl of Pembroke, brought to it a great accession of power and interest: Even earl Warrenne deserted the royal cause, which he had hitherto supported, and was induced to embrace the side of the confederates[t]: And as Robert de Winchelsey, archbishop of Canterbury, professed himself of the same party, he determined the body of the clergy, and consequently the people, to declare against the king and his minion. So predominant, at that time, was the power of the great nobility, that the combination of a few of them was always able to shake the throne; and such an universal concurrence became irresistible. The earl of Lancaster suddenly raised an army, and marched to York, where he found the king already removed to Newcastle[u]: He flew thither in pursuit of him; and Edward had just time to escape to Tinmouth, where he embarked, and sailed with Gavaston to Scarborough. He left his favourite in that fortress, which, had it been properly supplied with provisions, was deemed impregnable; and he marched forward to York, in hopes of raising an army, which might be able to support him against his enemies. Pembroke was sent by the confederates to besiege the castle of Scarborough;

CHAP. XIV.

1312.

[s] Brady's App. N° 53. Walsing. p. 98.
[u] Walsing. p. ibid.
[t] Trivet, cont. p. 4.

borough; and Gavaston, senfible of the bad condition of his garrison, was obliged to capitulate, and to surrender himself prisoner [w]. He stipulated, that he should remain in Pembroke's hands for two months; that endeavours should, during that time, be mutually used for a general accommodation; that if the terms proposed by the barons were not accepted, the castle should be restored to him in the same condition as when he surrendered it; and that the earl of Pembroke and Henry Piercy should, by contract, pledge all their lands for the fulfilling of these conditions [x]. Pembroke, now master of the person of this public enemy, conducted him to the castle of Dedington, near Banbury; where, on pretence of other business, he left him, protected by a feeble guard [y]. Warwic, probably in concert with Pembroke, attacked the castle: The garrison refused to make any resistance: Gavaston was yielded up to him, and conducted to Warwic castle: The Earls of Lancaster, Hereford, and Arundel, immediately repaired thither [z]: And without any regard, either to the laws or the military capitulation, they ordered the head of the obnoxious favourite to be struck off by the hands of the executioner [a].

THE king had retired northward to Berwic, when he heard of Gavaston's murder; and his resentment was proportioned to the affection which he had ever borne him while living. He threatened vengeance on all the nobility who had been active in that bloody scene, and he made preparations for war in all parts of England. But being less constant in his enmities than in his friendships, he soon after hearkened to terms of accommodation; granted the barons a pardon of all offences; and as they stipulated to ask him publicly pardon on their knees [b], he

---

[w] Walsing. p. 101.   [x] Rymer, vol. ii. p. 314.
[y] T. de la More, p. 593.   [z] Dugd. Baron. vol. II. p. 44.
[a] Walsing. p. 101. T. de la More, p. 593. Trivet, cont. p. 9.
[b] Ryley, p. 538. Rymer, vol. iii, p. 366.

EDWARD II.

was so pleased with these vain appearances of submission, that he seemed to have sincerely forgiven them all past injuries. But as they still pretended, notwithstanding their lawless conduct, a great anxiety for the maintenance of law, and required the establishment of their former ordinances as a necessary security for that purpose, Edward told them, that he was willing to grant them a free and legal confirmation of such of these ordinances as were not entirely derogatory to the prerogative of the crown. This answer was received, for the present, as satisfactory. The king's person, after the death of Gavaston, was now become less obnoxious to the public; and as the ordinances insisted on appeared to be nearly the same with those which had formerly been extorted from Henry III. by Mountfort, and which had been attended with so many fatal consequences, they were, on that account, demanded with less vehemence by the nobility and people. The minds of all men seemed to be much appeased: The animosities of faction no longer prevailed: And England, now united under its head, would henceforth be able, it was hoped, to take vengeance on all its enemies; particularly on the Scots, whose progress was the object of general resentment and indignation.

CHAP. XIV.

1312.

IMMEDIATELY after Edward's retreat from Scotland, Robert Bruce left his fastnesses, in which he intended to have sheltered his feeble army; and supplying his defect of strength by superior vigour and abilities, he made deep impression on all his enemies, foreign and domestic. He chaced lord Argyle, and the chieftain of the Macdowals, from their hills, and made himself entirely master of the high country: He thence invaded, with success, the Cummins in the low countries of the north: He took the castles of Inverness, Forfar, and Brechin: He daily gained some new accession of territory; and, what was a

War with Scotland.

CHAP. XIV.
1312.

more important acquisition, he daily reconciled the minds of the nobility to his dominion, and inlisted under his standard every bold leader, whom he enriched by the spoils of his enemies. Sir James Douglas, in whom commenced the greatness and renown of that warlike family, seconded him in all his enterprizes: Edward Bruce, Robert's own brother, distinguished himself by acts of valour: And the terror of the English power being now abated by the feeble conduct of the king, even the least sanguine of the Scots began to entertain hopes of recovering their independence; and the whole kingdom, except a few fortresses, which he had not the means to attack, had acknowledged the authority of Robert.

In this situation, Edward had found it necessary to grant a truce to Scotland; and Robert successfully employed the interval in consolidating his power, and introducing order into the civil government, disjointed by a long continuance of wars and factions. The interval was very short: The truce, ill observed on both sides, was at last openly violated; and war recommenced with greater fury than ever. Robert, not content with defending himself, had made successful inroads into England, subsisted his needy followers by the plunder of that country, and taught them to despise the military genius of a people who had long been the object of their terror. Edward, at last, rouzed from his lethargy, had marched an army into Scotland; and Robert, determined not to risque too much against an enemy so much superior, retired again into the mountains. The king advanced beyond Edinburgh; but, being destitute of provisions, and being ill supported by the English nobility, who were then employed in framing their ordinances, he was soon obliged to retreat, without gaining any advantage over the enemy. But the appearing union of all the parties in England,

EDWARD II.

England, after the death of Gavaston, seemed to restore that kingdom to its native force, opened again the prospect of reducing Scotland, and promised a happy conclusion to a war in which both the interests and passions of the nation were so deeply engaged.

CHAP.
XIV.

1311.

EDWARD assembled forces from all quarters, with a view of finishing, at one blow, this important enterprize. He summoned the most warlike of his vassals from Gascony: He inlisted troops from Flanders, and other foreign countries: He invited over great numbers of the disorderly Irish as to a certain prey: He joined to them a body of the Welsh, who were actuated by like motives: And assembling the whole military force of England, he marched to the frontiers with an army which, according to the Scotch writers, amounted to a hundred thousand men.

1314.

The army collected by Robert exceeded not thirty thousand combatants; but being composed of men who had distinguished themselves by many acts of valour, who were rendered desperate by their situation, and who were enured to all the varieties of fortune, they might justly, under such a leader, be deemed formidable to the most numerous and best appointed armies. The castle of Stirling, which, with Berwic, was the only fortress in Scotland that remained in the hands of the English, had long been besieged by Edward Bruce: Philip de Mowbray, the governor, after an obstinate defence, was at last obliged to capitulate, and to promise, that if, before a certain day which was now approaching, he were not relieved, he should open his gates to the enemy[c]. Robert, therefore, sensible that here was the ground on which he must expect the English, chose the field of battle with all the skill and prudence imaginable, and made

[c] Rymer, vol. iii. p. 481.

the necessary preparations for their reception. He posted himself at Bannockburn, about two miles from Stirling; where he had a hill on his right flank, and a morass on his left: And not content with having taken these precautions to prevent his being surrounded by the more numerous army of the English, he foresaw the superior strength of the enemy in cavalry, and made provision against it. Having a rivulet in front, he commanded deep pits to be dug along its banks, and sharp stakes to be planted in them; and he ordered the whole to be carefully covered over with turf [d]. The English arrived in sight on the evening, and a bloody conflict immediately ensued between two bodies of cavalry; where Robert, who was at the head of the Scots, engaged in single combat with Henry de Bohun, a gentleman of the family of Hereford, and at one stroke cleft his adversary to the chin with a battle-ax, in sight of the two armies. The English horse fled with precipitation to their main body.

The Scots, encouraged by this favourable event, and glorying in the valour of their prince, prognosticated a happy issue to the combat on the ensuing day: The English, confident in their numbers, and elated with former successes, longed for an opportunity of revenge: And the night, though extremely short in that season and in that climate, appeared tedious to the impatience of the several combatants. Early in the morning Edward drew out his army, and advanced towards the Scots. The earl of Glocester, his nephew, who commanded the left wing of the cavalry, impelled by the ardour of youth, rushed on to the attack without precaution, and fell among the covered pits, which had been prepared by Bruce for the reception of the enemy [e]. This body of horse was disordered: Glocester himself was overthrown and slain: Sir James Douglas, who commanded the Scot-

[d] T. de la Mote, p. 554.   [e] Ibid.

tish cavalry, gave the enemy no leisure to rally, but pushed them off the field with considerable loss, and pursued them in sight of their whole line of infantry. While the English army were alarmed with this unfortunate beginning of the action, which commonly proves decisive, they observed an army on the heights towards the left, which seemed to be marching leisurely in order to surround them; and they were distracted by their multiplied fears. This was a number of waggoners and sumpter-boys, whom Robert had collected; and having supplied them with military standards, gave them the appearance, at a distance, of a formidable body. The stratagem took effect: A panic seized the English: They threw down their arms, and fled: They were pursued with great slaughter, for the space of ninety miles, till they reached Berwic: And the Scots, besides an inestimable booty, took many persons of quality prisoners, and above 400 gentlemen, whom Robert treated with great humanity [f], and whose ransom was a new accession of wealth to the victorious army. The king himself narrowly escaped, by taking shelter in Dunbar, whose gates were opened to him by the earl of March; and he thence passed by sea to Berwic.

Such was the great and decisive battle of Bannockburn, which secured the independence of Scotland, fixed Bruce on the throne of that kingdom, and may be deemed the greatest overthrow that the English nation, since the conquest, has ever received. The number of slain on those occasions is always uncertain, and is commonly much magnified by the victors: But this defeat made a deep impression on the minds of the English; and it was remarked, that, for some years, no superiority of numbers could encourage them to keep the field against the Scots. Robert, in order to avail himself of his present success,

[f] Ypod. Neust. p. 504.

success, entered England, and ravaged all the northern counties without opposition: He besieged Carlisle; but that place was saved by the valour of Sir Andrew Harcla, the governor: He was more successful against Berwic, which he took by assault: And this prince, elated by his continued prosperity, now entertained hopes of making the most important conquests on the English. He sent over his brother Edward, with an army of 6000 men, into Ireland; and that nobleman assumed the title of King of that island: He himself followed soon after with more numerous forces: The horrible and absurd oppressions which the Irish suffered under the English government made them, at first, fly to the standard of the Scots, whom they regarded as their deliverers: But a grievous famine, which at that time desolated both Ireland and Britain, reduced the Scottish army to the greatest extremities; and Robert was obliged to return, with his forces much diminished, into his own country. His brother, after having experienced a variety of fortune, was defeated and slain near Dundalk by the English, commanded by lord Bermingham: And these projects, too extensive for the force of the Scottish nation, thus vanished into smoke.

EDWARD, besides suffering those disasters from the invasion of the Scots, and the insurrection of the Irish, was also infested with a rebellion in Wales; and, above all, by the factions of his own nobility, who took advantage of the public calamities, insulted his fallen fortunes, and endeavoured to establish their own independence on the ruins of the throne. Lancaster, and the barons of his party, who had declined attending him on his Scottish expedition, no sooner saw him return with disgrace, than they insisted on the renewal of their ordinances, which, they still pretended, had validity; and the king's unhappy situation obliged him to submit to their demands. The ministry was new modelled by the direction of Lancaster [t];

[t] Ryley, p. 569. Rymer, vol. iii. p. 712.

That

EDWARD II.

That prince was placed at the head of the council: It was declared, that all the offices should be filled, from time to time, by the votes of parliament, or rather by the will of the great barons [b]: And the nation, under this new model of government, endeavoured to put itself in a better posture of defence against the Scots. But the factious nobles were far from being terrified with the progress of these public enemies: On the contrary, they founded the hopes of their own future grandeur on the weakness and distresses of the crown: Lancaster himself was suspected, with great appearance of reason, of holding a secret correspondence with the king of Scots: And though he was entrusted with the command of the English armies, he took care that every enterprize should be disappointed, and every plan of operations prove unsuccessful.

ALL the European kingdoms, especially that of England, were at this time unacquainted with the office of a prime minister, so well understood at present in all regular monarchies; and the people could form no conception of a man, who, though still in the rank of a subject, possessed all the power of a sovereign, eased the prince of the burthen of affairs, supplied his want of experience or capacity, and maintained all the rights of the crown, without degrading the greatest nobles by their submission to his temporary authority. Edward was plainly, by nature, unfit to hold himself the reins of government: He had no vices, but was unhappy in a total incapacity for serious business: He was sensible of his own defects, and necessarily sought to be governed: Yet every favourite whom he successively chose was regarded as a fellow-subject exalted above his rank and station: He was the object of envy to the great nobility: His character and conduct were decried with the people: His authority

CHAP.
XIV.

1315.

[b] Brady, vol. II. p. 122. from the records, App. N° 61. Ryley, p. 560.

CHAP. XIV.

1315.

over the king and kingdom was confidered as an ufurpation: And unlefs the prince had embraced the dangerous expedient, of devolving his power on the earl of Lancafter, or fome mighty baron, whofe family intereft was fo extenfive as to be able alone to maintain his influence, he could expect no peace or tranquillity upon the throne.

Hugh le Defpenfer.

THE king's chief favourite, after the death of Gavafton, was Hugh le Defpenfer, or Spenfer, a young man of Englifh birth, of high rank, and of a noble family[f]. He poffeffed all the exterior accomplifhments of perfon and addrefs, which were fitted to engage the weak mind of Edward; but was deftitute of that moderation and prudence which might have qualified him to mitigate the envy of the great, and conduct him through all the perils of that dangerous ftation to which he was advanced. His father, who was of the fame name, and who, by means of his fon, had alfo attained great influence over the king, was a nobleman venerable from his years, refpected through all his paft life for wifdom, valour, and integrity, and well fitted, by his talents and experience, could affairs have admitted of any temperament, to have fupplied the defects both of the king and of his minion[h]. But no fooner was Edward's attachment declared for young Spenfer, than the turbulent Lancafter, and moft of the great barons, regarded him as their rival, made him the object of their animofity, and formed violent plans for his ruin[i]. They firft declared their difcontent by withdrawing from parliament; and it was not long ere they found a pretence for proceeding to greater extremities againft him.

1311. Civil commotions.

THE king, who fet no limits to his bounty towards his minions, had married the younger Spenfer to his niece, one of the co-heirs of the earl of Gloceſter, flain at

[f] Dugd. Baron. vol. I. p. 389. [h] T. de la More, p. 594.
[i] Walfingham, p. 113. T. de la More, p. 593. Murimoth, p. 55.

Bannockburn.

Bannockburn. The favourite, by his succession to that opulent family, had inherited great possessions in the marches of Wales[m]; and being desirous of extending still farther his influence in those quarters, he is accused of having committed injustice on the barons of Audley and Ammori, who had also married two sisters of the same family. There was likewise a baron in that neighbourhood, called William de Braoufe, lord of Gower, who had made a settlement of his estate on John de Mowbray, his son-in-law; and, in case of failure of that nobleman and his issue, had substituted the earl of Hereford in the succession to the barony of Gower. Mowbray, on the decease of his father-in-law, entered immediately in possession of the estate, without the formality of taking livery and seizin from the crown: But Spenser, who coveted that barony, persuaded the king to put in execution the rigour of the feudal law, to seize Gower as escheated to the crown, and to confer it upon him[n]. This transaction, which was the proper subject of a lawsuit, immediately excited a civil war in the kingdom. The earls of Lancaster and Hereford flew to arms: Audley and Ammori joined them with all their forces: The two Rogers de Mortimer and Roger de Clifford, with many others, disgusted, for private reasons, at the Spensers, brought a considerable accession to the party: And their army being now formidable, they sent a message to the king, requiring him immediately to dismiss or confine the younger Spenser; and menacing him, in case of refusal, with renouncing their allegiance to him, and taking revenge on that minister by their own authority. They scarcely waited for an answer; but immediately fell upon the lands of young Spenser, which they pillaged and destroyed; murdered his servants, drove off his cattle, and burned his houses[o]. They thence proceeded to

CHAP. XIV.

1311.

[m] Trivet, cont. p. 25. [n] Monach. Malmes. p. 36. [o] Murimarh,

commit

CHAP. XIV.

1321.

commit like devastations on the estates of Spenser the father, whose character they had hitherto seemed to respect: And having drawn and signed a formal association among themselves [p], they marched to London with all their forces, stationed themselves in the neighbourhood of that city, and demanded of the king the banishment of both the Spensers. These noblemen were then absent; the father abroad, the son at sea; and both of them employed in different commissions: The king therefore replied, that his coronation oath, by which he was bound to observe the laws, restrained him from giving his assent to so illegal a demand, or condemning noblemen who were accused of no crime, nor had any opportunity afforded them of making answer [q]. Equity and reason were but a feeble opposition to men who had arms in their hands, and who, being already involved in guilt, saw no safety but in success and victory. They entered London with their troops; and giving in to the parliament, which was then sitting, a charge against the Spensers, of which they attempted not to prove one article, they procured, by menaces and violence, a sentence of attainder and perpetual exile against these ministers [r]. This sentence was voted by the lay barons alone: For the commons, though now an estate in parliament, were yet of so little consideration, that their assent was not demanded; and even the votes of the prelates were neglected amidst the present disorders. The only symptom which these turbulent barons gave of their regard to law, was their requiring from the king an indemnity for their illegal proceedings [s]; after which they disbanded their army, and separated, in security, as they imagined, to their several castles.

[p] Tyrrel, vol. ii. p. 280. from the register of C. C. Canterbury.
[q] Walsing. p. 114. [r] Tottle's Collect. part 2. p. 50. Walsing. p. 114. [s] Tottle's Collect. part 2. p. 54. Rymer, vol. iii. p. 891.

THIS

THIS act of violence, in which the king was obliged to acquiesce, rendered his person and his authority so contemptible, that every one thought himself entitled to treat him with neglect. The queen, having occasion soon after to pass by the castle of Leeds in Kent, which belonged to the lord Badlesmere, desired a night's lodging, but was refused admittance; and some of her attendants, who presented themselves at the gate, were killed[t]. The insult upon this princess, who had always endeavoured to live on good terms with the barons, and who joined them heartily in their hatred of the younger Spenser, was an action which no body pretended to justify; and the king thought that he might, without giving general umbrage, assemble an army, and take vengeance on the offender. No one came to the assistance of Badlesmere; and Edward prevailed[u]: But having now some forces on foot, and having concerted measures with his friends throughout England, he ventured to take off the mask, to attack all his enemies, and to recall the two Spensers, whose sentence he declared illegal, unjust, contrary to the tenor of the Great Charter, passed without the assent of the prelates, and extorted by violence from him and the estate of barons[w]. Still the commons were not mentioned by either party.

THE king had now got the start of the barons; an advantage which, in those times, was commonly decisive: And he hastened with his army to the marches of Wales, the chief seat of the power of his enemies, whom he found totally unprepared for resistance. Many of the barons in those parts endeavoured to appease him by submission[x]: Their castles were seized, and their persons committed to custody. But Lancaster, in order to prevent the total ruin

[t] Rymer, vol. lii. p. 89. Walsing. p. 114, 115. T. de la More, p. 595. Murimuth, p. 56. [u] Walsing. p. 115. [w] Rymer, vol. lii. p. 907. T. de la More, p. 595. [x] Walsing. p. 115. Murimuth, p. 57.

of his party, summoned together his vassals and retainers; declared his alliance with Scotland, which had long been suspected; received the promise of a reinforcement from that country, under the command of Randolf earl of Murray, and Sir James Douglas [y]; and being joined by the earl of Hereford, advanced with all his forces against the king, who had collected an army of 30,000 men, and was superior to his enemies. Lancaster posted himself at Burton upon Trent, and endeavoured to defend the passages of the river [z]: But being disappointed in that plan of operations, this prince, who had no military genius, and whose personal courage was even suspected, fled with his army to the north, in expectation of being there joined by his Scottish allies [a]. He was pursued by the king; and his army diminished daily; till he came to Boroughbridge, where he found Sir Andrew Harcla posted with some forces on the opposite side of the river, and ready to dispute the passage with him. He was repulsed in an attempt which he made to force his way; the earl of Hereford was killed; the whole army of the rebels was disconcerted; Lancaster himself was become incapable of taking any measures either for flight or defence; and he was seized, without resistance, by Harcla, and conducted to the king [b]. In those violent times, the laws were so much neglected on both sides, that, even where they might, without any sensible inconvenience, have been observed, the conquerors deemed it unnecessary to pay any regard to them. Lancaster, who was guilty of open rebellion, and was taken in arms against his sovereign, instead of being tried by the laws of his country, which pronounced the sentence of death against him, was condemned by a court-martial [c], and led to execution. Edward, however little vindictive in

[y] Rymer, vol. III. p. 938. [z] Walsing. p. 115. [a] Ypod. Neust. p. 504. [b] T. de la More, p. 596. Walsing. p. 116. [c] Tyrrel, vol. III. p. 291. from the records.

his

his natural temper, here indulged his revenge, and employed against the prisoner the same indignities which had been exercised, by his orders, against Gavaston. He was clothed in a mean attire, placed on a lean jade without a bridle, a hood was put on his head, and in this posture, attended by the acclamations of the people, this prince was conducted to an eminence near Pontfret, one of his own castles, and there beheaded [4].

THUS perished Thomas earl of Lancaster, prince of the blood, and one of the most potent barons that had ever been in England. His public conduct sufficiently discovers the violence and turbulence of his character: His private deportment appears not to have been more innocent: And his hypocritical devotion, by which he gained the favour of the monks and populace, will rather be regarded as an aggravation than an alleviation of his guilt. Badlesmere, Giffard, Barret, Cheyney, Fleming, and about eighteen of the most notorious offenders, were afterwards condemned by a legal trial, and were executed. Many were thrown into prison: Others made their escape beyond sea: Some of the king's servants were rewarded from the forfeitures: Harcla received for his services the earldom of Carlisle, and a large estate, which he soon after forfeited with his life, for a treasonable correspondence with the king of Scotland. But the greater part of those vast escheats was seized by young Spenser, whose rapacity was insatiable. Many of the barons of the king's party were disgusted with this partial division of the spoils: The envy against Spenser rose higher than ever: The usual insolence of his temper, enflamed by success, impelled him to commit many acts of violence: The people, who always hated him, made him still more the object of aversion: All the relations of the attainted barons and gentlemen secretly vowed revenge:

[4] Leland's Coll. vol. i. p. 663.

venge: And though tranquillity was, in appearance, restored to the kingdom, the general contempt of the king, and odium against Spenser, bred dangerous humours, the source of future revolutions and convulsions.

In this situation, no success could be expected from foreign wars; and Edward, after making one more fruitless attempt against Scotland, whence he retreated with dishonour, found it necessary to terminate hostilities with that kingdom by a truce of thirteen years[*]. Robert, though his title to the crown was not acknowledged in the treaty, was satisfied with ensuring his possession of it during so long a time. He had repelled with gallantry all the attacks of England: He had carried war both into that kingdom and into Ireland: He had rejected with disdain the pope's authority, who pretended to impose his commands upon him, and oblige him to make peace with his enemies: His throne was firmly established, as well in the affections of his subjects as by force of arms: Yet there naturally remained some inquietude in his mind, while at war with a state which, however at present disordered by faction, was of itself so much an over-match for him, both in riches and in numbers of people. And this truce was, at the same time, the more seasonable for England, because the nation was at that juncture threatened with hostilities from France.

PHILIP the Fair, king of France, who died in 1315, had left the crown to his son Lewis Hutin, who, after a short reign, dying without male issue, was succeeded by Philip the Long, his brother, whose death soon after made way for Charles the Fair, the youngest brother of that family. This monarch had some grounds of complaint against the king's ministers in Guienne; and as there was no common or equitable judge in that strange species

[*] Rymer, vol. lii. p. 1022. Murimuth, p. 60.

of

of sovereignty, established by the feudal law, he seemed desirous to take advantage of Edward's weakness, and, under that pretence, to confiscate all his foreign dominions [f]. After an embassy by the earl of Kent, the king's brother, had been tried in vain, queen Isabella obtained permission to go over to Paris, and endeavour to adjust, in an amicable manner, the difference with her brother: But while she was making some progress in this negotiation, Charles started a new pretension, the justice of which could not be disputed, that Edward himself should appear in his court, and do homage for the fees which he held in France. But there occurred many difficulties in complying with this demand. Young Spenser, by whom the king was implicitly governed, had unavoidably been engaged in many quarrels with the queen, who aspired to the same influence; and though that artful princess, on her leaving England, had dissembled her animosity, Spenser, well acquainted with her secret sentiments, was unwilling to attend his master to Paris, and appear in a court, where her credit might expose him to insults, if not to danger. He hesitated no less on allowing the king to make the journey alone; both fearing, lest that easy prince should in his absence fall under other influence; and foreseeing the perils to which he himself should be exposed, if, without the protection of royal authority, he remained in England, where he was so generally hated. While these doubts occasioned delays and difficulties, Isabella proposed, that Edward should resign the dominion of Guienne to his son, now thirteen years of age; and that the prince should come to Paris, and do the homage which every vassal owed to his superior lord. This expedient, which seemed so happily to remove all difficulties, was immediately embraced: Spenser was charmed with the contrivance: Young Edward was sent to Paris: And the

[f] Rymer, vol. iv. p. 74. 98.

ruin,

352   HISTORY OF ENGLAND.

CHAP.
XIV.
ruin, covered under this fatal snare, was never perceived, or suspected by any of the English council.

1325.
THE queen, on her arrival in France, had there found a great number of English fugitives, the remains of the Lancastrian faction; and their common hatred of Spenser soon begat a secret friendship and correspondence between them and that princess. Among the rest was young Roger Mortimer, a potent baron in the Welsh marches, who had been obliged, with others, to make his submissions to the king; had been condemned for high treason; but having received a pardon for his life, was afterwards detained in the Tower, with an intention of rendering his confinement perpetual. He was so fortunate as to make his escape into France [a]; and being one of the most considerable persons now remaining of the party, as well as distinguished by his violent animosity against Spenser, he was easily admitted to pay his court to queen Isabella. The graces of his person and address advanced him quickly in her affections: He became her confident and counsellor in all her measures: And gaining ground daily upon her heart, he engaged her to sacrifice at last, to her passion, all the sentiments of honour and of fidelity to her husband [b]. Hating now the man whom she had injured, and whom she never valued, she entered ardently into all Mortimer's conspiracies; and having artfully gotten into her hands the young prince, and heir of the monarchy, she resolved on the utter ruin of the king, as well as of his favourite. She engaged her brother to take part in the same criminal purpose: Her court was daily filled with the exiled barons: Mortimer lived in the most declared intimacy with her: A correspondence was secretly carried on with the malcontent party in England: And when Edward, informed of those alarming circumstances, required

Conspiracy against the king.

[a] Rymer, vol. iv. p. 7, 8, 20. T. de la More, p. 596. Walsing. p. 120. Ypod. Neust. p. 506.   [b] T. de la More, p. 368. Murimuth. p. 65.

her

EDWARD II.

her speedily to return with the prince, she publicly replied, that she would never set foot in the kingdom, till Spenser was for ever removed from his presence and councils: A declaration, which procured her great popularity in England, and threw a decent veil over all her treasonable enterprizes.

CHAP. XIV.
1325.

EDWARD endeavoured to put himself in a posture of defence[1]; but, besides the difficulties arising from his own indolence and slender abilities, and the want of authority which of consequence attended all his resolutions, it was not easy for him, in the present state of the kingdom and revenue, to maintain a constant force ready to repel an invasion, which he knew not at what time or place he had reason to expect. All his efforts were unequal to the traiterous and hostile conspiracies, which, both at home and abroad, were forming against his authority, and which were daily penetrating farther even into his own family. His brother, the earl of Kent, a virtuous but weak prince, who was then at Paris, was engaged by his sister-in-law, and by the king of France, who was also his cousin-german, to give countenance to the invasion, whose sole object, he believed, was the expulsion of the Spensers: He prevailed on his elder brother, the earl of Norfolk, to enter secretly into the same design: The earl of Leicester, brother and heir of the earl of Lancaster, had too many reasons for his hatred of these ministers, to refuse his concurrence. Walter de Reynel, archbishop of Canterbury, and many of the prelates, expressed their approbation of the queen's measures: Several of the most potent barons, envying the authority of the favourite, were ready to fly to arms: The minds of the people, by means of some truths and many calumnies, were strongly disposed to the same party; And there needed but the appearance of the queen and prince, with such a body of foreign troops as

Insurrections.

[1] Rymer, vol. iv. p. 184. 188. 215.

VOL. II. A a might

354   HISTORY OF ENGLAND.

CHAP.
XIV.
might protect her against immediate violence, to turn all this tempest, so artfully prepared, against the unhappy Edward.

1326.

CHARLES, though he gave countenance and assistance to the faction, was ashamed openly to support the queen and prince against the authority of a husband and father; and Isabella was obliged to court the alliance of some other foreign potentate, from whose dominions she might set out on her intended enterprize. For this purpose, she affianced young Edward, whose tender age made him incapable to judge of the consequences, with Philippa, daughter of the count of Holland and Hainault[k]; and having, by the open assistance of this prince, and the secret protection of her brother, inlisted in her service near 3000 men, she set sail from the harbour of Dort, and landed safely, and without opposition, on the coast of Suffolk. The earl of Kent was in her company: Two other princes of the blood, the earl of Norfolk, and the earl of Leicester, joined her soon after her landing with all their followers: Three prelates, the bishops of Ely, Lincoln, and Hereford, brought her both the force of their vassals and the authority of their character[l]: Even Robert de Watteville, who had been sent by the king to oppose her progress in Suffolk, deserted to her with all his forces. To render her cause more favourable, she renewed her declaration, that the sole purpose of her enterprize was to free the king and kingdom from the tyranny of the Spensers, and of chancellor Baldoc, their creature[m]. The populace were allured by her specious pretences: The barons thought themselves secure against forfeitures by the appearance of the prince in her army:

24th Sept.

[k] T. de la More, p. 598.   [l] Walsing. p. 113. Ypod. Neust.
p. 507. T. de la More, p. 598. Murimoth, p. 66.   [m] Ypod.
Neust. p. 508.

And

EDWARD II.

And a weak irresolute king, supported by ministers generally odious, was unable to stem this torrent, which bore with such irresistible violence against him.

CHAP. XIV.
1326.

Edward, after trying in vain to rouze the citizens of London, to some sense of duty [a], departed for the west, where he hoped to meet with better reception; and he had no sooner discovered his weakness by leaving the city, than the rage of the populace broke out without controul against him and his ministers. They first plundered, then murdered all those who were obnoxious to them: They seized the bishop of Exeter, a virtuous and loyal prelate, as he was passing through the streets; and having beheaded him, they threw his body into the river [o]. They made themselves masters of the Tower by surprize; then entered into a formal association to put to death, without mercy, every one who should dare to oppose the enterprize of queen Isabella, and of the prince [p]. A like spirit was soon communicated to all other parts of England; and threw the few servants of the king, who still entertained thoughts of performing their duty, into terror and astonishment.

Edward was hotly pursued to Bristol by the earl of Kent, seconded by the foreign forces under John de Hainault. He found himself disappointed in his expectations with regard to the loyalty of those parts; and he passed over to Wales, where, he flattered himself, his name was more popular, and which he hoped to find uninfected with the contagion of general rage, which had seized the English [q]. The elder Spenser, created earl of Winchester, was left governor of the castle of Bristol; but the garrison mutinied against him, and he was delivered into the hands of his enemies. This venerable noble, who had nearly reached his ninetieth year, was instantly, without

[a] Walsing. p. 113. Murimuth, p. 66.
[o] Walsing. p. 124.
[p] Walsing. p. 124.
T. de la More, p. 599.
[q] Murimuth, p. 67.

356 HISTORY OF ENGLAND.

CHAP.
XIV.
1326.

trial, or witnefs, or accufation, or anfwer, condemned to death by the rebellious barons: He was hanged on a gibbet; his body was cut in pieces, and thrown to the dogs'; and his head was fent to Winchefter, the place whofe title he bore, and was there fet on a pole, and expofed to the infults of the populace.

THE king, difappointed anew in his expectations of fuccour from the Welfh, took fhipping for Ireland; but being driven back by contrary winds, he endeavoured to conceal himfelf in the mountains of Wales: He was foon difcovered, was put under the cuftody of the earl of Leicefter, and was confined in the caftle of Kenilworth. The younger Spenfer, his favourite, who alfo fell into the hands of his enemies, was executed, like his father, without any appearance of a legal trial ': The earl of Arundel, almoft the only man of his rank in England who had maintained his loyalty, was, without any trial, put to death at the inftigation of Mortimer: Baldoc, the chancellor, being a prieft, could not with fafety be fo fuddenly difpatched; but being fent to the bifhop of Hereford's palace in London, he was there, as his enemies probably forefaw, feized by the populace, was thrown into Newgate, and foon after expired, from the cruel ufage which he had received'. Even the ufual reference, paid to the facerdotal character, gave way, with every other confideration, to the prefent rage of the people.

The king dethroned.

THE queen, to avail herfelf of the prevailing delufion, fummoned, in the king's name, a parliament at Weftminfter; where, together with the power of her army, and the authority of her partizans among the barons, who were concerned to fecure their paft treafons by commit-

' Leland's Coll. vol. i. p. 673. T. de la More, p. 599. Walfing. p. 115. M. Froiffart, liv. l. chap. 13.   ' Walfing. p. 125. T pod. Neuft. p. 501.   t Walfing. p. 226. Motimoth, p. 68.

1   ting

EDWARD II.

ting new acts of violence against their sovereign, she expected to be seconded by the fury of the populace, the most dangerous of all instruments, and the least answerable for their excesses. A charge was drawn up against the king, in which, even though it was framed by his inveterate enemies, nothing but his narrow genius, or his misfortunes, were objected to him: For the greatest malice found no particular crime with which it could reproach this unhappy prince. He was accused of incapacity for government, of wasting his time in idle amusements, of neglecting public business, of being swayed by evil counsellors, of having lost, by his misconduct, the kingdom of Scotland, and part of Guienne; and to swell the charge, even the death of some barons, and the imprisonment of some prelates, convicted of treason, were laid to his account [v]. It was in vain, amidst the violence of arms and tumult of the people, to appeal either to law or to reason: The deposition of the king, without any appearing opposition, was voted by parliament: The prince, already declared regent by his party [w], was placed on the throne: And a deputation was sent to Edward at Kenilworth, to require his resignation, which menaces and terror soon extorted from him.

But it was impossible that the people, however corrupted by the barbarity of the times, still farther enflamed by faction, could for ever remain insensible to the voice of nature. Here, a wife had first deserted, next invaded, and then dethroned her husband; had made her minor son an instrument in this unnatural treatment of his father; had, by lying pretences, seduced the nation into a rebellion against their sovereign; had pushed them into violence and cruelties that had dishonoured them: All those circumstances were so odious in themselves, and

---

[v] Knyghton, p. 2765, 2766. Brady's App. N° 72.
[w] Rymer, vol. iv. p. 137. Walsing. p. 125.

CHAP. XIV.

1327.
25th Jan.

CHAP. XIV.
1327.

formed such a complicated scene of guilt, that the least reflection sufficed to open men's eyes, and make them detest this flagrant infringement of every public and private duty. The suspicions which soon arose of Isabella's criminal commerce with Mortimer, the proofs which daily broke out of this part of her guilt, encreased the general abhorrence against her; and her hypocrisy, in publicly bewailing with tears the king's unhappy fate[k], was not able to deceive even the most stupid and most prejudiced of her adherents. In proportion as the queen became the object of public hatred, the dethroned monarch, who had been the victim of her crimes and her ambition, was regarded with pity, with friendship, with veneration: And men became sensible, that all his misconduct, which faction had so much exaggerated, had been owing to the unavoidable weakness, not to any voluntary depravity, of his character. The earl of Leicester, now earl of Lancaster, to whose custody he had been committed, was soon touched with those generous sentiments; and besides using his prisoner with gentleness and humanity, he was suspected to have entertained still more honourable intentions in his favour. The king, therefore, was taken from his hands, and delivered over to lord Berkeley, and Mautravers, and Gournay, who were entrusted alternately, each for a month, with the charge of guarding him. While he was in the custody of Berkeley, he was still treated with the gentleness due to his rank and his misfortunes; but when the turn of Mautravers and Gournay came, every species of indignity was practised against him, as if their intention had been to break entirely the prince's spirit, and to employ his sorrows and afflictions, instead of more violent and more dangerous expedients, for the instruments of his murder[l]. It is reported that one day, when Edward was to be shaved, they ordered

[k] Walsing. p. 126.   [l] Anonymi Hist. p. 138.

cold

cold and dirty water to be brought from the ditch for that purpose; and when he desired it to be changed, and was still denied his request, he burst into tears, which bedewed his cheeks; and he exclaimed, that, in spite of their insolence, he should be shaved with clean and warm water [a]. But as this method of laying Edward in his grave appeared still too slow to the impatient Mortimer, he secretly sent orders to the two keepers, who were at his devotion, instantly to dispatch him; and these ruffians contrived to make the manner of his death as cruel and barbarous as possible. Taking advantage of Berkeley's sickness, in whose custody he then was, and who was thereby incapacitated from attending his charge [a], they came to Berkeley-castle, and put themselves in possession of the king's person. They threw him on a bed, held him down violently with a table, which they flung over him; thrust into his fundament a red-hot iron, which they inserted through a horn; and though the outward marks of violence upon his person were prevented by this expedient, the horrid deed was discovered to all the guards and attendants by the screams with which the agonizing king filled the castle, while his bowels were consuming.

GOURNAY and Mautravers were held in general detestation; and when the ensuing revolution in England threw their protectors from power, they found it necessary to provide for their safety by flying the kingdom. Gournay was afterwards seized at Marseilles, delivered over to the seneschal of Guienne, put on board a ship with a view of carrying him to England; but was beheaded at sea by secret orders, as was supposed, from some nobles and prelates in England, anxious to prevent any discovery which he might make of his accomplices. Mautravers concealed himself for several years in Ger-

[a] T. de la More, p. 602. [a] Cotton's Abridg. p. 8.

360   HISTORY OF ENGLAND.

C H A P.   many; but having found means of rendering some service
  XIV.   to Edward III., he ventured to approach his person, threw
1327.   himself on his knees before him, submitted to mercy, and
         received a pardon [b].

His charac-   It is not easy to imagine a man more innocent and in-
ter.   offensive than the unhappy king, whose tragical death
         we have related; nor a prince less fitted for governing
         that fierce and turbulent people subjected to his autho-
         rity. He was obliged to devolve on others the weight of
         government, which he had neither ability nor inclination
         to bear: The same indolence and want of penetration led
         him to make choice of ministers and favourites, who were
         not always the best qualified for the trust committed to
         them: The seditious grandees, pleased with his weakness,
         yet complaining of it; under pretence of attacking his
         ministers, insulted his person and invaded his authority:
         And the impatient populace, mistaking the source of their
         grievances, threw all the blame upon the king, and en-
         creased the public disorders by their faction and violence.
         It was in vain to look for protection from the laws, whose
         voice, always feeble in those times, was not heard amidst
         the din of arms: What could not defend the king was
         less able to give shelter to any of the people: The whole
         machine of government was torn in pieces with fury and
         violence: And men, instead of regretting the manners of
         their age, and the form of their constitution, which re-
         quired the most steady and most skilful hand to conduct
         them, imputed all errors to the person who had the misfor-
         tune to be entrusted with the reins of empire.

         But though such mistakes are natural and almost un-
         avoidable while the events are recent, it is a shameful
         delusion in modern historians, to imagine that all the
         ancient princes, who were unfortunate in their govern-
         ment, were also tyrannical in their conduct, and that the

[b] Cotton's Abridg. p. 66, &c. Rymer, vol. v. p. 600.

                                                    seditions

EDWARD II.

seditions of the people always proceeded from some invasion of their privileges by the monarch. Even a great and a good king was not in that age secure against faction and rebellion, as appears in the case of Henry II.; but a great king had the best chance, as we learn from the history of the same period, for quelling and subduing them. Compare the reigns and characters of Edward I. and II. The father made several violent attempts against the liberties of the people: His barons opposed him: He was obliged, at least found it prudent, to submit: But, as they dreaded his valour and abilities, they were content with reasonable satisfaction, and pushed no farther their advantages against him. The facility and weakness of the son, not his violence, threw every thing into confusion: The laws and government were overturned: An attempt to reinstate them was an unpardonable crime: And no atonement, but the deposition and tragical death of the king himself, could give those barons contentment. It is easy to see that a constitution, which depended so much on the personal character of the prince, must necessarily, in many of its parts, be a government of will, not of laws. But always to throw, without distinction, the blame of all disorders upon the sovereign, would introduce a fatal error in politics, and serve as a perpetual apology for treason and rebellion: As if the turbulence of the great, and madness of the people, were not, equally with the tyranny of princes, evils incident to human society, and no less carefully to be guarded against in every well-regulated constitution.

CHAP. XIV.
1317.

WHILE these abominable scenes passed in England, the theatre of France was stained with a wickedness equally barbarous, and still more public and deliberate. The order of knights templars had arisen during the first fervour of the Crusades; and uniting the two qualities, the most popular in that age, devotion and valour, and exercising both in the most popular of all enterprizes, the defence

Miscellaneous transactions during this reign.

fence of the Holy Land, they had made rapid advances in credit and authority, and had acquired, from the piety of the faithful, ample possessions in every country of Europe, especially in France. Their great riches, joined to the course of time, had, by degrees, relaxed the severity of these virtues; and the templars had in a great measure lost that popularity, which first raised them to honour and distinction. Acquainted from experience with the fatigues and dangers of those fruitless expeditions to the East, they rather chose to enjoy in ease their opulent revenues in Europe: And being all men of birth, educated, according to the custom of that age, without any tincture of letters, they scorned the ignoble occupations of a monastic life, and passed their time wholly in the fashionable amusements of hunting, gallantry, and the pleasures of the table. Their rival order, that of St. John of Jerusalem, whose poverty had as yet preserved them from like corruptions, still distinguished themselves by their enterprizes against the infidels, and succeeded to all the popularity, which was lost by the indolence and luxury of the templars. But though these reasons had weakened the foundations of this order, once so celebrated and revered, the immediate cause of their destruction proceeded from the cruel and vindictive spirit of Philip the Fair, who, having entertained a private disgust against some eminent templars, determined to gratify at once his avidity and revenge, by involving the whole order in an undistinguished ruin. On no better information than that of two knights, condemned by their superiors to perpetual imprisonment for their vices and profligacy, he ordered on one day all the templars in France to be committed to prison, and imputed to them such enormous and absurd crimes, as are sufficient of themselves to destroy all the credit of the accusation. Besides their being universally charged with murder, robbery, and

and vices the most shocking to nature; every one, it was pretended, whom they received into their order, was obliged to renounce his Saviour, to spit upon the cross [c], and to join to this impiety the superstition of worshipping a gilded head, which was secretly kept in one of their houses at Marseilles. They also initiated, it was said, every candidate by such infamous rites, as could serve to no other purpose, than to degrade the order in his eyes, and destroy for ever the authority of all his superiors over him [d]. Above a hundred of these unhappy gentlemen were put to the question, in order to extort from them a confession of their guilt: The more obstinate perished in the hands of their tormentors: Several, to procure immediate ease in the violence of their agonies, acknowledged whatever was required of them: Forged confessions were imputed to others: And Philip, as if their guilt were now certain, proceeded to a confiscation of all their treasures. But no sooner were the templars relieved from their tortures, than, preferring the most cruel execution to a life with infamy, they disavowed their confessions, exclaimed against the forgeries, justified the innocence of their order, and appealed to all the gallant actions, performed by them in ancient or later times, as a full apology for their conduct. The tyrant, enraged at this disappointment, and thinking himself now engaged in honour to proceed to extremities, ordered fifty-four of them, whom he branded as relapsed heretics, to perish by the punishment of fire in his capital: Great numbers expired after a like manner in other parts of the kingdom: And when he found, that the perseverance of these unhappy victims, in justifying to the last their innocence, had made deep impression on the spectators, he endeavoured to overcome the constancy of the templars by new inhu-

[c] Rymer, vol. iii p. pr. 101.
[d] It was pretended, that he kissed the knights who received him on the mouth, navel, and breech. Dupuy, p. 15, 16. Walf. p. 99.

manities.

manities. The grand master of the order, John de Molay, and another great officer, brother to the sovereign of Dauphiny, were conducted to a scaffold, erected before the church of Notredam, at Paris: A full pardon was offered them on the one hand; the fire, destined for their execution, was shown them on the other: These gallant nobles still persisted in the protestations of their own innocence and that of their order; and were instantly hurried into the flames by the executioner[e].

In all this barbarous injustice, Clement V. who was the creature of Philip, and then resided in France, fully concurred; and without examining a witness, or making any enquiry into the truth of facts, he summarily, by the plenitude of his apostolic power, abolished the whole order. The templars all over Europe were thrown into prison; their conduct underwent a strict scrutiny; the power of their enemies still pursued and oppressed them; but no where, except in France, were the smallest traces of their guilt pretended to be found. England sent an ample testimony of their piety and morals; but as the order was now annihilated, the knights were distributed into several convents, and their possessions were, by command of the pope, transferred to the order of St. John[f]. We now proceed to relate some other detached transactions of the present period.

The kingdom of England was afflicted with a grievous famine during several years of this reign. Perpetual rains and cold weather not only destroyed the harvest, but bred a mortality among the cattle, and raised every kind of food to an enormous price[g]. The parliament, in 1315, endeavoured to fix more moderate rates to commodities; not sensible that such an attempt was impracticable, and that, were it possible to reduce the price of provisions

[e] Vertot, vol. ii. p. 143. vol. iv. p. 47. Ypod. Neust. p. 506.
[f] Rymer, vol. III. p. 323. 956.
[g] Trivet, cont. p. 17, 18.

by any other expedient than by introducing plenty, nothing could be more pernicious and destructive to the public. Where the produce of a year, for instance, falls so far short, as to afford full subsistance only for nine months, the only expedient for making it last all the twelve, is to raise the prices, to put the people by that means on short allowance, and oblige them to save their food till a more plentiful season. But, in reality, the encrease of prices is a necessary consequence of scarcity; and laws, instead of preventing it, only aggravate the evil, by cramping and restraining commerce. The parliament accordingly, in the ensuing year, repealed their ordinance, which they had found useless and burdensome [b].

THE prices affixed by the parliament are somewhat remarkable: Three pounds twelve shillings of our present money for the best stalled ox; for other oxen, two pounds eight shillings: A fat hog of two years old, ten shillings: A fat wether unshorn, a crown; if shorn, three shillings and six-pence: A fat goose, seven-pence halfpenny: A fat capon, six-pence: A fat hen, three-pence: Two chickens, three-pence: Four pigeons, three-pence: Two dozen of eggs, three-pence [i]. If we consider these prices, we shall find that butcher's meat, in this time of great scarcity, must still have been sold, by the parliamentary ordinance, three times cheaper than our middling prices at present: Poultry somewhat lower; because, being now considered as a delicacy, it has risen beyond its proportion. In the country places of Ireland and Scotland, where delicacies bear no price, poultry is at present as cheap, if not cheaper, than butcher's meat. But the inference I would draw from the comparison of prices is still more considerable: I suppose that the rates, affixed by

[b] Walf. p. 107. Neust. p. 502.   [i] Rot. Parl. 7 Edw. II. n. 35. 36. Ypod.

parliament, were inferior to the usual market prices in those years of famine and mortality of cattle; and that these commodities, instead of a third, had really risen to a half of the present value. But the famine at that time was so consuming, that wheat was sometimes sold for above four pounds ten shillings a quarter [r], usually for three pounds [l]; that is, twice our middling prices: A certain proof of the wretched state of tillage in those ages. We formerly found, that the middling price of corn in that period was half of the present price; while the middling price of cattle was only an eighth part: We here find the same immense disproportion in years of scarcity. It may thence be inferred with certainty, that the raising of corn was a species of manufactory, which few in that age could practise with advantage: And there is reason to think, that other manufactures more refined, were sold even beyond their present prices: At least there is a demonstration for it in the reign of Henry VII. from the rates affixed to scarlet and other broad cloth by act of parliament. During all those times, it was usual for the princes and great nobility to make settlements of their velvet beds and silken robes, in the same manner as of their estates and manors [m]. In the list of jewels and plate which had belonged to the ostentatious Gavaston, and which the king recovered from the earl of Lancaster after the murder of that favourite, we find some embroidered girdles, flowered shirts, and silk waistcoats [s]. It was afterwards one article of accusation against that potent and opulent earl, when he was put to death, that he had purloined some of that finery of Gavaston's. The ignorance of those ages in manufactures, and still more, their unskilful husbandry, seem a clear proof that the country was then far from being populous.

[r] Murimuth, p. 48. Walsingham, p. 108, says it rose to six pounds.
[l] Ypod. Neust. p. 502. Trivet, cont. p. 18.
[m] Dugdale, passim. [s] Rymer, vol. III. p. 388.

EDWARD II.

ALL trade and manufactures indeed were then at a very low ebb. The only country in the northern parts of Europe, where they seem to have risen to any tolerable degree of improvement, was Flanders. When Robert, earl of that country, was applied to by the king, and was desired to break off commerce with the Scots, whom Edward called his rebels, and represented as excommunicated on that account by the church, the earl replied, that Flanders was always considered as common, and free and open to all nations [o].

THE petition of the elder Spenser to parliament, complaining of the devastation committed on his lands by the barons, contains several particulars which are curious, and discover the manners of the age [p]. He affirms, that they had ravaged sixty-three manors belonging to him, and he makes his losses amount to 46,000 pounds; that is, to 138,000 of our present money. Among other particulars, he enumerates 28,000 sheep, 1000 oxen and heifers, 1200 cows with their breed for two years, 560 cart horses, 2000 hogs, together with 600 bacons, 80 carcases of beef, and 600 muttons in the larder; ten tuns of cyder, arms for 200 men, and other warlike engines and provisions. The plain inference is, that the greater part of Spenser's vast estate, as well as the estates of the other nobility, was farmed by the landlord himself, managed by his stewards or bailiffs, and cultivated by his villains. Little or none of it was let on lease to husbandmen: Its produce was consumed in rustic hospitality by the baron or his officers: A great number of idle retainers, ready for any disorder or mischief, were maintained by him: All who lived upon his estate were absolutely at his disposal: Instead of applying to courts of justice, he usually sought redress by open force and vio-

[o] Rymer. v. L. iii. p. 770. [p] Brady's hist. vol. II. p. 143. from Claus. 15 Edw. II. M. 14. Dorf. in cedula.

lence:

lence: The great nobility were a kind of independent potentates, who, if they submitted to any regulations at all, were less governed by the municipal law, than by a rude species of the law of nations. The method, in which we find they treated the king's favourites and ministers, is a proof of their usual way of dealing with each other. A party, which complains of the arbitrary conduct of ministers, ought naturally to affect a great regard for the laws and constitution, and maintain at least the appearance of justice in their proceedings: Yet those barons, when discontented, came to parliament with an armed force, constrained the king to assent to their measures, and without any trial or witness or conviction, passed, from the pretended notoriety of facts, an act of banishment or attainder against the minister, which, on the first revolution of fortune, was reversed by like expedients. The parliament, during factious times, was nothing but the organ of present power. Though the persons, of whom it was chiefly composed, seemed to enjoy great independence, they really possessed no true liberty; and the security of each individual among them, was not so much derived from the general protection of law, as from his own private power and that of his confederates. The authority of the monarch, though far from absolute, was irregular, and might often reach him: The current of a faction might overwhelm him: A hundred considerations, of benefits and injuries, friendships and animosities, hopes and fears, were able to influence his conduct; and amidst these motives a regard to equity and law and justice was commonly, in those rude ages, of little moment. Nor did any man entertain thoughts of opposing present power, who did not deem himself strong enough to dispute the field with it by force, and was not prepared to give battle to the sovereign or the ruling party.

BEFORE

EDWARD II.

CHAP. XIV.
1317.

BEFORE I conclude this reign, I cannot forbear making another remark, drawn from the detail of losses given in by the elder Spenser; particularly, the great quantity of salted meat which he had in his larder, 600 bacons, 80 carcases of beef, 600 muttons. We may observe that the outrage, of which he complained, began after the third of May, or the eleventh new style, as we learn from the same paper. It is easy therefore to conjecture what a vast store of the same kind he must have laid up at the beginning of winter; and we may draw a new conclusion with regard to the wretched state of ancient husbandry, which could not provide subsistence for the cattle during winter, even in such a temperate climate as the south of England: For Spenser had but one manor so far north as Yorkshire. There being few or no inclosures, except perhaps for deer, no sown grass, little hay, and no other resource for feeding cattle; the barons, as well as the people, were obliged to kill and salt their oxen and sheep in the beginning of winter, before they became lean upon the common pasture: A precaution still practised with regard to oxen in the least cultivated parts of this island. The salting of mutton is a miserable expedient, which has every where been long disused. From this circumstance, however trivial in appearance, may be drawn important inferences, with regard to the domestic œconomy and manner of life in those ages.

THE disorders of the times, from foreign wars and intestine dissentions, but above all, the cruel famine, which obliged the nobility to dismiss many of their retainers, encreased the number of robbers in the kingdom; and no place was secure from their incursions[*]. They met in troops like armies, and over-ran the country. Two cardinals, themselves, the pope's legates, notwithstanding the numerous train which attended them, were

[*] Ypod. NeuR. p. 500. Walf. p. 107.

robbed,

CHAP.
XIV.

1327.

robbed, and despoiled of their goods and equipage, when they travelled on the highway[1].

AMONG the other wild fancies of the age, it was imagined, that the persons affected with leprosy, a disease at that time very common, probably from bad diet, had conspired with the Saracens to poison all the springs and fountains; and men being glad of any pretence to get rid of those who were a burthen to them, many of those unhappy people were burnt alive on this chimerical imputation. Several Jews also were punished in their persons, and their goods were confiscated on the same account[a].

STOWE, in his survey of London, gives us a curious instance of the hospitality of the ancient nobility in this period: It is taken from the accounts of the cofferer or steward of Thomas earl of Lancaster, and contains the expences of that earl during the year 1313, which was not a year of famine. For the pantry, buttery, and kitchen, 3405 pounds. For 369 pipes of red wine, and two of white, 104 pounds, &c. The whole 7309 pounds; that is, near 22,000 pounds of our present money; and making allowance for the cheapness of commodities, near a hundred thousand pounds.

I HAVE seen a French manuscript, containing accounts of some private disbursements of this king. There is an article, among others, of a crown paid to one for making the king laugh. To judge by the events of the reign, this ought not to have been an easy undertaking.

THIS king left four children, two sons, and two daughters: Edward, his eldest son and successor; John, created afterwards earl of Cornwal, who died young at Perth; Jane, afterwards married to David Bruce, king of Scotland; and Eleanor, married to Reginald, count of Guelders.

[1] Ypod. Neust. p. 503. T. de la More, p. 594. Trivet, cont. p. 22, Murimuth, p. 51. [a] Y. d. Neust. p. 504.

CHAP. XV.

EDWARD III.

War with Scotland——Execution of the Earl of Kent ——Execution of Mortimer, earl of March—— State of Scotland——War with that kingdom—— King's claim to the crown of France——Preparations for war with France——War——Naval victory——Domestic disturbances———Affairs of Britanny——Renewal of the war with France—— Invasion of France——Battle of Crecy——War with Scotland——Captivity of the king of Scots ——Calais taken.

THE violent party, which had taken arms against Edward II. and finally deposed that unfortunate monarch, deemed it requisite for their future security to pay so far an exterior obeisance to the law, as to desire a parliamentary indemnity for all their illegal proceedings; on account of the necessity, which, it was pretended, they lay under, of employing force against the Spensers and other evil counsellors, enemies of the kingdom. All the attainders also, which had passed against the earl of Lancaster and his adherents, when the chance of war turned against them, were easily reversed during the triumph of their party [*]; and the Spensers, whose former attainder had been reversed by parliament, were now again, in this change of fortune, condemned by the votes of their enemies. A council of regency was likewise appointed by parliament, consisting of twelve persons; five prelates, the archbishops of Canterbury and York,

CHAP. XV.
1327.
20th Jan.

[*] Rymer, vol. iv. p. 249, 257, 258, &c.

the bishops of Winchester, Worcester, and Hereford; and seven lay peers, the earls of Norfolk, Kent, and Surrey, and the lords Wake, Ingham, Piercy, and Ross. The earl of Lancaster was appointed guardian and protector of the king's person. But though it was reasonable to expect, that, as the weakness of the former king had given reins to the licentiousness of the barons, great domestic tranquillity would not prevail during the present minority; the first disturbance arose from an invasion by foreign enemies.

War with Scotland.

THE king of Scots declining in years and health, but retaining still that martial spirit which had raised his nation from the lowest ebb of fortune, deemed the present opportunity favourable for infesting England. He first made an attempt on the castle of Norham, in which he was disappointed; he then collected an army of 25,000 men on the frontiers, and having given the command to the earl of Murray and lord Douglas, threatened an incursion into the northern counties. The English regency, after trying in vain every expedient to restore peace with Scotland, made vigorous preparations for war; and besides assembling an English army of near sixty thousand men, they invited back John of Hainault, and some foreign cavalry, whom they had dismissed, and whose discipline and arms had appeared superior to those of their own country. Young Edward himself, burning with a passion for military fame, appeared at the head of these numerous forces; and marched from Durham, the appointed place of rendezvous, in quest of the enemy, who had already broken into the frontiers, and were laying every thing waste around them.

MURRAY and Douglas were the two most celebrated warriors, bred in the long hostilities between the Scots and English; and their forces, trained in the same school, and enured to hardships, fatigues, and dangers, were perfectly qualified, by their habits and manner of life,

for

for that defultory and deftructive war which they carried into England. Except a body of about 4000 cavalry, well armed, and fit to make a fteady impreffion in battle, the reft of the army were light-armed troops, mounted on fmall horfes, which found fubfiftence every where, and carried them with rapid and unexpected marches, whether they meant to commit depredations on the peaceable inhabitants, or to attack an armed enemy, or to retreat into their own country. Their whole equipage confifted of a bag of oat-meal, which, as a fupply in cafe of neceffity, each foldier carried behind him; together with a light plate of iron, on which he inftantly baked the meal into a cake, in the open fields. But his chief fubfiftence was the cattle which he feized; and his cookery was as expeditious as all his other operations. After fleaing the animal, he placed the fkin, loofe and hanging in the form of a bag, upon fome flakes; he poured water into it, kindled a fire below, and thus made it ferve as a caldron for the boiling of his victuals [r].

The chief difficulty which Edward met with, after compofing fome dangerous frays which broke out between his foreign forces and the Englifh [r], was to come up with an army fo rapid in its marches, and fo little incumbered in its motions. Though the flame and fmoke of burning villages directed him fufficiently to the place of their encampment, he found, upon hurrying thither, that they had already diflodged; and he foon difcovered, by new marks of devaftation, that they had removed to fome diftant quarter. After haraffing his army during fome time in this fruitlefs chace, he advanced northwards, and croffed the Tyne, with a refolution of awaiting them on their return homewards, and taking vengeance for all their depredations [s]. But that whole country was already fo much wafted by their frequent incurfions, that

[r] Froiffard, liv. iv. chap. 18. [r] Ibid. liv. i. chap. 17.
[s] Ibid. liv. iv. chap. 19.

CHAP.
XV.

1327.

it could not afford fubfiftence to his army; and he was obliged again to return fouthwards, and change his plan of operations. He had now loft all track of the enemy; and though he promifed the reward of a hundred pounds a year to any one who fhould bring him an account of their motions, he remained unactive fome days, before he received any intelligence of them [a]. He found at laft, that they had fixed their camp on the fouthern banks of the Were, as if they intended to await a battle; but their prudent leaders had chofen the ground with fuch judgment, that the Englifh, on their approach, faw it impracticable, without temerity, to crofs the river in their front, and attack them in their prefent fituation. Edward, impatient for revenge and glory, here fent them a defiance, and challenged them, if they dared, to meet him in an equal field, and try the fortune of arms. The bold fpirit of Douglas could ill brook this bravadoe, and he advifed the acceptance of the challenge; but he was over-ruled by Murray, who replied to Edward, that he never took the counfel of an enemy in any of his operations. The king, therefore, kept ftill his pofition oppofite to the Scots; and daily expected, that neceffity would oblige them to change their quarters, and give him an opportunity of overwhelming them with fuperior forces. After a few days, they fuddenly decamped, and marched farther up the river; but ftill pofted themfelves in fuch a manner, as to preferve the advantage of the ground, if the enemy fhould venture to attack them [b]. Edward infifted, that all hazards fhould be run, rather than allow thefe ravagers to efcape with impunity; but Mortimer's authority prevented the attack, and oppofed itfelf to the valour of the young monarch. While the armies lay in this pofition, an incident happened which had well nigh proved fatal to the Englifh. Douglas, having gotten the

[a] Rymer, vol. iv. p. 318. Froiffard, liv. iv. chap. 19. [b] Froiffard, liv. iv. chap. 19.

word,

word, and surveyed exactly the situation of the English camp, entered it secretly in the night-time, with a body of two hundred determined soldiers, and advanced to the royal tent, with a view of killing or carrying off the king, in the midst of his army. But some of Edward's attendants, awaking in that critical moment, made resistance; his chaplain and chamberlain sacrificed their lives for his safety; the king himself, after making a valorous defence, escaped in the dark: And Douglas, having lost the greater part of his followers, was glad to make a hasty retreat with the remainder[c]. Soon after, the Scottish army decamped without noise in the dead of night; and having thus gotten the start of the English, arrived without farther loss in their own country. Edward, on entering the place of the Scottish encampment, found only six Englishmen, whom the enemy, after breaking their legs, had tied to trees, in order to prevent their carrying any intelligence to their countrymen[d].

THE king was highly incensed at the disappointment which he had met with in his first enterprize, and at the head of so gallant an army. The symptoms, which he had discovered of bravery and spirit, gave extreme satisfaction, and were regarded as sure prognostics of an illustrious reign: But the general displeasure fell violently on Mortimer, who was already the object of public odium: And every measure, which he pursued, tended to aggravate, beyond all bounds, the hatred of the nation both against him and queen Isabella.

WHEN the council of regency was formed, Mortimer, though in the plenitude of his power, had taken no care to ensure a place in it; but this semblance of moderation was only a cover to the most iniquitous and most ambitious projects. He rendered that council entirely useless by usurping to himself the whole sovereign authority;

[c] Froissard, liv. iv. chap. 19. Hemingford, p. 268. Ypod. Neustr. p. 509. Knyghton, p. 2552. [d] Froissard, liv. iv. chap. 19.

CHAP.
XV.

1327.

he settled on the queen dowager the greater part of the royal revenues; he never consulted either the princes of the blood, or the nobility, in any public measure; the king himself was so besieged by his creatures, that no access could be procured to him; and all the envy, which had attended Gavaston and Spenser, fell much more deservedly on the new favourite.

1328.

MORTIMER, sensible of the growing hatred of the people, thought it requisite, on any terms, to secure peace abroad; and he entered into a negociation with Robert Bruce for that purpose. As the claim of superiority in England, more than any other cause, had tended to inflame the animosities between the two nations, Mortimer, besides stipulating a marriage between Jane, sister of Edward, and David, the son and heir of Robert, consented to resign absolutely this claim, to give up all the homages done by the Scottish parliament and nobility, and to acknowledge Robert as independent sovereign of Scotland [e]. In return for these advantages, Robert stipulated the payment of 30,000 marks to England. This treaty was ratified by parliament [f]; but was nevertheless the source of great discontent among the people, who, having entered zealously into the pretensions of Edward I. and deeming themselves disgraced by the successful resistance made by so inferior a nation, were disappointed, by this treaty, in all future hopes both of conquest and of vengeance.

THE princes of the blood, Kent, Norfolk, and Lancaster, were much united in their councils; and Mortimer entertained great suspicions of their designs against him. In summoning them to parliament, he strictly prohibited them, in the king's name, from coming attended by an armed force, an illegal but usual practice in that age. The three earls, as they approached to

[e] Rymer, p. 337. Heming. p. 270. Anon. Hist. p. 330.   [f] Ypod.
Neust. p. 510.

Salisbury,

Salisbury, the place appointed for the meeting of parliament, found, that, though they themselves, in obedience to the king's command, had brought only their usual retinue with them, Mortimer and his party were attended by all their followers in arms; and they began with some reason to apprehend a dangerous design against their persons. They retreated, assembled their retainers, and were returning with an army to take vengeance on Mortimer; when the weakness of Kent and Norfolk, who deserted the common cause, obliged Lancaster also to make his submissions[e]. The quarrel, by the interposition of the prelates, seemed, for the present, to be appeased.

But Mortimer, in order to intimidate the princes, determined to have a victim; and the simplicity, with the good intentions of the earl of Kent, afforded him soon after an opportunity of practising upon him. By himself and his emissaries, he endeavoured to persuade that prince, that his brother, king Edward, was still alive, and detained in some secret prison in England. The earl, whose remorses for the part which he had acted against the late king, probably inclined him to give credit to this intelligence, entered into a design of restoring him to liberty, of re-instating him on the throne, and of making thereby some atonement for the injuries which he himself had unwarily done him[b]. After this harmless contrivance had been allowed to proceed a certain length, the earl was seized by Mortimer, was accused before the parliament, and condemned by those slavish, though turbulent barons, to lose his life and fortune. The queen and Mortimer, apprehensive of young Edward's lenity towards his uncle, hurried on the execution, and the prisoner was beheaded next day: But so general was the

[e] Knyghton, p. 2554. [b] Avesbury, p. 8. Ang. Hist. p. 395.

affection

CHAP. XV.
1330.

affection borne him, and such pity prevailed for his unhappy fate, that, though peers had been easily found to condemn him, it was evening before his enemies could find an executioner to perform the office[1].

THE earl of Lancaster, on pretence of his having assented to this conspiracy, was soon after thrown into prison: Many of the prelates and nobility were prosecuted: Mortimer employed this engine to crush all his enemies, and to enrich himself and his family by the forfeitures. The estate of the earl of Kent was seized for his younger son, Geoffrey: The immense fortunes of the Spensers and their adherents were mostly converted to his own use: He affected a state and dignity equal or superior to the royal: His power became formidable to every one: His illegal practices were daily complained of: And all parties, forgetting past animosities, conspired in their hatred of Mortimer.

IT was impossible that these abuses could long escape the observation of a prince, endowed with so much spirit and judgment as young Edward, who, being now in his eighteenth year, and feeling himself capable of governing, repined at being held in fetters by this insolent minister. But so much was he surrounded by the emissaries of Mortimer, that it behoved him to conduct the project for subverting him, with the same secrecy and precaution, as if he had been forming a conspiracy against his sovereign. He communicated his intentions to lord Mountacute, who engaged the lords Molins and Clifford, Sir John Nevil of Hornby, Sir Edward Bohun, Ufford, and others, to enter into their views; and the castle of Nottingham was chosen for the scene of the enterprize. The queen-dowager and Mortimer lodged in that fortress: The king also was admitted, though with a few only of his attendants: And as the castle was strictly guarded,

[1] Heming. p. 271. Ypod. Neub. p. 510. Knyghton, p. 2555.

guarded, the gates locked every evening, and the keys carried to the queen, it became necessary to communicate the design to Sir William Eland, the governor, who zealously took part in it. By his direction, the king's associates were admitted through a subterraneous passage, which had formerly been contrived for a secret outlet from the castle, but was now buried in rubbish; and Mortimer, without having it in his power to make resistance, was suddenly seized in an apartment adjoining to the queen's[h]. A parliament was immediately summoned for his condemnation. He was accused, before that assembly, of having usurped regal power from the council of regency appointed by parliament; of having procured the death of the late king; of having deceived the earl of Kent into a conspiracy to restore that prince; of having solicited and obtained exorbitant grants of the royal demesnes; of having dissipated the public treasure; of secreting 20,000 marks of the money paid by the king of Scotland; and of other crimes and misdemeanors[l]. The parliament condemned him, from the supposed notoriety of the facts, without trial, or hearing his answer, or examining a witness; and he was hanged on a gibbet at the Elmes, in the neighbourhood of London. It is remarkable that this sentence was, near twenty years after, reversed by parliament, in favour of Mortimer's son; and the reason assigned, was the illegal manner of proceeding[m]. The principles of law and justice were established in England, not in such a degree as to prevent any iniquitous sentence against a person obnoxious to the ruling party; but sufficient, on the return of his credit, or that of his friends, to serve as a reason or pretence for its reversal.

Execution of Mortimer.
29th Nov.

[h] Avesbury, p. 9. 398. Knyghton, p. 2556.   [l] Brady's App. N° 83. Ann. Hist. p. 197.   [m] Cotton's Abridg. p. 85, 86.

JUSTICE

Justice was also executed, by a sentence of the house of peers, on some of the inferior criminals, particularly on Simon de Bereford: But the barons, in that act of jurisdiction, entered a protest, that though they had tried Bereford, who was none of their peers, they should not, for the future, be obliged to receive any such indictment. The queen was confined to her own house at Risings, near London: Her revenue was reduced to 4000 pounds a year [a]: And though the king, during the remainder of her life, paid her a decent visit once or twice a year, she never was able to reinstate herself in any credit or authority.

Edward, having now taken the reins of government into his own hands, applied himself with industry and judgment, to redress all those grievances which had proceeded, either from want of authority in the crown, or from the late abuses of it. He issued writs to the judges, enjoining them to administer justice, without paying any regard to arbitrary orders from the ministers: And as the robbers, thieves, murderers, and criminals of all kinds, had, during the course of public convulsions, multiplied to an enormous degree, and were openly protected by the great barons, who made use of them against their enemies, the king, after exacting from the peers a solemn promise in parliament that they would break off all connections with such malefactors [b], set himself in earnest to remedy the evil. Many of these gangs had become so numerous, as to require his own presence to disperse them; and he exerted both courage and industry in executing this salutary office. The ministers of justice, from his example, employed the utmost diligence in discovering, pursuing, and punishing, the criminals; and thus disorder was, by degrees, corrected, at least palliated; the utmost that could

[a] Cotton's Abridg. p. 10. [b] Cotton's Abridg.

EDWARD III.

be expected, with regard to a disease hitherto inherent in the constitution.

IN proportion as the government acquired authority at home, it became formidable to the neighbouring nations; and the ambitious spirit of Edward sought, and soon found, an opportunity of exerting itself. The wise and valiant Robert Bruce,' who had recovered by arms the independence of his country, and had fixed it by the last treaty of peace with England, soon after died, and left David, his son, a minor, under the guardianship of Randolf, earl of Murray, the companion of all his victories. It had been stipulated in this treaty, that both the Scottish nobility, who, before the commencement of the wars, enjoyed lands in England, and the English, who inherited estates in Scotland, should be restored to their respective possessions *p*: But, though this article had been executed pretty regularly on the part of Edward, Robert, who observed that the estates, claimed by Englishmen, were much more numerous and valuable than the others, either thought it dangerous to admit so many secret enemies into the kingdom, or found it difficult to wrest from his own followers the possessions bestowed on them as the reward of former services: And he had protracted the performance of his part of the stipulation. The English nobles, disappointed in their expectations, began to think of a remedy; and as their influence was great in the north, their enmity alone, even though unsupported by the king of England, became dangerous to the minor prince, who succeeded to the Scottish throne.

EDWARD BALIOL, the son of that John, who was crowned king of Scotland, had been detained some time a prisoner in England after his father was released; but having also obtained his liberty, he went over to France,

p Rymer, vol. iv. p. 384.

and

and refided in Normandy, on his patrimonial eftate in that country, without any thoughts of reviving the claims of his family to the crown of Scotland. His pretenfions, however plaufible, had been fo ftrenuoufly abjured by the Scots, and rejected by the Englifh, that he was univerfally regarded as a private perfon; and he had been thrown into prifon on account of fome private offence of which he was accufed. Lord Beaumont, a great Englifh baron, who, in the right of his wife, claimed the earldom of Buchan, in Scotland[q], found him in this fituation; and, deeming him a proper inftrument for his purpofe, made fuch intereft with the king of France, who was not aware of the confequences, that he recovered him his liberty, and brought him over with him to England.

THE injured nobles, poffeffed of fuch a head, began to think of vindicating their rights by force of arms; and they applied to Edward for his concurrence and affiftance. But there were feveral reafons, which deterred the king from openly avowing their enterprize. In his treaty with Scotland, he had entered into a bond of 20,000 pounds, payable to the pope, if within four years he violated the peace; and as the term was not yet elapfed, he dreaded the exacting of that penalty by the fovereign pontiff, who poffeffed fo many means of forcing princes to make payment. He was alfo afraid, that violence and injuftice would every where be imputed to him, if he attacked with fuperior force a minor king, and a brother-in-law, whofe independent title had fo lately been acknowledged by a folemn treaty. And as the regent of Scotland, on every demand which had been made of reftitution to the Englifh barons, had always confeffed the juftice of their claim, and had only given an evafive anfwer, grounded on plaufible pretences, Edward refolved

[q] Rymer, v. I, Iv. p. 251.

not to proceed by open violence, but to employ like artifices against him. He secretly encouraged Baliol in his enterprize; connived at his assembling forces in the north; and gave countenance to the nobles, who were disposed to join in the attempt. A force of near 2500 men was inlisted under Baliol, by Umfreville, earl of Angus, the lords Beaumont, Ferrars, Fitz-warin, Wake, Stafford, Talbot, and Moubray. As these adventurers apprehended that the frontiers would be strongly armed and guarded, they resolved to make their attack by sea; and, having embarked at Ravenspur, they reached, in a few days, the coast of Fife.

SCOTLAND was, at that time, in a very different situation from that in which it had appeared under the victorious Robert. Besides the loss of that great monarch, whose genius and authority preserved entire the whole political fabric, and maintained an union among the unruly barons, Lord Douglas, impatient of rest, had gone over to Spain, in a crusade against the Moors, and had there perished in battle[f] : The earl of Murray, who had long been declining through age and infirmities, had lately died, and had been succeeded, in the regency, by Donald earl of Marre, a man of much inferior talents: The military spirit of the Scots, though still unbroken, was left without a proper guidance and direction: And a minor king seemed ill qualified to defend an inheritance, which it had required all the consummate valour and abilities of his father to acquire and maintain. But, as the Scots were apprized of the intended invasion, great numbers, on the appearance of the English fleet, immediately ran to the shore, in order to prevent the landing of the enemy. Baliol had valour and activity, and he drove back the Scots with considerable loss[g]. He marched westward

[f] Froissard, liv. I. chap. 21. p. 131. Knyghton, p. 2562.   [g] Heming. p. 271. Walsing.

into the heart of the country; flattering himself that the ancient partizans of his family would declare for him. But the fierce animosities, which had been kindled between the two nations, inspiring the Scots with a strong prejudice against a prince supported by the English, he was regarded as a common enemy; and the regent found no difficulty in assembling a great army to oppose him. It is pretended, that Marre had no less than 40,000 men under his banners; but the same hurry and impatience that made him collect a force, which, from its greatness, was so disproportioned to the occasion, rendered all his motions unskilful and imprudent. The river Erne ran between the two armies; and the Scots, confiding in that security, as well as in their great superiority of numbers, kept no order in their encampment. Baliol passed the river in the night-time; attacked the unguarded and undisciplined Scots; threw them into confusion, which was encreased by the darkness and by their very numbers to which they trusted; and he beat them off the field with great slaughter[1]. But, in the morning, when the Scots were at some distance, they were ashamed of having yielded the victory to so weak a foe, and they hurried back to recover the honour of the day. Their eager passions urged them precipitately to battle, without regard to some broken ground, which lay between them and the enemy, and which disordered and confounded their ranks. Baliol seized the favourable opportunity, advanced his troops upon them, prevented them from rallying, and anew chaced them off the field with redoubled slaughter. There fell above 12,000 Scots in this action; and among these the flower of their nobility; the regent himself, the earl of Carric, a natural son of their late king, the earls of Athole and Monteith, lord Hay of Errol, constable, and the lords Keith and Lindsey. The loss of the Eng-

[1] Knyghton, p. 2562.

EDWARD III.

lish scarcely exceeded thirty men; a strong proof, among many others, of the miserable state of military discipline in those ages[u].

BALIOL soon after made himself master of Perth; but still was not able to bring over any of the Scots to his party. Patric Dunbar, earl of March, and Sir Archibald Douglas, brother to the lord of that name, appeared at the head of the Scottish armies, which amounted still to near 40,000 men; and they purposed to reduce Baliol and the English by famine. They blockaded Perth by land; they collected some vessels with which they invested it by water: But Baliol's ships, attacking the Scottish fleet, gained a complete victory; and opened the communication between Perth and the sea[w]. The Scotch armies were then obliged to disband, for want of pay and subsistence: The nation was, in effect, subdued by a handful of men: Each nobleman, who found himself most exposed to danger, successively submitted to Baliol: That prince was crowned at Scone: David, his competitor, was sent over to France, with his betrothed wife, Jane, sister to Edward: And the heads of his party sued to Baliol for a truce, which he granted them, in order to assemble a parliament in tranquillity, and have his title recognized by the whole Scottish nation.

CHAP.
XV.

1332.

27th Sept.

BUT Baliol's imprudence, or his necessities, making him dismiss the greater part of his English followers, he was, notwithstanding the truce, attacked of a sudden, near Annan, by Sir Archibald Douglas, and other chieftains of that party; he was routed; his brother John Baliol was slain; he himself was chaced into England in a

1333.

[u] Heming. p. 273. Walf. g. p. 131. Knyghton, p. 2561.
[w] Heming. p. 273. Knyghton, p. 2561.

miserable condition; and thus lost his kingdom by a revolution as sudden as that by which he had acquired it.

While Baliol enjoyed his short-lived and precarious royalty, he had been sensible, that, without the protection of England, it would be impossible for him to maintain possession of the throne; and he had secretly sent a message to Edward, offering to acknowledge his superiority, to renew the homage for his crown, and to espouse the princess Jane, if the pope's consent could be obtained for dissolving her former marriage, which was not yet consummated. Edward, ambitious of recovering that important concession, made by Mortimer during his minority, threw off all scruples, and willingly accepted the offer; but as the dethroning of Baliol had rendered this stipulation of no effect, the king prepared to re-instate him in possession of the crown; an enterprize which appeared from late experience so easy and so little hazardous. As he possessed many popular arts, he consulted his parliament on the occasion; but that assembly, finding the resolution already taken, declined giving any opinion, and only granted him, in order to support the enterprize, an aid of a fifteenth, from the personal estates of the nobility and gentry, and a tenth of the moveables of boroughs. And they added a petition, that the king would thenceforth live on his own revenue, without grieving his subjects by illegal taxes, or by the outrageous seizure of their goods in the shape of purveyance[a].

As the Scots expected that the chief brunt of the war would fall upon Berwic, Douglas, the regent, threw a strong garrison into that place, under the command of Sir William Keith, and he himself assembled a great army on the frontiers, ready to penetrate into England, as soon as Edward should have invested that place. The English

[a] Cotton's Abridg.

army was less numerous, but better supplied with arms and provisions, and retained in stricter discipline; and the king, notwithstanding the valiant defence made by Keith, had, in two months, reduced the garrison to extremities, and had obliged them to capitulate: They engaged to surrender, if they were not relieved within a few days by their countrymen [r]. This intelligence being conveyed to the Scottish army, which was preparing to invade Northumberland, changed their plan of operations, and engaged them to advance toward Berwic, and attempt the relief of that important fortress. Douglas, who had ever purposed to decline a pitched battle, in which he was sensible of the enemy's superiority, and who intended to have drawn out the war by small skirmishes, and by mutually ravaging each other's country, was forced, by the impatience of his troops, to put the fate of the kingdom upon the event of one day. He attacked the English at Halidown-hill, a little north of Berwic; and, though his heavy-armed cavalry dismounted, in order to render the action more steady and desperate, they were received with such valour by Edward, and were so galled by the English archers, that they were soon thrown into disorder, and, on the fall of Douglas, their general, were totally routed. The whole army fled in confusion, and the English, but much more the Irish, gave little quarter in the pursuit: All the nobles of chief distinction were either slain or taken prisoners: Near thirty thousand of the Scots fell in the action: While the loss of the English amounted only to one knight, one esquire, and thirteen private soldiers: An inequality almost incredible [s].

AFTER this fatal blow, the Scottish nobles had no other resource than instant submission; and Edward, leaving a considerable body with Baliol to complete the conquest of the kingdom, returned with the remainder of his army to England. Baliol was acknowledged king by a parliament assembled at Edinburgh [a]; the superiority of England was again recognized; many of the Scottish nobility swore fealty to Edward; and to complete the misfortunes of that nation, Baliol ceded Berwic, Dunbar, Roxborough, Edinburgh, and all the south-east counties of Scotland, which were declared to be for ever annexed to the English monarchy [b].

If Baliol, on his first appearance, was dreaded by the Scots, as an instrument employed by England for the subjection of the kingdom, this deed confirmed all their suspicions, and rendered him the object of universal hatred. Whatever submissions they might be obliged to make, they considered him, not as their prince, but as the delegate and confederate of their determined enemy: And neither the manners of the age, nor the state of Edward's revenue, permitting him to maintain a standing army in Scotland, the English forces were no sooner withdrawn, than the Scots revolted from Baliol, and returned to their former allegiance under Bruce. Sir Andrew Murray, appointed regent by the party of this latter prince, employed with success his valour and activity in many small but decisive actions against Baliol; and in a short time had almost wholly expelled him the kingdom. Edward was obliged again to assemble an army, and to march into Scotland: The Scots, taught by experience, withdrew into their hills and fastnesses: He destroyed the houses and ravaged the estates of those whom he called rebels: But this confirmed them still farther in their obstinate antipathy to England and to Baliol; and being now rendered desperate, they were ready to take advantage, on the first opportunity, of the retreat of their enemy,

[a] Rymer, vol. iv. p. 590.   [b] Ibid. p. 614.

and

and they soon re-conquered their country from the English. Edward made anew his appearance in Scotland with like success: He found every thing hostile in the kingdom, except the spot on which he was encamped: And though he marched uncontrouled over the low countries, the nation itself was farther than ever from being broken and subdued. Besides being supported by their pride and anger, passions difficult to tame, they were encouraged, amidst all their calamities, by daily promises of relief from France; and as a war was now likely to break out between that kingdom and England, they had reason to expect, from this incident, a great diversion of that force which had so long oppressed and overwhelmed them.

CHAP. XV.
1336.

WE now come to a transaction, on which depended the most memorable events, not only of this long and active reign, but of the whole English and French history, during more than a century; and it will therefore be necessary to give a particular account of the springs and causes of it.

1337. King's claim to the crown of France.

IT had long been a prevailing opinion, that the crown of France could never descend to a female; and, in order to give more authority to this maxim, and assign it a determinate origin, it had been usual to derive it from a clause in the Salian Code, the law of an ancient tribe among the Franks; though that clause, when strictly examined, carries only the appearance of favouring this principle, and does not really, by the confession of the best antiquaries, bear the sense commonly imposed upon it. But though positive law seems wanting among the French for the exclusion of females, the practice had taken place; and the rule was established beyond controversy on some antient, as well as some modern precedents. During the first race of the monarchy, the Franks were so rude and

Cc 3

barbarous

barbarous a people, that they were incapable of submitting to a female reign; and in that period of their history there were frequent instances of kings advanced to royalty in prejudice of females, who were related to the crown by nearer degrees of consanguinity. These precedents, joined to like causes, had also established the male succession in the second race; and though the instances were neither so frequent nor so certain during that period, the principle of excluding the female line seems still to have prevailed, and to have directed the conduct of the nation. During the third race, the crown had descended from father to son for eleven generations, from Hugh Capet to Lewis Hutin; and thus, in fact, during the course of nine hundred years, the French monarchy had always been governed by males, and no female, and none who founded his title on a female had ever mounted the throne. Philip the Fair, father of Lewis Hutin, left three sons, this Lewis, Philip the Long, and Charles the Fair, and one daughter, Isabella, queen of England. Lewis Hutin, the eldest, left at his death one daughter, by Margaret sister to Eudes, duke of Burgundy; and as his queen was then pregnant, Philip, his younger brother, was appointed regent, till it should appear whether the child proved a son or a daughter. The queen bore a male, who lived only a few days: Philip was proclaimed king: And as the duke of Burgundy made some opposition, and asserted the rights of his niece, the states of the kingdom, by a solemn and deliberate decree, gave her an exclusion, and declared all females for ever incapable of succeeding to the crown of France. Philip died after a short reign, leaving three daughters; and his brother, Charles, without dispute or controversy, then succeeded to the crown. The reign of Charles was also short: He left one daughter; but as his queen was pregnant, the next male heir was appointed regent,

regent, with a declared right of succession, if the issue should prove female. This prince was Philip de Valois, cousin-german to the deceased king; being the son of Charles de Valois, brother of Philip the Fair. The queen of France was delivered of a daughter: The regency ended; and Philip de Valois was unanimously placed on the throne of France.

The king of England, who was at that time a youth of fifteen years of age, embraced a notion that he was intitled, in right of his mother, to the succession of the kingdom, and that the claim of the nephew was preferable to that of the cousin-german. There could not well be imagined a notion weaker or worse grounded. The principle of excluding females was of old an established opinion in France, and had acquired equal authority with the most express and positive law: It was supported by ancient precedents: It was confirmed by recent instances, solemnly and deliberately decided: And what placed it still farther beyond controversy; if Edward was disposed to question its validity, he thereby cut off his own pretensions; since the three last kings had all left daughters, who were still alive, and who stood before him in the order of succession. He was therefore reduced to assert, that, though his mother, Isabella, was, on account of her sex, incapable of succeeding, he himself, who inherited through her, was liable to no such objection, and might claim by the right of propinquity. But, besides that this pretension was more favourable to Charles, king of Navarre, descended from the daughter of Lewis Hutin, it was so contrary to the established principles of succession in every country of Europe[b], was so repugnant to the practice, both in private and public inheritances, that no body in France thought of Edward's claim: Philip's title was universally recognized[c]: And

[b] Froissart, liv. I. chap. 4. [c] Id. liv. I. chap. 22.

CHAP. XV.

1337.

BUT though the youthful and ambitious mind of Edward had rashly entertained this notion, he did not think proper to insist on his pretensions, which must have immediately involved him, on very unequal terms, in a dangerous and implacable war with so powerful a monarch. Philip was a prince of mature years, of great experience, and, at that time, of an established character both for prudence and valour; and by these circumstances, as well as by the internal union of his people, and their acquiescence in his undoubted right, he possessed every advantage above a raw youth, newly raised, by injustice and violence, to the government of the most intractable and most turbulent subjects in Europe. But there immediately occurred an incident, which required that Edward should either openly declare his pretensions, or for ever renounce and abjure them. He was summoned to do homage for Guienne: Philip was preparing to compel him by force of arms: That country was in a very bad state of defence: And the forfeiture of so rich an inheritance was, by the feudal law, the immediate consequence of his refusing or declining to perform the duty of a vassal. Edward therefore thought it prudent to submit to present necessity: He went over to Amiens: Did homage to Philip: And, as there had arisen some controversy concerning the terms of this submission, he afterwards sent over a formal deed, in which he acknowledged that he owed liege homage to France[d]; which was in effect ratifying, and that in the strongest terms, Philip's title to the crown of that kingdom. His own claim indeed was so unreasonable, and so thoroughly disavowed by the whole French

Rymer. vol. iv. p. 477. 481. Froissard, liv. I. chap. 25. Anon. Hist. p. 394. Walfing. p. 130. Marimuth. p. 73.

nation,

EDWARD III. 393

nation, that to infift on it was no better than pretending to the violent conqueft of the kingdom; and it is probable that he would never have farther thoughts of it, had it not been for fome incidents which excited an animofity between the monarchs.

ROBERT of Artois was defcended from the blood royal of France, was a man of great character and authority, had efpoufed Philip's fifter, and, by his birth, talents, and credit, was entitled to make the higheft figure, and fill the moft important offices, in the monarchy. This prince had loft the county of Artois, which he claimed as his birthright, by a fentence, commonly deemed iniquitous, of Philip the Fair; and he was feduced to attempt recovering poffeffion by an action fo unworthy of his rank and character as a forgery[e]. The detection of this crime covered him with fhame and confufion: His brother-in-law not only abandoned him, but profecuted him with violence: Robert, incapable of bearing difgrace, left the kingdom, and hid himfelf in the Low Countries: Chaced from that retreat, by the authority of Philip, he came over to England; in fpite of the French king's menaces and remonftrances, he was favourably received by Edward[f]; and was foon admitted into the councils, and fhared the confidence of that monarch. Abandoning himfelf to all the movements of rage and defpair, he endeavoured to revive the prepoffeffion entertained by Edward in favour of his title to the crown of France, and even flattered him, that it was not impoffible for a prince of his valour and abilities, to render his claim effectual. The king was the more difpofed to hearken to fuggeftions of this nature, becaufe he had, in feveral particulars, found reafon to complain of Philip's conduct with regard to Guienne, and becaufe that prince had both given protection

CHAP. XV.

1337.

[e] Froiffard, liv. I. chap. 19. [f] Rymer, vol. iv. p. 747. Froiffard, liv. i. chap. 29.

CHAP. XV.

1337.

to the exiled David Bruce, and supported, at least encouraged, the Scots in their struggles for independence. Thus resentment gradually filled the breasts of both monarchs, and made them incapable of hearkening to any terms of accommodation proposed by the pope, who never ceased interposing his good offices between them. Philip thought that he should be wanting to the first principles of policy if he abandoned Scotland: Edward affirmed, that he must relinquish all pretensions to generosity, if he withdrew his protection from Robert. The former, informed of some preparations for hostilities which had been made by his rival, issued a sentence of felony and attainder against Robert, and declared, that every vassal of the crown, whether *within or without* the kingdom, who gave countenance to that traitor, would be involved in the same sentence; a menace easy to be understood: The latter, resolute not to yield, endeavoured to form alliances in the Low Countries and on the frontiers of Germany, the only places from which he either could make an effectual attack upon France, or produce such a diversion as might save the province of Guienne, which lay so much exposed to the power of Philip.

Preparations for war with France.

THE king began with opening his intentions to the count of Hainault, his father-in-law; and having engaged him in his interests, he employed the good offices and counsels of that prince in drawing into his alliance the other sovereigns of that neighbourhood. The duke of Brabant was induced, by his mediation, and by large remittances of money from England, to promise his concurrence [e]: The archbishop of Cologn, the duke of Gueldres, the marquis of Juliers, the count of Namur, the lords of Fauquemont and Baquen, were engaged by like motives to embrace the English alliance [b]. These sove-

[e] Rymer, vol. iv. p. 777.   [b] Froissart, liv. iv. chap. 29. 33. 36.

reign

reign princes could supply, either from their own states or from the bordering countries, great numbers of warlike troops; and naught was wanting to make the force on that quarter very formidable but the accession of Flanders; which Edward procured by means somewhat extraordinary and unusual.

As the Flemings were the first people in the northern parts of Europe that cultivated arts and manufactures, the lower ranks of men among them had risen to a degree of opulence unknown elsewhere to those of their station in that barbarous age; had acquired privileges and independence; and began to emerge from that state of vassalage, or rather of slavery, into which the common people had been universally thrown by the feudal institutions. It was probably difficult for them to bring their sovereign and their nobility to conform themselves to the principles of law and civil government, so much neglected in every other country: It was impossible for them to confine themselves within the proper bounds in their opposition and resentment against any instance of tyranny: They had risen in tumults: Had insulted the nobles: Had chaced their earl into France: And delivering themselves over to the guidance of a seditious leader, had been guilty of all that insolence and disorder, to which the thoughtless and enraged populace are so much inclined, wherever they are unfortunate enough to be their own masters[1].

THEIR present leader was James d'Arteville, a brewer in Ghent, who governed them with a more absolute sway than had ever been assumed by any of their lawful sovereigns: He placed and displaced the magistrates at pleasure: He was accompanied by a guard, who, on the least signal from him, instantly assassinated any man that happened to fall under his displeasure: All the cities of Flanders were full of his spies; and it was immediate death to

[1] Froissart, liv. I. chap. 30. Meyerus.

give him the smallest umbrage: The few nobles, who remained in the country, lived in continual terror from his violence: He seized the estates of all those whom he had either banished or murdered; and bestowing a part on their wives and children, converted the remainder to his own use [k]. Such were the first effects, that Europe saw, of popular violence; after having groaned, during so many ages, under monarchical and aristocratical tyranny.

James d'Arteville was the man to whom Edward addressed himself for bringing over the Flemings to his interests; and that prince, the most haughty and most aspiring of the age, never courted any ally with so much assiduity and so many submissions, as he employed towards this seditious and criminal tradesman. D'Arteville, proud of these advances from the king of England, and sensible that the Flemings were naturally inclined to maintain connexions with the English, who furnished them the materials of their woollen manufactures, the chief source of their opulence, readily embraced the interests of Edward, and invited him over into the Low Countries. Edward, before he entered on this great enterprize, affected to consult his parliament, asked their advice, and obtained their consent [l]. And the more to strengthen his hands, he procured from them a grant of 20,000 sacks of wool; which might amount to about a hundred thousand pounds: This commodity was a good instrument to employ with the Flemings; and the price of it with his German allies. He completed the other necessary sums by loans, by pawning the crown jewels, by confiscating, or rather robbing at once all the Lombards, who now exercised the invidious trade, formerly monopolized by the Jews, of lending on interest [m]; and being attended

[k] Froissard, liv. 1. chap. 30. [l] Cotton's Abridg.
[m] Dugd. Baron, vol. ii. p. 146.

by a body of English forces, and by several of his nobility, he sailed over to Flanders.

The German princes, in order to justify their unprovoked hostilities against France, had required the sanction of some legal authority; and Edward, that he might give them satisfaction on this head, had applied to Lewis of Bavaria, then emperor, and had been created by him *vicar of the empire*; an empty title, but which seemed to give him a right of commanding the service of the princes of Germany[a]. The Flemings, who were vassals of France, pretending like scruples with regard to the invasion of their liege lord; Edward, by the advice of d'Arteville, assumed, in his commissions, the title of king of France; and, in virtue of this right, claimed their assistance for dethroning Philip de Valois, the usurper of his kingdom[b]. This step, which, he feared, would destroy all future amity between the kingdoms, and beget endless and implacable jealousies in France, was not taken by him without much reluctance and hesitation: And not being in itself very justifiable, it has in the issue been attended with many miseries to both kingdoms. From this period we may date the commencement of that great animosity, which the English nation have ever since born to the French, which has so visible an influence on all future transactions, and which has been, and continues to be, the spring of many rash and precipitate resolutions among them. In all the preceding reigns since the conquest, the hostilities between the two crowns had been only casual and temporary; and as they had never been attended with any bloody or dangerous event, the traces of them were easily obliterated by the first treaty of pacification. The English nobility and gentry valued themselves on their

[a] Froissard. liv. I. chap. 35. p. 143. [b] Heming. p. 303. Walsingham.

French or Norman extraction: They affected to employ the language of that country in all public transactions, and even in familiar conversation: And both the English court and camp being always full of nobles, who came from different provinces of France, the two people were, during some centuries, more intermingled together than any two distinct nations whom we meet with in history. But the fatal pretensions of Edward III. dissolved all these connexions, and left the seeds of great animosity in both countries, especially among the English. For it is remarkable, that this latter nation, though they were commonly the aggressors, and by their success and situation were enabled to commit the most cruel injuries on the other, have always retained a stronger tincture of national antipathy; nor is their hatred retaliated on them to an equal degree by the French. That country lies in the middle of Europe, has been successively engaged in hostilities with all its neighbours, the popular prejudices have been diverted into many channels, and, among a people of softer manners, they never rose to a great height against any particular nation.

PHILIP made great preparations against the attack from the English, and such as seemed more than sufficient to secure him from the danger. Besides the concurrence of all the nobility in his own populous and warlike kingdom, his foreign alliances were both more cordial and more powerful than those which were formed by his antagonist. The pope, who, at this time, lived at Avignon, was dependant on France, and being disgusted at the connexions between Edward and Lewis of Bavaria, whom he had excommunicated, he embraced with zeal and sincerity the cause of the French monarch. The king of Navarre, the duke of Britanny, the count of Bar, were in the same interests; and on the side of Germany, the king of Bohemia, the Palatine, the dukes of Lorraine and Austria,

stria, the bishop of Liege, the counts of Deuxpont, Vaudemont, and Geneva. The allies of Edward were in themselves weaker; and having no object, but his money, which began to be exhausted, they were slow in their motions, and irresolute in their measures. The duke of Brabant, the most powerful among them, seemed even inclined to withdraw himself wholly from the alliance; and the king was necessitated, both to give the Brabanters new privileges in trade, and to contract his son Edward with the daughter of that prince, ere he could bring him to fulfil his engagements. The summer was wasted in conferences and negotiations before Edward could take the field; and he was obliged, in order to allure his German allies into his measures, to pretend that the first attack should be made upon Cambray, a city of the empire which had been garrisoned by Philip[p]. But finding, upon trial, the difficulty of the enterprize, he conducted them towards the frontiers of France; and he there saw, by a sensible proof, the vanity of his expectations: The count of Namur, and even the count of Hainault, his brother-in-law (for the old count was dead), refused to commence hostilities against their liege lord, and retired with their troops[q]. So little account did they make of Edward's pretensions to the crown of France!

CHAP. XV.

1338.

1339.

THE king, however, entered the enemy's country, and encamped on the fields of Vironfosse near Capelle, with an army of near 50,000 men, composed almost entirely of foreigners: Philip approached him with an army of near double the force, composed chiefly of native subjects; and it was daily expected that a battle would ensue. But the English monarch was averse to engage against so great a superiority: The French thought it sufficient if he

War with France.

[p] Froissard, liv. 1. chap. 39. Heming. p. 305. [q] Froissard, liv. 1. chap. 39.

eluded

eluded the attacks of his enemy, without running any unneceſſary hazard. The two armies faced each other for ſome days: Mutual defiances were ſent: And Edward, at laſt, retired into Flanders, and diſbanded his army [r].

Such was the fruitleſs, and almoſt ridiculous, concluſion of Edward's mighty preparations; and, as his meaſures were the moſt prudent that could be embraced in his ſituation, he might learn from experience in what a hopeleſs enterprize he was engaged. His expences, though they had led to no end, had been conſuming and deſtructive: He had contracted near 300,000 pounds of debt [s]; he had anticipated all his revenue; he had pawned every thing of value which belonged either to himſelf or his queen; he was obliged, in ſome meaſure, even to pawn himſelf to his creditors, by not failing to England, ti'l he obtained their permiſſion, and by promiſing, on his word of honour, to return in perſon, if he did not remit their money.

But he was a prince of too much ſpirit to be diſcouraged by the firſt difficulties of an undertaking; and he was anxious to retrieve his honour by more ſucceſsful and more gallant enterprizes. For this purpoſe he had, during the courſe of the campaign, ſent orders to ſummon a parliament by his ſon Edward, whom he had left with the title of guardian, and to demand ſome ſupply in his urgent neceſſities. The barons ſeemed inclined to grant his requeſt; but the knights, who often, at this time, acted as a ſeparate body from the burgeſſes, made ſome ſcruple of taxing the conſtituents without their conſent; and they deſired the guardian to ſummon a new parliament, which might be properly impowered for that purpoſe. The ſituation of the king and parliament was,

[r] Froiſſard, liv. l. chap. 41, 42, 43. Heming. p. 307. Walſing. p. 143.
[s] Cotton's Abridg. p. 17.

for the time, nearly similar to that which they constantly fell into about the beginning of the last century; and similar consequences began visibly to appear. The king, sensible of the frequent demands which he should be obliged to make on his people, had been anxious to ensure to his friends a seat in the house of commons, and at his instigation, the sheriffs and other placemen had made interest to be elected into that assembly; an abuse which the knights desired the king to correct by the tenor of his writ of summons, and which was accordingly remedied. On the other hand, the knights had professedly annexed conditions to their intended grant, and required a considerable retrenchment of the royal prerogatives, particularly with regard to purveyance, and the levying of the ancient feudal aids for knighting the king's eldest son, and marrying his eldest daughter. The new parliament, called by the guardian, retained the same free spirit; and, though they offered a large supply of 30,000 sacks of wool, no business was concluded; because the conditions, which they annexed, appeared too high to be compensated by a temporary concession. But when Edward himself came over to England, he summoned another parliament, and he had the interest to procure a supply on more moderate terms. A confirmation of the two charters, and of the privileges of boroughs, a pardon for old debts and trespasses, and a remedy for some abuses in the execution of common law, were the chief conditions insisted on; and the king, in return for his concessions on these heads, obtained from the barons and knights an unusual grant, for two years, of the ninth sheaf, lamb, and fleece on their estates; and from the burgesses, a ninth of their moveables at their true value. The whole parliament also granted a duty of forty shillings on each sack of wool exported, on each three hundred wool-fells, and on each last of leather for the same term of years; but dreading the arbitrary

bitrary spirit of the crown, they expressly declared, that this grant was to continue no longer, and was not to be drawn into precedent. Being soon after sensible that this supply, though considerable and very unusual in that age, would come in slowly, and would not answer the king's urgent necessities, proceeding both from his debts, and his preparations for war; they agreed, that 20,000 sacks of wool should immediately be granted him, and their value be deducted from the ninths which were afterwards to be levied.

But there appeared, at this time, another jealousy in the parliament, which was very reasonable, and was founded on a sentiment that ought to have engaged them rather to check, than support the king in all those ambitious projects so little likely to prove successful, and so dangerous to the nation, if they did. Edward, who, before the commencement of the former campaign, had, in several commissions, assumed the title of king of France, now more openly, in all public deeds, gave himself that appellation, and always quartered the arms of France with those of England in his seals and ensigns. The parliament thought proper to obviate the consequences of this measure, and to declare, that they owed him no obedience as king of France, and that the two kingdoms must for ever remain distinct and independent[1]. They undoubtedly foresaw, that France, if subdued, would, in the end, prove the seat of government; and they deemed this previous protestation necessary, in order to prevent their becoming a province to that monarchy. A frail security, if the event had really taken place!

As Philip was apprized, from the preparations which were making both in England and the Low Countries, that he must expect another invasion from Edward, he

[1] 14 Edward III.

EDWARD III.

fitted out a great fleet of 400 vessels, manned with 40,000 men; and he stationed them off Sluise, with a view of intercepting the king in his passage. The English navy was much inferior in number, consisting only of 240 sail; but whether it were by the superior abilities of Edward, or the greater dexterity of his seamen, they gained the wind of the enemy, and had the sun in their backs; and with these advantages began the action. The battle was fierce and bloody: The English archers, whose force and address were now much celebrated, galled the French on their approach: And when the ships grappled together, and the contest became more steady and furious, the example of the king, and of so many gallant nobles who accompanied him, animated to such a degree the seamen and soldiery, that they maintained every where a superiority over the enemy. The French also had been guilty of some imprudence in taking their station so near the coast of Flanders, and chusing that place for the scene of action. The Flemings, descrying the battle, hurried out of their harbours, and brought a reinforcement to the English; which, coming unexpectedly, had a greater effect than in proportion to its power and numbers. Two hundred and thirty French ships were taken: Thirty thousand Frenchmen were killed, with two of their admirals: The loss of the English was inconsiderable, compared to the greatness and importance of the victory". None of Philip's courtiers, it is said, dared to inform him of the event; till his fool or jester gave him a hint, by which he discovered the loss that he had sustained ".

CHAP. XV.

1340. Naval victory. 13th June.

THE lustre of this great success encreased the king's authority among his allies, who assembled their forces with expedition, and joined the English army. Edward

" Froissard, liv. 1. chap. 51. Avesbury, p. 56. Heming. p. 341.
" Walsing. p. 148.

D d 2 marched

CHAP.
XV.

1340.

marched to the frontiers of France at the head of above 100,000 men, consisting chiefly of foreigners, a more numerous army than, either before or since, has ever been commanded by any king of England [a]. At the same time the Flemings, to the number of 50,000 men, marched out under the command of Robert of Artois, and laid siege to St. Omer; but this tumultuary army, composed entirely of tradesmen unexperienced in war, was routed by a sally of the garrison, and notwithstanding the abilities of their leader, was thrown into such a panic, that they were instantly dispersed, and never more appeared in the field. The enterprizes of Edward, though not attended with so inglorious an issue, proved equally vain and fruitless. The king of France had assembled an army more numerous than the English; was accompanied by all the chief nobility of his kingdom; was attended by many foreign princes, and even by three monarchs, the kings of Bohemia, Scotland, and Navarre [b]: Yet he still adhered to the prudent resolution of putting nothing to hazard, and after throwing strong garrisons into all the frontier towns, he retired backwards, persuaded that the enemy, having wasted their force in some tedious and unsuccessful enterprize, would afford him an easy victory.

TOURNAY was, at that time, one of the most considerable cities of Flanders, containing above 60,000 inhabitants of all ages, who were affectionate to the French government; and, as the secret of Edward's designs had not been strictly kept, Philip learned that the English, in order to gratify their Flemish allies, had intended to open the campaign with the siege of this place: He took care therefore to supply it with a garrison of 14,000 men, commanded by the bravest nobility of France; and he reasonably expected that these forces, joined to the

[a] Rymer, vol. v. p. 197.   [b] Froissart, liv. 1. chap. 37.

inhabitants

inhabitants, would be able to defend the city against all the efforts of the enemy. Accordingly Edward, when he commenced the siege, about the end of July, found every where an obstinate resistance: The valour of one side was encountered with equal valour by the other: Every assault was repulsed, and proved unsuccessful: And the king was at last obliged to turn the siege into a blockade, in hopes that the great numbers of the garrison and citizens, which had enabled them to defend themselves against his attacks, would but expose them to be the more easily reduced by famine[*]. The count of Eu, who commanded in Tournay, as soon as he perceived that the English had formed this plan of operations, endeavoured to save his provisions, by expelling all the useless mouths; and the duke of Brabant, who wished no success to Edward's enterprizes, gave every one a free passage through his quarters.

AFTER the siege had continued ten weeks, the city was reduced to distress; and Philip, recalling all his scattered garrisons, advanced towards the English camp, at the head of a mighty army, with an intention of still avoiding any decisive action, but of seeking some opportunity for throwing relief into the place. Here Edward, irritated with the small progress he had hitherto made, and with the disagreeable prospect that lay before him, sent Philip a defiance by a herald; and challenged him to decide their claims for the crown of France, either by single combat, or by an action of a hundred against a hundred, or by a general engagement. But Philip replied, that Edward having done homage to him for the dutchy of Guienne, and having solemnly acknowledged him for his superior, it by no means became him to send a defiance to his liege lord and sovereign: That he was confident, notwithstanding all Edward's preparations, and

[* Froissard, liv. I. chap. 54.]

CHAP. XV.
1340.

his conjunction with the rebellious Flemings, he himself should soon be able to chace him from the frontiers of France: That as the hostilities from England had prevented him from executing his purposed crusade against the infidels, he trusted in the assistance of the Almighty, who would reward his pious intentions, and punish the aggressor, whose ill-grounded claims had rendered them abortive: That Edward proposed a duel on very unequal terms, and offered to hazard only his own person against both the kingdom of France, and the person of the king: But that, if he would encrease the stake, and put also the kingdom of England on the issue of the duel, he would, notwithstanding that the terms would still be unequal, very willingly accept of the challenge[a]. It was easy to see, that these mutual bravadoes were intended only to dazzle the populace, and that the two kings were too wise to think of executing their pretended purpose.

WHILE the French and English armies lay in this situation, and a general action was every day expected, Jane, countess dowager of Hainault, interposed with her good offices, and endeavoured to conciliate peace between the contending monarchs, and to prevent any farther effusion of blood. This princess was mother-in-law to Edward, and sister to Philip; and though she had taken the vows in a convent, and had renounced the world, she left her retreat on this occasion, and employed all her pious efforts, to allay those animosities which had taken place between persons so nearly related to her, and to each other. As Philip had no material claims on his antagonist, she found that he hearkened willingly to the proposals; and even the haughty and ambitious Edward, convinced of his fruitless attempt, was not averse to her

[a] Du Tillet, Recueil de Traites, &c. Heming. p. 325, 326. Walsing. p. 149.

negotiation,

negotiation. He was sensible, from experience, that he had engaged in an enterprize which far exceeded his force; and that the power of England was never likely to prevail over that of a superior kingdom, firmly united under an able and prudent monarch. He discovered, that all the allies whom he could gain by negotiation, were, at bottom, averse to his enterprize; and though they might second it to a certain length, would immediately detach themselves, and oppose its final accomplishment, if ever they could be brought to think, that there was seriously any danger of it. He even saw, that their chief purpose was to obtain money from him; and as his supplies from England came in very slowly, and had much disappointed his expectations, he perceived their growing indifference in his cause, and their desire of embracing all plausible terms of accommodation. Convinced, at last, that an undertaking must be imprudent, which could only be supported by means so unequal to the end, he concluded a truce, which left both parties in possession of their present acquisitions, and stopped all farther hostilities on the side of the Low Countries, Guienne, and Scotland, till Midsummer next [b]. A negotiation was soon after opened at Arras, under the mediation of the pope's legates; and the truce was attempted to be converted into a solid peace. Edward here required, that Philip should free Guienne from all claims of superiority, and entirely withdraw his protection from Scotland: But as he seemed not any wise entitled to make such high demands, either from his past successes, or future prospects, they were totally rejected by Philip, who agreed only to a prolongation of the truce.

The king of France soon after detached the emperor Lewis from the alliance of England, and engaged him to revoke the title of imperial vicar, which he had conferred

[b] Froissard, liv. 1. chap. 64. Avesbury, p. 65.

CHAP. XV.
1340.

Domestic disturbances.

on Edward [c]. The king's other allies on the frontiers of France, disappointed in their hopes, gradually withdrew from the confederacy. And Edward himself, harassed by his numerous and importunate creditors, was obliged to make his escape, by stealth, into England.

THE unusual tax of a ninth sheaf, lamb, and fleece, imposed by parliament, together with the great want of money, and still more, of credit in England, had rendered the remittances to Flanders extremely backward; nor could it be expected, that any expeditious method of collecting an imposition, which was so new in itself, and which yielded only a gradual produce, could possibly be contrived by the king or his ministers. And though the parliament, foreseeing the inconvenience, had granted, as a present resource, 20,000 sacks of wool, the only English goods that bore a sure price in foreign markets, and were the next to ready money; it was impossible, but the getting possession of such a bulky commodity, the gathering of it from different parts of the kingdom, and the disposing of it abroad, must take up more time than the urgency of the king's affairs would permit, and must occasion all the disappointments complained of during the course of the campaign. But though nothing had happened which Edward might not reasonably have foreseen, he was so irritated with the unfortunate issue of his military operations, and so much vexed and affronted by his foreign creditors, that he was determined to throw the blame somewhere off himself, and he came in very bad humour into England. He discovered his peevish disposition by the first act which he performed after his arrival: As he landed unexpectedly, he found the Tower negligently guarded; and he immediately committed to prison the constable, and all others who had the charge of that fortress, and he treated them with unusual rigour [d],

[c] Heming. p. 352. Ypod. Neust. p. 514. Knyghton, p. 2580.
[d] Ypod. Neust. p. 513.

His vengeance fell next on the officers of the revenue, the sheriffs, the collectors of the taxes, the undertakers of all kinds; and besides dismissing all of them from their employments, he appointed commissioners to enquire into their conduct; and these men, in order to gratify the king's humour, were sure not to find any person innocent who came before them[*]. Sir John St. Paul, keeper of the privy seal, Sir John Stonore, chief justice, Andrew Aubrey, mayor of London, were displaced and imprisoned; as were also the bishop of Chichester, chancellor, and the bishop of Litchfield, treasurer. Stratford, archbishop of Canterbury, to whom the charge of collecting the new taxes had been chiefly entrusted, fell likewise under the king's displeasure; but being absent at the time of Edward's arrival, he escaped feeling the immediate effects of it.

THERE were strong reasons which might discourage the kings of England, in those ages, from bestowing the chief offices of the crown on prelates and other ecclesiastical persons. These men had so entrenched themselves in privileges and immunities, and so openly challenged an exemption from all secular jurisdiction, that no civil penalty could be inflicted on them for any malversation in office; and as even treason itself was declared to be no canonical offence, nor was allowed to be a sufficient reason for deprivation or other spiritual censures, that order of men had ensured to themselves an almost total impunity, and were not bound by any political law or statute. But, on the other hand, there were many peculiar causes which favoured their promotion. Besides that they possessed almost all the learning of the age, and were best qualified for civil employments; the prelates enjoyed equal dignity with the greatest barons, and gave weight, by their personal authority, to the powers entrusted with them:

[*] Avesbury, p. 70. Hemingf. p. 326. Walsingham, p. 150.

While

CHAP.
XV.

1340.

While, at the same time, they did not endanger the crown by accumulating wealth or influence in their families, and were restrained, by the decency of their character, from that open rapine and violence so often practised by the nobles. These motives had induced Edward, as well as many of his predecessors, to entrust the chief departments of government in the hands of ecclesiastics, at the hazard of seeing them disown his authority as soon as it was turned against them.

1341.

This was the case with archbishop Stratford. That prelate, informed of Edward's indignation against him, prepared himself for the storm; and not content with standing upon the defensive, he resolved, by beginning the attack, to show the king that he knew the privileges of his character, and had courage to maintain them. He issued a general sentence of excommunication against all, who, on any pretext, exercised violence on the person or goods of clergymen; who infringed those privileges secured by the great charter, and by ecclesiastical canons; or who accused a prelate of treason or any other crime, in order to bring him under the king's displeasure [f]. Even Edward had reason to think himself struck at by this sentence; both on account of the imprisonment of the two bishops and that of other clergymen concerned in levying the taxes, and on account of his seizing their lands and moveables, that he might make them answerable for any balance which remained in their hands. The clergy, with the primate at their head, were now formed into a regular combination against the king; and many calumnies were spread against him, in order to deprive him of the confidence and affections of his people. It was pretended, that he meant to recal the general pardon, and the remission which he had granted of old debts,

[f] Heming. p. 339. Ang. Sacra, vol. i. p. 21, 22. Walsingham, p. 153.

and

and to impose new and arbitrary taxes without consent of parliament. The archbishop went so far, in a letter to the king himself, as to tell him, that there were two powers by which the world was governed, the holy pontifical apostolic dignity, and the royal subordinate authority: That of these two powers the clerical was evidently the supreme; since the priests were to answer, at the tribunal of the divine judgment, for the conduct of kings themselves: That the clergy were the spiritual fathers of all the faithful, and amongst others of kings and princes; and were intitled, by a heavenly charter, to direct their wills and actions, and to censure their transgressions: And that prelates had heretofore cited emperors before their tribunal, had sitten in judgment on their life and behaviour, and had anathematized them for their obstinate offences [a]. These topics were not well calculated to appease Edward's indignation; and when he called a parliament, he sent not to the primate, as to the other peers, a summons to attend it. Stratford was not discouraged at this mark of neglect or anger: He appeared before the gates, arrayed in his pontifical robes, holding the crosier in his hand, and accompanied by a pompous train of priests and prelates; and he required admittance as the first and highest peer in the realm. During two days, the king rejected his application: But sensible, either that this affair might be attended with dangerous consequences, or that in his impatience he had groundlessly accused the primate of malversation in his office, which seems really to have been the case, he at last permitted him to take his seat, and was reconciled to him [b].

EDWARD now found himself in a bad situation both with his own people and with foreign states; and it required all his genius and capacity to extricate himself

[a] Anglia Sacra, vol. I. p. 27, 39, 40, 41. [b] Anglia Sacra, vol. I. p. 38.

CHAP. XV.

1341.

from such multiplied difficulties and embarrassments. His unjust and exorbitant claims on France and Scotland had engaged him in an implacable war with these two kingdoms, his nearest neighbours: He had lost almost all his foreign alliances by his irregular payments: He was deeply involved in debts, for which he owed a consuming interest: His military operations had vanished into smoke; and except his naval victory, none of them had been attended even with glory or renown, either to himself or to the nation: The animosity between him and the clergy was open and declared: The people were discontented on account of many arbitrary measures, in which he had been engaged: And, what was more dangerous, the nobility, taking advantage of his present necessities, were determined to retrench his power, and by encroaching on the ancient prerogatives of the crown, to acquire to themselves independence and authority. But the aspiring genius of Edward, which had so far transported him beyond the bounds of discretion, proved at last sufficient to re-instate him in his former authority, and finally, to render his reign the most triumphant that is to be met with in English story: Though for the present he was obliged, with some loss of honour, to yield to the current, which bore so strongly against him.

THE parliament framed an act, which was likely to produce considerable innovations in the government. They premised, that, whereas the great charter had, to the manifest peril and slander of the king and damage of his people, been violated in many points, particularly by the imprisonment of free men, and the seizure of their goods, without suit, indictment, or trial, it was necessary to confirm it anew, and to oblige all the chief officers of the law, together with the steward and chamberlain of the household, the keeper of the privy-seal, the controller and treasurer of the wardrobe, and those who were entrusted with the education of the young prince, to swear to the regular observance of it. They also remarked, that the peers of the realm had formerly been arrested and imprisoned, and dispossessed of their temporalities and lands, and even some of them put to death, without judgment or trial; and they therefore enacted that such violences should henceforth cease, and no peer be punished but by the award of his peers *in parliament*. They required that, whenever any of the great offices above mentioned became vacant, the king should fill it by the advice of his council, and the consent of such barons as should at that time be found to reside in the neighbourhood of the court. And they enacted, that, on the third day of every session, the king should resume into his own hand all these offices, except those of justices of the two benches and the barons of exchequer; that the ministers should for the time be reduced to private persons; that they should in that condition answer before parliament to any accusation brought against them; and that, if they were found any wise guilty, they should finally be dispossessed of their offices, and more able persons be substituted in their place [l]. By these last regulations, the barons approached as near as they durst to those restrictions which had formerly been imposed on Henry III. and Edward II. and which, from the dangerous consequences attending them, had become so generally odious, that they did not expect to have either the concurrence of the people in demanding them, or the assent of the present king in granting them.

In return for these important concessions, the parliament offered the king a grant of 20,000 sacks of wool; and his wants were so urgent, from the clamours of his creditors, and the demands of his foreign allies, that he

[l] 15 Edward III.

CHAP. XV.

1341.

was obliged to accept of the supply on these hard conditions. He ratified this statute in full parliament; but he secretly entered a protest of such a nature, as were sufficient, one should imagine, to destroy all future trust and confidence with his people: He declared that, as soon as his convenience permitted, he would, from his own authority, revoke what had been extorted from him [k]. Accordingly, he was no sooner possessed of the parliamentary supply, than he issued an edict, which contains many extraordinary positions and pretensions. He first asserts, that that statute had been enacted contrary to law; as if a free legislative body could ever do any thing illegal. He next affirms, that, as it was hurtful to the prerogatives of the crown, which he had sworn to defend, he had only dissembled, when he seemed to ratify it, but that he had never in his own breast given his assent to it. He does not pretend, that either he or the parliament lay under force; but only that some inconvenience would have ensued, had he not seemingly affixed his sanction to that pretended statute. He therefore, with the advice of his council, and of *some* earls and barons, abrogates and annuls it; and though he professes himself willing and determined to observe such articles of it as were formerly law, he declares it to have thenceforth no force or authority [l]. The parliaments, that were afterwards assembled, took no notice of this arbitrary exertion of royal power, which, by a parity of reason, left all their laws at the mercy of the king; and during the course of two years, Edward had so far re-established his influence, and freed himself from his present necessities, that he then obtained from his parliament a legal repeal of the ob-

[k] Statutes at Large, 15 Edw. III. That this protest of the king's was *secret*, appears evidently, since otherwise it would have been ridiculous in the parliament to have accepted of his assent: Besides, the king owns that he *dissembled*, which would not have been the case, had his protest been public.
[l] Statutes at Large, 15 Edw. III.

noxious

EDWARD III. 415

noxious statute [m]. This transaction certainly contains remarkable circumstances, which discover the manners and sentiments of the age, and may prove what inaccurate work might be expected from such rude hands, when employed in legislation, and in rearing the delicate fabric of laws and a constitution.

CHAP. XV.

1344.

But though Edward had happily recovered his authority at home, which had been impaired by the events of the French war, he had undergone so many mortifications from that attempt, and saw so little prospect of success, that he would probably have dropped his claim, had not a revolution in Britanny opened to him more promising views, and given his enterprizing genius a full opportunity of displaying itself.

John III. duke of Britanny, had, during some years, found himself declining through age and infirmities; and having no issue, he was solicitous to prevent those disorders, to which, on the event of his demise, a disputed succession might expose his subjects. His younger brother, the count of Penthievre, had left only one daughter, whom the duke deemed his heir; and as his family had inherited the dutchy by a female succession, he thought her title preferable to that of the count of Mountfort, who, being his brother by a second marriage, was the male heir of that principality [n]. He accordingly purposed to bestow his niece in marriage on some person who might be able to defend her rights; and he cast his eye on Charles of Blois, nephew of the king of France, by his mother, Margaret of Valois, sister to that monarch. But as he both loved his subjects, and was beloved by them, he determined not to take this important step without their approbation; and having assembled the states of Britanny, he represented to them the advantages

Affairs of Britanny.

[m] Cotton's Abridgm. p. 38, 39. [n] Froissard, liv. 1, chap. 64.

CHAP. XV.

1341.

of that alliance, and the prospect, which it gave, of an entire settlement of the succession. The Bretons willingly concurred in his choice: The marriage was concluded: All his vassals, and among the rest, the count of Mountfort, swore fealty to Charles and to his consort as to their future sovereigns: And every danger of civil commotions seemed to be obviated, as far as human prudence could provide a remedy against them.

But on the death of this good prince, the ambition of the count of Mountfort broke through all these regulations, and kindled a war, not only dangerous to Britanny, but to a great part of Europe. While Charles of Blois was soliciting at the court of France the investiture of the dutchy, Mountfort was active in acquiring immediate possession of it; and by force or intrigue he made himself master of Rennes, Nantz, Brest, Hennebonne, and all the most important fortresses, and engaged many considerable barons to acknowledge his authority [o]. Sensible that he could expect no favour from Philip, he made a voyage to England, on pretence of soliciting his claim to the earldom of Richmond, which had devolved to him by his brother's death; and there, offering to do homage to Edward, as king of France, for the dutchy of Britanny, he proposed a strict alliance for the support of their mutual pretensions. Edward saw immediately the advantages attending this treaty: Mountfort, an active and valiant prince, closely united to him by interest, opened at once an entrance into the heart of France, and afforded him much more flattering views, than his allies on the side of Germany and the Low Countries, who had no sincere attachment to his cause, and whose progress was also obstructed by those numerous fortifications, which had been raised on that frontier. Robert of Artois was

[o] Froissart, liv. I. chap. 65, 66, 67, 68.

zealous

EDWARD III.

CHAP. XV.

1341.
Renewal of the war with France.

zealous in enforcing these considerations: The ambitious spirit of Edward was little disposed to sit down under those repulses which he had received, and which, he thought, had so much impaired his reputation: And it required a very short negociation to conclude a treaty of alliance between two men, who, though their pleas with regard to the preference of male or female succession were directly opposite, were intimately connected by their immediate interests [p].

As this treaty was still a secret, Mountfort, on his return, ventured to appear at Paris, in order to defend his cause before the court of peers; but observing Philip and his judges to be prepossessed against his title, and dreading their intentions of arresting him, till he should restore what he had seized by violence, he suddenly made his escape; and war immediately commenced between him and Charles of Blois [q]. Philip sent his eldest son, the duke of Normandy, with a powerful army, to the assistance of the latter; and Mountfort, unable to keep the field against his rival, remained in the city of Nantz, where he was besieged. The city was taken by the treachery of the inhabitants; Mountfort fell into the hands of his enemies; was conducted as a prisoner to Paris; and was shut up in the tower of the Louvre [r].

1342.

THIS event seemed to put an end to the pretensions of the count of Mountfort; but his affairs were immediately retrieved by an unexpected incident, which inspired new life and vigour into his party. Jane of Flanders, countess of Mountfort, the most extraordinary woman of the age, was roused, by the captivity of her husband, from those domestic cares to which she had hitherto limited

[p] Froissard, liv. I. chap. 69.   [q] Ibid. chap. 70, 71.
[r] Ibid. chap. 73.

her genius; and she courageously undertook to support the falling fortunes of her family. No sooner did she receive the fatal intelligence, than she assembled the inhabitants of Rennes, where she then resided, and carrying her infant son in her arms, deplored to them the calamity of their sovereign. She recommended to their care the illustrious orphan, the sole male remaining of their ancient princes, who had governed them with such indulgence and lenity, and to whom they had ever professed the most zealous attachment. She declared herself willing to run all hazards with them in so just a cause; discovered the resources which still remained in the alliance of England; and entreated them to make one effort against an usurper, who, being imposed on them by the arms of France, would in return make a sacrifice to his protector of the ancient liberties of Britanny. The audience, moved by the affecting appearance, and inspirited by the noble conduct of the princess, vowed to live and die with her in defending the rights of her family: All the other fortresses of Britanny embraced the same resolution: The countess went from place to place, encouraging the garrisons, providing them with every thing necessary for subsistence, and concerting the proper plans of defence; and after she had put the whole province in a good posture, she shut herself up in Hennebonne, where she waited with impatience the arrival of those succours which Edward had promised her. Mean while, she sent over her son to England, that she might both put him in a place of safety, and engage the king more strongly, by such a pledge, to embrace with zeal the interests of her family.

CHARLES OF BLOIS, anxious to make himself master of so important a fortress as Hennebonne, and still more to take the countess prisoner, from whose vigour and capacity all the difficulties to his succession in Britanny now proceeded, sat down before the place with a great army, composed of French, Spaniards, Genoese, and some Bretons; and he conducted the attack with indefatigable industry[1]. The defence was no less vigorous: The besiegers were repulsed in every assault: Frequent sallies were made with success by the garrison: And the countess herself being the most forward in all military operations, every one was ashamed not to exert himself to the utmost in this desperate situation. One day she perceived that the besiegers, entirely occupied in an attack, had neglected a distant quarter of their camp; and she immediately sallied forth at the head of a body of 200 cavalry, threw them into confusion, did great execution upon them, and set fire to their tents, baggage, and magazines: But when she was preparing to return, she found that she was intercepted, and that a considerable body of the enemy had thrown themselves between her and the gates. She instantly took her resolution: She ordered her men to disband, and to make the best of their way by flight to Brest: She met them at the appointed place of rendezvous, collected another body of 500 horse, returned to Hennebonne, broke unexpectedly through the enemy's camp, and was received with shouts and acclamations by the garrison, who, encouraged by this reinforcement, and by so rare an example of female valour, determined to defend themselves to the last extremity.

The reiterated attacks, however, of the besiegers had at length made several breaches in the walls; and it was apprehended, that a general assault, which was every hour expected, would overpower the garrison, diminished in numbers, and extremely weakened with watching and fatigue. It became necessary to treat of a capitulation; and the bishop of Leon was already engaged, for that purpose, in a conference with Charles of Blois; when the countess, who had mounted to a high tower,

[1] Froissard, liv. 1. chap. 81.

CHAP.
XV.
1342.

and was looking towards the sea with great impatience, descried some sails at a distance. She immediately exclaimed: *Behold the succours! the English succours! No capitulation*[1]. This fleet had on board a body of heavy-armed cavalry, and six thousand archers, whom Edward had prepared for the relief of Hennebonne, but who had been long detained by contrary winds. They entered the harbour under the command of Sir Walter Manny, one of the bravest captains of England; and having inspired fresh courage into the garrison, immediately sallied forth, beat the besiegers from all their posts, and obliged them to decamp.

But notwithstanding this success, the countess of Mountfort found that her party, overpowered by numbers, was declining in every quarter; and she went over to solicit more effectual succours from the king of England. Edward granted her a considerable reinforcement under Robert of Artois; who embarked on board a fleet of forty-five ships, and sailed to Britanny. He was met in his passage by the enemy; an action ensued, where the countess behaved with her wonted valour, and charged the enemy sword in hand; but the hostile fleets, after a sharp action, were separated by a storm, and the English arrived safely in Britanny. The first exploit of Robert was the taking of Vannes, which he mastered by conduct and address[u]: But he survived a very little time this prosperity. The Breton noblemen of the party of Charles assembled secretly in arms, attacked Vannes of a sudden, and carried the place; chiefly by reason of a wound received by Robert, of which he soon after died at sea on his return to England[w].

After the death of this unfortunate prince, the chief author of all the calamities with which his country was

[1] Froissard, liv. i. chap. 81.   [u] Ibid. chap. 93.
[w] Ibid. chap. 94.

overwhelmed for more than a century, Edward undertook in person the defence of the countess of Mountfort; and as the last truce with France was now expired, the war, which the English and French had hitherto carried on as allies to the competitors for Britanny, was thenceforth conducted in the name and under the standard of the two monarchs. The king landed at Morbian, near Vannes, with an army of 12,000 men; and, being master of the field, he endeavoured to give a lustre to his arms, by commencing at once three important sieges, that of Vannes, of Rennes, and of Nantz. But by undertaking too much, he failed of success in all his enterprizes. Even the siege of Vannes, which Edward, in person, conducted with vigour, advanced but slowly *; and the French had all the leisure requisite for making preparations against him. The duke of Normandy, eldest son of Philip, appeared in Britanny at the head of an army of 30,000 infantry, and 4000 cavalry; and Edward was now obliged to draw together all his forces, and to entrench himself strongly before Vannes, where the duke of Normandy soon after arrived, and in a manner invested the besiegers. The garrison and the French camp were plentifully supplied with provisions; while the English, who durst not make any attempt upon the place in the presence of a superior army, drew all their subsistence from England, exposed to the hazards of the sea, and sometimes to those which arose from the fleet of the enemy. In this dangerous situation, Edward willingly hearkened to the mediation of the pope's legates, the cardinals of Palestine and Frescati, who endeavoured to negociate, if not a peace, at least a truce between the two kingdoms. A treaty was concluded for a cessation of arms during three years *; and Edward had the abilities, notwithstanding his present dangerous situation, to procure to himself very equal and

honourable

CHAP. XV.
1343.

honourable terms. It was agreed, that Vannes should be sequestered, during the truce, in the hands of the legates, to be disposed of afterwards as they pleased; and though Edward knew the partiality of the court of Rome towards his antagonists, he saved himself, by this device, from the dishonour of having undertaken a fruitless enterprize. It was also stipulated, that all prisoners should be released, that the places in Britanny should remain in the hands of the present possessors, and that the allies on both sides should be comprehended in the truce[a]. Edward, soon after concluding this treaty, embarked with his army for England.

THE truce, though calculated for a long time, was of very short duration; and each monarch endeavoured to throw on the other the blame of its infraction. Of course, the historians of the two countries differ in their account of the matter. It seems probable, however, as is affirmed by the French writers, that Edward, in consenting to the truce, had no other view than to extricate himself from a perilous situation into which he had fallen, and was afterwards very careless in observing it. In all the memorials which remain on this subject, he complains chiefly of the punishment inflicted on Oliver de Cliffon, John de Montauban, and other Breton noblemen, who, he says, were partizans of the family of Mountfort, and consequently under the protection of England[a]. But it appears, that, at the conclusion of the truce, those noblemen had openly, by their declarations and actions, embraced the cause of Charles of Blois[b]; and if they had entered into any secret correspondence and engagements with Edward, they were traitors to their party, and were justly punishable by Philip and Charles, for their breach of faith; nor had Edward

[a] Heming. p. 359. 376. Heming. p. 376.
[a] Rymer, vol. v. p. 433, 454, 459, 466.
[b] Froissard, liv. I. chap. 96. p. 200.

any

any ground of complaint againſt France for ſuch ſeverities. But when he laid theſe pretended injuries before the parliament, whom he affected to conſult on all occaſions, that aſſembly entered into the quarrel, adviſed the king not to be amuſed by a fraudulent truce, and granted him ſupplies for the renewal of the war: The counties were charged with a fifteenth for two years, and the boroughs with a tenth. The clergy conſented to give a tenth for three years.

THESE ſupplies enabled the king to complete his military preparations; and he ſent his couſin, Henry earl of Derby, ſon of the earl of Lancaſter, into Guienne, for the defence of that province [c]. This prince, the moſt accompliſhed in the Engliſh court, poſſeſſed to a high degree the virtues of juſtice and humanity, as well as thoſe of valour and conduct [d], and, not content with protecting and cheriſhing the province committed to his care, he made a ſucceſsful invaſion on the enemy. He attacked the count of Liſle, the French general, at Bergerac, beat him from his entrenchments, and took the place. He reduced a great part of Perigord, and continually advanced in his conqueſts, till the count of Liſle, having collected an army of ten or twelve thouſand men, ſat down before Aubèroche, in hopes of recovering that place, which had fallen into the hands of the Engliſh. The earl of Derby came upon him by ſurprize with only a thouſand cavalry, threw the French into diſorder, puſhed his advantages, and obtained a complete victory. Liſle himſelf, with many conſiderable nobles, was taken pri-

[c] Froiſſard, liv. 1. chap. 103. Aveſbury, p. 121.
[d] It is reported of this prince, that, having once, before the attack of a town, promiſed the ſoldiers the plunder, one private man happened to fall upon a great cheſt full of money, which he immediately brought to the earl, as thinking it too great for himſelf to keep poſſeſſion of it. But Derby told him, that his promiſe did not depend on the greatneſs or ſmallneſs of the ſum; and ordered him to keep it all for his own uſe.

sooner. After this important success, Derby made a rapid progress in subduing the French provinces. He took Monsegur, Monsepat, Villefranche, Miremont, and Tonnins, with the fortress of Damassen. Aiguillon, a fortress deemed impregnable, fell into his hands from the cowardice of the governor. Angouleme was surrendered after a short siege. The only place where he met with considerable resistance was Reole, which, however, was at last reduced, after a siege of above nine weeks. He made an attempt on Blaye, but thought it more prudent to raise the siege, than waste his time before a place of small importance.

The reason why Derby was permitted to make, without opposition, such progress on the side of Guienne, was the difficulties under which the French finances then laboured, and which had obliged Philip to lay on new impositions, particularly the duty on salt, to the great discontent, and almost mutiny of his subjects. But after the court of France was supplied with money, great preparations were made; and the duke of Normandy, attended by the duke of Burgundy, and other great nobility, led towards Guienne a powerful army, which the English could not think of resisting in the open field. The earl of Derby stood on the defensive, and allowed the French to carry on, at leisure, the siege of Angouleme, which was their first enterprize. John lord Norwich, the governor, after a brave and vigorous defence, found himself reduced to such extremities, as obliged him to employ a stratagem, in order to save his garrison, and to prevent his being reduced to surrender at discretion. He appeared on the walls, and desired a parley with the duke of Normandy. The prince there told Norwich, that he supposed he intended

tended to capitulate. "Not at all," replied the governor: "But as to-morrow is the feast of the Virgin, to whom, I know, that you, Sir, as well as myself, bear a great devotion, I desire a cessation of arms for that day." The proposal was agreed to; and Norwich, having ordered his forces to prepare all their baggage, marched out next day, and advanced towards the French camp. The besiegers, imagining they were to be attacked, ran to their arms; but Norwich sent a messenger to the duke, reminding him of his engagement. The duke, who piqued himself on faithfully keeping his word, exclaimed, *I see the governor has outwitted me: But let us be content with gaining the place*: And the English were allowed to pass through the camp unmolested [b]. After some other successes, the duke of Normandy laid siege to Aiguillon; and as the natural strength of the fortress, together with a brave garrison under the command of the earl of Pembroke, and Sir Walter Manny, rendered it impossible to take the place by assault, he purposed, after making several fruitless attacks [i], to reduce it by famine: But, before he could finish this enterprize, he was called to another quarter of the kingdom, by one of the greatest disasters that ever befel the French monarchy [k].

EDWARD, informed by the earl of Derby of the great danger to which Guienne was exposed, had prepared a force with which he intended, in person, to bring it relief. He embarked, at Southampton, on board a fleet of near a thousand sail of all dimensions; and carried with him, besides all the chief nobility of England, his eldest son, the prince of Wales, now fifteen years of age. The winds proved long contrary [l]; and the king, in despair of arriving in time at Guienne, was at last persuaded by Geoffrey d'Harcourt, to change the destination of his en-

[b] Froissard, liv. l. chap. 120.
[b] Ibid. chap. 154.

[i] Ibid. chap. 111.
[l] Avesbury, p. 123.

terprize. This nobleman was a Norman by birth, had long made a confiderable figure in the court of France, and was generally efteemed for his perfonal merit and his valour; but, being difobliged and perfecuted by Philip, he had fled into England; had recommended himfelf to Edward, who was an excellent judge of men; and had fucceeded to Robert of Artois in the invidious office of exciting and affifting the king in every enterprize againft his native country. He had long infifted, that an expedition to Normandy promifed, in the prefent circumftances, more favourable fuccefs than one to Guienne; that Edward would find the northern provinces almoft deftitute of military force, which had been drawn to the fouth; that they were full of flourifhing cities, whofe plunder would enrich the Englifh; that their cultivated fields, as yet unfpoiled by war, would fupply them with plenty of provifions; and that the neighbourhood of the capital rendered every event of importance in thofe quarters [m]. Thefe reafons, which had not before been duly weighed by Edward, began to make more impreffion, after the difappointments which he met with in his voyage to Guienne: He ordered his fleet to fail to Normandy, and fafely difembarked his army at la Hogue.

This army, which, during the courfe of the enfuing campaign, was crowned with the moft fplendid fuccefs, confifted of four thoufand men at arms, ten thoufand archers, ten thoufand Welfh infantry, and fix thoufand Irifh. The Welfh and the Irifh were light diforderly troops, fitter for doing execution in a purfuit, or fcouring the country, than for any ftable action. The bow was always efteemed a frivolous weapon, where true military difcipline was known, and regular bodies of well-armed foot maintained. The only folid force in this army were the men at arms; and even thefe, being cavalry, were,

[m] Foifard, liv. i. chap. 111.

on that account, much inferior, in the shock of battle, to good infantry: And as the whole were new levied troops, we are led to entertain a very mean idea of the military force of those ages, which, being ignorant of every other art, had not properly cultivated the art of war itself, the sole object of general attention.

The king created the earl of Arundel constable of his army, and the earls of Warwic and Harcourt, marefchals: He bestowed the honour of knighthood on the prince of Wales and several of the young nobility, immediately upon his landing. After destroying all the ships in la Hogue, Barfleur, and Cherbourg, he spread his army over the whole country, and gave them an unbounded licence of burning, spoiling, and plundering, every place of which they became masters. The loose discipline, then prevalent, could not be much hurt by these disorderly practices; and Edward took care to prevent any surprize, by giving orders to his troops, however they might disperse themselves in the day-time, always to quarter themselves at night near the main body. In this manner, Montebourg, Carentan, St. Lo, Valognes, and other places in the Cotentin, were pillaged without resistance; and an universal consternation was spread over the province [a].

The intelligence of this unexpected invasion soon reached Paris; and threw Philip into great perplexity. He issued orders, however, for levying forces in all quarters, and dispatched the count of Eu, constable of France, and the count of Tancarville, with a body of troops, to the defence of Caën, a populous and commercial, but open city, which lay in the neighbourhood of the English army. The temptation of so rich a prize soon allured Edward to approach it; and the inhabitants, encouraged by their numbers, and by the reinforcements which

[a] Froissart, liv. l. chap. 126.

they

they daily received from the country, ventured to meet him in the field. But their courage failed them on the first shock: They fled with precipitation: The counts of Eu and Tancarville were taken prisoners: The victors entered the city along with the vanquished, and a furious massacre commenced, without distinction of age, sex, or condition. The citizens, in despair, barricadoed their houses, and assaulted the English with stones, bricks, and every missile weapon: The English made way by fire to the destruction of the citizens: Till Edward, anxious to save both his spoil and his soldiers, stopped the massacre; and having obliged the inhabitants to lay down their arms, gave his troops licence to begin a more regular and less hazardous plunder of the city. The pillage continued for three days: The king reserved for his own share the jewels, plate, silks, fine cloth, and fine linen; and he bestowed all the remainder of the spoil on his army. The whole was embarked on board the ships, and sent over to England; together with three hundred of the richest citizens of Caën, whose ransom was an additional profit, which he expected afterwards to levy*. This dismal scene passed in the presence of two cardinal legates, who had come to negociate a peace between the kingdoms.

THE king moved next to Roüen in hopes of treating that city in the same manner; but found, that the bridge over the Seine was already broken down, and that the king of France himself was arrived there with his army. He marched along the banks of that river towards Paris, destroying the whole country, and every town and village which he met with on his road *p*. Some of his light troops carried their ravages even to the gates of Paris; and the royal palace of St. Germans, together with Nanterre, Ruelle, and other villages, was reduced to ashes within sight of the capital. The English intended to pass the river at Poissy, but found the French army encamped on

* Froissard, liv. l. chap. 114.   *p* Ibid. chap. 125.

the opposite banks, and the bridge at that place, as well as all others over the Seine, broken down by orders from Philip. Edward now saw, that the French meant to enclose him in their country, in hopes of attacking him with advantage on all sides: But he saved himself, by a stratagem, from this perilous situation. He gave his army orders to dislodge, and to advance farther up the Seine; but immediately returning by the same road, he arrived at Poissy, which the enemy had already quitted in order to attend his motions. He repaired the bridge with incredible celerity, passed over his army, and having thus disengaged himself from the enemy, advanced by quick marches towards Flanders. His vanguard, commanded by Harcourt, met with the townsmen of Amiens, who were hastening to reinforce their king, and defeated them with great slaughter [q]: He passed by Beauvais, and burned the suburbs of that city: But, as he approached the Somme, he found himself in the same difficulty as before: All the bridges on that river were either broken down, or strongly guarded: An army, under the command of Godemar de Faye, was stationed on the opposite banks: Philip was advancing on him from the other quarter, with an army of an hundred thousand men: And he was thus exposed to the danger of being enclosed, and of starving in an enemy's country. In this extremity, he published a reward to any one that should bring him intelligence of a passage over the Somme. A peasant, called Gobin Agace, whose name has been preserved by the share which he had in these important transactions, was tempted on this occasion to betray the interests of his country; and he informed Edward of a ford below Abbeville which had a found bottom, and might be passed without difficulty at low water [r]. The king hastened thither, but found Godemar de Faye on the opposite banks. Be-

CHAP.
XV.

1346.

[q] Froissard. liv. I. chap. 123.   [r] Ibid. chap. 126, 127.

ing

CHAP. XV.
1346.

ing urged by necessity, he deliberated not a moment; but threw himself into the river, sword in hand, at the head of his troops; drove the enemy from their station; and pursued them to a distance on the plain*. The French army, under Philip, arrived at the ford when the rear-guard of the English were passing. So narrow was the escape which Edward, by his prudence and celerity, made from this danger! The rising of the tide prevented the French king from following him over the ford, and obliged that prince to take his route over the bridge at Abbeville, by which some time was lost.

It is natural to think that Philip, at the head of so vast an army, was impatient to take revenge on the English, and to prevent the disgrace to which he must be exposed, if an inferior enemy should be allowed, after ravaging so great a part of his kingdom, to escape with impunity. Edward, also, was sensible that such must be the object of the French monarch; and, as he had advanced but a little way before his enemy, he saw the danger of precipitating his march over the plains of Picardy, and of exposing his rear to the insults of the numerous cavalry, in which the French camp abounded.

Battle of Crecy. 25th Aug.

He took therefore a prudent resolution: He chose his ground with advantage, near the village of Crecy; he disposed his army in excellent order; he determined to await, in tranquillity, the arrival of the enemy; and he hoped that their eagerness to engage and to prevent his retreat, after all their past disappointments, would hurry them on to some rash and ill-concerted action. He drew up his army on a gentle ascent, and divided them into three lines: The first was commanded by the prince of Wales, and under him, by the earls of Warwic and Oxford, by Harcourt, and by the lords Chandos, Holland, and other noblemen: The earls of Arundel and

* Froissart, liv. I. chap. 127.

Northampton,

EDWARD III.

Northampton, with the lords Willoughby, Basset, Roos, and Sir Lewis Tufton, were at the head of the second line: He took to himself the command of the third division, by which he purposed either to bring succour to the two first lines, or to secure a retreat in case of any misfortune, or to push his advantages against the enemy. He had likewise the precaution to throw up trenches on his flanks, in order to secure himself from the numerous bodies of the French, who might assail him from that quarter; and he placed all his baggage behind him in a wood, which he also secured by an intrenchment [f].

THE skill and order of this disposition, with the tranquillity in which it was made, served extremely to compose the minds of the soldiers; and the king, that he might farther inspirit them, rode through the ranks with such an air of cheerfulness and alacrity, as conveyed the highest confidence into every beholder. He pointed out to them the necessity to which they were reduced, and the certain and inevitable destruction which awaited them, if, in their present situation, enclosed on all hands in an enemy's country, they trusted to any thing but their own valour, or gave that enemy an opportunity of taking revenge for the many insults and indignities which they had of late put upon him. He reminded them of the visible ascendant, which they had hitherto maintained, over all the bodies of French troops that had fallen in their way; and assured them, that the superior numbers of the army, which at present hovered over them, gave them not greater force, but was an advantage easily compensated by the order in which he had placed his own army, and the resolution which he expected from them. He demanded nothing, he said, but that they would imitate his own example, and that of the prince of Wales; and as the honour, the lives, the liberties of all, were

[f] Froissard, liv. i. chap. 158.

now

now exposed to the same danger, he was confident, that they would make one common effort to extricate themselves from the present difficulties, and that their united courage would give them the victory over all their enemies.

It is related by some historians * that Edward, besides the resources which he found in his own genius and presence of mind, employed also a new invention against the enemy, and placed in his front some pieces of artillery, the first that had yet been made use of on any remarkable occasion in Europe. This is the epoch of one of the most singular discoveries that has been made among men; a discovery which changed, by degrees, the whole art of war, and by consequence many circumstances in the political government of Europe. But the ignorance of that age, in the mechanical arts, rendered the progress of this new invention very slow. The artillery, first framed, were so clumsy and of such difficult management, that men were not immediately sensible of their use and efficacy: And even to the present times, improvements have been continually making on this furious engine, which, though it seemed contrived for the destruction of mankind, and the overthrow of empires, has in the issue rendered battles less bloody, and has given greater stability to civil societies. Nations, by its means, have been brought more to a level: Conquests have become less frequent and rapid: Success in war has been reduced nearly to be a matter of calculation: And any nation, overmatched by its enemies, either yields to their demands, or secures itself by alliances against their violence and invasion.

The invention of artillery was at this time known in France as well as in England *; but Philip, in his hurry

* Jean Villani, lib. xii. cap. 66.   * Du Cange Gloss. in verb.

EDWARD III.

to overtake the enemy, had probably left his cannon behind him, which he regarded as a useless incumbrance. All his other movements discovered the same imprudence and precipitation. Impelled by anger, a dangerous counsellor, and trusting to the great superiority of his numbers, he thought that all depended on forcing an engagement with the English; and that, if he could once reach the enemy in their retreat, the victory on his side was certain and inevitable. He made a hasty march, in some confusion, from Abbeville; but after he had advanced above two leagues, some gentlemen, whom he had sent before to take a view of the enemy, returned to him, and brought him intelligence, that they had seen the English drawn up in great order, and awaiting his arrival. They therefore advised him to defer the combat till the ensuing day, when his army would have recovered from their fatigue, and might be disposed into better order than their present hurry had permitted them to observe. Philip assented to this counsel; but the former precipitation of his march, and the impatience of the French nobility, made it impracticable for him to put it in execution. One division pressed upon another: Orders to stop were not seasonably conveyed to all of them: This immense body was not governed by sufficient discipline to be manageable: And the French army, imperfectly formed into three lines, arrived, already fatigued and disordered, in presence of the enemy. The first line, consisting of 15,000 Genoese cross-bow men, was commanded by Anthony Doria and Charles Grimaldi: The second was led by the count of Alençon, brother to the king: The king himself was at the head of the third. Besides the French monarch, there were no less than three crowned heads in this engagement: The king of Bohemia, the king of the Romans, his son, and the king of Majorca; with all the nobility and great vassals of the crown of France. The army now consisted of above 120,000

120,000 men, more than three times the number of the enemy. But the prudence of one man was superior to the advantage of all this force and splendor.

The English, on the approach of the enemy, kept their ranks firm and immoveable; and the Genoese first began the attack. There had happened, a little before the engagement, a thunder-shower, which had moistened and relaxed the strings of the Genoese cross-bows; their arrows, for this reason, fell short of the enemy. The English archers, taking their bows out of their cases, poured in a shower of arrows upon this multitude who were opposed to them, and soon threw them into disorder. The Genoese fell back upon the heavy-armed cavalry of the count of Alençon[x]; who, enraged at their cowardice, ordered his troops to put them to the sword. The artillery fired amidst the crowd; the English archers continued to send in their arrows among them; and nothing was to be seen in that vast body but hurry and confusion, terror and dismay. The young prince of Wales had the presence of mind to take advantage of this situation, and to lead on his line to the charge. The French cavalry, however, recovering somewhat their order, and encouraged by the example of their leader, made a stout resistance; and having at last cleared themselves of the Genoese runaways, advanced upon their enemies, and, by their superior numbers, began to hem them round. The earls of Arundel and Northampton now advanced their line to sustain the prince, who, ardent in his first feats of arms, set an example of valour which was imitated by all his followers. The battle became, for some time, hot and dangerous; and the earl of Warwic, apprehensive of the event from the superior numbers of the French, dispatched a messenger to the king, and entreated him to send succours to the relief of the prince. Edward had chosen his station on the top of the hill; and he surveyed in tranquillity

[x] Froissard, liv. I. chap. 130.

quillity the scene of action. When the messenger accosted him, his first question was, whether the prince were slain or wounded? On receiving an answer in the negative, *Return*, said he, *to my son, and tell him that I reserve the honour of the day to him: I am confident that he will shew himself worthy of the honour of knighthood which I so lately conferred upon him: He will be able, without my assistance, to repel the enemy*[r]. This speech being reported to the prince and his attendants, inspired them with fresh courage: They made an attack with redoubled vigour on the French, In which the count of Alençon was slain: That whole line of cavalry was thrown into disorder: The riders were killed, or dismounted: The Welsh infantry rushed into the throng, and with their long knives cut the throats of all who had fallen; nor was any quarter given that day by the victors[s].

THE king of France advanced in vain with the rear to sustain the line commanded by his brother: He found them already discomfited; and the example of their rout encreased the confusion which was before but too prevalent in his own body. He had himself a horse killed under him: He was remounted; and, though left almost alone, he seemed still determined to maintain the combat; when John of Hainault seized the reins of his bridle, turned about his horse, and carried him off the field of battle. The whole French army took to flight, and was followed and put to the sword, without mercy, by the enemy; till the darkness of the night put an end to the pursuit. The king, on his return to the camp, flew into the arms of the prince of Wales, and exclaimed, *My brave son! Persevere in your honourable cause: You are my son; for valiantly have you acquitted yourself to-day: You have shewn yourself worthy of empire*[t].

[r] Froissart, liv. l. chap. 130. [s] Ibid. [t] Ibid. chap. 131.

THIS

This battle, which is known by the name of the battle of Crecy, began after three o'clock in the afternoon, and continued till evening. The next morning was foggy; and as the English observed that many of the enemy had lost their way in the night and in the mist, they employed a stratagem to bring them into their power: They erected on the eminences some French standards which they had taken in the battle; and all who were allured by this false signal were put to the sword, and no quarter given them. In excuse for this inhumanity, it was alleged that the French king had given like orders to his troops; but the real reason probably was, that the English, in their present situation, did not chuse to be encumbered with prisoners. On the day of battle, and on the ensuing, there fell, by a moderate computation, 1200 French knights, 1400 gentlemen, 4000 men at arms, besides about 30,000 of inferior rank [b]: Many of the principal nobility of France, the dukes of Lorraine and Bourbon, the earls of Flanders, Blois, Vaudemont, Aumale, were left on the field of battle. The kings also of Bohemia and Majorca were slain: The fate of the former was remarkable: He was blind from age; but being resolved to hazard his person, and set an example to others, he ordered the reins of his bridle to be tied on each side to the horses of two gentlemen of his train; and his dead body, and those of his attendants, were afterwards found among the slain, with their horses standing by them in that situation [c]. His crest was three ostrich feathers; and his motto these German words, *Ich dien*, *I serve:* Which the prince of Wales and his successors adopted in memorial of this great victory. The action may seem no less remarkable for the small loss sustained by the English, than for the great slaughter of the French: There were killed in it only

[b] Froissard, liv. I. chap. 131. Knyghton, p. 2588.   [c] Froissard, liv. I. chap. 130. Walsingham, p. 166.

one

one esquire and three knights[d], and very few of inferior rank; a demonstration, that the prudent disposition planned by Edward, and the disorderly attack made by the French, had rendered the whole rather a rout than a battle; which was indeed the common case with engagements in those times.

THE great prudence of Edward appeared not only in obtaining this memorable victory, but in the measures which he pursued after it. Not elated by his present prosperity, so far as to expect the total conquest of France, or even that of any considerable provinces; he purposed only to secure such an easy entrance into that kingdom, as might afterwards open the way to more moderate advantages. He knew the extreme distance of Guienne: He had experienced the difficulty and uncertainty of penetrating on the side of the Low Countries, and had already lost much of his authority over Flanders by the death of d'Arteville, who had been murdered by the populace themselves, his former partizans, on his attempting to transfer the sovereignty of that province to the prince of Wales[e]. The king, therefore, limited his ambition to the conquest of Calais; and after the interval of a few days, which he employed in interring the slain, he marched with his victorious army, and presented himself before the place.

JOHN of Vienne, a valiant knight of Burgundy, was governor of Calais, and being supplied with every thing necessary for defence, he encouraged the townsmen to perform to the utmost their duty to their king and country. Edward, therefore, sensible from the beginning that it was in vain to attempt the place by force, purposed only to reduce it by famine: He chose a secure station for his camp; drew entrenchments around the whole city; raised huts for his soldiers, which he covered with straw or broom; and provided his army with all the

[d] Knyghton, p. 2588. [e] Froissard, liv. i. chap. 136.

conve-

conveniences, necessary to make them endure the winter season, which was approaching. As the governor soon perceived his intention, he expelled all the useless mouths; and the king had the generosity to allow these unhappy people to pass through his camp, and he even supplied them with money for their journey[f].

WHILE Edward was engaged in this siege, which employed him near a twelvemonth, there passed in different places many other events; and all to the honour of the English arms.

THE retreat of the duke of Normandy from Guienne left the earl of Derby master of the field; and he was not negligent in making his advantage of the superiority. He took Mirebeau by assault: He made himself master of Lusignan in the same manner: Taillebourg and St. Jean d'Angeli fell into his hands; Poictiers opened its gates to him; and Derby having thus broken into the frontiers on that quarter, carried his incursions to the banks of the Loire, and filled all the southern provinces of France with horror and devastation[g].

THE flames of war were at the same time kindled in Britanny. Charles of Blois invaded that province with a considerable army, and invested the fortress of Roche de Rien; but the countess of Mountfort, reinforced by some English troops under Sir Thomas Dagworth, attacked him during the night in his entrenchments, dispersed his army, and took Charles himself prisoner[h]. His wife, by whom he enjoyed his pretensions to Britanny, compelled by the present necessity, took on her the government of the party, and proved herself a rival in every shape, and an antagonist to the countess of Mountfort, both in the field and in the cabinet. And while these heroic dames presented this extraordinary scene to the world, another

[f] Froissart, liv. I. chap. 133.   [g] Ibid. chap. 136.   [h] Ibid. chap. 145. Walsingham, p. 168. Ypod. Neust. p. 517, 518.

princess

princess in England, of still higher rank, showed herself no less capable of exerting every manly virtue.

The Scottish nation, after long defending, with incredible perseverance, their liberties against the superior force of the English, recalled their king, David Bruce, in 1342. Though that prince, neither by his age nor capacity, could bring them great assistance, he gave them the countenance of sovereign authority; and as Edward's wars on the continent proved a great diversion to the force of England, they rendered the balance more equal between the kingdoms. In every truce which Edward concluded with Philip, the king of Scotland was comprehended; and when Edward made his last invasion upon France, David was strongly solicited by his ally to begin also hostilities, and to invade the northern counties of England. The nobility of his nation being always forward in such incursions, David soon mustered a great army, entered Northumberland at the head of above 50,000 men, and carried his ravages and devastations to the gates of Durham[j]. But queen Philippa, assembling a body of little more than 12,000 men[k], which she entrusted to the command of Lord Piercy, ventured to approach him at Neville's Cross near that city; and riding through the ranks of her army, exhorted every man to do his duty, and to take revenge on these barbarous ravagers[l]. Nor could she be persuaded to leave the field, till the armies were on the point of engaging. The Scots have often been unfortunate in the great pitched battles which they fought with the English; even though they commonly declined such engagements where the superiority of numbers was not on their side: But never did they receive a more fatal blow than the present. They were broken and chaced off the field: Fifteen thousand of them, some

CHAP.
XV.

1346.
War with
Scotland.

17th Oct.

[j] Froissard, liv. l. chap. 137.   [k] Ibid. chap. 138.
[l] Ibid. chap. 138.

CHAP. XV.

1346.
Captivity of the king of Scots.

hiftorians fay twenty thoufand, were flain; among whom were Edward Keith, earl Marefchal, and Sir Thomas Charteris, chancellor: And the king himfelf was taken prifoner, with the earls of Southerland, Fife, Monteith, Carric, lord Douglas, and many other noblemen [n].

PHILIPPA, having fecured her royal prifoner in the Tower [o], croffed the fea at Dover; and was received in the Englifh camp before Calais with all the triumph due to her rank, her merit, and her fuccefs. This age was the reign of chivalry and gallantry: Edward's court excelled in thefe accomplifhments as much as in policy and arms: And if any thing could juftify the obfequious devotion then profeffed to the fair fex, it muft be the appearance of fuch extraordinary women as fhone forth during that period.

1347.
Calais taken.

THE town of Calais had been defended with remarkable vigilance, conftancy, and bravery by the townfmen, during a fiege of unufual length: But Philip, informed of their diftreffed condition, determined at laft to attempt their relief; and he approached the Englifh with an immenfe army, which the writers of that age make amount to 200,000 men. But he found Edward fo furrounded with moraffes, and fecured by entrenchments, that, without running on inevitable deftruction, he concluded it impoffible to make an attempt on the Englifh camp. He had no other refource than to fend his rival a vain challenge to meet him in the open field; which being refufed, he was obliged to decamp with his army, and difperfe them into their feveral provinces [p].

JOHN of Vienne, governor of Calais, now faw the neceffity of furrendering his fortrefs, which was reduced

[n] Froiffard, liv. L. chap. 139. | [o] Rymer, vol. v. p. 537.
[p] Froiffard, liv. L. chap. 144, 145. Avefbury, p. 161, 162.

to the laſt extremity, by famine and the fatigue of the inhabitants. He appeared on the walls, and made a ſignal to the Engliſh centinels that he deſired a parley. Sir Walter Manny was ſent to him by Edward. "Brave "knight," cried the governor, "I have been entruſted "by my ſovereign with the command of this town: It "is almoſt a year ſince you beſieged me; and I have "endeavoured, as well as thoſe under me, to do our "duty. But you are acquainted with our preſent con- "dition: We have no hopes of relief; we are periſhing "with hunger; I am willing therefore to ſurrender, and "deſire, as the ſole condition, to enſure the lives and "liberties of theſe brave men, who have ſo long ſhared "with me every danger and fatigue?."

MANNY replied, that he was well acquainted with the intentions of the king of England; that that prince was incenſed againſt the townſmen of Calais for their pertinacious reſiſtance, and for the evils which they had made him and his ſubjects ſuffer; that he was determined to take exemplary vengeance on them; and would not receive the town on any condition which ſhould confine him in the puniſhment of theſe offenders. "Conſider," replied Vienne, "that this is not the treatment to which "brave men are intitled: If any Engliſh knight had "been in my ſituation, your king would have expected the "ſame conduct from him. The inhabitants of Calais "have done for their ſovereign what merits the eſteem "of every prince; much more of ſo gallant a prince as "Edward. But I inform you, that, if we muſt periſh, "we ſhall not periſh unrevenged; and that we are not "yet ſo reduced, but we can ſell our lives at a high price "to the victors. It is the intereſt of both ſides to pre- "vent theſe deſperate extremities; and I expect that

? Froiſſard, liv. l. chap. 146.

"you

"you yourself, brave knight, will interpose your good offices with your prince in our behalf."

Manny was struck with the justness of these sentiments, and represented to the king the danger of reprisals, if he should give such treatment to the inhabitants of Calais. Edward was at last persuaded to mitigate the rigour of the conditions demanded: He only insisted that six of the most considerable citizens should be sent to him, to be disposed of as he thought proper; that they should come to his camp carrying the keys of the city in their hands, bareheaded and barefooted, with ropes about their necks: And, on these conditions, he promised to spare the lives of all the remainder[r].

When this intelligence was conveyed to Calais, it struck the inhabitants with new consternation. To sacrifice six of their fellow-citizens to certain destruction for signalizing their valour in a common cause, appeared to them even more severe than that general punishment with which they were before threatened; and they found themselves incapable of coming to any resolution in so cruel and distressful a situation. At last one of the principal inhabitants, called Eustace de St. Pierre, whose name deserves to be recorded, stepped forth, and declared himself willing to encounter death for the safety of his friends and companions: Another, animated by his example, made a like generous offer: A third and a fourth presented themselves to the same fate; and the whole number was soon completed. These six heroic burgesses appeared before Edward in the guise of malefactors, laid at his feet the keys of their city, and were ordered to be led to execution. It is surprising that so generous a prince should ever have entertained such a barbarous purpose against such men; and still more that he should seriously persist

[r] Froissard, liv. i. chap. 146.

in the refolution of executing it [*]. But the entreaties of his queen faved his memory from that infamy: She threw herfelf on her knees before him, and, with tears in her eyes, begged the lives of thefe citizens. Having obtained her requeſt, ſhe carried them into her tent, ordered a repaſt to be ſet before them, and, after making them a prefent of money and clothes, difmiffed them in fafety [†].

CHAP.
XV.

1347.

THE king took poffeffion of Calais; and immediately executed an act of rigor, more juſtifiable, becaufe more neceffary, than that which he had before refolved on. He knew that, notwithſtanding his pretended title to the crown of France, every Frenchman regarded him as a mortal enemy: He therefore ordered all the inhabitants of Calais to evacuate the town, and be peopled it anew with Engliſh; a policy which probably preferved fo long to his fucceffors the dominion of that important fortrefs. He made it the ſtaple of wool, leather, tin, and lead; the four chief, if not the fole commodities of the kingdom, for which there was any confiderable demand in foreign markets. All the Engliſh were obliged to bring thither thefe goods: Foreign merchants came to the fame place in order to purchafe them: And at a period when pofts were not eſtabliſhed, and when the communication between ſtates was fo imperfect, this inſtitution, though it hurt the navigation of England, was probably of advantage to the kingdom.

4th Auguſt.

THROUGH the mediation of the pope's legates, Edward concluded a truce with France; but, even during this ceffation of arms, he had very nearly loſt Calais, the fole fruit of all his boaſted victories. The king had entruſted that place to Aimery de Pavie, an Italian, who had difcovered bravery and conduct in the wars,

1348.

[*] See note [H] at the end of the volume.
[†] Froiffard, liv. L chap. 146.

but

but was utterly destitute of every principle of honour and fidelity. This man agreed to deliver up Calais for the sum of 20,000 crowns; and Geoffrey de Charni, who commanded the French forces in those quarters, and who knew that, if he succeeded in this service, he should not be disavowed, ventured, without consulting his master, to conclude the bargain with him. Edward, informed of this treachery by means of Aimery's secretary, summoned the governor to London on other pretences; and having charged him with the guilt, promised him his life, but on condition that he would turn the contrivance to the destruction of the enemy. The Italian easily agreed to this double treachery. A day was appointed for the admission of the French; and Edward, having prepared a force of about a thousand men, under Sir Walter Manny, secretly departed from London, carrying with him the prince of Wales; and, without being suspected, arrived the evening before at Calais. He made a proper disposition for the reception of the enemy, and kept all his forces and the garrison under arms. On the appearance of Charni, a chosen band of French soldiers was admitted at the postern; and Aimery, receiving the stipulated sum, promised that, with their assistance, he would immediately open the great gate to the troops, who were waiting with impatience for the fulfilling of his engagement. All the French who entered were immediately slain, or taken prisoners: The great gate opened: Edward rushed forth with cries of battle and of victory: The French, though astonished at the event, behaved with valour: A fierce and bloody engagement ensued. As the morning broke, the king, who was not distinguished by his arms, and who fought as a private man under the standard of Sir Walter Manny, remarked a French gentleman, called Eustace de Ribaumont, who exerted himself with singular vigour and bravery; and he was seized with a desire of trying a single combat with him. He stepped forth from his troop, and challenging

challenging Ribaumont by name (for he was known to him), began a sharp and dangerous encounter. He was twice beaten to the ground by the valour of the Frenchman: He twice recovered himself: Blows were redoubled with equal force on both sides: The victory was long undecided; till Ribaumont, perceiving himself to be left almost alone, called out to his antagonist, *Sir knight, I yield myself your prisoner*; and at the same time delivered his sword to the king. Most of the French, being overpowered by numbers, and intercepted in their retreat, lost either their lives or their liberty[*].

THE French officers who had fallen into the hands of the English were conducted into Calais; where Edward discovered to them the antagonist with whom they had the honour to be engaged, and treated them with great regard and courtesy. They were admitted to sup with the prince of Wales and the English nobility; and, after supper, the king himself came into the apartment, and went about, conversing familiarly with one or other of his prisoners. He even addressed himself to Charni, and avoided reproaching him, in too severe terms, with the treacherous attempt which he had made upon Calais during the truce: But he openly bestowed the highest encomiums on Ribaumont; called him the most valorous knight that he had ever been acquainted with; and confessed that he himself had at no time been in so great danger as when engaged in combat with him. He then took a string of pearls, which he wore about his own head, and throwing it over the head of Ribaumont, he said to him, "Sir Eustace, I bestow this present upon "you as a testimony of my esteem for your bravery: "And I desire you to wear it a year for my sake: I "know you to be gay and amorous, and to take delight "in the company of ladies and damsels: Let them all

[*] Froissart, liv. 1. chap. 140, 141, 142.

"know

"know from what hand you had the present: You are no longer a prisoner; I acquit you of your ransom; and you are at liberty to-morrow to dispose of yourself as you think proper."

Nothing proves more evidently the vast superiority assumed by the nobility and gentry above all the other orders of men during those ages, than the extreme difference which Edward made in his treatment of these French knights, and that of the six citizens of Calais, who had exerted more signal bravery in a cause more justifiable, and more honourable.

CHAP. XVI.

EDWARD III.

Inſtitution of the garter——State of France——Battle of Poictiers——Captivity of the king of France——State of that kingdom——Invaſion of France——Peace of Bretigni——State of France——Expedition into Caſtile——Rupture with France——Ill ſucceſs of the Engliſh——Death of the prince of Wales——Death——and character of the king——Miſcellaneous tranſactions in this reign.

THE prudent conduct and great ſucceſs of Edward in his foreign wars had excited a ſtrong emulation and a military genius among the Engliſh nobility; and theſe turbulent barons, overawed by the crown, gave now a more uſeful direction to their ambition, and attached themſelves to a prince who led them to the acquiſition of riches and of glory. That he might farther promote the ſpirit of emulation and obedience, the king inſtituted the order of the Garter, in imitation of ſome orders of a like nature, religious as well as military, which had been eſtabliſhed in different parts of Europe. The number received into this order conſiſted of twenty-five perſons, beſides the ſovereign; and as it has never been enlarged, this badge of diſtinction continues as honourable as at its firſt inſtitution, and is ſtill a valuable, though a cheap preſent, which the prince can confer on his greateſt ſubjects. A vulgar ſtory prevails, but is not ſupported by any ancient authority, that, at a court-ball,

CHAP. XVI.
1349.

Inſtitution of the Garter.

ball, Edward's miſtreſs, commonly ſuppoſed to be the counteſs of Saliſbury, dropped her garter; and the king, taking it up, obſerved ſome of the courtiers to ſmile, as if they thought that he had not obtained this favour merely by accident: Upon which he called out, *Honi ſoit qui mal y penſe*, Evil to him that evil thinks; and as every incident of gallantry among thoſe ancient warriors was magnified into a matter of great importance *, he inſtituted the order of the Garter in memorial of this event, and gave theſe words as the motto of the order. This origin, though frivolous, is not unſuitable to the manners of the times; and it is indeed difficult by any other means to account, either for the ſeemingly unmeaning terms of the motto, or for the peculiar badge of the garter, which ſeems to have no reference to any purpoſe either of military uſe or ornament.

But a ſudden damp was thrown over this feſtivity and triumph of the court of England, by a deſtructive peſtilence which invaded that kingdom, as well as the reſt of Europe; and is computed to have ſwept away near a third of the inhabitants in every country which it attacked. It was probably more fatal in great cities than in the country; and above fifty thouſand ſouls are ſaid to have periſhed by it in London alone[1]. This malady firſt diſcovered itſelf in the north of Aſia, was ſpread over all that country, made its progreſs from one end of Europe to the other, and ſenſibly depopulated every ſtate through which it paſſed. So grievous a calamity, more than the pacific diſpoſition of the princes, ſerved to maintain and prolong the truce between France and England.

* See note [1] at the end of the volume.
[1] Stowe's Survey, p. 478. There were buried 50,000 bodies in one church-yard, which Sir Walter Manny had bought for the uſe of the poor. The ſame author ſays, that there died above 50,000 perſons of the plague in Norwich, which is quite incredible.

DURING

EDWARD III.

DURING this truce, Philip de Valois died, without being able to re-establish the affairs of France, which his bad success against England had thrown into extreme disorder. This monarch, during the first years of his reign, had obtained the appellation of *Fortunate*, and acquired the character of prudent; but he ill maintained either the one or the other; less from his own fault, than because he was overmatched by the superior fortune and superior genius of Edward. But the incidents in the reign of his son John, gave the French nation cause to regret even the calamitous times of his predecessor. John was distinguished by many virtues, particularly a scrupulous honour and fidelity: He was not deficient in personal courage: But as he wanted that masterly prudence and foresight, which his difficult situation required, his kingdom was at the same time disturbed by intestine commotions, and oppressed with foreign wars. The chief source of its calamities was Charles king of Navarre, who received the epithet of the *bad* or *wicked*, and whose conduct fully entitled him to that appellation. This prince was descended from males of the blood royal of France; his mother was daughter of Lewis Hutin; he had himself espoused a daughter of king John: But all these ties, which ought to have connected him with the throne, gave him only greater power to shake and overthrow it. With regard to his personal qualities, he was courteous, affable, engaging, eloquent; full of insinuation and address; inexhaustible in his resources; active and enterprising. But these splendid accomplishments were attended with such defects, as rendered them pernicious to his country, and even ruinous to himself: He was volatile, inconstant, faithless, revengeful, malicious: Restrained by no principle or duty: Insatiable in his pretensions: And whether successful or unfortunate in one enterprize, he immediately undertook another, in which he was never deterred

CHAP. XVI.

1350.

1354. State of France.

deterred from employing the moſt criminal and moſt diſhonourable expedients.

1354. The conſtable of Eu, who had been taken priſoner by Edward at Caën, recovered his liberty, on the promiſe of delivering as his ranſom the town of Guiſnes, near Calais, of which he was ſuperior lord: But as John was offended at this ſtipulation, which, if fulfilled, opened ſtill farther that frontier to the enemy; and, as he ſuſpected the conſtable of more dangerous connections with the king of England, he ordered him to be ſeized, and, without any legal or formal trial, put him to death in priſon. Charles de la Cerda was appointed conſtable in his place; and had a like fatal end: The king of Navarre ordered him to be aſſaſſinated; and ſuch was the weakneſs of the crown, that this prince, inſtead of dreading puniſhment, would not even agree to aſk pardon for his offence, but on condition that he ſhould receive an acceſſion of territory: And he had alſo John's ſecond ſon put into his hands as a ſecurity for his perſon, when he came to court, and performed this act of mock penitence and humiliation before his ſovereign [a].

1355. The two French princes ſeemed entirely reconciled; but this diſſimulation, to which John ſubmitted from neceſſity, and Charles from habit, did not long continue; and the king of Navarre knew, that he had reaſon to apprehend the moſt ſevere vengeance for the many crimes and treaſons which he had already committed, and the ſtill greater, which he was meditating. To enſure himſelf of protection, he entered into a ſecret correſpondence with England, by means of Henry earl of Derby, now earl of Lancaſter, who at that time was employed in fruitleſs negociations for peace at Avignon, under the mediation of the pope. John detected this correſpondence;

[a] Froiſſard, liv. i. chap. 144.

and to prevent the dangerous effects of it, he sent forces into Normandy, the chief seat of the king of Navarre's power, and attacked his castles and fortresses. But, hearing that Edward had prepared an army to support his ally, he had the weakness to propose an accommodation with Charles, and even to give this traitorous subject the sum of a hundred thousand crowns as the purchase of a feigned reconcilement, which rendered him still more dangerous. The king of Navarre, insolent from past impunity, and desperate from the dangers which he apprehended, continued his intrigues; and associating himself with Geoffrey d'Harcourt, who had received his pardon from Philip de Valois, but persevered still in his factious disposition, he encreased the number of his partizans in every part of the kingdom. He even seduced, by his address, Charles the king of France's eldest son, a youth of seventeen years of age, who was the first that bore the appellation of Dauphin, by the re-union of the province of Dauphiny to the crown. But this prince, being made sensible of the danger and folly of these connexions, promised to make atonement for the offence by the sacrifice of his associates; and, in concert with his father, he invited the king of Navarre, and other noblemen of the party, to a feast at Roüen, where they were betrayed into the hands of John. Some of the most obnoxious were immediately led to execution; the king of Navarre was thrown into prison [w]: But this stroke of severity in the king, and of treachery in the Dauphin, was far from proving decisive in maintaining the royal authority. Philip of Navarre, brother to Charles, and Geoffrey d'Harcourt, put all the towns and castles belonging to that prince in a posture of defence; and had immediate recourse to the protection of England in this desperate extremity.

[w] Froissard, liv. i. chap. 146. Avesbury, p. 243.

CHAP. XVI.
1355.

The truce between the two kingdoms, which had always been ill observed on both sides, was now expired; and Edward was entirely free to support the French malcontents. Well pleased that the factions in France had at length gained him some partizans in that kingdom, which his pretensions to the crown had never been able to accomplish, he purposed to attack his enemy both on the side of Guienne, under the command of the prince of Wales, and on that of Calais, in his own person.

Young Edward arrived in the Garronne with his army, on board a fleet of three hundred sail, attended by the earls of Warwic, Salisbury, Oxford, Suffolk, and other English noblemen. Being joined by the vassals of Gascony, he took the field; and, as the present disorders in France prevented every proper plan of defence, he carried on with impunity his ravages and devastations, according to the mode of war in that age. He reduced all the villages and several towns in Languedoc to ashes: He presented himself before Thoulouse; passed the Garronne, and burned the suburbs of Carcassonne; advanced even to Narbonne, laying every place waste around him: And after an incursion of six weeks, returned with a vast booty and many prisoners to Guienne, where he took up his winter-quarters [n]. The constable of Bourbon, who commanded in those provinces, received orders, though at the head of a superior army, on no account to run the hazard of a battle.

The king of England's incursion from Calais was of the same nature, and attended with the same issue. He broke into France at the head of a numerous army; to which he gave a full licence of plundering and ravaging the open country. He advanced to St. Omer, where the king of France was posted; and on the retreat of that

[n] Froissard, liv. I. chap. 144. 146.

prince, followed him to Hesdin [y]. John still kept at a distance, and declined an engagement: But, in order to save his reputation, he sent Edward a challenge to fight a pitched battle with him; a usual bravadoe in that age, derived from the practice of single combat, and ridiculous in the art of war. The king, finding no sincerity in this defiance, retired to Calais, and thence went over to England, in order to defend that kingdom against a threatened invasion of the Scots.

CHAP. XVI.

1355.

THE Scots, taking advantage of the king's absence, and that of the military power of England, had surprized Berwic; and had collected an army with a view of committing ravages upon the northern provinces: But, on the approach of Edward they abandoned that place, which was not tenable while the castle was in the hands of the English; and retiring to their mountains, gave the enemy full liberty of burning and destroying the whole country from Berwic to Edinburgh [z]. Baliol attended Edward on this expedition; but finding, that his constant adherence to the English had given his countrymen an unconquerable aversion to his title, and that he himself was declining through age and infirmities, he finally resigned into the king's hands his pretensions to the crown of Scotland [a], and received, in lieu of them, an annual pension of 2000 pounds, with which he passed the remainder of his life in privacy and retirement.

DURING these military operations, Edward received information of the encreasing disorders in France, arising from the imprisonment of the king of Navarre; and he sent Lancaster, at the head of a small army, to support the partizans of that prince in Normandy. The war was conducted with various success; but chiefly to the disadvantage of the French malcontents; till an important

[y] Froissard, liv. I. chap. 144. Avesbury, p. 106. Walsing. p. 171.
[z] Walsing. p. 171. [a] Rymer, vol. v. p. 823. Ypod. Neust. p. 511.

454 HISTORY OF ENGLAND.

CHAP. XVI. event happened in the other quarter of the kingdom, which had well nigh proved fatal to the monarchy of France, and threw every thing into the utmost confusion.

1356. THE prince of Wales, encouraged by the success of the preceding campaign, took the field with an army, which no historian makes amount to above 12,000 men, and of which not a third were English; and, with this small body, he ventured to penetrate into the heart of France. After ravaging the Agenois, Quercy, and the Limousin, he entered the province of Berry; and made some attacks, though without success, on the towns of Bourges and Issoudun. It appeared, that his intentions were to march into Normandy, and to join his forces with those of the earl of Lancaster and the partizans of the king of Navarre; but finding all the bridges on the Loire broken down, and every pass carefully guarded, he was obliged to think of making his retreat into Guienne [b]. He found this resolution the more necessary, from the intelligence which he received of the king of France's motions. That monarch, provoked at the insult offered him by this incursion, and entertaining hopes of success from the young prince's temerity, collected a great army of above 60,000 men, and advanced, by hasty marches, to intercept his enemy. The prince, not aware of John's near approach, lost some days on his retreat before the castle of Remorantin [c]; and thereby gave the French an opportunity of overtaking him. They came within sight at Maupertuis near Poictiers; and Edward, sensible that his retreat was now become impracticable, prepared for battle with all the courage of a young hero, and with all the prudence of the oldest and most experienced commander.

Battle of Poictiers.

BUT the utmost prudence and courage would have proved insufficient to save him in this extremity, had the

[b] Walsing. p. 171. [c] Froissard, liv. l. chap. 158. Walsing. p. 171.

king

EDWARD III.

king of France known how to make use of his present
advantages. His great superiority in numbers enabled
him to surround the enemy; and, by intercepting all provisions, which were already become scarce in the English
camp, to reduce this small army, without a blow, to the
necessity of surrendering at discretion. But such was the
impatient ardour of the French nobility, and so much had
their thoughts been bent on overtaking the English as
their sole object, that this idea never struck any of the
commanders; and they immediately took measures for the
assault, as for a certain victory. While the French army
was drawn up in order of battle, they were stopped by the
appearance of the cardinal of Perigord; who, having
learned the approach of the two armies to each other,
had hastened, by interposing his good offices, to prevent
any farther effusion of Christian blood. By John's permission, he carried proposals to the prince of Wales;
and found him so sensible of the bad posture of his affairs,
that an accommodation seemed not impracticable. Edward told him, that he would agree to any terms consistent with his own honour and that of England; and he
offered to purchase a retreat, by ceding all the conquests which he had made during this and the former
campaign, and by stipulating not to serve against France
during the course of seven years. But John, imagining
that he had now got into his hands a sufficient pledge for
the restitution of Calais, required that Edward should
surrender himself prisoner with a hundred of his attendants; and offered, on these terms, a safe retreat to the
English army. The prince rejected the proposal with
disdain; and declared, that whatever fortune might attend him, England should never be obliged to pay the
price of his ransom. This resolute answer cut off all
hopes of accommodation; but, as the day was already
spent

CHAP.
XVI.

1356.

19th Sept.

spent in negociating, the battle was delayed till the next morning [a].

The cardinal of Perigord, as did all the prelates of the court of Rome, bore a great attachment to the French interest; but the most determined enemy could not, by any expedient, have done a greater prejudice to John's affairs, than he did them by this delay. The prince of Wales had leisure, during the night, to strengthen, by new intrenchments, the post which he had before so judiciously chosen; and he contrived an ambush of 300 men at arms, and as many archers, whom he put under the command of the Captal de Buche, and ordered to make a circuit, that they might fall on the flank or rear of the French army during the engagement. The van of his army was commanded by the earl of Warwic, the rear by the earls of Salisbury and Suffolk, the main body by the prince himself. The lords Chandos, Audeley, and many other brave and experienced commanders, were at the head of different corps of his army.

John also arranged his forces in three divisions, nearly equal: The first was commanded by the duke of Orleans, the king's brother; the second by the Dauphin, attended by his two younger brothers; the third by the king himself, who had by his side Philip, his fourth son and favourite, then about fourteen years of age. There was no reaching the English army but through a narrow lane, covered on each side by hedges; and in order to open this passage, the marefchals Audrehen and Clermont were ordered to advance with a separate detachment of men at arms. While they marched along the lane, a body of English archers, who lined the hedges, plyed them on each side with their arrows; and being very near them, yet placed in perfect safety, they coolly took their aim against the enemy, and slaughtered them with impunity.

[a] Froissard, liv. i, chap. 161.

The

The French detachment, much discouraged by the unequal combat, and diminished in their number, arrived at the end of the lane, where they met on the open ground the prince of Wales himself, at the head of a chosen body, ready for their reception. They were discomfited and overthrown: One of the marefchals was slain; the other taken prisoner: And the remainder of the detachment, who were still in the lane, and exposed to the shot of the enemy, without being able to make resistance, recoiled upon their own army, and put every thing into disorder[*]. In that critical moment, the Captal de Buche unexpectedly appeared, and attacked in flank the Dauphin's line, which fell into some confusion. Landas, Bodenai, and St. Venant, to whom the care of that young prince and his brothers had been committed, too anxious for their charge or for their own safety, carried them off the field, and set the example of flight, which was followed by that whole division. The duke of Orleans, seized with a like panic, and imagining all was lost, thought no longer of fighting, but carried off his division by a retreat, which soon turned into a flight. Lord Chandos called out to the prince, that the day was won; and encouraged him to attack the division, under king John, which, though more numerous than the whole English army, were somewhat dismayed with the precipitate flight of their companions. John here made the utmost efforts to retrieve by his valour, what his imprudence had betrayed; and the only resistance made that day was by his line of battle. The prince of Wales fell with impetuosity on some German cavalry placed in the front, and commanded by the counts of Sallebruche, Nydo, and Nosto: A fierce battle ensued: One side were encouraged by the near prospect of so great a victory: The other were stimulated by the shame of quitting the field to an

[*] Froissard, liv. I, chap. 162.

enemy

CHAP. XVI.

13, 6.

enemy so much inferior: But the three German generals, together with the duke of Athens, constable of France, falling in battle, that body of cavalry gave way, and left the king himself exposed to the whole fury of the enemy. The ranks were every moment thinned around him: The nobles fell by his side, one after another: His son, scarce fourteen years of age, received a wound, while he was fighting valiantly in defence of his father: The king himself, spent with fatigue, and overwhelmed by numbers, might easily have been slain; but every English gentleman, ambitious of taking alive the royal prisoner, spared him in the action, exhorted him to surrender, and offered him quarter: Several who attempted to seize him, suffered for their temerity. He still cried out, *Where is my cousin, the prince of Wales?* and seemed unwilling to become prisoner to any person of inferior rank.

Captivity of the king of France.

But being told, that the prince was at a distance on the field, he threw down his gauntlet, and yielded himself to Dennis de Morbec, a knight of Arras, who had been obliged to fly his country for murder. His son was taken with him [f].

The prince of Wales, who had been carried away in pursuit of the flying enemy, finding the field entirely clear, had ordered a tent to be pitched, and was reposing himself after the toils of battle; enquiring still with great anxiety concerning the fate of the French monarch. He dispatched the earl of Warwic to bring him intelligence; and that nobleman came happily in time to save the life of the captive prince, which was exposed to greater danger than it had been during the heat of the action. The English had taken him by violence from Morbec: The Gascons claimed the honour of detaining the royal prisoner: And some brutal soldiers, rather than yield the prize to their rivals, had threatened to put him to death [g].

[f] Rymer, vol. vi. p. 72. 154. Froissard, liv. l. chap. 164.
[g] Froissard, liv. i. chap. 164.

Warwic

Warwic overawed both parties, and approaching the king with great demonstrations of respect, offered to conduct him to the prince's tent.

HERE commences the real and truly admirable heroism of Edward: For victories are vulgar things in comparison of that moderation and humanity displayed by a young prince of twenty-seven years of age, not yet cooled from the fury of battle, and elated by as extraordinary and as unexpected success as had ever crowned the arms of any commander. He came forth to meet the captive king with all the marks of regard and sympathy; administered comfort to him amidst his misfortunes; paid him the tribute of praise due to his valour; and ascribed his own victory merely to the blind chance of war, or to a superior providence, which controuls all the efforts of human force and prudence [b]. The behaviour of John showed him not unworthy of this courteous treatment: His present abject fortune never made him forget a moment that he was a king: More touched by Edward's generosity than by his own calamities, he confessed, that, notwithstanding his defeat and captivity, his honour was still unimpaired; and that, if he yielded the victory, it was at least gained by a prince of such consummate valour and humanity.

EDWARD ordered a repast to be prepared in his tent for the prisoner; and he himself served at the royal captive's table, as if he had been one of his retinue: He stood at the king's back during the meal; constantly refused to take a place at table; and declared, that, being a subject, he was too well acquainted with the distance between his own rank, and that of royal majesty, to assume such freedom. All his father's pretensions to the crown of France were now buried in oblivion: John, in captivity, received the honours of a king, which were refused him when seated on the throne: His misfortunes, not his title, were respected; and the French prisoners,

[b] Pool. Croull. p. 197.

conquered by this elevation of mind, more than by their late discomfiture, burst into tears of admiration; which were only checked by the reflection, that such genuine and unaltered heroism in an enemy must certainly in the issue prove but the more dangerous to their native country [1].

All the English and Gascon knights imitated the generous example set them by their prince. The captives were every where treated with humanity, and were soon after dismissed, on paying moderate ransoms to the persons into whose hands they had fallen. The extent of their fortunes was considered; and an attention was given, that they should still have sufficient means left to perform their military service in a manner suitable to their rank and quality. Yet so numerous were the noble prisoners, that these ransoms, added to the spoils gained in the field, were sufficient to enrich the prince's army; and as they had suffered very little in the action, their joy and exultation was complete.

The prince of Wales conducted his prisoner to Bourdeaux; and not being provided with forces so numerous as might enable him to push his present advantages, he concluded a two years' truce with France [k], which was also become requisite, that he might conduct the captive king with safety into England. He landed at Southwark, and was met by a great concourse of people, of all ranks and stations. The prisoner was clad in royal apparel, and mounted on a white steed, distinguished by its size and beauty, and by the richness of its furniture. The conqueror rode by his side in a meaner attire, and carried by a black palfry. In this situation, more glorious than all the insolent parade of a Roman triumph, he passed through the streets of London, and presented the king of France to his father, who advanced to meet

[1] Froissard, liv. i, chap. 169.   [k] Rymer, vol. vi. p. 3.

him,

him, and received him with the same courtesy, as if he had been a neighbouring potentate, that had voluntarily come to pay him a friendly visit¹. It is impossible, in reflecting on this noble conduct, not to perceive the advantages which resulted from the otherwise whimsical principles of chivalry, and which gave men, in those rude times, some superiority even over people of a more cultivated age and nation.

CHAP.
XVI.

1357.

THE king of France, besides the generous treatment which he met with in England, had the melancholy consolation of the wretched, to see companions in affliction. The king of Scots had been eleven years a captive in Edward's hands; and the good fortune of this latter monarch had reduced at once the two neighbouring potentates, with whom he was engaged in war, to be prisoners in his capital. But Edward, finding that the conquest of Scotland was nowise advanced by the captivity of its sovereign, and that the government, conducted by Robert Stuart, his nephew and heir, was still able to defend itself, consented to restore David Bruce to his liberty, for the ransom of 100,000 marks sterling; and that prince delivered the sons of all his principal nobility as hostages for the payment ᵐ.

MEANWHILE, the captivity of John, joined to the preceding disorders of the French government, had produced in that country a dissolution, almost total, of civil authority, and had occasioned confusions, the most horrible and destructive that had ever been experienced in any age or in any nation. The dauphin, now about eighteen years of age, naturally assumed the royal power during his father's captivity; but though endowed with an excellent capacity, even in such early years, he possessed neither experience nor authority sufficient to defend a

1358.
State of France.

¹ Froissard, liv. i. chap. 177. ᵐ Rymer, vol. vi. p. 45, 46, 51. 56. Froissard, liv. i. chap. 174. Walsingham, p. 173.

state,

CHAP. XVI.

1355.

state, assailed at once by foreign power and shaken by intestine faction. In order to obtain supply, he assembled the states of the kingdom: That assembly, instead of supporting his administration, were themselves seized with the spirit of confusion; and laid hold of the present opportunity to demand limitations of the prince's power, the punishment of past malversations, and the liberty of the king of Navarre. Marcel, provost of the merchants, and first magistrate of Paris, put himself at the head of the unruly populace; and from the violence and temerity of his character, pushed them to commit the most criminal outrages against the royal authority. They detained the dauphin in a sort of captivity; they murdered in his presence Robert de Clermont and John de Conflans, mareschals, the one of Normandy, the other of Burgundy; they threatened all the other ministers with a like fate; and when Charles, who was obliged to temporize and dissemble, made his escape from their hands, they levied war against him, and openly erected the standard of rebellion. The other cities of the kingdom, in imitation of the capital, shook off the dauphin's authority; took the government into their own hands; and spread the disorder into every province. The nobles, whose inclinations led them to adhere to the crown, and were naturally disposed to check these tumults, had lost all their influence; and being reproached with cowardice on account of the base desertion of their sovereign in the battle of Poictiers, were treated with universal contempt by the inferior orders. The troops, who, from the deficiency of pay, were no longer retained in discipline, threw off all regard to their officers, sought the means of subsistence by plunder and robbery, and associating to them all the disorderly people, with whom that age abounded, formed numerous bands, which infested all parts of the kingdom. They desolated the open country; burned and plundered the villages; and by cutting off all means of communication or subsistence, fistence, reduced even the inhabitants of the walled towns to the most extreme necessity. The peasants, formerly oppressed, and now left unprotected by their masters, became desperate from their present misery; and rising every where in arms, carried to the last extremity those disorders, which were derived from the sedition of the citizens and disbanded soldiers [a]. The gentry, hated for their tyranny, were every where exposed to the violence of popular rage; and instead of meeting with the regard due to their past dignity, became only, on that account, the object of more wanton insult to the mutinous peasants. They were hunted like wild beasts, and put to the sword without mercy: Their castles were consumed with fire, and levelled to the ground: Their wives and daughters were first ravished, then murdered: The savages proceeded so far as to impale some gentlemen, and roast them alive before a slow fire: A body of nine thousand of them broke into Meaux, where the wife of the dauphin, with above 300 ladies, had taken shelter: The most brutal treatment and most atrocious cruelty were justly dreaded by this helpless company: But the Captal de Buche, though in the service of Edward, yet moved by generosity and by the gallantry of a true knight, flew to their rescue, and beat off the peasants with great slaughter. In other civil wars, the opposite factions, falling under the government of their several leaders, commonly preserve still the vestige of some rule and order: But here the wild state of nature seemed to be renewed: Every man was thrown loose and independent of his fellows: And the populousness of the country, derived from the preceding police of civil society, served only to encrease the horror and confusion of the scene.

AMIDST these disorders, the king of Navarre made his escape from prison, and presented a dangerous leader to

[a] Froissard, liv. 1. chap. 182, 183, 184.

the furious malcontents [*]. But the splendid talents of this prince qualified him only to do mischief, and to encrease the public distractions: He wanted the steadiness and prudence requisite for making his intrigues subservient to his ambition, and forming his numerous partizans into a regular faction. He revived his pretensions, somewhat obsolete, to the crown of France: But while he advanced this claim, he relied entirely on his alliance with the English, who were concerned in interest to disappoint his pretensions; and who, being public and inveterate enemies to the state, served only, by the friendship which they seemingly bore him, to render his cause the more odious. And in all his operations, he acted more like a leader of banditti, than one who aspired to be the head of a regular government, and who was engaged, by his station, to endeavour the re-establishment of order in the community.

The eyes, therefore, of all the French, who wished to restore peace to their miserable and desolated country, were turned towards the dauphin; and that young prince, though not remarkable for his military talents, possessed so much prudence and spirit, that he daily gained the ascendant over all his enemies. Marcel, the seditious provost of Paris, was slain, while he was attempting to deliver the city to the king of Navarre and the English; and the capital immediately returned to its duty [*]. The most considerable bodies of the mutinous peasants were dispersed, and put to the sword: Some bands of military robbers underwent the same fate: And though many grievous disorders still remained, France began gradually to assume the face of a regular civil government, and to form some plan for its defence and security.

During the confusion in the dauphin's affairs, Edward seemed to have a favourable opportunity for pushing

[*] Froissard, liv. i. chap. 181. [*] Ibid. chap. 187.

his

his conquests: But besides that his hands were tied by the truce, and he could only assist underhand the faction of Navarre; the state of the English finances and military power, during those ages, rendered the kingdom incapable of making any regular or steady effort, and obliged it to exert its force at very distant intervals, by which all the projected ends were commonly disappointed. Edward employed himself, during a conjuncture so inviting, chiefly in negociations with his prisoner; and John had the weakness to sign terms of peace, which, had they taken effect, must have totally ruined and dismembered his kingdom. He agreed to restore all the provinces which had been possessed by Henry II. and his two sons, and to annex them for ever to England, without any obligation of homage or fealty on the part of the English monarch. But the dauphin and the states of France rejected this treaty, so dishonourable and pernicious to the kingdom[q]; and Edward, on the expiration of the truce, having now, by subsidies and frugality, collected some treasure, prepared himself for a new invasion of France.

THE great authority and renown of the king and the prince of Wales, the splendid success of their former enterprizes, and the certain prospect of plunder from the defenceless provinces of France, soon brought together the whole military power of England; and the same motives invited to Edward's standard all the hardy adventurers of the different countries of Europe[r]. He passed over to Calais, where he assembled an army of near a hundred thousand men; a force which the dauphin could not pretend to withstand in the open field: That prince, therefore, prepared himself to elude a blow which it was impossible for him to resist. He put all the considerable towns in a posture of defence; ordered them to be sup-

[q] Froissard, liv. i. chap. 207.   [r] Ibid chap. 205.

plied with magazines and provisions; distributed proper garrisons in all places; secured every thing valuable in the fortified cities; and chose his own station at Paris, with a view of allowing the enemy to vent their fury on the open country.

The king, aware of this plan of defence, was obliged to carry along with him six thousand waggons, loaded with the provisions necessary for the subsistence of his army. After ravaging the province of Picardy, he advanced into Champagne; and having a strong desire of being crowned king of France at Rheims, the usual place in which this ceremony is performed, he laid siege to that city, and carried on his attacks, though without success, for the space of seven weeks[s]. The place was bravely defended by the inhabitants, encouraged by the exhortations of the archbishop, John de Craon; till the advanced season (for this expedition was entered upon in the beginning of winter) obliged the king to raise the siege. The province of Champagne, meanwhile, was desolated by his incursions; and he thence conducted his army, with a like intent, into Burgundy. He took and pillaged Tonnerre, Gaillon, Avalon, and other small places; but the duke of Burgundy, that he might preserve his country from farther ravages, consented to pay him the sum of 100,000 nobles[t]. Edward then bent his march towards the Nivernois, which saved itself by a like composition: He laid waste Brie and the Gatinois; and after a long march, very destructive to France, and somewhat ruinous to his own troops, he appeared before the gates of Paris, and taking up his quarters at Bourg-la-Reine, extended his army to Long-jumeau, Mont-rouge, and Vaugirard. He tried to provoke the dauphin to ha-

[s] Froissard, liv. i. chap. 208. Walsing. p. 174. p. 161. Walsing. p. 174. [t] Rymer, vol. vi.

zard a battle, by sending him a defiance; but could not make that prudent prince change his plan of operations. Paris was safe from the danger of an assault by its numerous garrison; from that of a blockade by its well supplied magazines: And as Edward himself could not subsist his army in a country wasted by foreign and domestic enemies, and left also empty by the precaution of the dauphin, he was obliged to remove his quarters; and he spread his troops into the provinces of Maine, Beausse, and the Chartraine, which were abandoned to the fury of their devastations [a]. The only repose which France experienced, was during the festival of Easter, when the king stopped the course of his ravages. For superstition can sometimes restrain the rage of men, which neither justice nor humanity is able to controul.

CHAP. XVI.
1360.

WHILE the war was carried on in this ruinous manner, the negociations for peace were never interrupted: But as the king still insisted on the full execution of the treaty, which he had made with his prisoner at London, and which was strenuously rejected by the dauphin, there appeared no likelihood of an accommodation. The earl, now duke of Lancaster (for this title was introduced into England during the present reign) endeavoured to soften the rigour of these terms, and to finish the war on more equal and reasonable conditions. He insisted with Edward, that, notwithstanding his great and surprising successes, the object of the war, if such were to be esteemed the acquisition of the crown of France, was not become any nearer than at the commencement of it; or rather, was set at a greater distance by those very victories and advantages which seemed to lead to it. That his claim of succession had not from the first procured him one partizan in the kingdom; and the continuance of these destructive hostilities had united every Frenchman in the

[a] Walsing. p. 175.

most

most implacable animosity against him. That though intestine faction had creeped into the government of France, it was abating every moment; and no party, even during the greatest heat of the contest, when subjection under a foreign enemy usually appears preferable to the dominion of fellow-citizens, had ever adopted the pretensions of the king of England. That the king of Navarre himself, who alone was allied with the English, instead of being a cordial friend, was Edward's most dangerous rival, and, in the opinion of his partizans, possessed a much preferable title to the crown of France. That the prolongation of the war, however it might enrich the English soldiers, was ruinous to the king himself, who bore all the charges of the armament, without reaping any solid or durable advantage from it. That if the present disorders of France continued, that kingdom would soon be reduced to such a state of desolation that it would afford no spoils to its ravagers; if it could establish a more steady government, it might turn the chance of war in its favour, and by its superior force and advantages, be able to repel the present victors. That the dauphin, even during his greatest distresses, had yet conducted himself with so much prudence, as to prevent the English from acquiring one foot of land in the kingdom; and it were better for the king to accept by a peace what he had in vain attempted to acquire by hostilities, which, however hitherto successful, had been extremely expensive, and might prove very dangerous: And that Edward having acquired so much glory by his arms, the praise of moderation was the only honour to which he could now aspire; an honour so much the greater, as it was durable, was united with that of prudence, and might be attended with the most real advantages [w].

[w] Froissard, liv. 1. chap. 211.

These

EDWARD III.

THESE reasons induced Edward to accept of more moderate terms of peace; and it is probable that, in order to palliate this change of resolution, he ascribed it to a vow made during a dreadful tempest, which attacked his army on their march, and which ancient historians represent as the cause of this sudden accommodation [a]. The conferences between the English and French commissioners were carried on during a few days at Bretigni in the Chartraine, and the peace was at last concluded on the following conditions [y]: It was stipulated that king John should be restored to his liberty, and should pay as his ransom three millions of crowns of gold, about 1,500,000 pounds of our present money [z]; which was to be discharged at different payments: That Edward should for ever renounce all claim to the crown of France, and to the provinces of Normandy, Maine, Touraine, and Anjou, possessed by his ancestors; and should receive in exchange the provinces of Poictou, Xaintonge, l'Agenois, Perigort, the Limousin, Quercy, Rovergue, l'Angoumois, and other districts in that quarter, together with Calais, Guisnes, Montreuil, and the county of Ponthieu, on the other side of France: That the full sovereignty of all these provinces, as well as that of Guienne, should be vested in the crown of England, and that France should renounce all title to feudal jurisdiction, homage, or appeal from them: That the king of Navarre should be restored to all his honours and possessions: That Edward should renounce his confederacy with the Flemings, John his connexions with the Scots: That the disputes concerning the succession of Britanny, between the families of Blois and Mountfort, should be decided by arbiters appointed by the two kings; and if the competitors refused to submit to the award,

CHAP. XVI.

1360. Peace of Bretigni.

8th May,

[a] Froissard, liv. I. chap. 211.
Froissard, liv. I. chap. 212.
[y] Rymer, vol. vi. p. 178.
[z] See note [K] at the end of the volume.

the dispute should no longer be a ground of war between the kingdoms: And that forty hostages, such as should be agreed on, should be sent to England as a security for the execution of all these conditions [a].

IN consequence of this treaty, the king of France was brought over to Calais; whither Edward also soon after repaired: And there, both princes solemnly ratified the treaty. John was sent to Boulogne; the king accompanied him a mile on his journey; and the two monarchs parted, with many professions, probably cordial and sincere, of mutual amity [b]. The good disposition of John made him fully sensible of the generous treatment which he had received in England, and obliterated all memory of the ascendant gained over him by his rival. There seldom has been a treaty of so great importance so faithfully executed by both parties. Edward had scarcely, from the beginning, entertained any hopes of acquiring the crown of France: By restoring John to his liberty, and making peace at a juncture so favourable to his arms, he had now plainly renounced all pretensions of this nature: He had sold at a very high price that chimerical claim: And had at present no other interest than to retain those acquisitions which he had made with such singular prudence and good fortune. John, on the other hand, though the terms were severe, possessed such fidelity and honour, that he was determined, at all hazards, to execute them, and to use every expedient for satisfying a mo-

[a] The hostages were the two sons of the French king, John and Lewis; his brother Philip duke of Orleans, the duke of Bourbon, James de Bourbon count de Ponthieu, the counts d'Eu, de Longueville, de St. Pol, de Harcourt, de Vendome, de Couci, de Craon, de Montmorency, and many of the chief nobility of France. The princes were mostly released on the fulfilling of certain articles: Others of the hostages, and the duke of Berry among the rest, were permitted to return upon their parole, which they did not keep. Rymer, vol. vi. p. 278. 285. 287.
[b] Froissard, liv. i. chap. 213.

march who had indeed been his greatest political enemy, but had treated him personally with singular humanity and regard. But, notwithstanding his endeavours, there occurred many difficulties in fulfilling his purpose; chiefly from the extreme reluctance which many towns and vassals in the neighbourhood of Guienne expressed against submitting to the English dominion^c; and John, in order to adjust these differences, took a resolution of coming over himself to England. His council endeavoured to dissuade him from this rash design; and probably would have been pleased to see him employ more chicanes for eluding the execution of so disadvantageous a treaty: But John replied to them, that, though good faith were banished from the rest of the earth, she ought still to retain her habitation in the breasts of princes. Some historians would detract from the merit of this honourable conduct, by representing John as enamoured of an English lady, to whom he was glad, on this pretence, to pay a visit: But besides that this surmise is not founded on any good authority, it appears somewhat unlikely on account of the advanced age of that prince, who was now in his fifty-sixth year. He was lodged in the Savoy; the palace where he had resided during his captivity, and where he soon after sickened and died. Nothing can be a stronger proof of the great dominion of fortune over men, than the calamities which pursued a monarch of such eminent valour, goodness, and honour, and which he incurred merely by reason of some slight imprudences, which, in other situations, would have been of no importance. But though both his reign and that of his father proved extremely unfortunate to their kingdom, the French crown acquired, during their time, very confiderable accessions, those of Dauphiny and Burgundy. This latter province, however, John had the imprudence again to dismember

CHAP. XVI.

1360.

1363.

1364.

8th April.

^c Froissart, liv. 1. chap. 214.

by bestowing it on Philip, his fourth son, the object of his most tender affections[f]; a deed which was afterwards the source of many calamities to the kingdom.

John was succeeded in the throne by Charles, the dauphin, a prince educated in the school of adversity, and well qualified, by his consummate prudence and experience, to repair all the losses which the kingdom had sustained from the errors of his two predecessors. Contrary to the practice of all the great princes of those times, which held nothing in estimation but military courage, he seems to have fixed it as a maxim never to appear at the head of his armies; and he was the first king in Europe that showed the advantage of policy, foresight, and judgment, above a rash and precipitate valour. The events of his reign, compared with those of the preceding, are a proof how little reason kingdoms have to value themselves on their victories, or to be humbled by their defeats; which in reality ought to be ascribed chiefly to the good or bad conduct of their rulers, and are of little moment towards determining national characters and manners.

State of France.

Before Charles could think of counterbalancing so great a power as England, it was necessary for him to remedy the many disorders to which his own kingdom was exposed. He turned his arms against the king of Navarre, the great disturber of France during that age: He defeated this prince by the conduct of Bertrand du Guesclin, a gentleman of Britanny, one of the most accomplished characters of the age, whom he had the discernment to chuse as the instrument of all his victories[g]: And he obliged his enemy to accept of moderate terms of peace. Du Guesclin was less fortunate in the wars of Britanny, which still continued, notwithstanding the me-

[f] Rymer, vol. vi. p. 418. [g] Froissard, liv. l. chap. 119.

EDWARD III.

diation of France and England: He was defeated and taken prisoner at Auray by Chandos: Charles of Blois was there slain, and the young count of Mountfort soon after got entire possession of that dutchy [b]. But the prudence of Charles broke the force of this blow: He submitted to the decision of fortune: He acknowledged the title of Mountfort, though a zealous partizan of England; and received the proffered homage for his dominions. But the chief obstacle which the French king met with in the settlement of the state proceeded from obscure enemies, whom their crimes alone rendered eminent, and their number dangerous.

ON the conclusion of the treaty of Bretigni, the many military adventurers, who had followed the standard of Edward, being dispersed into the several provinces, and possessed of strong holds, refused to lay down their arms, or relinquish a course of life to which they were now accustomed, and by which alone they could gain a subsistence [i]. They associated themselves with the banditti, who were already enured to the habits of rapine and violence; and under the name of the *companies* and *companions*, became a terror to all the peaceable inhabitants. Some English and Gascon gentlemen of character, particularly Sir Matthew Gournay, Sir Hugh Calverly, the chevalier Verte, and others, were not ashamed to take the command of these ruffians, whose numbers amounted on the whole to near 40,000, and who bore the appearance of regular armies, rather than bands of robbers. These leaders fought pitched battles with the troops of France, and gained victories; in one of which Jaques de Bourbon, a prince of the blood, was slain [k]: And they proceeded to such a height, that they wanted little but regular establishments to become princes, and thereby sanctify, by the maxims of

CHAP. XVI.

1364.

[b] Froissard, liv. l. chap. 227, 228, &c. Walsing. p. 180.
[i] Froissard, liv. l. chap. 214. [k] Ibid. chap. 214, 215.

the

the world, their infamous profession. The greater spoil they committed on the country, the more easy they found it to recruit their number: All those who were reduced to misery and despair flocked to their standard: The evil was every day encreasing: And, though the pope declared them excommunicated, these military plunderers, however deeply affected with the sentence, to which they paid a much greater regard than to any principles of morality, could not be induced by it to betake themselves to peaceable or lawful professions.

As Charles was not able by power to redress so enormous a grievance, he was led by necessity, and by the turn of his character, to correct it by policy, and to contrive some method of discharging into foreign countries this dangerous and intestine evil.

Peter, king of Castile, stigmatized by his contemporaries and by posterity with the epithet of *Cruel*, had filled with blood and murder his kingdom and his own family; and having incurred the universal hatred of his subjects, he kept, from present terror alone, an anxious and precarious possession of the throne. His nobles fell every day the victims of his severity: He put to death several of his natural brothers from groundless jealousy: Each murder, by multiplying his enemies, became the occasion of fresh barbarities: And as he was not destitute of talents, his neighbours, no less than his own subjects, were alarmed at the progress of his violence and injustice. The ferocity of his temper, instead of being softened by his strong propensity to love, was rather inflamed by that passion, and took thence new occasion to exert itself. Instigated by Mary de Padilla, who had acquired the ascendant over him, he threw into prison Blanche de Bourbon, his wife, sister to the queen of France; and soon after made way, by poison, for the espousing of his mistress.

HENRY,

HENRY, count of Transtamare, his natural brother, seeing the fate of every one who had become obnoxious to this tyrant, took arms against him; but being foiled in the attempt, he sought for refuge in France, where he found the minds of men extremely inflamed against Peter, on account of his murder of the French princess. He asked permission of Charles to enlist the *companies* in his service, and to lead them into Castile; where, from the concurrence of his own friends, and the enemies of his brother, he had the prospect of certain and immediate success. The French king, charmed with the project, employed du Guesclin in negociating with the leaders of these banditti. The treaty was soon concluded. The high character of honour which that general possessed, made every one trust to his promises: Though the intended expedition was kept a secret, the companies implicitly inlisted under his standard: And they required no other condition before their engagement, than an assurance that they were not to be led against the prince of Wales in Guienne. But that prince was so little averse to the enterprize, that he allowed some gentlemen of his retinue to enter into the service under du Guesclin.

DU GUESCLIN, having completed his levies, led the army first to Avignon, where the pope then resided, and demanded, sword in hand, an absolution for his soldiers, and the sum of 200,000 livres. The first was readily promised him; some more difficulty was made with regard to the second. "I believe that my fellows," replied du Guesclin, "may make a shift to do without "your absolution; but the money is absolutely neces- "sary." The pope then extorted from the inhabitants in the city and neighbourhood the sum of a hundred thousand livres, and offered it to du Guesclin. "It is not my "purpose," cried that generous warrior, "to oppress the "innocent people. The pope and his cardinals themselves

"can

CHAP.
XVI.

1369.

" can well spare me that sum from their own coffers.
" This money, I infist, must be restored to the owners.
" And should they be defrauded of it, I shall myself re-
" turn from the other side of the Pyrenees, and oblige
" you to make them restitution." The pope found the
necessity of submitting, and paid him, from his treasury,
the sum demanded [d]. The army, hallowed by the blessings, and enriched by the spoils of the church, proceeded
on their expedition.

These experienced and hardy soldiers, conducted by
so able a general, easily prevailed over the king of Castile,
whose subjects, instead of supporting their oppressor, were
ready to join the enemy against him [m]. Peter fled from
his dominions, took shelter in Guienne, and craved the
protection of the prince of Wales, whom his father had
invested with the sovereignty of these conquered provinces, by the title of the principality of Aquitaine [n].
The prince seemed now to have entirely changed his sentiments with regard to the Spanish transactions: Whether
that he was moved by the generosity of supporting a distressed prince, and thought, as is but too usual among sovereigns, that the rights of the people were a matter of
much less consideration; or dreaded the acquisition of so
powerful a confederate to France as the new king of Castile; or, what is most probable, was impatient of rest and
ease, and sought only an opportunity for exerting his military talents, by which he had already acquired so much
renown. He promised his assistance to the dethroned
monarch; and having obtained the consent of his father,
he levied a great army, and set out upon his enterprize.
He was accompanied by his younger brother, John of
Gaunt, created duke of Lancaster, in the room of the
good prince of that name, who had died without any male

1367.
Expedition
against Castile.

[d] Hist. du Guesclin.   [m] Froissard, liv. l. chap. 230.
[l] Rymer, vol. vi. p. 534.   Froissard, liv. i. chap. 131.

issue,

issue, and whose daughter he had espoused. Chandos also, who bore among the English the same character, which du Guesclin had acquired among the French, commanded under him in this expedition.

THE first blow which the prince of Wales gave to Henry of Transtamare, was the recalling of all the *companies* from his service; and so much reverence did they bear to the name of Edward, that great numbers of them immediately withdrew from Spain, and inlisted under his banners. Henry, however, beloved by his new subjects, and supported by the king of Arragon and others of his neighbours, was able to meet the enemy with an army of 100,000 men; forces three times more numerous than those which were commanded by Edward. Du Guesclin, and all his experienced officers, advised him to delay any decisive action, to cut off the prince of Wales's provisions, and to avoid every engagement with a general, whose enterprizes had hitherto been always conducted with prudence, and crowned with success. Henry trusted too much to his numbers; and ventured to encounter the English prince at Najara*. Historians of that age are commonly very copious in describing the shock of armies in battle, the valour of the combatants, the slaughter and various successes of the day: But though small rencounters in those times were often well disputed, military discipline was always too imperfect to preserve order in great armies; and such actions deserve more the name of routs than of battles. Henry was chaced off the field, with the loss of above 20,000 men: There perished only four knights and forty private men on the side of the English.

PETER, who so well merited the infamous epithet which he bore, purposed to murder all his prisoners in cold blood; but was restrained from this barbarity by the

* Froissart, liv. I. chap. 241.

remon-

CHAP. XVI.

1367.

remonstrances of the prince of Wales. All Castile now submitted to the victor: Peter was restored to the throne: And Edward finished this perilous enterprize with his usual glory. But he had soon reason to repent his connexions with a man like Peter, abandoned to all sense of virtue and honour. The ungrateful tyrant refused the stipulated pay to the English forces; and Edward, finding his soldiers daily perish by sickness, and even his own health impaired by the climate, was obliged, without receiving any satisfaction on this head, to return into Guienne [p].

The barbarities exercised by Peter over his helpless subjects, whom he now regarded as vanquished rebels, revived all the animosity of the Castilians against him; and, on the return of Henry of Transtamare, together with du Guesclin, and some forces levied anew in France, the tyrant was again dethroned, and was taken prisoner. His brother, in resentment of his cruelties, murdered him with his own hand; and was placed on the throne of Castile, which he transmitted to his posterity. The duke of Lancaster, who espoused, in second marriage, the eldest daughter of Peter, inherited only the empty title of that sovereignty, and, by claiming the succession, encreased the animosity of the new king of Castile against England.

1368.
Rupture with France.

But the prejudice which the affairs of prince Edward received from this splendid, though imprudent expedition, ended not with it. He had involved himself in so much debt, by his preparations and the pay of his troops, that he found it necessary, on his return, to impose on his principality a new tax, to which some of the nobility consented with extreme reluctance, and to which

[p] Froissard, liv. I. chap. 240, 243. Willingham, p. 182.

others

others absolutely refused to submit[q]. This incident revived the animosity which the inhabitants bore to the English, and which all the amiable qualities of the prince of Wales were not able to mitigate or assuage. They complained, that they were considered as a conquered people, that their privileges were disregarded, that all trust was given to the English alone, that every office of honour and profit was conferred on these foreigners, and that the extreme reluctance, which most of them had expressed to receive the new yoke, was likely to be long remembered against them. They cast, therefore, their eyes towards their ancient sovereign, whose prudence, they found, had now brought the affairs of his kingdom into excellent order; and the counts of Armagnac, Comminge, and Perigord, the lord d'Albret, with other nobles, went to Paris, and were encouraged to carry their complaints to Charles, as to their lord paramount, against these oppressions of the English government[r].

IN the treaty of Bretigni it had been stipulated that the two kings should make renunciations, Edward of his claim to the crown of France, and to the provinces of Normandy, Maine, and Anjou; John of the homage and fealty due for Guienne, and the other provinces ceded to the English. But when that treaty was confirmed and renewed at Calais, it was found necessary, as Edward was not yet in possession of all the territories, that the mutual renunciations should for some time be deferred;

[q] This tax was a livre upon a hearth; and it was imagined that the imposition would have yielded 1,200,000 livres a year, which supposes so many hearths in the provinces possessed by the English. But such loose conjectures have commonly no manner of authority, much less in such ignorant times. There is a strong instance of it in the present reign. The house of commons granted the king a tax of twenty-two shillings on each parish, supposing that the amount of the whole would be 50,000 pounds. But they were found to be in a mistake of near five to one. Cotton, p. 3. And the council afterwards the power of augmenting the tax upon each parish.

[r] Froissard, liv. I. chap. 244.

and

CHAP. XVI.

and it was agreed, that the parties, meanwhile, should make no use of their respective claims against each other.

1368. Though the failure in exchanging these renunciations had still proceeded from France, Edward appears to have taken no umbrage at it; both because this clause seemed to give him entire security, and because some reasonable apology had probably been made to him for each delay. It was, however, on this pretence, though directly contrary to treaty, that Charles resolved to ground his claim, of still considering himself as superior lord of those provinces, and of receiving the appeals of his sub-vassals.

1369. But as views of policy, more than those of justice, enter into the deliberations of princes; and as the mortal injuries received from the English, the pride of their triumphs, the severe terms imposed by the treaty of peace, seemed to render every prudent means of revenge honourable against them; Charles was determined to take this measure, less by the reasonings of his civilians and lawyers, than by the present situation of the two monarchies. He considered the declining years of Edward, the languishing state of the prince of Wales's health, the affection which the inhabitants of all these provinces bore to their ancient master, their distance from England, their vicinity to France, the extreme animosity expressed by his own subjects against these invaders, and their ardent thirst of vengeance; and having silently made all the necessary preparations, he sent to the prince of Wales a summons to appear in his court at Paris, and there to justify his conduct towards his vassals. The prince replied, that he would come to Paris; but it should be at the head of sixty thousand men. The unwarlike cha-

racter

racter of Charles kept prince Edward, even yet, from thinking, that that monarch was in earnest, in this bold and hazardous attempt.

CHAP XVI.
1370.

It soon appeared what a poor return the king had received by his distant conquests for all the blood and treasure expended in the quarrel, and how impossible it was to retain acquisitions, in an age when no regular force could be maintained sufficient to defend them against the revolt of the inhabitants, especially if that danger was joined with the invasion of a foreign enemy. Charles fell first upon Ponthieu, which gave the English an inlet into the heart of France: The citizens of Abbeville opened their gates to him[x]: Those of St. Valori, Rue, and Crotoy imitated the example, and the whole country was in a little time reduced to submission. The dukes of Berri and Anjou, brothers to Charles, being assisted by du Guesclin, who was recalled from Spain, invaded the southern provinces; and by means of their good conduct, the favourable dispositions of the people, and the ardour of the French nobility, they made every day considerable progress against the English. The state of the prince of Wales's health did not permit him to mount on horseback, or exert his usual activity: Chandos, the constable of Guienne, was slain in one action[y]: The Captal de Buche, who succeeded him in that office, was taken prisoner in another[z]: And when young Edward himself was obliged by his encreasing infirmities to throw up the command, and return to his native country, the affairs of the English in the south of France seemed to be menaced with total ruin.

Ill success of the English.

The king, incensed at these injuries, threatened to put to death all the French hostages who remained in his hands; but on reflection abstained from that ungenerous revenge. After resuming, by advice of parliament, the

[x] Walsingham, p. 183. [y] Froissard, liv. 1. chap. 277. Walsingham, p. 185. [z] Froissard, liv. 1. chap. 310.

vain

vain title of king of France[a], he endeavoured to send succours into Gascony; but all his attempts, both by sea and land, proved unsuccessful. The earl of Pembroke was intercepted at sea, and taken prisoner with his whole army near Rochelle by a fleet, which the king of Castile had fitted out for that purpose[b]: Edward himself embarked for Bourdeaux with another army; but was so long detained by contrary winds, that he was obliged to lay aside the enterprize[c]. Sir Robert Knolles, at the head of 30,000 men, marched out of Calais, and continued his ravages to the gates of Paris, without being able to provoke the enemy to an engagement: He proceeded in his march to the provinces of Maine and Anjou, which he laid waste; but part of his army being there defeated by the conduct of du Guesclin, who was now created constable of France, and who seems to have been the first consummate general that had yet appeared in Europe, the rest were scattered and dispersed, and the small remains of the English forces, instead of reaching Guienne, took shelter in Britanny, whose sovereign had embraced the alliance of England[d]. The duke of Lancaster, some time after, made a like attempt with an army of 25,000 men; and marched the whole length of France from Calais to Bourdeaux; but was so much harassed by the flying parties which attended him, that he brought not the half of his army to the place of their destination. Edward, from the necessity of his affairs, was at last obliged to conclude a truce with the enemy[e]; after almost all his ancient possessions in France had been ravished from him, except Bourdeaux and Bayonne, and all his conquests, except Calais.

[a] Rymer, vol. vi. p. 621. Cotton's Abridg. p. 108. [b] Froissard, liv. I. chap. 301, 303, 304. Walsingham, p. 186. [c] Froissard, liv. I. chap. 311. Walsingham, p. 187. [d] Froissard, liv. I. chap. 291. Walsingham, p. 185. [e] Froissard, liv. I. chap. 321. Walsingham, p. 187.

THE

EDWARD III.

THE decline of the king's life was expofed to many mortifications, and correfponded not to the fplendid and noify fcenes which had filled the beginning and the middle of it. Befides feeing the lofs of his foreign dominions, and being baffled in every attempt to defend them; he felt the decay of his authority at home, and experienced, from the fharpnefs of fome parliamentary remonftrances, the great inconftancy of the people, and the influence of prefent fortune over all their judgments[f]. This prince, who, during the vigour of his age, had been chiefly occupied in the purfuits of war and ambition, began, at an unfeafonable period, to indulge himfelf in pleafure; and being now a widower, he attached himfelf to a lady of fenfe and fpirit, one Alice Pierce, who acquired a great afcendant over him, and by her influence gave fuch general difguft, that, in order to fatisfy the parliament, he was obliged to remove her from court[g]. The indolence alfo, naturally attending old age and infirmities, had made him, in a great meafure, refign the adminiftration into the hands of his fon, the duke of Lancafter, who, as he was far from being popular, weakened extremely the affection which the Englifh bore to the perfon and government of the king. Men carried their jealoufies very far againft the duke; and as they faw, with much regret, the death of the prince of Wales every day approaching, they apprehended, left the fucceffion of his fon, Richard, now a minor, fhould be defeated by the intrigues of Lancafter, and by the weak indulgence of the old king. But Edward, in order to fatisfy both the people and the prince on this head, declared in parliament his grandfon heir and fucceffor to the crown; and thereby cut off all the hopes of the duke of Lancafter, if he ever had the temerity to entertain any.

CHAP. XVI.

1376.

[f] Walfingham, p. 189. Ypod. Neuft. p. 530.
[g] Walfingham, p. 189.

CHAP. XVI.

1376.
8th June.
Death of the prince of Wales.

THE prince of Wales, after a lingering illness, died in the forty-sixth year of his age; and left a character, illustrious for every eminent virtue, and from his earliest youth, till the hour he expired, unstained by any blemish. His valour and military talents formed the smallest part of his merit: His generosity, humanity, affability, moderation, gained him the affections of all men; and he was qualified to throw a lustre, not only on that rude age in which he lived, and which nowise infected him with its vices, but on the most shining period of ancient or modern history. The king survived about a year this melancholy incident: England was deprived at once of both these princes, its chief ornament and support: He expired in the sixty-fifth year of his age and the fifty-first of his reign; and the people were then sensible, though too late, of the irreparable loss which they had sustained.

1377.
21st June.
Death

and character of the king.

THE English are apt to consider with peculiar fondness the history of Edward III. and to esteem his reign, as it was one of the longest, the most glorious also, that occurs in the annals of their nation. The ascendant which they then began to acquire over France, their rival and supposed national enemy, makes them cast their eyes on this period with great complacency, and sanctifies every measure which Edward embraced for that end. But the domestic government of this prince is really more admirable than his foreign victories; and England enjoyed, by the prudence and vigour of his administration, a longer interval of domestic peace and tranquillity than she had been blest with in any former period, or than she experienced for many ages after. He gained the affections of the great, yet curbed their licentiousness: He made them feel his power, without their daring, or even being inclined, to murmur at it: His affable and obliging behaviour, his munificence and generosity, made them submit with pleasure to his dominion; his valour and conduct

7 made

EDWARD III.

made them succefsful in moſt of their enterprizes; and their unquiet ſpirits, directed againſt a public enemy, had no leiſure to breed thoſe diſturbances to which they were naturally ſo much inclined, and which the frame of the government ſeemed ſo much to authorize. This was the chief benefit, which reſulted from Edward's victories and conqueſts. His foreign wars were, in other reſpects, neither founded in juſtice, nor directed to any ſalutary purpoſe. His attempt againſt the king of Scotland, a minor and a brother-in-law, and the revival of his grandfather's claim of ſuperiority over that kingdom, were both unreaſonable and ungenerous; and he allowed himſelf to be too eaſily ſeduced, by the glaring proſpect of French conqueſts, from the acquiſition of a point, which was practicable, and which, if attained, might really have been of laſting utility to his country and his ſucceſſors. The ſucceſs which he met with in France, though chiefly owing to his eminent talents, was unexpected; and yet, from the very nature of things, not from any unforeſeen accidents, was found, even during his life-time, to have procured him no ſolid advantages. But the glory of a conqueror is ſo dazzling to the vulgar, the animoſity of nations is ſo violent, that the fruitleſs deſolation of ſo fine a part of Europe as France, is totally diſregarded by us, and is never conſidered as a blemiſh in the character or conduct of this prince. And indeed, from the unfortunate ſtate of human nature, it will commonly happen, that a ſovereign of genius, ſuch as Edward, who uſually finds every thing eaſy in his domeſtic government, will turn himſelf towards military enterprizes, where alone he meets with oppoſition, and where he has full exerciſe for his induſtry and capacity.

EDWARD had a numerous poſterity by his queen, Philippa of Hainault. His eldeſt ſon was the heroic Edward, uſually denominated the Black Prince, from the colour of his armour. This prince eſpouſed his couſin Joan, commonly

CHAP.
XVI.
1377.

monly called the *Fair Maid of Kent*, daughter and heir of his uncle, the earl of Kent, who was beheaded in the beginning of this reign. She was first married to Sir Thomas Holland, by whom she had children. By the prince of Wales, she had a son, Richard, who alone survived his father.

THE second son of king Edward (for we pass over such as died in their childhood) was Lionel duke of Clarence, who was first married to Elizabeth de Burgh, daughter and heir of the earl of Ulster, by whom he left only one daughter, married to Edmund Mortimer, earl of Marche. Lionel espoused in second marriage, Violante, the daughter of the duke of Milan[h], and died in Italy soon after the consummation of his nuptials, without leaving any posterity by that princess. Of all the family, he resembled most his father and elder brother in his noble qualities.

EDWARD's third son was John of Gaunt, so called from the place of his birth: He was created duke of Lancaster; and from him sprang that branch which afterwards possessed the crown. The fourth son of this royal family was Edmund, created Earl of Cambridge by his father, and duke of York by his nephew. The fifth son was Thomas, who received the title of earl of Buckingham from his father, and that of duke of Glocester from his nephew. In order to prevent confusion, we shall always distinguish these two princes by the titles of York and Glocester, even before they were advanced to them.

THERE were also several princesses born to Edward by Philippa; to wit, Isabella, Joan, Mary, and Margaret, who espoused, in the order of their names, Ingelram de Coucy earl of Bedford, Alphonso king of Castile, John of Mountfort duke of Britanny, and John Hastings earl of Pembroke. The princess Joan died at Bourdeaux before the consummation of her marriage.

Miscellaneous transactions of this reign.

IT is remarked by an elegant historian[i], that conquerors, though usually the bane of human kind, proved

[h] Rymer, vol. vi. p. 564. [i] Dr. Robertson's Hist. of Scotland, B. I.

often,

often, in those feudal times, the most indulgent of sovereigns: They stood most in need of supplies from their people; and, not being able to compel them by force to submit to the necessary impositions, they were obliged to make them some compensation by equitable laws and popular concessions. This remark is, in some measure, though imperfectly, justified by the conduct of Edward III. He took no steps of moment without consulting his parliament and obtaining their approbation, which he afterwards pleaded as a reason for their supporting his measures [i]. The parliament, therefore, rose into greater consideration during his reign, and acquired more regular authority than in any former time; and even the house of commons, which, during turbulent and factious periods, was naturally depressed by the greater power of the crown and barons, began to appear of some weight in the constitution. In the later years of Edward, the king's ministers were impeached in parliament, particularly lord Latimer, who fell a sacrifice to the authority of the commons [k]; and they even obliged the king to banish his mistress by their remonstrances. Some attention was also paid to the election of their members; and lawyers, in particular, who were at that time men of a character somewhat inferior, were totally excluded the house during several parliaments [l].

One of the most popular laws enacted by any prince, was the statute which passed in the twenty-fifth of this reign [m], and which limited the cases of high treason, before vague and uncertain, to three principal heads, conspiring the death of the king, levying war against him, and adhering to his enemies; and the judges were prohibited, if any other cases should occur, from inflicting the penalty of treason without an application to parliament. The bounds of treason were indeed so much

[i] Cotton's Abridg. p. 108, 120. [k] Ibid. p. 122.
[l] Cotton's Abridg. p. 12. [m] Chap. 2.

limited by this statute, which still remains in force without any alteration, that the lawyers were obliged to enlarge them, and to explain a conspiracy for levying war against the king, to be equivalent to a conspiracy against his life; and this interpretation, seemingly forced, has, from the necessity of the case, been tacitly acquiesced in. It was also ordained, that a parliament should be held once a year, or oftner, if need be: A law which, like many others, was never observed, and lost its authority by disuse [a].

EDWARD granted above twenty parliamentary confirmations of the Great Charter; and these concessions are commonly appealed to as proofs of his great indulgence to the people, and his tender regard for their liberties. But the contrary presumption is more natural. If the maxims of Edward's reign had not been, in general, somewhat arbitrary, and if the Great Charter had not been frequently violated, the parliament would never have applied for these frequent confirmations, which could add no force to a deed regularly observed, and which could serve to no other purpose than to prevent the contrary precedents from turning into a rule, and acquiring authority. It was indeed the effect of the irregular government during those ages, that a statute which had been enacted some years, instead of acquiring, was imagined to lose force by time, and needed to be often renewed by recent statutes of the same sense and tenor. Hence, likewise, that general clause so frequent in old acts of parliament, that the statutes enacted by the king's progenitors should be observed [b]; a precaution which, if we do not consider the circumstances of the times, might appear absurd and ridiculous. The frequent confirmations, in general terms, of the privileges of the church, proceeded from the same cause.

[a] 4 Edw. III. chap. 14. cap. 1, &c. [b] 36 Edw. III. cap. 1. 37 Edw. III.

IT is a clause in one of Edward's statutes, that no man, of what estate or condition soever, shall be put out of land or tenement, nor taken nor imprisoned, nor disherited, nor put to death, without being brought in answer by due process of the law[p]. This privilege was sufficiently secured by a clause of the Great Charter, which had received a general confirmation in the first chapter of the same statute. Why then is the clause so anxiously, and, as we may think, so superfluously repeated? Plainly, because there had been some late infringements of it, which gave umbrage to the commons[q].

BUT there is no article in which the laws are more frequently repeated during this reign, almost in the same terms, than that of purveyance, which the parliament always calls an *outrageous* and *intolerable* grievance, and the source of *infinite* damage to the people[r]. The parliament tried to abolish this prerogative altogether, by prohibiting any one from taking goods without the consent of the owners[s], and by changing the *buissus nems* of *purveyors*, as they term it, into that of *buyers*[t]: But the arbitrary conduct of Edward still brought back the grievance upon them; though contrary both to the Great Charter, and to many statutes. This disorder was in a great measure derived from the state of the public finances and of the kingdom; and could therefore the less admit of remedy. The prince frequently wanted ready money; yet his family must be subsisted: He was therefore obliged to employ force and violence for that purpose, and to give tallies, at what rate he pleased, to the owners of the goods which he laid hold of. The kingdom also abounded so little in commodities, and the interior communication was so imperfect, that, had the owners been strictly protected

---

[p] 28 Edw. III. cap. 3.   [q] They affert, in the 15th of this reign, that there had been such instances. Cotton's Abridg. p. 51. They repeat the same in the 21st year. See p. 59.   [r] 36 Edw. III. art.
[s] 14 Edw. III. cap. 19.   [t] 36 Edw. III. cap. 2.

by

490   HISTORY OF ENGLAND.

CHAP. XVI.

1377.

by law, they could easily have exacted any price from the king; especially in his frequent progresses, when he came to distant and poor places, where the court did not usually reside, and where a regular plan for supplying it could not easily be established. Not only the king, but several great lords, insisted upon this right of purveyance within certain districts*.

THE magnificent castle of Windsor was built by Edward III. and his method of conducting the work may serve as a specimen of the condition of the people in that age. Instead of engaging workmen by contracts and wages, he assessed every county in England to send him a certain number of masons, tilers, and carpenters, as if he had been levying an army*.

THEY mistake, indeed, very much the genius of this reign, who imagine that it was not extremely arbitrary. All the high prerogatives of the crown were to the full exerted in it; but what gave some consolation, and promised in time some relief to the people, they were always complained of by the commons: Such as the dispensing power *; the extension of the forests *; erecting monopolies *; exacting loans *; stopping justice by particular warrants *; the renewal of the commission of *trailbaton* *; pressing men and ships into the public service *; levying arbitrary and exorbitant fines *; extending the authority of the privy council or star-chamber to the decision of private causes *; enlarging the power of the mareschal's and other arbitrary courts *; imprisoning members for freedom of speech in parliament *; obliging people, without any rule, to send recruits of men at arms, archers, and hoblers, to the army *.

* 7 Rich. II. cap. 8.   * Ashmole's Hist. of the Garter, p. 129.
* Cotton's Abridg. p. 148.   * Cotton, p. 71.   * Cotton's
Abridg. p. 56. 64. 112.   * Pynner, vol. 1. p. 491. 574. Cotton's
Abridg. p. 56.   * Cotton, p. 114.   * Ibid. p. 67.   * Cotton's
Abridg. p. 47. 70. 113.   * Ibid. p. 32.   * Ibid. p. 74.   * Ibid.
* Walsing. p. 179, 190.   * Tyrrel's Hist. vol. viii. p. 554. from the records.

BUT

But there was no act of arbitrary power more frequently repeated in this reign, than that of imposing taxes without consent of parliament. Though that assembly granted the king greater supplies than had ever been obtained by any of his predecessors, his great undertakings, and the necessity of his affairs, obliged him to levy still more; and after his splendid success against France had added weight to his authority, these arbitrary impositions became almost annual and perpetual. Cotton's Abridgment of the records affords numerous instances of this kind, in the first [i] year of his reign, in the thirteenth year [k], In the fourteenth [l], in the twentieth [m], in the twenty-first [n], in the twenty-second [o], in the twenty-fifth [p], in the thirty-eighth [q], in the fiftieth [r], and in the fifty-first [s].

The king openly avowed and maintained this power of levying taxes at pleasure. At one time he replied to the remonstrance made by the commons against it, that the impositions had been exacted from great necessity, and had been assented to by the prelates, earls, barons, and *some* of the commons [t]; at another, that he would advise with his council [u]. When the parliament desired that a law might be enacted for the punishment of such as levied these arbitrary impositions, he refused compliance [w]. In the subsequent year, they desired that the king might renounce this pretended prerogative; but his answer was, that he would levy no taxes without necessity, for the defence of the realm, and where he reasonably might use that authority [x]. This incident passed a few days before his death; and these were, in a manner, his last words to his people. It would seem, that the famous charter or statute of Edward I. *de tallagio non*

CHAP. XVI.

1377.

[i] Rymer, vol. iv. p. 363. [k] P. 17, 18. [l] Rymer, vol. iv. p. 39. [m] P. 47. [n] P. 52, 53, 57, 58. [o] P. 69. [p] P. 76. [q] P. 101. [r] P. 138. [s] P. 150.
[t] Cotton, p. 33. He repeats the same answer in p. 82, *Some of the commons were such as be should be pleased to consult with.* [u] Cotton, p. 57. [w] Ibid. p. 138. [x] Ibid. p. 132.

concedendo,

CHAP.
XVI.

1377.

commendando, though never repealed, was supposed to have already lost, by age, all its authority.

These facts can only show the *practice* of the times: For as to the *right*, the continual remonstrances of the commons may seem to prove that it rather lay on their side: At least, these remonstrances served to prevent the arbitrary practices of the court from becoming an established part of the constitution. In so much a better condition were the privileges of the people, even during the arbitrary reign of Edward III. than during some subsequent ones, particularly those of the Tudors, where no tyranny or abuse of power ever met with any check or opposition, or so much as a remonstrance, from parliament.

In this reign we find, according to the sentiments of an ingenious and learned author, the first strongly marked, and probably contested, distinction between a proclamation by the king and his privy-council, and a law which had received the assent of the lords and commons [y].

It is easy to imagine that a prince of so much sense and spirit as Edward, would be no slave to the court of Rome. Though the old tribute was paid during some years of his minority [z], he afterwards withheld it; and when the pope, in 1367, threatened to cite him to the court of Rome for default of payment, he laid the matter before his parliament. That assembly unanimously declared, that king John could not, without a national consent, subject his kingdom to a foreign power: And that they were therefore determined to support their sovereign against this unjust pretension [a].

During this reign, the statute of provisors was enacted, rendering it penal to procure any presentations to benefices from the court of Rome, and securing the rights of all patrons and electors, which had been extremely encroached on by the pope [b]. By a subsequent statute,

[y] Observations on the statutes, p. 193. [z] Rymer, vol. iv. p. 434.
[a] Cotton's Abridg. p. 110. [b] 25 Edw. III. 27 Edw. III.

every

every person was outlawed who carried any cause by appeal to the court of Rome[c].

THE laity, at this time, seem to have been extremely prejudiced against the papal power, and even somewhat against their own clergy, because of their connexions with the Roman pontiff. The parliament pretended that the usurpations of the pope were the cause of all the plagues, injuries, famine, and poverty of the realm; were more destructive to it than all the wars; and were the reason why it contained not a third of the inhabitants and commodities which it formerly possessed: That the taxes levied by him, exceeded five times those which were paid to the king: That every thing was venal in that sinful city of Rome; and that even the patrons in England had thence learned to practise simony without shame or remorse[d]. At another time they petition the king to employ no churchman in any office of state[e]; and they even speak in plain terms, of expelling by force the papal authority, and thereby providing a remedy against oppressions, which they neither could nor would any longer endure[f]. Men who talked in this strain were not far from the reformation: But Edward did not think proper to second all this zeal: Though he passed the statute of provisors, he took little care of its execution; and the parliament made frequent complaints of his negligence on this head[g]. He was content with having reduced such of the Romish ecclesiastics as possessed revenues in England, to depend entirely upon him by means of that statute.

As to the police of the kingdom during this period, it was certainly better than during times of faction, civil war, and disorder, to which England was so often exposed: Yet were there several vices in the constitution, the bad consequences of which, all the power and vigi-

[c] 27 Edw. III. 38 Edw. III. [d] Cotton, p. 74. 118, 119. [e] Ibid. p. 112. [f] Cotton, p. 48. [g] Ibid. p. 119. 118, 129, 130, 148.

lance of the king could not prevent. The barons, by their confederacies with those of their own order, and by supporting and defending their retainers in every iniquity [b], were the chief abettors of robbers, murderers, and ruffians of all kinds; and no law could be executed against those criminals. The nobility were brought to give their promise in parliament, that they would not avow, retain, or support, any felon or breaker of the law [i]; yet this engagement, which we may wonder to see exacted from men of their rank, was never regarded by them. The commons make continual complaints of the multitude of robberies, murders, rapes, and other disorders, which, they say, were become numberless in every part of the kingdom, and which they always ascribe to the protection that the criminals received from the great [k]. The king of Cyprus, who paid a visit to England in this reign, was robbed and stripped on the highway, with his whole retinue [l]. Edward himself contributed to this dissolution of law, by his facility in granting pardons to felons from the solicitation of the courtiers. Laws were made to retrench this prerogative [m], and remonstrances of the commons were presented against the abuse of it [n]: But to no purpose. The gratifying of a powerful nobleman continued still to be of more importance than the protection of the people. The king also granted many franchises, which interrupted the course of justice, and the execution of the laws [o].

Commerce and industry were certainly at a very low ebb during this period. The bad police of the country alone affords a sufficient reason. The only exports were wool, skins, hydes, leather, butter, tin, lead, and such unmanufactured goods, of which wool was by far the most considerable. Knyghton has asserted, that 100,000

[b] 11 Edw. III. cap. 14.   [q] Edw. III. cap. 2.   [l] 15 Edw. III. cap. 4.
[c] Cotton, p. 10.   [h] Ibid. p. 51. 62. 64. 70. 160.
[i] Walsing. p. 170.   [m] 10 Edw. III. cap. 2.   [n] 7 Edw. III. cap. 2.
[k] Cotton, p. 75.   [o] Ibid. p. 54.

licks

sacks of wool were annually exported, and sold at twenty pounds a sack, money of that age. But he is widely mistaken, both in the quantity exported and in the value. In 1349, the parliament remonstrate that the king, by an illegal imposition of forty shillings on each sack exported, had levied 60,000 pounds a year [?]: Which reduces the annual exports to 30,000 sacks. A sack contained twenty-six stone, and each stone fourteen pounds [*]; and at a medium was not valued at above five pounds a sack [*], that is, fourteen or fifteen pounds of our present money. Knyghton's computation raises it to sixty pounds, which is near four times the present price of wool in England. According to this reduced computation, the export of wool brought into the kingdom about 450,000 pounds of our present money, instead of six millions, which is an extravagant sum. Even the former sum is so high, as to afford a suspicion of some mistake in the computation of the parliament with regard to the number of sacks exported. Such mistakes were very usual in those ages.

EDWARD endeavoured to introduce and promote the woollen manufacture, by giving protection and encouragement to foreign weavers [*], and by enacting a law, which prohibited every one from wearing any cloth but of English fabric [*]. The parliament prohibited the exportation of woollen goods, which was not so well judged, especially while the exportation of unwrought wool was so much allowed and encouraged. A like injudicious law was made against the exportation of manufactured iron [*].

IT appears from a record in the Exchequer, that in 1354 the exports of England amounted to 294,184 pounds seventeen shillings and two-pence: The imports to 38,970 pounds three shillings and six-pence money of that time. This is a great balance, considering that it arose wholly from the exportation of raw wool and other rough materials. The import was chiefly linen and fine cloth, and some wine. England seems to have been extremely drained at this time by Edward's foreign expeditions and foreign subsidies, which probably was the reason why the exports so much exceed the imports.

THE first toll we read of in England, for mending the highways, was imposed in this reign: It was that for repairing the road between St. Giles's and Temple-Bar[w].

IN the first of Richard II. the parliament complain extremely of the decay of shipping during the preceding reign, and assert, that one sea-port formerly contained more vessels than were then to be found in the whole kingdom. This calamity they ascribe to the arbitrary seizure of ships by Edward for the service of his frequent expeditions[x]. The parliament in the fifth of Richard renew the same complaint[y]; and we likewise find it made in the forty-sixth of Edward III. So false is the common opinion, that this reign was favourable to commerce.

THERE is an order of this king, directed to the mayor and sheriffs of London, to take up all ships of forty ton and upwards, to be converted into ships of war[z].

THE parliament attempted the impracticable scheme of reducing the price of labour after the pestilence, and also that of poultry[a]. A reaper, in the first week of August, was not allowed above two-pence a day, or near sixpence of our present money; in the second week a third more. A master carpenter was limited through the whole year to three-pence a day, a common carpenter to two-pence, money of that age[b]. It is remarkable that, in the same reign, the pay of a common soldier, an archer, was six-pence a day; which, by the change both in denomination and value, would be equivalent to near

w Rymer, vol. v. p. 520.
x Rymer, vol. iv. p. 664.
b 25 Edw. III. cap. 1. 3.
a Cotton, p. 155. 164.
s 37 Edw. III. cap. 3.
y Cap. 3.

five

EDWARD III.

five shillings of our present money[e]. Soldiers were then inlisted only for a very short time: They lived idle all the rest of the year, and commonly all the rest of their lives: One successful campaign, by pay and plunder, and the ransom of prisoners, was supposed to be a small fortune to a man; which was a great allurement to enter into the service[d].

THE staple of wool, wool-fells, leather, and lead, was fixed by act of parliament in particular towns of England[e]. Afterwards it was removed by law to Calais: But Edward, who commonly deemed his prerogative above law, paid little regard to these statutes; and when the parliament remonstrated with him on account of those acts of power, he plainly told them, that he would proceed in that matter as he thought proper[f]. It is not easy to assign the reason of this great anxiety for fixing a staple; unless perhaps it invited foreigners to a market, when they knew, beforehand, that they should there meet with great choice of any particular species of commodity. This policy of inviting foreigners to Calais was carried so far, that all English merchants were prohibited by law from exporting any English goods from the staple; which was in a manner the total abandoning of all foreign navigation, except that to Calais[g]. A contrivance seemingly extraordinary.

---

[c] Dugdale's Baronage, vol. I. p. 784. Brady's hist. vol. II. App. N° 92. The pay of a man at arms was quadruple. We may therefore conclude, that the numerous armies, mentioned by historians in those times, consisted chiefly of ragamuffins, who followed the camp, and lived by plunder. Edward's army before Calais consisted of 31,294 men; yet his pay for sixteen months was only 127,201 pounds. Brady, ibid.

[d] Commodities seem to have risen since the Conquest. Instead of being ten times cheaper than at present, they were, in the age of Edward III. only three or four times. This change seems to have taken place in a great measure since Edward I. The allowance granted by Edward III. to the earl of Murray, then a prisoner in Nottingham castle, is one pound a week; whereas the bishop of St. Andrews, the primate of Scotland, had only six pence a day allowed him by Edward I.

[e] 27 Edw. III.   [f] Cotton, p. 117.   [g] 27 Edw. III. cap. 7.

CHAP.
XVI.

1379.

It was not till the middle of this century that the English began to extend their navigation even to the Baltic [h]; nor till the middle of the subsequent, that they sailed to the Mediterranean [i].

Luxury was complained of in that age, as well as in others of more refinement; and attempts were made by parliament to restrain it, particularly on the head of apparel, where surely it is the most obviously innocent and inoffensive. No man under a hundred a year was allowed to wear gold, silver, or silk in his clothes: Servants also were prohibited from eating flesh meat, or fish, above once a day [k]. By another law it was ordained, that no one should be allowed, either for dinner or supper, above three dishes in each course, and not above two courses: And it is likewise expressly declared, that *soused* meat is to count as one of these dishes [l]. It was easy to foresee that such ridiculous laws must prove ineffectual, and could never be executed.

The use of the French language, in pleadings and public deeds, was abolished [m]. It may appear strange, that the nation should so long have worn this badge of conquest: But the king and nobility seem never to have become thoroughly English, or to have forgotten their French extraction, till Edward's wars with France gave them an antipathy to that nation. Yet still, it was long before the use of the English tongue came into fashion. The first English paper which we meet with in Rymer is in the year 1386, during the reign of Richard II. [n] There are Spanish papers in that collection of more ancient date [o]: And the use of the Latin and French still continued.

[h] Anderson, vol. i. p. 151.   [i] Id. p. 177.   [k] 37 Edw. III. cap. 8, 9, 10, &c.   [l] 10 Edw. III.   [m] 36 Edw. III. cap. 15.
[n] Rymer, vol. vii. p. 526. This paper, by the style, seems to have been drawn by the Scots, and was signed by the wardens of the marches only.
[o] Rymer, vol. vi. p. 554.

We may judge of the ignorance of this age in geography, from a story told by Robert of Avesbury. Pope Clement VI. having, in 1344, created Lewis of Spain prince of *the fortunate islands*, meaning the Canaries, then newly discovered; the English ambassador at Rome, and his retinue, were seized with an alarm that Lewis had been created king of England; and they immediately hurried home, in order to convey this important intelligence. Yet such was the ardour for study at this time, that Speed, in his Chronicle, informs us, there were then 30,000 students in the university of Oxford alone. What was the occupation of all these young men? To learn very bad Latin, and still worse Logic.

In 1364, the commons petitioned, that in consideration of the preceding pestilence, such persons as possessed manors holding of the king in chief, and had let different leases without obtaining licences, might continue to exercise the same power, till the country were become more populous[p]. The commons were sensible that this security of possession was a good means for rendering the kingdom prosperous and flourishing; yet durst not apply, all at once, for a greater relaxation of their chains.

There is not a reign among those of the ancient English monarchs, which deserves more to be studied than that of Edward III. nor one where the domestic transactions will better discover the true genius of that kind of mixed government which was then established in England. The struggles, with regard to the validity and authority of the great charter, were now over: The king was acknowledged to lie under some limitations: Edward himself was a prince of great capacity, not governed by favourites, not led astray by any unruly passion, sensible that nothing could be more essential to his interests than

[p] Cotton, p. 97.

CHAP.
XVI.

1277.

to keep on good terms with his people: Yet, on the whole, it appears that the government, at beſt, was only a barbarous monarchy, not regulated by any fixed maxims, or bounded by any certain undiſputed rights, which in practice were regularly obſerved. The king conducted himſelf by one ſet of principles; the barons by another; the commons by a third; the clergy by a fourth. All theſe ſyſtems of government were oppoſite and incompatible: Each of them prevailed in its turn, as incidents were favourable to it: A great prince rendered the monarchical power predominant: The weakneſs of a king gave reins to the ariſtocracy: A ſuperſtitious age ſaw the clergy triumphant: The people, for whom chiefly government was inſtituted, and who chiefly deſerve conſideration, were the weakeſt of the whole. But the commons, little obnoxious to any other order, though they ſunk under the violence of tempeſts, ſilently reared their head in more peaceable times; and, while the ſtorm was brewing, were courted by all ſides, and thus received ſtill ſome acceſſion to their privileges, or, at worſt, ſome confirmation of them.

It has been an eſtabliſhed opinion, that gold coin was not ſtruck till this reign: But there has lately been found proof that it is as ancient as Henry III.¹

¹ See obſervations on the more antient Statutes, p. 375. 2d Edit.

NOTES

TO THE

SECOND VOLUME.

NOTE [A], p. 36.

MADOX, in his Baronia Anglica, cap. 14. tells us, That in the 30th of Henry II. thirty-three cows and two bulls cost but eight pounds seven shillings, money of that age; 500 sheep, twenty-two pounds ten shillings, or about ten pence three farthings per sheep; sixty-six oxen, eighteen pounds three shillings; fifteen breeding mares, two pounds twelve shillings and six-pence; and twenty-two hogs, one pound two shillings. Commodities seem then to have been about ten times cheaper than at present; all except the sheep, probably on account of the value of the fleece. The same author, in his *Formulare Anglicanum*, p. 17. says, That in the 10th year of Richard I. mention is made of ten per cent. paid for money: but the Jews frequently exacted much higher interest.

NOTE [B], p. 253.

RYMER, vol. ii. p. 216. 845. There cannot be the least question, that the homage usually paid by the kings of Scotland was not for their crown, but for some other territory. The only question remains, what that territory was?

It was not always for the earldom of Huntingdon, nor the honour of Penryth; because we find it sometimes done at a time when these possessions were not in the hands of the kings of Scotland. It is probable, that the homage was performed in general terms without any particular specification of territory; and this inaccuracy had proceeded either from some dispute between the two kings about the territory and some opposite claims, which were compromised by the general homage, or from the simplicity of the age, which employed few words in every transaction. To prove this we need but look into the letter of king Richard, where he resigns the homage of Scotland, reserving the usual homage. His words are, *Sæpedictus W. Rex ligius homo noster devenict de omnibus terris de quibus antecessores sui antecessorum nostrorum ligii homines fuerunt, et nobis atque hæredibus nostris fidelitatem jurarunt.* Rymer, vol. i. p. 65. These general terms were probably copied from the usual form of the homage itself.

It is no proof that the kings of Scotland possessed no lands or baronies in England, because we cannot find them in the imperfect histories and records of that age. For instance, it clearly appears, from another passage of this very letter of Richard, that the Scottish king held lands both in the county of Huntingdon and elsewhere in England; though the earldom of Huntingdon itself was then in the person of his brother David; and we know at present of no other baronies which William held. It cannot be expected that we should now be able to specify all his fees which he either possessed or claimed in England; when it is probable that the two monarchs themselves, and their ministers, would at that very time have differed in the list: The Scottish king might possess some to which his right was disputed; he might claim others, which he did not possess: And neither of the two kings was willing to resign his pretensions by a particular enumeration.

A late author of great industry and learning, but full of prejudices, and of no penetration, Mr. Carte, has taken advantage of the undefined terms of the Scotch homage, and has pretended that it was done for Lothian and Galloway; that is, all the territories of the country now called Scotland, lying south of the Clyde and Forth. But to refute this pretension at

once,

once, we need only confider, that if thefe territories were held in fee of the Englifh kings, there would, by the nature of the feudal law, as eftablifhed in England, have been continual appeals from them to the courts of the Lord Paramount; contrary to all the hiftories and records of that age. We find that, as foon as Edward really eftablifhed his fuperiority, appeals immediately commenced from all parts of Scotland: And that king, in his writ to the king's bench, confiders them as a neceffary confequence of the feudal tenure. Such large territories alfo would have fupplied a confiderable part of the Englifh armies, which never could have efcaped all the hiftorians. Not to mention that there is not any inftance of a Scotch prifoner of war being tried as a rebel, in the frequent hoftilities between the kingdoms, where the Scottifh armies were chiefly filled from the fouthern counties.

Mr. Carte's notion with regard to Galloway, which comprehends, in the language of that age, or rather in that of the preceding, moft of the fouth-weft counties of Scotland; his notion, I fay, refts on fo flight a foundation, that it fcarcely merits being refuted. He will have it (and merely becaufe he will have it) that the Cumberland, yielded by king Edmund to Malcolm I. meant not only the county in England of that name, but all the territory northwards to the Clyde. But the cafe of Lothian deferves fome more confideration.

It is certain, that in very ancient language, Scotland means only the country north of the friths of Clyde and Forth. I fhall not make a parade of literature to prove it; becaufe I do not find that this point is difputed by the Scots themfelves. The fouthern country was divided into Galloway and Lothian; and the latter comprehended all the fouth-eaft counties. This territory was certainly a part of the ancient kingdom of Northumberland, and was entirely peopled by Saxons, who afterwards received a great mixture of Danes among them. It appears from all the Englifh hiftories, that the whole kingdom of Northumberland paid very little obedience to the Anglo-Saxon monarchs, who governed after the diffolution of the heptarchy; and the northern and remote parts of it feem to have fallen into a kind of anarchy, fometimes pillaged by the

Danes,

Danes, sometimes joining them in their ravages upon other parts of England. The kings of Scotland, lying nearer them, took at last possession of the country, which had scarcely any government; and we are told by Matthew of Westminster, p. 163. that king Edgar made a grant of the territory to Kenneth III. that is, he resigned claims which he could not make effectual, without bestowing on them more trouble and expence than they were worth: For these are the only grants of provinces made by kings; and so ambitious and active a prince as Edgar would never have made presents of any other kind. Though Matthew of Westminster's authority may appear small with regard to so remote a transaction; yet we may admit it in this case, because Ordericus Vitalis, a good authority, tells us, p. 701. that Malcolm acknowledged to William Rufus, that the Conqueror had confirmed to him the former grant of Lothian. But it follows not, because Edgar made this species of grant to Kenneth, that therefore he exacted homage for that territory. Homage, and all the rites of the feudal law, were very little known among the Saxons; and we may also suppose that the claim of Edgar was so antiquated and weak, that, in resigning it, he made no very valuable conceffion; and Kenneth might well refuse to hold, by so precarious a tenure, a territory which he at present held by the sword. In short, no author says he did homage for it.

The only colour indeed of authority for Mr. Carte's notion is, that Matthew Paris, who wrote in the reign of Henry III. before Edward's claim of superiority was heard of, says that Alexander III. did homage to Henry III. *pro Laudiano et aliis terris*. See page 555. This word seems naturally to be interpreted Lothian. But, in the first place, Matthew Paris's testimony, though confiderable, will not outweigh that of all the other historians, who say that the Scotch homage was always done for lands in England. Secondly, if the Scotch homage was done in general terms (as has been already proved), it is no wonder that historians should differ in their account of the object of it, since, it is probable, the parties themselves were not fully agreed. Thirdly, there is reason to think that

Laudianum,

Laudianum, in Matthew Paris, does not mean the Lothians now in Scotland. There appears to have been a territory, which anciently bore that or a similar name, in the north of England. For (1) The Saxon Chronicle, p. 197, says, that Malcolm Kenmure met William Rufus in Lodene in England. (2) It is agreed by all historians, that Henry II. only reconquered from Scotland the northern counties of Northumberland, Cumberland, and Westmorland. See Newbriggs, p. 383. Wykes, p. 30. Hemingford, p. 492. Yet the same country is called by other historians Loidis, comitatus Lodonensis, or some such name. See M. Paris, p. 68. M. West. p. 217. Annal. Waverl. p. 159. and Diceto, p. 531. (3) This last mentioned author, when he speaks of Lothian in Scotland, calls it Loheneis, p. 574. though he had called the English territory Loidis.

I thought this long note necessary, in order to correct Mr. Carte's mistake, an author whose diligence and industry has given light to many passages of the more ancient English history.

NOTE [C], p. 253.

RYMER, vol. ii. p. 543. It is remarkable that the English chancellor spoke to the Scotch parliament in the French tongue. This was also the language commonly made use of by all parties on that occasion. Ibid. passim. Some of the most considerable among the Scotch, as well as almost all the English barons, were of French origin; they valued themselves upon it; and pretended to despise the language and manners of the island. It is difficult to account for the settlement of so many French families in Scotland, the Bruces, Baliols, St. Clairs, Montgomeries, Somervilles, Gordons, Frasers, Cummins, Colvilles, Umfrevilles, Mowbrays, Hays, Maules, who were not supported there, as in England, by the power of the sword. But the superiority of the smallest civility and knowledge over total ignorance and barbarism, is prodigious.

NOTES TO THE SECOND VOLUME.

NOTE [D], p. 259.

SEE Rymer, vol. ii. p. 533. where Edward writes to the King's Bench to receive appeals from Scotland. He knew the practice to be new and unusual; yet he establishes it as an infallible consequence of his superiority. We learn also from the same collection, p. 603, that immediately upon receiving the homage, he changed the style of his address to the Scotch king, whom he now calls *dilecto & fideli*, instead of *fratri dilecto & fideli*, the appellation which he had always before used to him; see p. 109. 124. 168. 280. 1064. This is a certain proof that he himself was not deceived, as was scarcely indeed possible, but that he was conscious of his usurpation. Yet he solemnly swore afterwards to the justice of his pretensions, when he defended them before pope Boniface.

NOTE [E], p. 276.

THROUGHOUT the reign of Edw. I. the assent of the commons is not once expressed in any of the enacting clauses; nor in the reigns ensuing, till the 9 Edw. III. nor in any of the enacting clauses of 16 Rich. II. Nay even so low as Hen. VI. from the beginning till the 8th of his reign, the assent of the commons is not once expressed in any enacting clause. See preface to Ruffhead's edit. of the Statutes, p. 7. If it should be asserted, that the commons had really given their assent to these statutes, though they are not expressly mentioned, this very omission, proceeding, if you will, from carelessness, is a proof how little they were respected. The commons were so little accustomed to transact public business, that they had no speaker till after the parliament 6th Edw. III. See Prynne's preface to Cotton's Abridg.: Not till the first of Richard II. in the opinion of most antiquaries. The commons were very unwilling to meddle in any state affairs, and commonly either referred themselves to the lords, or desired a select committee of that house to assist them, as appears from Cotton. 5 E. III. n. 5; 15 E. III. n. 17; 21 E. III. n. 5; 47 E. III. n. 5; 50 E. III. n. 10; 51 E. III. n. 18; 1 R. II. n. 12; 2 R. II. n. 12; 5 R. II. n. 14; 2 parl. 6 R. II. n. 14; parl. 2. 6 R. II. n. 6, &c.

NOTES TO THE SECOND VOLUME.

NOTE [F], p. 277.

IT was very agreeable to the maxims of all the feudal governments, that every order of the state should give their consent to the acts which more immediately concerned them; and as the notion of a political system was not then so well understood, the other orders of the state were often not consulted on these occasions. In this reign, even the merchants, though no public body, granted the king impositions on merchandize, because the first payments came out of their pockets. They did the same in the reign of Edward III. but the commons had then observed that the people paid these duties, though the merchants advanced them; and they therefore remonstrated against this practice. Cotton's Abridg. p. 39. The taxes imposed by the knights on the counties were always lighter than those which the burgesses laid on the boroughs; a presumption, that in voting those taxes the knights and burgesses did not form the same house. See Chancellor West's enquiry into the manner of creating peers, p. 8. But there are so many proofs that those two orders of representatives were long separate, that it is needless to insist on them. Mr. Carte, who had carefully consulted the rolls of parliament, affirms, that they never appear to have been united till the 16th of Edward III. See Hist. vol. ii. p. 451. But it is certain that this union was not even then final: in 1372, the burgesses acted by themselves, and voted a tax after the knights were dismissed. See Tyrrel, Hist. vol. iii. p. 734. from Rot. Clauf. 46 Edw. III. n. 9. In 1376 they were the knights alone who passed a vote for the removal of Alice Pierce from the king's person, if we may credit Walsingham, p. 189. There is an instance of a like kind in the reign of Richard II. Cotton, p. 193. The different taxes voted by those two branches of the lower house naturally kept them separate: But as their petitions had mostly the same object, namely, the redress of grievances, and the support of law and justice, both against the crown and the barons, this cause as naturally united them, and was the reason why they at last joined in one house for the dispatch of business. The barons had few petitions. Their privileges

NOTES TO THE SECOND VOLUME.

were of more ancient date: Grievances seldom affected them: They were themselves the chief oppressors. In 1333, the knights by themselves concurred with the bishops and barons in advising the king to stay his journey into Ireland. Here was a petition which regarded a matter of state, and was supposed to be above the capacity of the burgesses. The knights, therefore, acted apart in this petition. See Cotton, Abridg. p. 13. Chief baron Gilbert thinks, that the reason why taxes always began with the commons or burgesses was, that they were limited by the instructions of their boroughs. See Hist. of the Exchequer, p. 37.

NOTE [G], p. 278.

THE chief argument from ancient authority, for the opinion that the representatives of boroughs preceded the forty-ninth of Henry III. is the famous petition of the borough of St. Albans, first taken notice of by Selden, and then by Petyt, Brady, Tyrrel, and others. In this petition, presented to the parliament in the reign of Edward II. the town of St. Albans asserts, that though they held *in capite* of the crown, and owed only for all other service, their attendance in parliament, yet the sheriff had omitted them in his writs; whereas both in the reign of the king's father, and all his predecessors, they had always sent members. Now, say the defenders of this opinion, if the commencement of the house of commons were in Henry III.'s reign, this expression could not have been used. But Madox, in his History of the Exchequer, p. 522, 523, 524, has endeavoured, and with great reason, to destroy the authority of this petition for the purpose alleged. He asserts, first, That there was no such tenure in England as that of holding by attendance in parliament, instead of all other service. Secondly, That the borough of St. Albans never held of the crown at all, but was always demesne land of the abbot. It is no wonder, therefore, that a petition which advances two falsehoods, should contain one historical mistake, which indeed amounts only to an inaccurate and exaggerated expression; no strange matter in ignorant burgesses of that age. Accordingly St. Albans continued still to belong to the

abbot,

NOTES TO THE SECOND VOLUME.

abbot. It never held of the crown till after the dissolution of the monasteries. But the assurance of these petitioners is remarkable. They wanted to shake off the authority of their abbot, and to hold of the king; but were unwilling to pay any services even to the crown: Upon which they framed this idle petition, which later writers have made the foundation of so many inferences and conclusions. From the tenor of the petition it appears, that there was a close connection between holding of the crown, and being represented in parliament: The latter had scarcely ever place without the former: Yet we learn from Tyrrel's Append. vol. iv. that there were some instances to the contrary. It is not improbable that Edward followed the roll of the earl of Leicester, who had summoned, without distinction, all the considerable boroughs of the kingdom; among which there might be some few that did not hold of the crown. Edward also found it necessary to impose taxes on all the boroughs in the kingdom without distinction. This was a good expedient for augmenting his revenue. We are not to imagine, because the house of commons have since become of great importance, that the first summoning of them would form any remarkable and striking epoch, and be generally known to the people even seventy or eighty years after. So ignorant were the generality of men in that age, that country burgesses would readily imagine an innovation, seemingly so little material, to have existed from time immemorial, because it was beyond their own memory, and perhaps that of their fathers. Even the parliament in the reign of Henry V. say, that Ireland had, from the beginning of time, been subject to the crown of England. (See Brady.) And surely, if any thing interests the people above all others, it is war and conquests, with their dates and circumstances.

NOTE [H], p. 443.

THIS story of the six burgesses of Calais, like all other extraordinary stories, is somewhat to be suspected; and so much the more, as Avesbury, p. 167, who is particular in his narration of the surrender of Calais, says nothing of it: and, on the contrary, extols in general the king's generosity and lenity to the inhabitants. The numberless mistakes of Froissard,

NOTES TO THE SECOND VOLUME.

fard, proceeding either from negligence, credulity, or love of the marvellous, invalidate very much his testimony, even though he was a contemporary, and though his history was dedicated to queen Philippa herself. It is a mistake to imagine, that the patrons of dedications read the books, much less vouch for all the contents of them. It is not a slight testimony, that should make us give credit to a story so dishonourable to Edward, especially after that proof of his humanity, in allowing a free passage to all the women, children, and infirm people, at the beginning of the siege; at least, it is scarcely to be believed, that, if the story has any foundation, he seriously meant to execute his menaces against the six townsmen of Calais.

NOTE [I], p. 448.

THERE was a singular instance about this time of the prevalence of chivalry and gallantry in the nations of Europe. A solemn duel of thirty knights against thirty was fought between Bembrough, an Englishman, and Beaumanoir, a Breton, of the party of Charles of Blois. The knights of the two nations came into the field; and before the combat began, Beaumanoir called out, that it would be seen that day who had the fairest mistresses. After a bloody combat the Bretons prevailed; and gained for their prize, full liberty to boast of their mistresses beauty. It is remarkable, that two such famous generals as Sir Robert Knolles and Sir Hugh Calverley drew their swords in this ridiculous contest. See Pere Daniel, vol. ii. p. 536, 537, &c. The women not only instigated the champions to those rough, if not bloody frays of tournament; but also frequented the tournaments during all the reign of Edward, whose spirit of gallantry encouraged this practice. See Knyghton, p. 2597.

NOTE [K], p. 469.

THIS is a prodigious sum, and probably near the half of what the king received from the parliament during the whole course of his reign. It must be remarked, that a tenth and fifteenth (which was always thought a high grant) were, in the eighth year of his reign, fixed at about 39,000 pounds;

pounds: There were said to be near 30,000 sacks of wool exported every year: A sack of wool was, at a medium, sold for five pounds. Upon these suppositions it would be easy to compute all the parliamentary grants, taking the list as they stand in Tyrrel, vol. iii. p. 780: Though somewhat must still be left to conjecture. This king levied more money on his subjects than any of his predecessors; and the parliament frequently complain of the poverty of the peop'e, and the oppressions under which they laboured. But it is to be remarked, that a third of the French king's ransom was yet unpaid when war broke out anew between the two crowns: His son chose rather to employ his money in combating the English, than in enriching them. See Rymer, vol. viii. p. 315.

END OF THE SECOND VOLUME.

www.ingramcontent.com/pod-product-compliance
Lightning Source LLC
Chambersburg PA
CBHW020858020526
44116CB00029B/358